6th

E D I T I O N

Creating Compositions

Harvey S. Wiener

The City University of New York

McGraw-Hill, Inc.
New York St. Louis San Francisco Auckland Bogotá
Caracas Lisbon London Madrid Mexico City Milan
Montreal New Delhi San Juan Singapore
Sydney Tokyo Toronto

Creating Compositions

14 15 16 17 18 19 20   QPF/QPF   0 5 4 3 2 1

ISBN 0-07-070178-4

Acknowledgments appear on pages 457–458, and on this page by reference.

This book was set in Times Roman by Ruttle, Shaw & Wetherill, Inc.
The editors were Lesley Denton, Lyn Beamesderfer, and David Dunham.
the designer was Robin Hoffmann.
The photo editor was Anne Manning.
The photo researcher was Elyse Rieder.
Arcata Graphics/Martinsburg was printer and binder.

Chapter-Opening Photo Credits

1. Eugene Richards/Magnum
2. Peter Menzel/Stock, Boston
3. Burt Glinn/Magnum
4. David Hurn/Magnum
5. Joseph Schuyler/Stock, Boston
6. Richard Karvar/Magnum
7. David Hurn/Magnum
8. Eugene Richards/Magnum

Library of Congress Cataloging-in-Publication Data

Wiener, Harvey S.
    Creating compositions / Harvey S. Wiener. —6th ed.
        p.   cm.
    Includes index.
    ISBN 0-07-070178-4
    1. English language—Rhetoric.   2. English language—
    Grammar—1950—   I. Title.
    PE 1408.W5819   1992   91-16733
    808'.042—dc20   CIP

This book is printed on acid-free paper.

About the Author

Harvey S. Wiener, professor of English at LaGuardia Community College, is University Dean for Academic Affairs of the City University of New York, where he coordinates new program review on the seventeen campuses of CUNY. As Director of the Instructional Resource Center, he oversees publications and seminars to advance the teaching of reading and writing. He also is adjunct professor of Adult and Higher Education at Columbia Teachers College. He was founding president of the Council of Writing Program Administrators.

He is the author of many books on reading and writing for college students and their teachers, including *The Writing Room* (Oxford, 1981). His book for parents, *Any Child Can Write*, was a Book-of-the-Month Club alternate. A revised edition appeared in 1990. He has written two other books for parents, *Talk With Your Child* (1988) and *Any Child Can Read Better* (1990). He has written for network television and was trained in Columbia Broadcasting System's daytime television Writer Development Project. He is a member of the Standing Committee on Assessment of the National Council of Teachers of English and he was chair of the Teaching of Writing Division of the Modern Language Association (1987).

Born in Brooklyn, he has worked in public education for thirty years. He has taught writing and literature at every level of education from elementary school to graduate school. A Phi Beta Kappa graduate from Brooklyn College, he holds a Ph.D. from Fordham University. He has won grants from the National Endowment for the Humanities, the Fund for Improvement of Postsecondary Education, the Exxon Education Foundation, and the Ford Foundation.

TO THE MEMORY OF DON MARION WOLFE
whose ideas take on new power
with each generation of writers

AND TO MY STUDENTS
who illustrate with every theme they write
the eternal freshness of those ideas

Contents

Part II
Writing Essays   **107**

Chapter 4   Writing Essays   107

Chapter 8 Writing a Brief Research Essay   251

Part III
Word and Sentence Skills   281

Part IV
A Minibook of Eight Special Skills 420

Appendixes 448

Preface

Since 1973 *Creating Compositions* has helped many college students learn to improve their writing. As in previous versions the sixth edition builds upon its prior successes by addressing new theories and practices as it maintains its established approach to learning how to write well.

This edition marks a dramatic change in the content and organization of *Creating Compositions*. I have trimmed Part I, "Writing Paragraphs," and have expanded Part II, "Writing Essays." Each chapter no longer has a thematic core, meaning that students and teachers have a wider range of available topics for exploration. Chapters continue to focus on important rhetorical strategies such as description, narration, illustration, comparison and contrast, and so on.

Another organizational change in the text is Part III, "Word and Sentence Skills," which includes alphabetically arranged instruction in basic concepts of grammar, usage, and sentence structure. In past editions, language skills instruction and practice exercises were spread throughout the chapters in Parts I and II. Including this material in a separate section allows considerable flexibility as students may consult areas of correctness when the need arises. Also the chapters in the first two parts now focus on the writing process without having to sidetrack for attention to grammar and other important language skills. As an aid to exploring these skills chapter by chapter, however, I suggest possible areas of study by making cross-references to activities in Part III. I also have expanded the The Professionals Speak section by adding essays to reinforce the rhetorical concept at hand. Additionally, I have pared down the "Minibook" considerably, integrating necessary instruction in the main chapters and eliminating any material not essential for beginning writers.

Despite all these changes the basic philosophy of *Creating Compositions* remains unaltered. The text continues to affirm that if you live by feeling and observing and hearing and responding, then you can write. The individual's life is a major source for writing; experience—the countless moments of pleasure and sorrow and surprise that fill each day—lays the groundwork for excellent compositions. Once you learn to recreate your experiences in written words, then you can move easily into the world of abstract ideas where details other than those based upon experience are often needed to support a written assignment. Most chapters urge class discussions well before actual writing begins so that you can share ideas and listen to other people's thoughts about a topic.

The new format of *Creating Compositions* will help writers succeed even more than in the past. In each chapter, vocabulary exercises present words helpful for the assignment at hand, words you might want to use in your own writing.

A section in each chapter on building composition skills explains different techniques in the construction of paragraphs and essays. You will learn how to expand and combine sentences for variety in your writing. You will also learn about and practice writing the different kinds of details required to support a topic idea—from details alive with sensory experience to details built upon statistics and quotations from reliable sources.

In each chapter a section on writing the paragraph or writing the essay offers specific goals for your compositions. You'll find instruction on prewriting in every chapter and you will practice a variety of prewriting exercises including brainstorming, making lists, and doing timed writing, among others. Before you write your paper, you will read examples of what other students wrote in response to the same assignment. You'll see in each chapter a student's rough draft and a final draft for the paragraph or essay. The questions that appear after the student models suggest directions for your own writing; so does the checklist of goals that remind you of the specific skills you are trying to build. Suggested topics will give you additional ideas for your own themes.

The section called The Professionals Speak provides essays to illustrate how professional writers deal with the same kinds of materials you treat in your writing. Many new pieces make this section even more valuable than in earlier editions.

Part III, "Word and Sentence Skills," looks at typical problems in written communication: the run-on error, the sentence fragment, problems with subject and verb agreement, punctuation skills, and a number of others. Clearly marked model sentences illustrate principles by example more often than by rule and without the sometimes confusing language of grammatical terminology. Exercises often require that you apply each skill in the language of your own sentences. You probably will not need to do all the activities, and you can omit those that deal with skills that you and your instructor agree you already know. As your instructor identifies errors in your writing, simply check the error in the alphabetically arranged section, study the explanations, and do the necessary practice exercises. Perforated pages make it possible for your instructor to collect the work you do directly in the book.

Part IV, "A Minibook of Eight Special Skills," presents briefly a number of important areas of communication for successful college work, including how to write a resume and job application letter, how to answer essay exam questions, and several other skills.

● Acknowledgments

As in the past, I have many debts to friends and colleagues who helped me with *Creating Compositions*. From Don Marion Wolfe comes the philosophy of sensory language in writing and the need for exploring individual moments in order to write with meaning. His too are the ideas for using model paragraphs as the heart of any composition program and for using activities in language that require students to call upon their own resources in communication. Karen Greenberg at Hunter College made innumerable comments about the text through many editions and I thank her for her keen insights and support; similarly, Don Linder provided excellent suggestions for revision. To my wife Barbara Koster Wiener go thanks for her patience during the preparation of this edition and for her skills as a teacher of reading, which made her assistance invaluable. My daughter Melissa brought many fresh concepts to this sixth edition and helped shape it; I am in her debt for her hard work and dynamic ideas. Dee Shedd typed the manuscript often under great pressure, and I thank her for all her hard work.

To my colleagues throughout the City University of New York who used *Creating Compositions* and who made valuable suggestions for improvement I am deeply grateful, as I am to those colleagues in colleges across the country who sent comments to me. Robert Esch at the University of Texas at El Paso has guided more revisions than I can count, and I thank him.

McGraw-Hill and I would like to thank the following reviewers for their many helpful comments and suggestions: Carol Adams, Delaware Technical and Community College; Robert Esch, University of Texas—El Paso; Karen Greenberg, The City University of New York—Hunter College; Bettie Horne, Lander College; Sturgis Monteith, Northwestern Mississippi Community College; Aleene Rose, Old Dominion University; and Philip Skerry, Lakeland Community College.

Finally, it is to the students in my writing courses who prove each term anew the infinite resources of their own lives and their ability to commit those vital elements into words—it is to them I owe special thanks.

Harvey S. Wiener

e chart
flecting
be

Description in Action

●

INTRODUCTION TO DESCRIPTION

Because many writing tasks require accurate details, description is a basic element in the writer's craft. As a writer, you have to observe the details of your subject with great care; and you have to present them faithfully so that readers know exactly what you see. This first paragraph assignment in description requires that you make a specific person, place, or object come to life through your writing. What can you describe well? Perhaps it's the crotchety old man who owns the corner hardware store, a treehouse in a rotting oak tree, a tattered brown couch in the living room. Each of us can recall some particular person, place, or object that has fixed itself clearly in our minds. To reproduce such an image in words is to describe for others the details that make it come alive. Selecting some place filled with colors, noises, and people in the midst of actions, you can present a scene that is clear and vivid for any reader to appreciate. If you choose instead to write about a person or an object, you also need to provide enough details to appeal to all the reader's senses. You will call upon your sense impressions of sound, color, smell, touch, and action to describe your major reaction to your subject. Before you write your paragraph, you will read what students before you have written in response to the same assignment.

● Journal Entry

The best way to begin thinking about an assignment is to write a journal entry. A journal, like a diary, is a place to record your private early impressions of the assignment. In a separate notebook, keep a journal and write down your ideas for each chapter assignment in this book. Unless you and your teacher agree otherwise, your journal is for your eyes only.

In your journal write a few sentences about some person, place, or object you might choose to describe for this assignment. Think about some unforgettable person in your high school, some vivid place you recall from summer vacation, an unusual or puzzling object you saw recently. Talk to yourself in writing about how you might turn one of these elements into a strong descriptive paragraph.

● Vocabulary

Step 1. Words to Describe Situations.   These words specify reactions you may have to the subject you are describing. Write definitions on the blank lines below. Use a dictionary if necessary.

1. personable _____
2. stately   _____
3. tranquil   _____
4. bustling   _____
5. somber   _____

6. formidable _____
7. elegant   _____
8. aggravating _____
9. cluttered _____
10. decrepit   _____

Step 2. Applying Vocabulary.   After you are sure of the meanings of the above words, write:

1. a word to describe someone or something dignified _____
2. a word that means peaceful _____

3. a word to describe a gloomy place _____

4. a word to indicate something or someone feared or respected _____

5. a word to describe something or someone graceful _____

6. a word that means irritating _____

7. a word to show noisy, energetic activity _____

8. a word that means pleasing in personality or appearance _____

9. a word that means broken down from age or hard use _____

10. a word to show things heaped in a disorderly way _____

Step 3. Words That Name Sounds. For the writer of description, words that indicate sounds are very important. For each word in italics below, write a definition that explains the word accurately. Use a dictionary when you need one.

EXAMPLE

He *chortled* at the jokes, his whole body shaking with delight.
laughed with a snorting, joyful chuckle

1. The senator tried to speak over the *din* of the reporters. _____

2. She spoke so low that her words were *inaudible*. _____

3. The baby *squealed* with delight whenever she was tickled. _____

4. Drumrolls *reverberated* in the empty concert hall. _____

● Building Composition Skills

Sensory Language

Step 1. Listening Well. Listen a moment to the sound of the room in which you are now sitting. Write two sentences that tell sounds you hear. Use a color in each sentence.

EXAMPLES

I hear the thump of a guitar from behind the green wall.

Pink gum cracks as Paul blows a bubble at his seat.

1. Some parts of wall are darked color sense the light is not reflecting off to thouse parts.

2. As I listen carefuly, I hear the clock ticking.

Step 2. Action and Color. Look around. Write two sentences that show some action in the room. Use a specific color in each sentence.

EXAMPLES

In front of me Marina munches on yellow corn chips.

Jeff's orange pen darts back and forth across the clean white page.

1. _____

_____

2. _____

_____

Step 3. What You Feel. Touch your desk, your shirt or sweater, your pen, or your wristwatch. Move around and touch the walls, the doors, the windows, and other objects in your room. Write two sentences that include a word to show what you feel. Use a color or a sound as well.

EXAMPLES

The blue walls feel damp with mildew.

I hear the squeak of my chair as I touch its smooth wooden sides.

1. I feel the table has not been cleaned properly, seree it's sticky.

2. I feel the writing in graved on the side of the pen.

Steps 1, 2, and 3 above demonstrate an important technique in writing: *concrete sensory detail. Concrete* means specific, solid; *sensory* means relating to any of the senses. The highly specific pictures that result are called *images*. Notice in the two following columns how the images in Column I are general and have little sensory appeal, while the examples in Column II are concrete because they appeal strongly to the senses.

I	II
EXAMPLES	
a tie	*a red silk tie painted with bright yellow daisies*
a chair	*a mahogany rocking chair that clacks and groans*
1. the ceiling	_____
2. a refrigerator	_____
3. a pen	_____

Step 4. Concrete Details.   In the blank spaces under Column II, above, write concrete sensory details for the general pictures in Column I.

Step 5. Naming Specifically.   One way to create pictures is to use the exact word you want rather than a general term that needs too many descriptive words to make the picture specific. Readers prefer the word *elm* or *oak* to *tree* because they get an added identification for the object through the exactness of the name.

For each general term in Column I, write in Column II three different *specific* terms to replace it.

I	II
EXAMPLE	
tool	*hammer, pliers, screwdriver*
1. car	_____
2. book	_____
3. flower	_____

Topic Sentences

The key to a good paragraph is its topic sentence. For your purposes at this point, the topic sentence should always come as the first sentence of the paragraph.

Look at these three sentences and try to judge which you think most effective as the opening topic sentence in a paragraph:

1. It all happened last night.
2. My room is on the second floor of our house.
3. My room is the messiest room on the second floor of our house.

If you selected 3, you rejected 1 and 2 for good reason. Sentence 1, though typical of many papers by beginning writers, lacks a clear statement of topic. What is the *it*? The element of suspense the writer tries to achieve can be lost in a drift away from the topic. Not having stated the topic clearly at the beginning, the writer can easily lose control. Besides, the "It all happened . . ." opening is so familiar and overused by now that it pays to avoid it.

Sentences 2 and 3 are superior because they both state the topic immediately: it's clear to readers that they will be reading descriptions of rooms. Sentence 2, however, is merely a statement of fact. It gives the writer too little control over the topic. What details can be included? What details can be left out? Sentence 3, on the other hand, by introducing the word *messiest,* states an opinion about the room and helps the writer determine which details to use in the description. The writer would omit any image not contributing to the overall effect of *messiness.*

The best topic sentences are those that state both the topic and the writer's opinion of or attitude toward that topic. The box below highlights the qualities of topic sentences.

• A Topic Sentence Reminder •

Topic Sentences	**Why**
1. Introduce the topic immediately.	So that your reader knows what you will write about. So you know what you will write about. **Hint:** Do not surprise your readers. Tell them immediately what you want to write about.
2. Limit the topic.	So that you will not have too much to write about. So that you will have enough to write about. So that you will focus on only one major feature or point.
3. Give an opinion or an attitude or a reaction or an impression that the writer has about the topic.	You get readers interested in the topic: they will want to find out why you feel the way you do about your subject. You can introduce a key word that will help you relate all your supporting ideas to one dominant impression.

Here are two more topic sentences, which are successful because they introduce a limited topic clearly *and* give the writer's opinion about that topic.

1. Everyone in my writing class
    this Monday morning looks
    restless and uncomfortable.

    Topic: people in the writing class
    Monday morning
    Opinion: restlessness

2. Last Friday night I realized the
    bitterness in my husband's
    character.

    Topic: my husband last Friday night
    Opinion: bitterness

The writer of sentence 1 above would need to show in the sentences that follow it just why everyone appears to be restless.

The writer of sentence 2 would need to show specific details of her husband's bitterness.

Step 1. Determining Topics and Opinions.   In the following topic sentences, underline the topic and circle the word(s) that tell the opinion or attitude.

EXAMPLE

Most new students are shocked at college registration procedures.

1. My twentieth birthday was the saddest day of my life.
2. Family dinners at my house are noisy and comical.
3. Little brothers are nothing but trouble.
4. On this chilly October morning I am sitting in the students' cafeteria, watching the commotion around me.

Step 2. Improving Topic Sentences.   The following topic sentences need words of opinion or attitude that will help limit and specify the topic. Rewrite the sentences in the space provided. You may wish to change the idea of some of the sentences as you introduce opinions. Try to avoid overused words like *good, nice, pleasant, enjoyable* by using some of the vocabulary in Appendix A.

EXAMPLE

I have a collection of old coins.

My collection of old coins is the envy of my Uncle Dave.

1. My room is on the fifth floor of the dormitory.

2. Jesse watches TV every day after school.

3. I called my father from Florida late last night.

4. I spent many summer afternoons in my grandmother's attic.

    _____

5. Rose knits sweaters for her grandchildren.

    _____

Step 3. Clearing Up Topics.   The topic sentences below fail to specify the topic to be developed in the paragraph. Many lack key words to express opinions. Others give important details, but fail to clarify exactly what the topic will be. On separate paper rewrite the sentences to make them clearer and more effective paragraph openings.

EXAMPLE

I will never forget what happened last winter.

One evening last winter I watched in amazement as a calf was born.

1. People lined up for the sale at the supermarket.
2. I will drive to Phoenix next Saturday.
3. Our dog barks whenever a stranger appears.

Step 4. Details and Topic Sentences.   The most effective way to construct your sentence is to decide beforehand on those details you wish to discuss. Suppose you wanted to write a paragraph on pollution and you wanted to discuss these two issues.

1. machines, such as cars and trains and lawn mowers, as major pollutants
2. humans as careless destroyers of our air and water

Here is a topic sentence that would permit the writer to discuss those two issues:

Both machines and human beings share the awful guilt of polluting our air and water.

The topic is clearly stated. Which words give the opinion or attitude?
    Suppose the topic sentence were

Pollution is a terrible problem.

The writer would then have presented too broad a topic for treatment in a composition of limited length. There are just too many possibilities to consider with such a topic sentence, and the writer would tend to treat too quickly many points without examining closely two or three that are especially important.

For each group of three details in Column I, write a topic sentence (including opinion and limited topic) in Column II.

I

DETAILS IN PARAGRAPH

II

TOPIC SENTENCE

1. On our vacation in San Francisco it rained for three days.
   The cable car operators went on strike.
   My wife had the flu.

2. The smell of varnish filled the room.
   Power saws buzzed.
   The pounding of hammers echoed through the halls.

3. Inflation hurts old people who are living on fixed incomes.
   Inflation affects the poor who are struggling to pay their bills.
   Inflation hurts young people raising a family.

1. _____
   _____
   _____

2. _____
   _____
   _____

3. _____
   _____
   _____

Step 5. Predicting Topics. A good topic sentence suggests for the reader some of the details to be found in the paragraph. For each topic sentence below, write two kinds of information you might expect to find in the paragraph. Use separate paper.

TOPIC SENTENCE

DETAILS IN PARAGRAPH

EXAMPLE

In this complex society there are many vital reasons to explain why teenagers drop out of school.

a. *pressure by friends to cut classes*
b. *personal problems at home*

1. My brother always feels happy on the first day of school.
2. Microwaves play an important role in many homes.
3. The new mall is a confusing place to spend a day.
4. Owning a car often presents many problems.

5. Traveling by public transportation in our city is always an adventure.

6. Joining a community action group can be a very rewarding experience.

Step 6. More Topic Sentence Practice.   For each general topic, note in Column II details that you might develop in a paragraph. Then write a topic sentence in Column III.

I	II	III
GENERAL TOPIC	DETAILS FOR PARAGRAPH	TOPIC SENTENCE

EXAMPLE

diets

A crash diet I went on to lose weight always left me hungry. It made me very sick. I gained back all the weight I lost anyhow.

I learned from a crash diet I foolishly followed to lose weight that serious problems may result from an unwise eating program.

1. your high school graduation
   _____ _____
   _____ _____
   _____ _____
   _____ _____
   _____ _____

2. cooking
   _____ _____
   _____ _____
   _____ _____
   _____ _____
   _____ _____

3. shopping for clothes
   _____ _____
   _____ _____
   _____ _____
   _____ _____
   _____ _____

Transitions

In a descriptive composition, the writer can move smoothly from one feature of the description to another by using *transitional expressions*. A transitional expression is a connector; it is a bridge between statements and ideas in paragraphs. Here are some transitions that can relate ideas in a descriptive paragraph; they will be valuable as you write because they help move your reader from one part of a place to another, or from one aspect of the person or object to another.

there	against	next to	surrounding
behind	on	in the rear	beyond
up above	at	in front of	near the back
to the left	beside	in back of	forward
to the right	far off	up front	through
nearby	inside	over	from
below	alongside	around	under

Step 1. Seeing Transitions at Work.   Examine the sentences in Column I below. The ideas seem unrelated and unclear. By adding transitional expressions in the blank spaces in the same sentences under Column II, make the relation between ideas clearer. You may want to add a word or two after the transition as well.

I

As I cleaned Paul's bedroom, I realized what a sad and lonely place it had become since my brother had joined the army last November. I saw his dusty football trophies, which he had polished so carefully. I passed his blue and gold football jacket, which hung proudly. I picked up one of several detective novels Paul loved to read; the tattered bookmark indicated that he had never finished the story. I suddenly heard my mother call me. Taking one last look, I slowly closed the door.

II

As I cleaned Paul's bedroom, I realized what a sad and lonely place it had become since my brother had joined the army last November. _____ ____ I saw his dusty football trophies, which he had polished so carefully. _____ I passed his blue and gold football jacket, which hung proudly _____. _____ I picked up one of several detective novels Paul loved to read; the tattered bookmark indicated that he had never finished the story. _____ I suddenly heard my mother call me. Taking one last look, I slowly closed the door _____.

Coordination

Read the sentences below. Then write on the blank line your first reaction to the way the sentences sound. (You will find it helpful to study "A Sentence Review" on pages 403–407.)

The Nursery

(1) My baby's room is the happiest room in our home. (2) I love to spend time there. (3) The walls are painted a sunny yellow. (4) Above the crib hangs a musical mobile. (5) It plays Brahms' Lullaby. (6) Stuffed dogs and cats rest on the floor. (7) The sweet smell of talcum powder is in the air. (8) A brown rocking horse sits in the corner. (9) My baby sucks his little pink thumb. (10) He suddenly awakens. (11) He doesn't see me in the corner. (12) He rests his head on the pillow. (13) I tiptoe quietly to the door.

Did you write *choppy* or *childish*? If you did, you probably sensed that some of the sentences needed to be joined in some way. Although very brief statements as sentences are often effective in writing, there are several other ways of structuring sentences for a clear development of ideas.

One way is to use *coordination*. The words *and, but, or, for, nor* (called *conjunctions*), and the semicolon (;) are called coordinators. Coordinators help ideas flow smoothly in a paragraph by joining two complete thoughts together so that they both are equal in importance and strength. When you use *and, but, or, for,* or *nor* to join complete sentences, always use a comma before the coordinators.

	WHAT THEY MEAN	HOW TO USE THEM	
and	The information that follows in the second complete thought is true along with, in addition to, the related information in the first complete thought.	The boys sat in the schoolyard with their shirts off, **and** they enjoyed sunning themselves.	[comma] [This part of the sentence tells what the boys do in addition to sitting in the schoolyard with their shirts off.]
but	The information that follows in the second complete thought is something you would not expect to happen, according to the information in the first complete thought. Idea two tells an *exception* to idea one.	I wanted to see that Japanese film on television, **but** I had too much homework.	[comma] [You wouldn't expect someone who wanted to watch the program (as stated in the first part of the sentence) to miss it.]
for	The information in the second complete thought tells why the events in the first	We were not permitted to visit the baby, **for** we both had colds.	[This tells why the visit (stated in the first thought) could not occur.] [comma]

complete thought
happened or should
happen.

or The information in the
second complete
thought is an alterna-
tive—another possibil-
ity—to the informa-
tion in the first. *Or*
suggests that only one
of the two ideas will
be possible.

You must arrive on time,   [comma]
or you will miss the
first part of the exami-
nation.

[This will occur only if what is told in
the first part of the sentence does not
occur.]

nor *Nor* continues into the
second complete
thought some negative
idea begun in the first.

[This word begins
the negative idea.]

He never ate candy, **nor**   [comma]
did he miss the taste of
sweetness.

[This continues the negative idea.]

The semicolon indicates
close relationship
between both complete
thoughts.

It was time for a new car;   [semicolon]
even his father agreed
to that.

[This thought depends for its sense on
the thought before the semicolon.]

Hint

Remember to use a comma whenever you use a conjunction to connect two complete thoughts.

Notice how well sentences 1 and 2 in the paragraph called "The Nursery" may be coordinated.

My baby's room is the happiest room in our home, and I love to spend time there.

Similarly, sentences 10 and 11 may be united.

He suddenly awakens, but he doesn't see me in the corner.

What other sentences might be coordinated effectively?

Three Important Hints

1. Too many coordinated sentences can weaken prose style. Use coordination sparingly.
2. Don't coordinate a whole string of complete sentences with conjunctions. Your paragraph
    will be just as dull as if you had not used any coordinators. Sometimes semicolons or a
    combination of semicolon and conjunction may be used effectively to coordinate *three*
    complete thoughts.

    Example
    *We drove carefully through the strange neighborhood; all of us watched the street signs, but nothing
    looked familiar.*

3. Make sure that the two complete thoughts you coordinate make sense together.

Step 1. You Pick the Coordinator. Here are five coordinated sentences written by professional writers. The coordinator in each case is left out. Write in the blank space the best coordinator from the choices given on the right.

1. The big patch of shadow might be a hut cer-   for   ;   but
   tainly, _____ it might be a cove leading
   down into the very depths of the earth.
   —Leo Tolstoy

2. A breeze must have blown outside, _____   or   for   nor
   the net on the basket moved. . . .
   —Philip Roth

3. Small children and babies perched on every lap   for   and   but
   available, _____ men leaned on the
   shelves or on each other.
   —Maya Angelou

4. . . . the last corn went flying into the silo with a   but   ;   for
   clackety roar and a smell as sweet as honey
   _____ the beans were harvested in a half
   day, like an afterthought _____ on the
   porch and out by the roadside stood mountains   but   ;   nor
   of pumpkins.
   —John Gardner

5. Marijuana smoke contains 150 chemicals in ad-   for   but   and
   dition to THC, _____ the effects of most
   of these are not known.
   —Jane E. Brody

Step 2. Completing Sentences. Basing your choice upon the coordinator used in each statement below, add a complete thought to the beginning word group that appears. Make sure that your final sentence makes sense. Look at the example.

EXAMPLE

Jimmy found 5 dollars, but *he tried not to spend it.* _____

1. We stopped for lunch at a cheap hamburger stand, for _____

   _____

2. The dog barked wildly; _____

   _____

3. A husband should never take his wife's love for granted, nor _____

    _____

4. We may go to the beach, but _____

    _____

5. Turn up the fan, or _____

    _____

Step 3. Coordinators in Your Sentences.   Using any of the methods of coordination, write a sentence about the topics listed below. Use each type of coordinator at least once. Be sure a complete thought (containing subject and verb) follows each coordinator. Use your own paper.

1. autumn   6.   amusement parks
2. democracy   7.   college instructors
3. your kitchen   8.   parents
4. soap operas   9.   your childhood
5. junk food   10. inflation

Ending a Paragraph

A paragraph must have a closing, some indication that the writer has finished developing ideas and has not simply run out of things to say. In one-paragraph papers, the closing may be made effectively in just one sentence. Often two or three sentences may conclude the paragraph. Here are a few pointers to help you write closing sentences:

1. The closing sentence should leave no doubt in the reader's mind that you are finished with the paragraph.
2. The closing sentence should leave the reader with a feeling that you have done what you intended to do. It should clinch the main point of your theme.
3. The closing sentence should perform one or a combination of these functions:

    a. Restate the main idea by referring back to the topic sentence

    Hint

    You do not have to use the same words that appear in the topic sentence. Find synonyms for the opinion word and the words that state the topic.

    b. Summarize one or more of the subtopics
    c. Give the dominant impression of the experience being described
    d. Suggest some action that could be taken based on the paragraph

    e. Form a judgment based upon information in the paragraph

4.   When needed, use transitions to help you conclude: *therefore, as a result, consequently,* and others are good for concluding, summarizing, and showing results.

5.   Make the conclusion fit the tone of the paragraph. A funny, brief, clever conclusion might suit a humorous paragraph about jobs. But a serious paragraph about employment problems would require something more formal.

Here are the things you should *not* do in closing sentences:

1.   Don't start a new topic.

2.   Don't contradict the point you have tried to make. A one-paragraph paper that tries to show why factory workers dislike their jobs should not end in the way that one student chose: "Some of them like their job, however."

3.   Don't make statements that are obvious or overused. A paragraph dealing with the high costs of job training would gain little by a conclusion like this: "Money is the root of all evil."

4.   Don't apologize for your lack of knowledge, lack of resources, or lack of interest. If you are not qualified to write about the topic, select a topic for which you are qualified.

5.   Don't end with a hasty statement that indicates that your paragraph is over. *Avoid* endings like these:

And that's all I have to say.	You see what I mean.
The end.	That's all.
That's how it happened.	It may sound unbelievable but it's true.
I hope you have enjoyed my story.	Therefore, what I have said is true.

6.   Don't be wordy. Be brief, to the point, and clear.

7.   Don't make any sweeping statements that admit no possibilities of other ideas or actions. To conclude a paragraph with "Therefore, all workers can learn to improve their job performance" overstates your case by an *absolute* conclusion, that is, a conclusion that has no conditions or possible exceptions or limitations. Try to soften your point with words that permit other possibilities: *perhaps, it seems, we may conclude, I am in favor, a good suggestion is.*

8.   Don't make your closing statement too obvious by saying things like: "As I have shown in my paragraph . . ." or "So my closing sentence is . . . ."

Step 1. Picking Good Endings.   Column I gives the topic sentence of a paragraph. Circle, in Column II, the closing sentence you think would best suit the paragraph. Explain your choice.

I	II
1. Students realistically must take into account the job market when choosing a major, but they must also choose careers that will be emotionally satisfying.	*a.* But some students are just out for big money. *b.* As I have indicated to you, emotions are important, too. *c.* We may conclude that a blend of financial and emotional considerations is the best way to choose a major.
2. Our society must realize that children have legal job rights that must not be ignored.	*a.* Since I am not a lawyer, I don't know all the legal rights of children, but something should be done. *b.* As I have shown you in the above paragraph, this is a serious problem. *c.* Therefore, the legal rights of our children as American workers must be upheld.
3. The job forecast for humanities or creative-arts majors is rather bleak for the 1990s.	*a.* It is unfortunate that many qualified writers, philosophers, and artists may be unemployed in the next decade. *b.* However, a rolling stone gathers no moss, and so future employees must continue to search everywhere for jobs. *c.* Since I don't really know anything about art, I don't know how bad the situation really will be in the 1990s.

Step 2. Rewriting Closing Sentences.   Answer the following questions. Use separate paper.

1. Read "My Old Friend" on page 24. How does the closing sentence give a summary and dominant impression of the object?

   Write a different closing sentence that will *suggest some consequence of the actions told about in the paragraph.*

2. Read "The Gloom Room," on page 23. How does the closing sentence give the *dominant impression of the experience?*

   Write a different closing sentence that will *summarize* the main point.

3. Read "A Family Gathering," on page 22. How does the closing sentence *restate the main idea* and *suggest some action that could be taken* based upon the ideas expressed in the paragraph?

   Rewrite the closing sentences so that it *forms a judgment* based upon the information in the paragraph.

Word and Sentence Skills: Suggested Topics for Study

Sentence Review, pages 403–407.
Run-on Sentences, pages 313–320.
Mirror Words (Homophones), pages 345–357.

● Writing a Descriptive Paragraph

Assignment

Write a paragraph of at least ten sentences in which you describe an object, place, or person that is clear in your mind. To *describe* means to use concrete sensory detail that create images. Make it possible for the reader to experience what you did. For other specific elements to consider as you write, see the checklist on pages 29–31.

Suggested Topics

Think about some indoor or outdoor place, memorable person, or meaningful object that has stuck in your mind; and plan to write a paragraph describing your subject clearly. You might want to choose one of these topics:

1. a concert auditorium
2. a toy bear or doll
3. a teacher
4. a relative
5. a favorite restaurant
6. a hotel or motel room
7. your neighbor
8. your car
9. your mechanic
10. your typewriter
11. an exchange student you know
12. a bus terminal
13. an assertive salesperson
14. a museum
15. your doctor or dentist
16. a health food store
17. an antique
18. a disco nightclub
19. a gym
20. your kitchen or dining room table

Prewriting

Handing in a paper written for someone else to read is the last in a series of steps writers take to produce their work. Writing begins long before writers put pens to paper. A convenient word to describe many of the steps that lead up to the actual writing of a first draft is *prewriting*.

What Is Prewriting?

Prewriting is a set of activities writers use to stimulate ideas and details before writing begins. In order to limit a topic and to uncover possible ideas about it, you have to let your thoughts take shape informally. It is very helpful to get opinions and advice about your drafts from people you trust. Plan on showing your drafts to other students in your class, your friends, or relatives. When you actually begin writing a paragraph, then you can develop and refine ideas you have already had a chance to examine.

1. making lists
2. brainstorming
3. making subject trees
4. preparing scratch outlines or other kinds of groupings for ideas
5. looking at what other writers have written on the same topic
6. doing timed writing
7. limiting broad topics
8. doing free association
9. doing research
10. conducting interviews

Various chapters in this book define and explain these techniques so that you will have a chance to practice them for different writing tasks.

Making Lists

Since good descriptive writing requires a number of strong sensory images, recording those images in lists is a valuable prewriting technique. With a list of many images before you, you can build a descriptive paper alive in detail.

● Prewriting: Making Lists of Sensory Images ●

Topic: Gino's Pizza Parlor

Sight	*Sound*	*Smell*
fingers kneading white dough	*ring of a cash register*	*tangy smell of garlic and pepper*
bubbling mozzarella cheese	*quarters and dimes clinking on the blue counter*	*cigarette smoke*
red tomato paste	*cries of "One slice and a Coke"*	*hot dough*
crisp brown crust	*rumble of the juke box*	*sweet orange drink*

Touch	*Taste*
wave of heat from the oven	*spicy sauce*
hot olive oil on my fingers	*fiery sausage*
cool ceramic counter	*hot, bland cheese*
icy cup of Coke	
greasy dollar	

—*Lisa Roth*

Step 1. Exploring Lists of Images. Look at Lisa Roth's lists of sensory images. Answer these questions about them.

1. Which image do you find most original? Where does the writer combine senses to create especially clear pictures?

2. Using any one or a combination of images on her list, write a complete sentence alive in sensory language.

3. What single dominant impression could you suggest to help the writer organize her details? How would you incorporate that impression in a topic sentence?

Step 2. Listing Ideas in Groups. Once you have selected the object, place, or person you want to describe, develop images (see pages 3–5) under various sense headings. Write *sight, sound, smell, touch,* and *taste* above five columns on a blank sheet of paper. Under each heading, develop images about the subject you are describing. (Remember, images of action and color go under *sight*. And you may not be able to come up with images under *taste*, the most difficult of the senses to convey in language.)

Practice making lists of this kind with one of the topics suggested below if you are not yet sure about your own topic. Study Lisa Roth's example above.

1. an elderly person you know well (a grandparent, for example)

2. a local bar

3. the college library

4. your old gym sneakers

5. your favorite dessert

Student Samples: Drafting and Revising

Your first assignment is to write a paragraph of at least ten sentences that bring to life an individual, an object, or a particular setting. You are going to have the chance to develop your ideas about this topic before you actually begin writing your paragraph. You should plan to write several drafts of your paper. A *draft* is an attempt that you work over and re-create until your writing fully expresses what you want to say.

When you revise a draft, you try to improve its clarity and precision. You move sentences around, adding and changing words and phrases in order to make your ideas easier to understand. You combine some thoughts, shift some to different parts of your paper, eliminate others. Much revision consists of cutting or removing excess or repetitive or vague language that does not enhance your point.

Mess up your working drafts all you like. Draw arrows. Cross out words. Draw pictures. Use purple ink or crayon or pencil. Use scissors to cut out words and sentences. Paste or tape the words in new positions where they make more sense. Discard pages you don't like, and start again. Remember, your drafts are work sheets. They help you find out what you want to say. (When you submit a paper for evaluation, you do have to follow accepted conventions for preparing your work. See page 27.)

As you prepare your drafts and before you develop your final copy, be sure to examine the section called Progress Reminder: A Checklist on pages 29–31. Presented in question form, this checklist will remind you of the goals for your descriptive paragraph.

Step 1. Examining Drafts.   Read the two drafts of "A Family Gathering" by Marie Mikulka, and answer the questions that follow. (Don't be surprised to discover errors in *both* drafts.) What changes do you notice from the early draft to the revised draft?

DRAFT

```
                    A Family Gathering

The wind roared against the dining room window on that brisk November
day, as we gathered around the table for a peaceful Thanksgiving
dinner. The aroma of apple pies still baking filled the air. The dining
room is cozy, with light brown paneling, and dark wood notches. There
are beige cape cod curtains hanging on the windows. The freshly waxed
floor shines brilliantly. My mother used the white lace tablecloth that
she keeps in the bottom drawer of the small antique china closet, to
decorate the table. In the center of the table are two white
candlesticks that give the room a soft glow. In between the two
candlesticks, lies a basket of wild daisies. My father, in his crisp
white shirt, sits at the head of the table. He is eying the sizzling
brown turkey, that my mother placed in front of him to carve. Before he
carved the turkey, my parents, sisters, brother, a I join hands for a
silent prayer to thank God for all his blessings. For one moment the
room is silent, except for the beating of the wind against the window,
and the sound of the steam surging up the radiator. Soon my father
```

started carving the turkey. My brother Tommy asks for the turkey leg with the crisp skin I ask for a juicy white piece of the breast. Next everyone is passing each other the whipped potatoes with melted butter, the firm broccoli with cheese sauce, the golden brown stuffing, and the cranberry sauce. My mother also prepared sweet potatoes for my father and mashed turnips for her and my sister Laura. Everyone is busy eating, and talking about the upcoming national election, or the football game that will start in about twenty minutes. We slowly begin to excuse ourselves from the table, to go sit in the living room, to watch the football game between the University of Southern California, and Michigan State. We are so full from all the food my mother prepared. The apple pie will have to wait until later. When I think of our family gatherings. A tranquil feeling always flows through me.

REVISED DRAFT

A Family Gathering

The wind roars against the dining room window on this brisk November day as the family gathers around the table for a memorable Thanksgiving dinner. With light brown paneling and dark notches, and with the aroma of apple pies drifting in from the kitchen, the dining room has a soft warm glow. Mother has washed and starched the beige curtains hanging on the windows and the freshly waxed floor gleams. To cover the table, Mother used the white lace cloth. In the center now are two old white candlesticks; between them lies a basket of wild daisies. My father, in his crisp white shirt, sits at the head of the table. He is eyeing a sizzling turkey that my mother has placed in front of him to carve. Before he makes the first cut, my parents, sisters, brothers and I join hands for a silent prayer to thank God for all his blessings. For one tranquil moment the room is quiet, except for the beating of the wind against the window, and the sound of the steam surging up the radiator. Then my father starts carving the turkey and the room bursts into action. "I want the leg, the piece with the crisp skin," my brother Tommy begs. I ask for a piece of the juicy white breast. Next, everyone is passing the potatoes with melted butter, the broccoli with cheese sauce, the stuffing flecked with mushrooms and sausage, and the cranberry sauce. My mother also has prepared sweet potatoes for my father and mashed turnips for her and my sister Laura. Dishes clatter, voices rise and fall, laughter fills the room. Everyone is busy eating and talking about the upcoming national election, or the football game that will start in about twenty minutes. After we're full, we slowly begin to excuse ourselves from the table and drift into the living room to watch the football game between the University of Southern California and Michigan State. We are so full that the apple pie and the dishes will have to wait until later. After a family gathering like this one, I know the meaning of comfort and happiness.

-Marie Mikulka

1. What additions of concrete sensory language do you notice in the revised draft? How do these additions improve the visual quality of the draft?

2. In the revised draft the writer has added exact words spoken by her brother Tommy. How do they compare with the sentence in the earlier draft that indicates only indirectly what Tommy says? Which do you prefer? Why?

3. The second sentence in the revised draft combines elements of several sentences in the early draft. What is your opinion of the change? Does it improve the paragraph? How? What other sentences has the writer combined in the revised draft?

4. What words, phrases, or sentences has the writer eliminated from the early draft? Do you like the cuts? Why or why not?

5. What errors in grammar or spelling has the writer corrected in the revision?

6. What further changes would you recommend that Marie Mikulka make? How might she improve the revision even further?

Step 2. More Student Samples. Read the final drafts of these students' paragraphs written in response to the same assignment you are doing. As you read, look especially at the topic sentences and at the use of concrete sensory detail.

The Gloom Room

On this dreary October afternoon in my writing class here on the second floor of Boylan Hall at Brooklyn College, a shadow of gloom hangs over the people and things that surround me. The atmosphere is depressing. There is an old brown chair beside the teacher's desk, a mahogany bookcase with a missing shelf, and this ugly desk of mine filled with holes and scratches. As I rub my hand across its surface, there is a feeling of coldness. Even the gray walls and the rumble of thunder outside reflect the atmosphere of seriousness as we write our first theme of the semester. When some air sails through an open window beside me, there is the annoying smell of coffee grounds from a garbage pail not far off. My classmates, too, show this mood of tension. Mary, a slim blonde at my right, chews frantically the inside of her lower lip. Only one or two words in blue ink stand upon her clean white page. David Harris, slouched in his seat in the third row, nibbles each finger of each hand. Then he plays inaudibly with a black collar button that stands open on the top of his red plaid shirt. There is a thump as he uncrosses his legs and his scuffed shoe hits the floor. A painful cough slices the air from behind me. I hear a woman's heels click from the hall beyond the closed door and a car engine whine annoyingly from Bedford Avenue. If a college classroom should be a place of delight and pleasure, that could never be proved by the tension in this room.

—*Harry Golden*

1. Underline the topic sentence.

2. What key word (or words) shows Harry Golden's opinion of the subject he is writing about?

3. There are two things in particular that Harry Golden will discuss about his writing class, and he announces them both in the topic sentence. What are they?

4. Pick out three groups of words that describe sounds.

5. Pick out three word groups that use color to paint a picture.

6. Tell in your own words two specific actions you see in Harry Golden's theme.

7. Which sentence appeals to the sense of smell?

8. Which words include an appeal to the sense of touch?

9. Which word picture, in your opinion, is most vivid?

10. Why does Harry Golden mention the time of year and time of day in the first sentence?

My Old Friend

As I settle myself comfortably on the gray blanket on my bed, I fondly study Dumbo the elephant, my oldest and most faithful stuffed animal. He greets me warmly, his fuzzy gray body propped up against my pillows. His blue, cone-shaped hat with the white pom-pom on top once stood stiffly, but now tilts rakishly to the left. The threadbare cloth has recently torn, revealing a white cotton stuffing inside. Dumbo's huge, droopy ears, too, are well worn, and the pink side, the front, is faded. Yet however faded, those ears even now are inviting to me when I need to talk and no one else has time to listen. Next, I examine my friend's gray face, and I touch his small trunk curving up and ending just between his eyes. Those eyes, flat blue and black ovals, look reassuringly at me as they have ever since I was very young. Once so carefully painted, the colors are now scratched off in some spots, but the eyes still have their cheerful sparkle. When I was four, my father brought Dumbo home for me from a trip to California. Then, Dumbo's body, from his neck to the tops of his short gray legs and arms, was pure white, clean as a new sheet. The white is now soiled, and the fur, once plush and fluffy, has become matted from the little hands that snuggled and stroked it every night. Now I pick Dumbo up, and he rests in the crook of my arm as I write. I give him a quick hug, an apology for scrutinizing him, and I breathe in his slightly musty scent. It is a comforting smell, a smell that I've grown up with. For a moment, nostalgia takes over, and I am again five years old and Mommy has sent me to my room for misbehaving. As always, Dumbo is ready to listen and to soak up my tears.

—*Melissa Grace*

1. How does the topic sentence introduce the subject? What is the writer's attitude toward the subject?

2. What words of touch and smell does the writer use?

3. From the writer's descriptions, can you tell how Dumbo has changed? Write down two or three words from the paragraph that describe Dumbo when the writer was young and a few other words that tell how he looks now.

Richard

Richie Fries sits confidently atop the brown desk before us on this English theme day in late November. He speaks immediately, brown eyes sparkling at his audience of fellow classmates. His pressed blue shirt stresses his tall straight posture as his hand motions express words. He scratches his neat black hair as if in thought. "Next question!" he says. "Gotta wake you up. Ya look like you're falling asleep." The class watches his every expression, but there is no sign of nervousness in Richard, not a drop of sweat falling from his brow. "Look at me," his apple cheeks shout. "Look at me," his smile says. "Look," his position at the edge of the table screams. "Look at me. This is my moment of glory." His actual words race by at record pace. "My father tells me I should think in seventy-eight and talk in thirty-three," Rich speedily adds. Susan asks him to smile and change his position. Propping himself upon his elbow, he leans back on the desk. "Hey, why isn't this guy in Hollywood?" I think to myself. His eyes dance. They illuminate when he talks and glow softly when he is silent. His exciting brown eyes hold the class in a strong grip. They are only brown, same as so many other eyes, but they twinkle and they bubble and they look squarely at their audience without so much as a nervous blink. His eyes smile even when his lips fall. The girls like him: he is lively, has a good physique—I suppose it is understandable. Michelle asks where he goes to meet girls and the class giggles squeamishly. After a long, funny answer Richie leans back, the edges of his lips pushing his cheeks up. His brown eyes now stare at no one. Everybody is writing. He takes a deep breath. Then, in a sudden leap from the table Richie returns to his seat like a conqueror.

—Debbie Osher

1. What one word in the topic sentence gives away the writer's opinion of Richie?

2. What does the writer mean by "His actual words *race by at record pace*," "His eyes *dance*," and "His exciting brown eyes *hold the class in a strong grip*"?

3. How does the description of Richie as "like a conqueror" in the concluding sentence relate to the topic sentence?

A Birth Room

At General Hospital there I lay on stark white sheets in a stark white room, only a large clock with black hands, a worm-eaten chair, and a window in my view, as I waited with fear for the arrival of my first born. While the sulky, snowy January dawn rolled lazily through the window, I could see the wind making snow drifts outside and could feel it blow crystals through the rotting window sill. Overhead loomed a menacing light pressed to a vast white ceiling. In front of me an orderly in a green nylon gown cheerily imprisoned my ankles in metal stirrups. "Don't fret none honey," she said. "You ain't the first to have a baby." I forced a smile, but then a sharp pain in my back made me twitch. It passed in a moment although I swore I saw black spots growing on the empty walls. I looked to my left as I ran my fingers over the worn leather straps that held my wrists. The thin second hand moved swiftly on the clock near the door. It was five after seven. Behind me the anesthetist, all in white with mask in hand, fussed with some metal tools, and I saw his intense black eyes darting swiftly. The sudden smell of alcohol nauseated me. In the distance I heard moans reverberating down the corridors—moans of women in labor. I felt reassured about this, for I was one step higher. I was in the delivery room; they still suffered in the labor rooms. To my right Dr. Kassop paced inaudibly, his rubber shoes sliding on the polished green tiles. Then he moved close and with warm fingers touched my brow. How such a small thing can be so comforting! Near my feet Nurse Day bustled about adjusting the tubes from a bottle hanging upside down on a metal stand. No sympathy for a frightened person from her, I thought. To her it was just another birth. Then as I stared at those erupting black spots on the walls I heard a liquid splashing. Suddenly I felt the icy coldness of antiseptic between my thighs as a cry of "Oye!" from a Spanish woman far off rang in my ears. A great pain made me scream and the stark white room reeled. Was that my new baby's cry? That's all I remember. The anesthetist covered my nose with the sharp, welcome smell of his medicine as everything went blank, my fears and the white birth room lost in sleep.

—*Gwendolyn Wellington*

1. What words in the closing sentence go back to the topic and attitude expressed in the topic sentence?

2. Which words best name sounds? smells? actions?

3. What are some transitions the writer uses?

4. Why does the writer call the room *stark*? Why does she say "Overhead *loomed* a *menacing* light" instead of "Overhead *was* a light"?

Collaboration: Getting Reader Response

After you have done your prewriting, write a first draft of your descriptive paragraph and bring it to class. In groups of three, read each other's papers and make either written or spoken comments to help the writer move on to the next draft. As discussion guidelines, answer the questions listed below for each paper you read and refer to the checklist on pages 29–31, especially items 7 to 10 and 13 to 14.

1. Which sensory images are sharp and concrete? Which images need more vivid details?

2. Which senses are not adequately represented? Where in the paragraph could the writer develop those senses?

3. Which transitions help you to follow the writer's movement from one part of the description to another?

4. What dominant impression of the subject has the writer given you?

5. What general suggestions can you make for improving the paper?

Manuscript Form

A manuscript is the final copy of a writer's created work. You must prepare your manuscript carefully before you submit it. Your instructor will insist that your paper be clean and easy to read and that you follow procedures most professional writers follow before they share their final efforts with others.

1. Leave wide margins (1 to 1 1/2 inches) on all four sides.

2. Write in ink on one side of each page only. Use regulation theme paper if you write by hand. If you type, use sturdy bond, 8 1/2- by 11-inch typing paper. Do not use onionskin. Use blue or black ink: nothing fancy.

3. Make sure your name, your class, and the date appear where your instructor asks for them.

4. If you write by hand, *print* all your capital letters (this makes them easier to read). Leave a large space after each end mark. Make periods firm and clear. They remind you that you are starting a new idea in a new sentence.

5. Check your theme by proofreading (see below) for any careless errors.

6. Occasional errors may be corrected with correction fluid or with a good ink or typewriter eraser.

If You Write Your Paper in Class

1. Do not plan on rewriting: you will not have time.

2. Think for several minutes about the topic. Spend a minute or two examining the topic sentence you write.

3. Jot down some ideas on scrap paper. If an outline helps you, draw one up quickly (see pages 204–206).

4. You are still responsible for errors. Check your theme by proofreading (see below) for careless mistakes. Save at least five minutes at the end of the session to proofread.

5. Most instructors encourage you to use a dictionary and thesaurus even when you write your composition in class. Check with your teacher, and if it is all right, look up words to check spelling errors.

Proofreading

Proofreading is a convenient term to name what writers do when they look over their work for errors.

As a writer you should not expect to proofread your writing at all stages of creation. There's not much point in worrying about being correct when you are trying to develop ideas in a rough draft. In fact, the *last* thing you want to think about as your ideas first take shape on paper is correctness. Drafts are for putting thoughts down clearly and logically.

When you revise each draft, you look especially for ways of improving your language and the structure of your sentences. Part of that process will involve correcting major sentence errors of the kinds explained in this chapter and in other parts of the book.

Productive proofreading takes place at two critical stages in the writing of any paper. First, you need to check for errors in the draft that you will turn into a final manuscript. Next, you need to check over your final manuscript itself to make sure that no errors have slipped by.

The suggestions below will help you locate careless mistakes that may appear in your writing.

Tips for Effective Proofreading

1. Read *slowly*. This is not a job done by skimming. Look at—and read aloud, if necessary—every word. Don't let your eyes move too swiftly from one word to the next.

2. Use a ruler or a blank sheet of paper below each line; this will help you locate spelling errors by cutting off later words from your line of vision. Block any words that may distract you on the line you are checking. The fewer words you examine at a time, the easier it is to find spelling errors.

3. Examine each syllable of each word. Try pointing at each word as you pronounce it to see if it is correct.

4. Be aware of your own usual errors. A glance at your Progress Sheet (page 454) before you do any written work puts you on your guard. If you're a chronic run-on writer, know the run-on Stop Signs. If you write fragments, know the fragment Stop Signs. (See pages 334 and 335.) If you usually confuse *its* and *it's* and you have used one of those words in your paragraph, stop for a second to analyze the spelling you've chosen.

5. If you are writing in class, cross out or erase errors neatly. Some writers like to skip lines in order to insert any words or ideas left out through carelessness. If you've left out a word or words, draw a caret (∧) below the line and insert what was omitted. Do it this way:

> *went*
> *So we awakened early and ˄ to the beach.*

6. You can't look up every word to check spelling, but you do know which words you are unsure of. *Look them up in a dictionary.* And keep a record of the words you usually spell wrong (see Your Own Demon List, page 434).

7. You can make minor corrections on your final manuscript, but if too many errors require corrections there, you should consider it as a draft and should write another manuscript to submit.

Practice with Proofreading.   Correct the errors by following the suggestions above.

The nicest think about raining days in our old house was the oportunity to to play in the attic. Our attic was with old stage costumes witch are grandparents wore many years a go. There collection of wigs and beeded dresses kept us busy for hours, for instance, i was always pretended that I was a beautiful princes who would be rescued by a hansome Prince. I whish I could relive those child hood days.

Follow-up: After Your Instructor Returns Your Graded Theme

1. Check your paper to make sure that you understand your instructor's writing and any correction symbols used in the margin.

2. Correct all errors in mechanics—grammar, spelling, and punctuation.

3. Rewrite your entire paper if your instructor suggests that you do so. Correct problems in content and thought development, using the comments in the margin to guide you.

4. Enter on page 434 any words you misspelled.

5. Enter on the Theme Progress Sheet (Appendix B) the total number of errors you made in each category listed on top of the page. In that way you can see before you write the next theme just what kinds of mistakes you usually make.

Progress Reminders: A Checklist

Ask yourself these questions as you prepare your drafts and examine them for revision. Check off each item as you evaluate your own writing. When you hand in your paragraph, submit the checklist along with it.

1. Have I chosen my topic carefully, selecting for description   _____
   someone or something which is especially clear in my mind
   and which I can bring alive with concrete sensory detail?

2. Have I done prewriting? (See pages 18–20.) Have I exam-   _____
   ined the prewriting model on page 19 and the model student
   themes on pages 21–26?

3. From my prewriting activities, have I prepared a rough draft?   _____

4. Have I developed subsequent drafts to shape and clarify my   _____
   ideas further? Have I followed guidelines on page 27 in
   preparing my final manuscript?

5. Have I shared my draft with someone else in the class, either   _____
   in the activity listed on page 26 or in some other way my
   instructor suggests? Have I used a reader's response to revise
   my draft?

6. Have I avoided jumping too quickly from one feature of my   _____
   subject to another? As I described some person, place, or
   object, have I written two or three sentences to show clearly
   what I saw before I moved on to another aspect of my
   subject?   _____

7. Have I mentioned time and place as early as possible in the
   paragraph?   _____

8. Have I used at least three words that appeal to the sense of
   sound? (See page 3 for some new "sound" vocabulary.)

   Here is one sound image from my paragraph. _____

   _____

9. Have I used at least three colors in different places through-   _____
   out the theme?

10. Have I used at least one group of words to appeal to the sense   _____
    of touch and one group of words to appeal to the sense of
    smell?

11. *a.* Have I written one sentence that uses the semicolon cor-   _____
    rectly? (See pages 2–3.)

    b. Have I tried to use one or two words from the vocabulary   _____
    introduced at the beginning of this chapter? (See page
    392.)

12. Have I named people and shown them as they perform some   _____
    action? Harry Golden says that Mary chews the inside of her
    lip.

13. Have I written a topic sentence that includes an opinion and   _____
    states clearly what my topic will be? Do my descriptive

details support the opinion word I stated in my topic sentence? Here is my topic sentence: _____

_____

14. Have I used words and phrases like *up front, to my left,* _____
    nearby, across the room, far away, above, beside, in the
    corner to help me move from one aspect of my subject to
    another?

15. Have I given my paragraph a title? (A title is not a topic _____
    sentence. If you can use part of the topic in your title, you
    must still repeat the topic in the topic sentence. See pages 48–
    49.) Here is my title: _____

    _____

16. Have I proofread my paper twice: once before I prepared my _____
    final manuscript and once after I prepared it? (See pages 28–
    29.)

17. Have I checked my paper for my usual errors, especially for _____
    run-ons and for spelling problems? (See pages 313–320 and
    421–433.)

● The Professionals Speak

Concrete details are essential parts of a good description. Writers know that to make a firm impression on the reader's mind, they must give lively sensory images so that the subject may be easily visualized.

Read the descriptions below and answer the questions that follow.

SOME WORDS TO KNOW BEFORE YOU READ

obscurity—darkness

motes—small particles; specks

frazzly—frayed; tattered

contemplate—think about

murky—dark or gloomy

Our Little Store

Our Little Store rose right up from the sidewalk; standing in a street of family houses, it alone hadn't any yard in front, any tree or flowerbed. It was a plain frame building covered over with brick. Above the door, a little railed porch ran across on an upstairs level and four windows with shades were looking out. But I didn't catch on to those.

Running in out of the sun, you met what seemed total obscurity inside. There were almost tangible smells—licorice recently sucked in a child's cheek, dill-pickle brine that had leaked through a paper sack in a fresh trail across the wooden floor, ammonia-loaded ice that had been hoisted from wet croker sacks and slammed into the icebox with its sweet butter at the door, and perhaps the smell of still untrapped mice.

Then through the motes of cracker dust, cornmeal dust, the Gold Dust of the Gold Dust Twins that the floor had been swept out with, the realities emerged. Shelves climbed to high reach all the way around, set out with not too much of any one thing but a lot of things—lard, molasses, vinegar, starch, matches, kerosene, Octagon soap (about a year's worth of octagon-shaped coupons cut out and saved brought a signed ring addressed to you in the mail. Furthermore, when the postman arrived at your door, he blew a whistle). It was up to you to remember what you came for while your eye traveled from cans of sardines to ice cream salt to harmonicas to flypaper (over your head, batting around on a thread beneath the blades of the ceiling fan, stuck with its testimonial catch).

Its confusion may have been in the eye of its beholder. Enchantment is cast upon you by all those things you weren't supposed to have need for, it lures you close to wooden tops you'd outgrown, boy's marbles and agates in little net pouches, small rubber balls that wouldn't bounce straight, frazzly kitestring, clay bubblepipes that would snap off in your teeth, the stiffest scissors. You could contemplate those long narrow boxes of sparklers gathering dust while you waited for it to be the Fourth of July or Christmas, and noisemakers in the shape of tin frogs for somebody's birthday party you hadn't been invited to yet, and see that they were all marvelous.

You might not have even looked for Mr. Sessions when he came around his store cheese (as big as a doll's house) and in front of the counter looking for you. When you'd finally asked him for, and received from him in its paper bag, whatever single thing it was that you had been sent for, the nickel that was left over was yours to spend.

Down at a child's eye level, inside those glass jars with mouths in their sides through which the grocer could run his scoop or a child's hand might be invited to reach for a choice, were wineballs, all-day suckers, gumdrops, peppermints. Making a row under the glass of a counter were the Tootsie Rolls, Hershey Bars, Goo-Goo Clusters, Baby Ruths. And whatever was the name of those pastilles that came stacked in a cardboard cylinder with a cardboard lid? They were thin and dry, about the size of tiddlywinks, and in the shape of twisted rosettes. A kind of chocolate dust came out with them when you shook them out in your hand. Were they chocolate? I'd say rather they were brown. They didn't taste of anything at all, unless it was wood. Their attraction was the number you got for a nickel.

Making up your mind, you circled the store around and around, around the pickle barrel, around the tower of Cracker Jack boxes; Mr. Sessions had built it for us himself on top of a packing case, like a house of cards.

If it seemed too hot for Cracker Jacks, I might get a cold drink. Mr. Sessions might have already stationed himself by the cold-drinks barrel, like a mind reader. Deep in ice water that looked black as ink, murky shapes that would come up as Coca-Colas, Orange Crushes; and various flavors of pop, were all swimming around together. When you gave the word, Mr. Sessions plunged his bare arm in to the elbow and fished out your choice, first try. I favored a locally bottled concoction called Lake's Celery. (What else could it be called? It was made by a Mr. Lake out of celery. It was a popular drink here for years but was not known universally, as I found out when I arrived in New York and ordered one in the Astor bar.) You drank on the premises, with feet set wide apart to miss the drip, and gave him back his bottle.

But he didn't hurry you off. A standing scales was by the door, with a stack of iron weights and a brass slide on the balance arm, that would weigh you up to three hundred pounds. Mr. Sessions, whose hands were gentle and smelled of carbolic, would lift you up and set your feet on the platform, hold your loaf of bread for you, and taking his time while you stood still for him, he would make certain of what you weighed today. He could even remember what you weighed the last time, so you could subtract and announce how much you'd gained. That was goodby.

—*Eudora Welty*

1. Which images best show action? Which verbs do you find particularly clear and specific?
2. Where does Welty use color in her description?
3. Identify the sensory appeals here to sound, smell, and touch. Which images are most original, do you think?
4. *Mood*, or atmosphere, is an important element in descriptive writing. What mood has Welty created in this description? What feeling is she trying to give you about her little grocery store? Which words help establish the mood?

SOME WORDS TO KNOW BEFORE YOU READ

deviation—a stepping aside from the norm

ragged—torn; tattered

meticulousness—great care about details; fussiness

fastidious—overly fussy; hard to please

Uncle Kwok

Among the workers in Daddy's factory, Uncle Kwok was one of the strangest—a large-framed, awkward, unshaven man whose worn clothes hung on him as if they did not belong to him. Each afternoon around three-thirty, as some of the workers were about to go home to prepare their early dinners, Uncle Kwok slowly and deliberately ambled in through the Wong front door, dragging his feet heavily, and gripping in one hand the small black satchel from which he was never separated.

Going to his own place at the sewing machine, he took off his battered hat and ragged coat, hung both up carefully, and then sat down. At first Jade Snow was rather afraid of this extraordinary person, and unseen, watched his actions from a safe distance. After Uncle Kwok was settled in his chair, he took off his black, slipperlike shoes. Then, taking a piece of stout cardboard from a miscellaneous pile which he kept in a box near his sewing machine, he traced the outline of his shoes on the cardboard. Having closely examined the blades of his scissors and tested their sharpness, he would cut out a pair of cardboard soles, squinting critically through his inaccurate glasses. Next he removed from both shoes the cardboard soles he had made the day before and inserted the new pair. Satisfied with his inspection of his renewed footwear, he got up, went to the waste can some seventy-five feet away, disposed of the old soles, and returned to his machine. He had not yet said a word to anyone.

Daily this process was repeated without deviation.

The next thing Uncle Kwok always did was to put on his own special apron, homemade from double thicknesses of heavy burlap and fastened at the waist by strong denim ties. This long apron covered his thin, patched trousers and protected him from dirt and draft. After a half hour had been consumed by these chores, Uncle Kwok was ready to wash his hands. He sauntered into the Wong kitchen, stationed himself at the one sink which served both family and factory, and with characteristic meticulousness, now proceeded to clean his hands and fingernails.

It was Mama's custom to begin cooking the evening meal at this hour so that the children could have their dinner before they went to the Chinese school, but every day she had to delay her preparations at the sink until slow-moving Uncle Kwok's last clean fingernail passed his fastidious inspection. One day, however, the inconvenience tried her patience to its final limit.

Trying to sound pleasantly persuasive, she said, "Uncle Kwok, please don't be so slow and awkward. Why don't you wash your hands at a different time, or else wash them faster?"

Uncle Kwok loudly protested the injustice of her comment. "Mama, I am not awkward. The only awkward thing about my life is that it has not yet prospered!" And he strode off, too hurt to even dry his hands finger by finger, as was his custom.

—Jade Snow Wong

1. How does the opening paragraph introduce the subject of "Uncle Kwok"? Does it effectively state the writer's opinion about the subject? Where?

2. What concrete sensory images does Wong use to describe Uncle Kwok's appearance? How does she describe his clothes? What action verbs show how Uncle Kwok moves?

3. Which sentence in paragraph five contains a coordinator?

4. How many transition words or phrases can you find in "Uncle Kwok"? How do they help you move smoothly from one action to the next?

2

Narration: Telling a Story

●

INTRODUCTION: WRITING A NARRATIVE PAPER

We all remember outstanding moments—thrilling, tender, embarrassing, startling moments—that stand out vividly in our minds. If you have ever slid into home plate to break a tie, tripped while crossing a room to meet a friend, or thought someone was following you down a dimly lit street, you surely remember the experience clearly, along with the pride, embarrassment, or terror you felt. Perhaps you recall your grandmother's encouraging words as you first tried to ride a bicycle, or the thrill you felt the first time you visited an amusement park. Or perhaps instead of being directly involved, you were a spectator to some unforgettable moment. Perhaps you witnessed an automobile accident, watched a robin build its nest, observed a child learning how to read, or attended a concert featuring your favorite musical group. Both as observer and participant you can no doubt recall many moments that stirred emotions in you that you may feel even now as you think about the experiences.

These distinct moments are the subjects for your next writing assignment. The paragraph you write will narrate (tell a story about) a brief, meaningful event that you experienced.

● Journal Entry

Write a few sentences about some outstanding moment in your life. Try to identify an event that took place over a short period of time. Choose an event that is alive in color and action. Don't go too far back in the past because you might have trouble recalling the key details.

● Vocabulary

Step 1. Words for Actions. These words are useful in describing actions and help create specific pictures. Check a dictionary and write the definitions in the blank spaces.

1. grimace _____
2. stagger _____
3. hurl _____
4. amble _____
5. slither _____

6. plunge _____
7. veer _____
8. bellow _____
9. collapse _____
10. lunge _____

Step 2. Using New Vocabulary. Fill in each blank with a word from the list in Step 1 so that the sentences make sense.

1. When the workmen had finished testing the microphones, the announcer's

   voice _____ through the vast, empty arena.

2. Grunting as he spun around in order to gather momentum, Ricardo

   _____ the shot put for a new county record.

3. She balanced herself carefully on the high diving board and then, suddenly,

   _____ into the icy water.

4. Hurt, exhausted, and dirty, the defeated football players _____ into the dressing room.

5. Shoeless in the mud, she _____ to the edge of the lake.

6. The old man _____ slowly across the open field, enjoying the warm spring day.

7. Because the driver was tired, his old blue sedan _____ from one side of the road to the other.

8. Sarah _____ at her opponent and pinned her to the ground.

9. After two overtimes, the team _____ on the bench with exhaustion.

10. At the thought of spending a whole day with such an unpleasant child, Mr. Lee

_____, his face twisted with annoyance.

Step 3. How People Do or Say Things.   The following words, all ending in *-ly,* are helpful in conveying actions accurately. Check them in a dictionary and write definitions.

1. irresponsibly _____
2. joyously _____
3. sullenly _____
4. exhaustedly _____
5. longingly _____

6. brazenly _____
7. precariously _____
8. painstakingly _____
9. infrequently _____
10. vehemently _____

Step 4. Seeing the Words at Work.

1. When would you do something *vehemently?* _____

_____

2. If a team played *infrequently,* how well would you expect it to play? _____

_____

3. How could you tell if someone did something *exhaustedly?* _____

_____

4. Why might a teenager behave *sullenly?* _____

_____

5. What types of workers would perform their jobs *precariously?* _____

_____

6. If someone danced *joyously,* how would you expect her to look? _____

_____

7. What kind of job would you do *painstakingly?* _____

_____

8. How could you tell if someone acted *brazenly?* _____

_____

9. How could you tell if someone were looking *longingly* at an expensive new car in a showroom window? _____

_____

10. How would a group of demonstrators have to act for you to say that they were acting *irresponsibly*? _____

_____

Step 5. *-ing* Words for Liveliness. The words below, in their *-ing* forms, will help you improve your writing style (see pages 44–47). Check a dictionary for any you don't know; write the definition in the blank space.

> **Hint**
>
> Look up the word in its infinitive form. Look up *sputter*, not *sputtering*, for example.

1. sputtering _____
2. asserting _____
3. lamenting _____
4. reiterating _____
5. assenting _____

Step 6. Naming the Action. From the list above, write in each blank a word that would show:

1. that someone was repeating _____
2. agreement _____
3. expressing grief for _____
4. a manner of excited and unclear speech _____
5. someone making a statement she thought was true _____

● Building Composition Skills

Finding the Topic

One of the best ways to get ideas on any topic is to talk about and listen to the ideas of the people around you. Thus you can air out your own thoughts and can see how they sound before you begin to put them on paper. You also can recall ideas about your own experiences when you hear the ideas your friends may have.

Step 1. Talking About the Topic. Pick any word group below and read it aloud, adding your own ending. Then, in a few more sentences, explain what you said. Or, if your instructor suggests, write a few brief sentences to complete any of the statements.

1. I played well when _____

_____

2. At my high school graduation I felt _____

_____

3. An exciting sport I like is _____

_____

4. The first time I got a flat tire _____

_____

5. I felt happiest when I _____

_____

6. Jogging makes me feel _____

_____

7. One thing I hate about school is _____

_____

8. The most eventful day I had was _____

_____

9. I was most embarrassed when _____

_____

10. I wish my son (daughter) would _____

_____

11. The first time I ever drove a car, I _____

_____

12. When it comes to the outdoors, I _____

_____

13. I learned who my real friends were when _____

_____

14. On my first bicycle trip I _____

_____

15. I laughed hard when _____

_____

Here are some students' responses:

An exciting sport I like is skiing because the cold mountain air, the steep slopes, and the heart-pounding speed make me feel alive.

—Richard Young

I wish my son would play basketball more for enjoyment than for a victory over the other team. He takes the sport too seriously, and he broods over a loss for days.

—*Willa Brown*

I first learned who my real friends were when Dee and John dropped everything to drive my son Mike and me to the hospital when Mike fell off a swing and broke his collarbone.

—*Winnie Evans*

Expanding the Topic Sentence

You can limit a topic sentence if you name your topic specifically and if you give your opinion about the topic. (If you need a quick review, see Chapter 1.) You can further limit the topic sentence—especially when you write a paragraph that tells a story—by showing where and when the event you are writing about takes place. By *where* we mean the room, the outdoor setting, the physical location in which the moment happened. By *when* we mean not the date but the season or month of the year, the part of the day, the day of the week. Sometimes a word of color or sound or touch helps the *when* and *where* details come to life. Here are two topic sentences that give the topic and opinion, that tell when or where, and that use a sense word.

       [time]   [place]   [opinion]

One winter evening in our school gymnasium I learned the importance of team-work in basketball as the final bell clanged to end the game.

                        [sound]

Topic: teamwork in basketball

    [time]   [place]   [opinion]

Every morning in the park I experience the agony of the long-distance runner as I jog ten miles through the gray dawn.

                       [color]

Topic: jogging ten miles

Step 1. Adding Details. Add details of time or place or both to the topic sentences below, and rewrite them. If possible, use a sound, color, or touch word. Use your own paper.

EXAMPLE

My husband relaxes by washing our car.

On Saturday mornings outside our apartment building my husband relaxes by washing our old blue Chevy.

1. Our energetic cheerleaders always helped our teams to win.
2. Snorklers should always exercise caution.
3. My mother embarrassed me in front of all my friends.
4. Our school's parade was a flop.
5. I enjoy watching horror movies.

Step 2. Writing Sentence Openers. For each subject in Column I, write a topic sentence that includes time and place, gives an opinion, and appeals in some way to one of the senses. Try to put the words that tell *where* or *when* right at the beginning of the sentence.

I

EXAMPLE

team practice sessions

II

Every Saturday morning I hate dragging my football equipment to Washington Field to practice for the next week's game.

_____

1. eating in a neighborhood restaurant

_____

_____

_____

2. canoeing over the rapids

_____

_____

_____

3. learning to drive

_____

_____

_____

_____

Step 3. Analyzing the Topic Sentence. Turn to the top of page 39. Look at the topic sentences numbered 1 and 2. Which words tell the time of the event? Which of the topic sentences tells *place*?

Chronology

Whenever you narrate events, they are most easily understood when you write of them in the time order in which they happened. The arrangement of details or events according to time is *chronology*. Look at the two paragraphs below. The sentences on the right present the events in their order of occurrence while those on the left jump around without logic from event to event.

CONFUSED

On Wednesday evenings my uncle and I spend an enjoyable hour playing racquetball. On the way home we sometimes stop for ice cream; of course, the loser always pays the bill. We usually go into the sauna for ten minutes before hitting the showers. We change our clothing in the locker room, and play an exciting but exhausting hour of racquetball. My uncle picks me up in his station wagon and we zoom over to the Bethpage Racquetball Center. When I get home, I'm ready for a good night's sleep.

CHRONOLOGICAL

On Wednesday evenings my uncle and I spend an enjoyable hour playing racquetball. After dinner, my uncle picks me up in his station wagon and we zoom over to the Bethpage Racquetball Center. After a quick change of clothing in the locker room, we play an exciting but exhausting hour of racquetball. Then we usually go into the sauna for ten minutes before hitting the showers. On the way home, we sometimes stop for ice cream; of course, the loser always pays the bill. When I get home, I'm ready for a good night's sleep.

Step 1. Chronology. Write four sentences in chronological order about each subject named below.

1. catching a fish

    a. _____

    b. _____

    c. _____

    d. _____

2. changing a bicycle tire

    a. _____

    b. _____

    c. _____

    d. _____

3. watching a television program

   a. _____

   b. _____

   c. _____

   d. _____

Step 2. Telling the Order.   Here is a topic sentence that calls for a paragraph in chronological order. Write six or seven sentences in which you tell details in the order in which they might have occurred. Use a separate sheet of paper.

Driving along frozen mountain passes can be a hazardous experience on a dark February morning.

Expanding Sentences for Variety: Using the *-ly* Opener

One way to avoid writing a paragraph whose sentences are too much alike is to start one or two of them with a word that ends in *-ly*. You have a number of these words (called *adverbs*) in your vocabulary already (for example, *swiftly, slowly, annoyingly, suddenly*). Step 3 of the Vocabulary section introduces some new *-ly* words.

Step 1. *-ly* Words for Variety.   On a separate sheet of paper, use each *-ly* word in Step 3 of the Vocabulary section to open a sentence of your own.

EXAMPLE

Brazenly, my cousin announced, "I'm the best!"

Step 2. Two *-ly* Openers.   An effective technique for opening sentences is to use two *-ly* words at the beginning. Separate the *-ly* words either with a comma or with *and* or *but*. Don't use two *-ly* words that mean exactly the same thing.

EXAMPLE

Slowly, annoyingly, the actor's voice filled the theater.
Strongly and cautiously, the lion stalked its prey.

   Write a sentence about each subject indicated below, starting each sentence with two *-ly* words. Use words from your own vocabulary and from the words in Step 3 of the Vocabulary section. Use a separate sheet of paper.

1. a pitcher facing a powerful hitter with bases loaded
2. a racing car speeding out of control

3. getting out of bed in the morning
4. trying to clean the bedroom
5. sneaking twenty minutes late into a classroom

Expanding Sentences: Verb-Part Openers

You can improve sentence variety further by opening a sentence with a verb part or with a group of words containing part of a verb. (See A Sentence Review, pages 403–407.)

Using the *-ing* Opener

An *-ing* word—called a *present participle*—may be used effectively to open a sentence. Note how we can expand this sentence:

An old gray Ford inched to the stop sign.

An *-ing* word may be added at the beginning.

[comma here]

Sputtering, an old gray Ford inched to the stop sign.

Hint

A comma must follow an introductory *-ing* word or an introductory group of words that contain an *-ing* word.

A word that tells *how, when,* or *where* may be placed after the *-ing* word.

[how] [comma here]

Sputtering *loudly,* an old gray Ford inched to the stop sign.

A group of words that tell *why* or *how* or *where* or *when* may now be added after the *-ly* word.

[These words tell where.] [comma here]

Sputtering loudly *down Sixth Street,* an old gray Ford inched to the stop sign.

Sometimes a subordinator (see pages 86–94) may appear as the first word in verb-part opener:

[subordinator] [comma here]

While sputtering loudly down Sixth Street, an old gray Ford inched to the stop sign.

Hint

Make sure that the first two or three words after the comma tell *who* or *what* is doing the action of the *-ing* word with which you have opened the sentence. See pages 320–323 for some work with incorrect verb-part openers.

Step 1. Opening a Sentence Strongly.   Add opening word groups to the complete sentences that follow by selecting an item first from Column I, then from Column II, then from Column III. You should have three new sentences for each numbered statement below.

I	II	III
(-ing WORD)	(ONE WORD TO TELL HOW, WHEN, WHERE)	(A WORD GROUP TO TELL HOW, WHEN, WHERE, WHY)
coughing	gracefully	in the sky
trembling	noisily	below the hill
leaping	clumsily	near me
soaring	there	through an open window
roaring	yesterday	in darkness
speeding	above	on a warm summer night
moaning	innocently	with a whine
creeping	swiftly	beyond the gray mountains
dancing	today	at noon
cheering	slowly	in a soft voice
speaking	excitedly	beneath a pale cloud
crying	softly	across a stream
hurtling	deliberately	from their seats
drifting		at the campfire
pleading		beside an old oak tree

EXAMPLE

The boat returned home.

a. *Speeding, the boat returned home.*

b. *Trembling noisily, the boat returned home.*

c. *Drifting slowly across a stream, the boat returned home.*

1. A child clung to her mother's skirts.

    a. Very Quitly, a child clung to her mothe's skirts.

    b. runing throw the hall, a child clung to he mothor's skirts,

    c. _____

2. The raging stream raced to the canyon.

    a. _____

    b. _____

    c. _____

3. The ballet dancer gave his best performance ever.

    a. _____

    b. _____

    c. _____

4. The soldier smiled.

    a. _____

    b. _____

    c. _____

5. The cat sprang quickly away.

    a. As I sneezed, the cat sprang Quickly away.

    b. From the sound of the door bell, the cat sprang Quickly away.

    c. _____

Step 2. Using New Words.   Use the words given in the new -*ing* vocabulary (on page 38) to open three sentences of your own. Use separate paper.

Step 3. -*ing* at the End.   The -*ing* construction also works nicely at the ends of sentences. On a separate sheet of paper, rewrite any five sentences you wrote in Step 1 or Step 2 above, this time placing the -*ing* word group at the end.

Sentence from Step 1: Drifting slowly across a stream, the boat returned home quietly.

Rewritten sentence: The boat returned home, *drifting slowly across a stream.*

Step 4. Two -*ing* Words.   Two -*ing* words at the beginning produce an effective sentence. Complete each sentence below that begins with a double -*ing* construction by adding your own complete thought. Use your own paper.

EXAMPLE

Laughing and shouting,

Laughing and shouting, the children shouted, "Trick or Treat!"

> ### Hint
>
> The first few words after the comma must tell who or what does the action of the *-ing* words. See pages 320–323 for errors that may arise in the use of the *-ing* opener.

1. Pushing and screaming,
2. Gasping for breath and gripping the stair rail,
3. Brushing his hair and smiling into the mirror,
4. Groping in the dark and calling her name,
5. Whistling softly and shaking her head,

Using Infinitives as Openers

If you want to tell *why* the subject of a sentence performs some action, you can open the sentence with a word group that starts with an infinitive. (An infinitive is made up of the word *to* and the present tense of the verb: *to hope, to sing, to laugh* are just three examples.)

[This tells *why* he had the tires checked.]

To ensure the safety of his car, he had the tires checked carefully.
[comma here]

Step 5. Using Infinitives as Openers. Use each of the following infinitive word groups in front of your own complete sentence.

> ### Hint
>
> Use a comma after an infinitive word group when a complete sentence follows it.

EXAMPLE

To achieve high grades

To achieve high grades, a student needs discipline.

1. To lead a large corporation

   _____

2. To repair a faulty carburetor

   _____

3. To write well

   _____

4. To learn computer programming

   _____

Other Verb Parts as Openers

Word groups with verb parts that end in *-ed, -n, -en,* or *-t* (*past participles*) may also be used to start sentences. Again, a comma must come after the introductory word group, and the first words after the comma must tell who performs the action of the verb part used in that introductory word group.

Spoken in a loud voice, the announcer's words reached the whole audience.
   [verb part]   [comma here]   [This tells *what*
                                was spoken.]

     [verb part]

Concerned about her choice of medical schools, Joyce consulted her academic adviser.
                         [comma]   [This tells *who*
                                         was concerned.]

Step 6. Using Other Verb Parts as Openers. On separate paper, begin a sentence of your own with each of the following verb-part openers. Be sure you study the examples given above.

1. Stimulated by the biologist's lecture
2. Drawn with a broken pencil
3. Encouraged by my teammates
4. Terrified by the darkness
5. Awakened by the ring of the doorbell

How to Write Titles

The title is a helpful feature for the reader since titles give the first hint of what appears within the paragraph or essay.

● How to Write a Strong Title ●

1. Give the main idea of your paragraph in the title.

2. If you don't want to tell the topic in your title, pick out a word or word group from the paragraph that will hint at the kind of topic you are treating.

3. Arouse the reader's curiosity by the title.

● What Not to Do in a Title ●

1. *Do not* make the title the only statement of the topic. *A title is not a topic sentence.* If you tell the topic in the title, repeat the topic in the topic sentence.

2. *Do not* try to be cute. If you want a funny title, be sure your paragraph deals with a humorous subject.

• How to Write a Strong Title •

4. Write the title last, after you have finished the paragraph.

5. If you can write an interesting, exciting title, good. If not, don't worry. It's better to be clear and to give a title that suits the paragraph than to be brilliant, clever, or original.

6. When you write your title, put it on top of page one. Capitalize all important words.

Hint: Do not capitalize words like *and, the, an, a, but,* or any of the short direction words like *in, on, to,* or *for* unless one of these words is the first or last word in your title.

• What Not to Do in a Title •

3. *Do not* use overworn expressions as your title: "A Stitch in Time Saves Nine" or "Love Makes the World Go Round" would be inappropriate titles for themes about prompt action and love because these titles are too familiar.

4. *Do not* write titles that are too long. A long full sentence is rarely used as a title.

5. *Do not* write a title that is too general.

6. *Do not* use quotation marks or underlining in your title when it appears in your composition.

Step 1. Seeing Effective Titles. Each statement in Column I is the topic sentence of a paragraph. Column II gives a title that is weak for one of the reasons explained in the boxed chart. In Column III, write why you think the title is poor; in Column IV, try to write your own title.

I	II	III	IV
EXAMPLE			
Many members of my family contributed to my happiness as a child.	Relatives	*too general*	*Relatives and Childhood Pleasure*
1. One frightening experience I recall is the awful time I was locked in a butcher's refrigerator for three hours.	Keeping Cool		
2. Skiing with my dad is always an adventure.	I Go Skiing with My Dad Every Winter		

I	II	III	IV
EXAMPLE			

3. Learning to enjoy foreign films takes concentration and energy.   Digging Flicks

4. I experienced the true meaning of friendship while playing varsity basketball.   Dribble Trouble

5. I remember the terrible trouble I got myself into when I lied to my parents about breaking Mr. Collins' window.   Honesty Is the Best Policy

Step 2. More Practice with Titles.   List titles of several books, motion pictures, or television shows. Explain why you think the titles are effective or why they lack appeal for you. What might you add to the titles to make them stronger?

Word and Sentence Skills: Suggested Topics for Study

Using Quotation Marks, pages 400–403 and 391
Fragments, pages 329–345

● Writing a Narrative Paragraph

Assignment

Your assignment for this theme is to write a paragraph of at least twelve to fifteen sentences to narrate one moment in which you reveal some memorable experience you had. To *narrate* means to tell a story in such a way that your reader easily can follow the sequence of events in the experience you choose to relate. As with descriptive writing, narration also makes use of vivid and concrete details and images. Before you write, take a look at the checklist on pages 58–59.

As you write this narrative, confine the action to a single moment. These suggestions will help you:

1. A "moment" is a memorable instance in your life that illustrates some opinion or idea you want to write about.
2. A "moment" is limited as much as possible in time; it is a brief span of time that you recall sharply.
3. You must make this "moment" as vivid for your reader as it was for you when you experienced it. In order to do this, you need to fill in details with concrete sensory language. Remember that you create pictures (images) by using sensory words that will let the reader share your experience.
4. What kinds of details do you need to make the moment come alive? Show some images of the setting (where the moment occurs) through color, smell, touch, and sound; describe the people who participate in the moment (show their faces and actions); use bits of important dialogue that people speak as the moment develops.

Suggested Topics

In case you need help in finding a moment about which to write, one of these titles may give you an idea.

1. My Brother's Temper	11. Proving Myself
2. Accidents Happen	12. A Walk Alone
3. The New Kid	13. A Practical Joke
4. The Meaning of Friendship	14. Skiing Thrills
5. Touchdown!	15. In an Elementary School Classroom
6. The Day I Lost My Wallet	16. A Moment with My Friends
7. Training for Victory	17. From the Grandstand
8. My Moment of Glory	18. My Big Scare
9. A Vacation I Won't Forget	19. Dead Last
10. Learning from Losing	20. Cooking Disaster

For more topic ideas, turn to pages 38–39 and reread the sentences in Step 1.

Prewriting: Brainstorming

Another prewriting strategy (see page 19) to loosen up ideas on a topic is *brainstorming*. Brainstorming is usually a technique in which a group of people meet in order to stimulate thinking on some idea or problem. People who brainstorm ask lots of questions about the problem at hand, trying then to answer them. To brainstorm on your own about some topic you are considering, make up questions that can generate information and details. On a scratch page write the words *Who? What? Where? When? Why?* and *How?* Then, try to answer the questions in short word groups or in full sentences.

Brainstorming

                    Topic: Baseball Game
        Who? my brother Pete and I
        What? helped lose the game
        Where? Highland Park in Fairfield, New Jersey
        When? last July, a humid afternoon
        Why? both poor players, inexperienced, clumsy, nervous
        How? I struck out 3 times, Pete dropped 2 fly balls
                                        —Jerome Haag

Another kind of brainstorming involves the writer in more detailed questioning about the topic. You think on paper in question form about all the various things you want to ask in regard to the subject you have identified.

Brainstorming

                    Topic: Learning to Swim
    When did I learn to swim? I was eight years old, and I remember
    being scared. Why? Fell into the creek at Cole's Farm three years
    before. Who helped me learn? My sister Bertie. How did she get me
    to do it? Why was I stupid enough to try again, being so scared?
    She dared me. When was this? June afternoon on the way home from
    school on the very last day. We were at the creek again. What did
    the scene look like? What did Bertie say? How did I feel when she
    held me under my stomach, making me kick my feet and move my arms?
    How did the water feel? What did I smell, feel, hear at my first
    swimming lesson?
                                        —Wilma Hanson

Hint

In brainstorming activities concentrate on getting ideas down on paper. Don't worry about spelling or other matters of correctness. And don't censor any of your ideas.

As with any other prewriting activity, the exercise in brainstorming allows you to develop a rough draft that expands on some or all of the ideas you have generated. You might need to group some of the thoughts you've written in brainstorming before you attempt your first draft.

Step 1. Stirring Up Ideas.   Write your topic in a word or two on the top of a blank page. Next, list at 2- or 3-inch intervals along the left-hand margin the questions *Who? What? Where? When? Why?* and *How?* Then start filling in your responses. Or, you might wish to generate more detailed questions about the topic, questions you try to answer after you write them. Look at the two samples above.

Student Samples: Drafting and Revising

As you write and revise your own drafts of your narrative paragraph, refer to the sections called Progress Reminders: A Checklist of Questions on pages 58–59 and Drafting and Revising on pages 20–21.

Step 1. Examining Drafts.   Read these two drafts of a paragraph about a race on horseback. How does the revised draft compare with the early draft? Answer the questions after you read.

DRAFT

The Horse Race

One exciting July morning, my Fiance and I decided to horse race across the green grass of Pelham Park. This was my first time racing Miguel, for he is a far better rider than I, but this didn't bother me because I was excited I felt like a winner today. Sometimes you just feel luck in your bones, and today was my day. As we walked across the high grass, I felt the moist wind kiss my face, and this made me giggle with excitement. Miguel flashed me a sideways glance as thought he were wondering whether I had something up my sleeve or not. I smiled back broadly, and ran to the chocolate brown horses, Cocoa and Fudge. My horse, Fudge was a deep rich brown with a white spot behind his left ear. I stroked the horses. Miguel got the saddles from the horse trainer. We quickly saddled the horses, and climbed on them. After we climbed on them we galloped through the grass to gain speed. I turned to Miguel and teased, "Are you ready to lose, Hon?" But he just flashed me a great sparkling smile, which puts a twinkle in his green eyes. He has beautiful green eyes that are always sparkling. Now we were ready to compete. And as we raced across the green pasture, I lowered my head to the level of Fudge's neck. Holding on tight to the black leather reins, I held my place ahead of Miguel and Cocoa. As all this was taking place, I remember thinking of how the smell of fresh pine reminded me of Christmas. This thought was soon interrupted with the sight of that uneven wooden fence. Now I knew that once over this fence I would be the winner. I snapped the black leather reins with my feeling of excitement. Fudge started running faster and faster as if we were flying. We got closer and closer to the fence finally Fudge jumped I held on for dear life as we flew over so high we almost touched the blue-gray sky. Down we came with Fudge dethroning me into the smelly green pines, but I had won. I beat Miguel!

REVISED DRAFT

The Horse Race

One exciting July morning, my fiancé and I raced horses across
the sparse grass of Pelham Park. This was my first time racing Miguel,
for he is a far better rider than I; however, his skill did not bother
me because I felt like a winner today. As we ambled across the high
grass to the stables, the moist wind on my face excited me and I
giggled. Miguel, in a yellow shirt open at the collar, wrinkled his
brow and glanced at me sideways as though I kept a dark secret from
him. I smiled back broadly, and ran to the familiar horses, Cocoa and
Fudge. My horse, Fudge, had a deep rich brown coat with a white spot
behind his left ear. Cocoa too was silky brown with penetrating brown
eyes. I stroked the horses while Miguel ran off for the saddles from
the trainer. We quickly saddled the horses, and climbed up. As we
galloped through the grass, gaining speed, I turned to Miguel and
teased, "Are you ready to lose, Hon?" But he just flashed me a great
sparkling smile, which puts a twinkle in his green eyes. Miguel's black
hair bounced up and down on his forehead as we raced across the
pasture. I joyously lowered my head to the level of Fudge's neck.
"Let's go, baby," I whispered to him gently. I felt his mane scratch
against my ear. Holding on tight to the black leather reins, I took my
place ahead of Miguel and Cocoa. I remember the smell of fresh pine
around me; it reminded me of Christmas, and my mind wandered. But the
sight of an uneven wooden fence interrupted my thoughts. Now I knew
that once over this fence I would be the winner. With a feeling of
excitement I snapped the black leather reins. Fudge raced faster and
faster as if we were flying. We drew closer and closer to the fence,
and Fudge jumped. I held on tightly, my eyes shut and my heart pounding
as we flew so high we almost touched the sky. Down we came with Fudge
dethroning me painfully amid the pines I had admired a short while
before. But I really didn't mind; I had won. I had beaten Miguel!

—Lisa Guadalupe

1. The second draft provides more descriptive detail than the first. What is your opinion of the added image of Miguel's clothing and action early in the paragraph? What other concrete sensory details sharpen the scene for you?

2. The sentence about the smell of fresh pine has been revised. Which do you prefer: the sentence in the revised draft or the sentence in the original draft? Why?

3. Which words and phrases has the writer eliminated? Were these wise deletions? Why?

4. Which topic sentence do you prefer, the one in the early draft or the one in the revision? Why?

5. What further changes would you recommend that Lisa Guadalupe make in her narrative paragraph? Where could she make her thoughts clearer? Where could she eliminate sentences? Where might she combine sentences?

Step 2. More Student Samples.   Examine these narrative paragraphs. When you finish reading, answer the questions on expanded topic sentences, sensory language, chronological order, and sentence variety.

Chicken

One hot July afternoon at Hecksher State Park Pool I finally tried diving but suffered defeat. I was in the water when I suddenly noticed someone on the diving platform. Quickly and gracefully the muscular young man bounced off the blue board. As he hit the water, a small splash leaped up. He made it seem so simple and so much fun that suddenly I wanted to try it. I could do it; I knew I could. Brazenly I scampered out of the water and ran across the hot concrete floor to the ladder, stepping in small puddles that I passed. As I looked up, I saw someone in a bright yellow bikini stepping down. She looked into my eyes and confessed, "I've changed my mind. That's too high and the water's too deep for me." "Chicken," I thought to myself and slowly climbed the steps one by one. Suddenly I thought to myself, "What if I don't make it? What if I drown? Think positive; you'll do it, and then you'll be able to dive every time you come to the pool." I kept repeating those words to myself as I nervously reached the top. I stood there proudly, yards above everyone at the pool. "Hey, everybody, look at me, I'm going to dive." Placing one foot in front of the other, I inched my way to the tip of the board. Looking down into the clear blue water, I saw my faint reflection. The water looked so cool and inviting as I felt the hot sun burning my back. The smell of chlorine drifted up. I heard the screams and laughter of the young children below me. As I glanced around, red and blue sun umbrellas whirled together in front of my eyes. "Hurry it up, will you," someone behind me said. "Okay, okay," I said, "here I go." I bounced once, then twice. I smiled as I swung my arms in front of me, still not daring to jump. I counted aloud, "One, two, three." Then suddenly I stopped bouncing, quickly balanced myself and did an about-face. Staggering back to the ladder, I pushed everyone aside as I stepped down. When I reached the hot pool deck, I realized what I had done. I looked into a pair of brown, sympathetic eyes and muttered, "I couldn't do it." Touching my shoulder, my sister replied, "Maybe some other time, Liz." "Yes, maybe," I said, but I thought to myself, "Chicken."

—Elizabeth Santiago

1. What is the topic of this paragraph? What is the writer's opinion about the topic?

2. Which quotation sentence is most realistic, one that includes words you think a person might really say in the situation?

3. Which image in the paragraph is most clear? Where has Elizabeth Santiago used color most effectively? Which actions are especially well presented?

4. Why is the title a good one?

5. What does *scampered* mean? Why does the writer say "scampered out of the water" instead of "went out of the water"?

6. Which sentence opens with two *-ly* words?

7. The events in the selection you read follow a strict chronological arrangement. Below, several important details from the selection are listed. But they appear in the wrong time sequence. Put number 1 in front of the first event that occurred; number 2 in front of the second; and so on.

_____ Liz pushed everyone aside as she stepped down.

_____ Liz heard the screams and laughter of the young children.

_____ Liz scampered out of the water and ran quickly over to the ladder.

_____ Liz said to her sister, "I couldn't do it."

_____ Liz saw the muscular young man bounce off the diving board.

Buck Fever

One blustery November morning I thought I would experience the thrill of shooting my first deer, but at the last moment I was seized by that dreaded hunter's ailment, buck fever. I was staying at my sister's house when, early in the morning, my brother-in-law Frank came into my room. The clumping of his boots on the bare wooden floors woke me in an instant. In a whisper Frank made my dream come true. "Do you want to go hunting with me this morning at the farm?" he asked. I leaped out of bed and jumped into my gray longjohns, my woolen hunting suit, and my orange plastic vest. Following Frank into his navy Ford pickup, I quickly pulled my yellow knit cap tightly over my head and ears. He started driving us over fifteen miles of slick, ice-covered country roads across the state line to Frank's father's farm. We parked behind the farmhouse and trudged through the snow-covered fields. The deep mysterious smell of the woods surrounded me, and as the pink light of dawn guided our way, I heard the wind rustle eerily through the bare birch and poplar trees. To encircle the meadow, we split up. Frank turned left and I trekked right. We had been apart for about fifteen minutes when I saw the soft, brown skin of a deer down in the creek bed at the bottom of the meadow. Stealthily, cautiously, I tiptoed forward so I wouldn't startle the deer, although I was sure that my heartbeat sounded like cannons firing. The small deer heard me and looked up. I even stopped breathing for fear he would run away. Luckily he lowered his head again and foraged for some sprouts of grass under the snow. At that, I brought my rifle up to my shoulder and took careful aim through the cold, steel sight. The deer brought his head up again and stared right at me. Through the sight I could see drops of moisture at the corners of his eyes. It was at that moment that buck fever struck me, the paralysis that comes when you think too much about the life you are about to take. It's the disease all hunters fear, and it overtook me so suddenly that I started shaking. I dropped the rifle from my shoulder to my side. The thump of the wood and metal slapping against my leg startled the deer who jumped in surprise and darted away through the woods. I never recovered from buck fever: I never went hunting again.

—John Scoville

1. What is your reaction to the topic sentence? Does it state the topic clearly? Does it give an opinion?

2. How does the title serve the writer's purpose in the paragraph?

3. Which images are most original? Identify pictures that appeal to the sense of sight, smell, and sound.

4. Is the sequence of events clear? Which transitions does the writer use to help the reader move easily through time?

Jungle Boy

A suppertime conversation one fall evening several years ago shows how both my parents can join forces to make me feel worse than I already do. My mother slammed the knives and forks upon the table with a startling clatter and stormed back to the sink. A bright yellow tablecloth with red roses did nothing to counteract the tension that hung about our usually cheery kitchen. Quizzically my father glanced at me, but I lowered my eyes quickly and labored at my grapefruit until I squeezed it dry. My brother solemnly leaned over his lamb chops and string beans. The large black, yellow, and blue marks on his arm stood out, the result of a fight with me that afternoon. Again mother stalked to the table, her brown eyes moist, the glass salt shaker clenched in her hand. She let loose her rage in a violent burst of words. "Are you crazy? Do you want to break your brother's arm?" I slouched lower in my chair, taking a piece of broiled meat in my mouth but unable to swallow it. My father looked at me through steel gray eyes. "I told you never to raise your hands in anger in this house," his voice boomed. The words echoed in my head as I felt my face warm. My mother shrieked at the top of her voice, "Why can't you get along with your brother the way your cousins do. They laugh together and play together, but not you, not Allen of the jungle, you have to fight and punch your brother." Quietly, sternly, my father said, "I've never hit you, Allen, without first discussing the situation with you like civilized people, have I?" I stirred uncomfortably in my chair and murmured an acknowledgment. My father's words weakened the wall that I built to fight my mother's assault. "I've brought you up to respect your brother and him you. We won't speak about this again, but in the future you'd better think before raising your hands." Feeling ashamed for my childish behavior, I excused myself from the table and tramped off sullenly to my cave.

—Allen Zuckerman

1. What is the topic of this paragraph? What is the writer's attitude toward his topic?

2. Which word group, in your opinion, gives the picture you see most clearly?

3. Which quotation sentence includes words you think a person might really say in the situation?

4. Why is the use of color in the sentence about the tablecloth so effective? Where else is color effectively used?

5. Do you think the title is a good one for this paragraph? Why?

6. What does the word *stalked* mean? Why does the writer say *stalked* instead of *walked* or *came*?

Collaboration: Getting Reader Response

Give a draft of your paragraph to a classmate along with the checklist below. Ask him or her to fill it out as completely as possible after reading your paper. Read the responses and then spend fifteen to twenty minutes brainstorming on each of your paragraphs. "Yes and No" questions should be answered *Yes, No,* or *Unsure;* other responses should be as detailed as possible.

1. Is the topic clearly stated?   _____

   The topic as I understand it is _____

   _____

2. Are the sensory images clear and specific?   _____

   The best sensory images are _____

3. Is the time sequence in the story clear enough?   _____

   Is there any point where you are confused by a "jump" in   _____
   the action?

4. Is the "moment" of the experience limited enough?   _____

5. Are the six brainstorming questions suggested on pages 51–52   _____
   sufficiently answered for you?

   If not, which ones need to be described in more detail?   _____

   _____

Progress Reminders: A Checklist

Ask yourself these questions as you prepare your drafts and revise them. Check off the items as you evaluate your own writing.

1. Have I carefully selected my topic so that it is limited to one   _____
   brief moment for narration? (Review the definition of *mo-ment* on page 51.)

2. Have I used a prewriting strategy that was comfortable for   _____
   me, such as the brainstorming technique that answers the
   questions *Who? What? When? Where? Why?* and *How?*
   about a topic? (See pages 51–52.)

3. As I wrote various drafts, did I include more details to make   _____
   my ideas clearer to the reader?

4. Did I present a clear sequence of events as I narrated my _____
   moment?

5. Have I included rich sensory detail to bring that moment to
   life? Here is one sensory image from my paragraph. _____

   _____

6. Did I use images of *color* in several places in the paragraph? _____

7. Did I show people as they performed various actions? _____

8. Did I pay particular attention to describing the faces of the _____
   people I wrote about? The eyes are particularly easy to describe; you can combine color with another sense like
   touch—*moist, hard, soft,* and so on.

9. Did I use several words that appeal to the sense of *sound?* The _____
   essay "Chicken" (page 55) includes "screams and laughter of
   young children," and "Buck Fever" contains such words as
   whisper and *clumping.*

10. Did I show touch and smell details of the scene in which the _____
    moment occurs? Elizabeth Santiago writes about the smell of
    chlorine and about the hot sun burning her back.

11. Did I write a topic sentence that states a limited topic through
    some opinion or attitude word? Here is the topic sentence: _____

    _____

12. Did I name time (month, part of the day, season) and place (a _____
    special room, a street, a sport arena, a gym) as soon as
    possible in my paragraph, preferably in the topic sentence?

13. Did I start at least one sentence with an *-ly* word? _____

    Did I start another sentence with two *-ly* words separated by a _____
    comma or *and?*

    These two words are _____ and _____.

14. Did I use any new words on page 37? _____

15. Did I make sure to include at least one quotation sentence that _____
    gives someone's exact words? (Check the review charts on
    pages 401–402 for correct punctuation.)

16. Did I check my theme for errors, especially fragments and _____
    run-ons? (See Word and Sentence Skills section.)

    Did I examine my Theme Progress Sheet (page 454) and my _____
    Individual Spelling List (page 434)?

17. Did I proofread my paragraph at least twice: once *before* I _____
    prepared my final manuscript and once *after* it?

18. Did I give my paragraph a lively title? _____

● The Professionals Speak

Read the excerpts below, and answer the questions.

SOME WORDS TO KNOW BEFORE YOU READ

essence—the most important property of something

luminous—bright and shining

pious—religious

oleomargarined—spread with a kind of margarine

narcotizing—soothing

quiescent—at rest

ingested—swallowed

abetting—encouraging

Java Jive

For several mornings at the age of three I stood quietly by the living-room window in our little one-story house in Ocean Springs, Mississippi, and studied the way a spider trapped a fly in his web and carefully devoured her. Why I thought the fly was a she and the spider a he would be tough to explain, but that was the way it played in my literal head of dream pictures, whose images, now that I think about it, were clearly made up of tiny quivering dots the way magazine or newspaper photos look when you subject them to intensive magnification.

Words didn't come easily for what I was seeing, yet somehow I knew deep beneath or beyond what little mind I must've had by then that I was glimpsing a mystery of some kind; some important, worldly essence was being vividly played out before my unblinking eyes.

Then, finally, it all fell into place. The sun—like a hot, luminous magnet—happened to be shining powerfully that antique afternoon. My father was busy being his auto mechanic self, and I could see him through the dusty window screen out there in the grass and dirt and clay of the side-yard driveway, fixing on our dark blue Chevy coupe, grease all over his face and forearms; black on black. Pious as a minister or metaphysician, he was bent on fixing that car.

My mother was in the next room, the kitchen, fixing red beans and rice. My very intestines were tingling with gladness, for red beans and rice as far as I was concerned, had no parallel; there simply wasn't anything like it anywhere in the world, whatever the world was. To dine every day on red beans and rice—or to breakfast, lunch, or snack on them—would've suited me just fine. Lifetimes from my spider-and-fly moment, just before nightfall, I knew we children would be gobbling our portions of dinner—complete with chopped onions and oleomargarined slices of white Bond bread—on the linoleum down under the kitchen table with newspaper for placemats. And I'd be spoiling to tell everybody about the spider and how he'd stuck it to the fly with his web, even though it was going to be years—and I seem to have glimpsed this too—before I'd be able to make heads or tails of any of it, in words anyway.

From the big Zenith radio console, the wood case shining with furniture oil, probably lemon, the Ink Spots were singing "Java Jive." Except for "I like coffee/I like tea," the words made no sense to me, but I liked the way the tune kept winding around and around to make its point, and I loved the way they came out of it all with: "A cup/ a cup/a cup/a cup/a cup, ahhhhhhh!" That sigh at the tag meant everything, said it all: it signaled my Aunt Ethel, the big coffee addict in the family, who, even then, always came to mind with her lips cradling the edge of some hot cup, breathing and exhaling steam and steaminess; big fogs of warmth in which sugar and sweetmilk or Pet Milk played some part. Watching her I could not fail to get the idea that something glad was going on between Aunt Ethel and that coffee of hers. If you or anyone else had taken time out to explain that the coffee bean and its narcotizing effect on people everywhere was an industry that involved colored peoples doing the picking all over the world, I wouldn't have connected with what you were saying any more than I would've understood the meaning of the Man in the Moon, but I might've had a notion. Around the same time, you see, the Andrews Sisters were drawing checks off something called "They've Got an Awful Lot of Coffee in Brazil."

Being three, you see, isn't that much different from being a hundred and three, particularly when you begin to understand it's all a matter of putting two and two together.

July seeped into the room, quiescent with harmony and heat, the beat; the beating of the fly's wings as the spider ingested her from head to toe, boodie and sole. I stood there. I stood still. Time stood still and the whole of Mississippi, maybe the whole world, stood there soaking up the three-year old's vision of how the world really works whether you realize it or not. It was as if, for me at least at that moment, my father had pried open the engine of life itself and motioned me over to have a look at how it worked and then, without so much as a seventh-grade shop class explanation, snapped the lid back on, leaving me the idea that there was something, some mechanism or cause, that lay behind any and everything I would ever experience in this ever-shifting, not to be believed existence that mystics—when you boil what they say down to a simmering, low gravy—say is only a movie, the acting out of something vaster than ourselves; the cosmic drama, if you will.

I wanted to taste this java, sample this coffee, this tea they were rhythmizing so invitingly. Feeling my insides beginning to gladden, I rushed out into the yard to hear my father say, "Hey, Skippy! C'mere, boy, and gimme some sugar!"—meaning: *Let me kiss you smack on the jaw.* I liked that. I liked it so much, I got confused. I wanted to race over and blurt out to him everything I'd just figured out about the spider and the world and the mystery and the tingling I felt inside, even though I didn't feel ready yet to pull the words together. There were no words, really; there was only this soundless understanding puffing up with feeling like a rainbow-colored balloon filling up all too fast with smooth summer air.

Just then, just as I was about to make my move toward Daddy, I saw a bright aquaplane zoom in close overhead, low enough for me to see the pilot, a white man, making me think at once of a crisp, airborne Nabisco saltine. He was wearing one of those old-time aviator helmets with earflaps and goggles. He waved at me. He waved and smiled and now, millions of mind-hours later, I can draw a wayward cloud of comic strip balloon over his head that shows him thinking: "Long as I'm up here foolin around, lemme just wave at that lil ole colored boy on the ground down there and give him a thrill!"

This bubbling moment and all that led up to it—like the family's first tentative move to Detroit and the unbelievable coldness of ice and snow and the tight light of what my folks kept calling "movin upnorth to the city"—are etched into me like the lines of some play; a kind of play that's had to settle for being sliced up over the years into what I eventually learned to call poetry or prose.

We lived close enough to the Gulf of Mexico for low-flying aquaplanes to be a commonplace, but that was the very first time I'd ever seen a pilot up close. It was entirely different from those blackout nights when coastal air raid alerts were up, when Ella Mae Morse would be on the Zenith singing "The House of Blue Lights," and there we'd be, me and my brothers, sprawled on the floor or blanketed down in bed, listening and remembering, with those blue emergency lightbulbs screwed into the lamp and ceiling sockets, their cooling glow softening the edge that was forever cutting a line between the seeable and the hearable worlds.

I rushed into my father's arms, gave him that sugar, wondering why we called those people crackers and why kids weren't supposed to fool with coffee.

As for the spider and the fly and my insights into the mystery of that spectacle, all I can say is that the craziness of my excitement has thickened over the years. Now I'm given to believing that the web is only the world, the spider desire, and the fly the fickle, innocent, and positively neutral nature of existence. Beyond that stands some youthful presence, more consciousness than thing, taking it all in with astonishment and, as a matter of fact, aiding and abetting and allowing it all to happen as if—like the web—it were either staged or created by design.

—Al Young

1. What words does Young use in his topic sentence that show where and when the event he describes took place?
2. Which sensory images of sight, sound, touch, and taste are most vivid?
3. Does Young narrate the event chronologically? Explain.
4. What are the three present participles that help vary the way the sentences begin?

SOME WORDS TO KNOW BEFORE YOU READ

maize—corn

permanganate—acid used to kill germs

besought—begged

Echoes of Grief

After a certain age—and for some of us that can be very young—there are no new people, beasts, dreams, faces, events: it has all happened before, masked differently, wearing different clothes, another nationality, another colour; but the same, the same, and everything is an echo and a repetition; and there is no grief even that it is not a recurrence of something long out of memory that expresses itself in unbelievable anguish, days of tears, loneliness, knowledge of betrayal—and all for a small, thin, dying cat.

I was sick that winter. It was inconvenient because my big room was due to be whitewashed. I was put in the little room at the end of the house. The house, nearly but not quite on the crown of the hill, always seemed as if it might slide off into the maize fields below. This tiny room, not more than a slice off the end of the house, had a door, always open, and windows, always open, in spite of the windy cold of a July whose skies were an interminable light clear blue. The sky, full of sunshine; the field, sunlit. But cold, very cold. The cat, a bluish-grey Persian, arrived purring on my bed, and settled down to share my sickness, my food, my pillow, my sleep. When I woke in the mornings, my face turned to half-frozen linen; the outside of the fur blanket on the bed was cold; the smell of fresh whitewash from next door was cold and antiseptic; the wind lifting and laying the dust outside the door was cold—but in the crook of my arm, a light purring warmth, the cat, my friend.

At the back of the house a wooden tub was let into the earth, outside the bathroom, to catch the bathwater. No pipes carrying water to taps on that farm: water was fetched by ox-drawn cart when it was needed, from the well a couple of miles off. Through the months of the dry season the only water for the garden was the dirty bathwater. The cat fell into this tub when it was full of hot water. She screamed, was pulled out into a chill wind, washed in permanganate, for the tub was filthy and held leaves and dust as well as soapy water, was dried, and put into my bed to warm. But she sneezed and sneezed and then grew burning hot with fever. She had pneumonia. We dosed her with what there was in the house, but that was before antibiotics, and so she died. For a week she lay in my arms purring, purring, in a rough trembling hoarse little voice that became weaker, then was silent; licked my hand; opened enormous green eyes when I called her name and besought her to live; closed them, died, and was thrown into the deep shaft—over a hundred feet deep it was—which had gone dry, because the underground water streams had changed their course one year and left what we had believed was a reliable well a dry, cracked, rocky shaft that was soon half filled with rubbish, tin cans, and corpses.

That was it. Never again. And for years I matched cats in friends' houses, cats in shops, cats on farms, cats in the street, cats on walls, cats in memory, with that gentle blue-gray purring creature which for me was the cat, the Cat, never to be replaced.

And besides, for some years my life did not include extras, unnecessaries, adornments. Cats had no place in an existence spent always moving from place to place, room to room. A cat needs a place as much as it needs a person to make its own.

And so it was not till twenty-five years later that my life had room for a cat.

—Doris Lessing

1. Why does the narrator talk about memories and grief to introduce the topic of this selection? How does the event that she narrates illustrate the idea she presents in the first paragraph?

2. What is the main point of this selection?

3. At the end of paragraph 2, how does the narrator use sensory images to illustrate her relationship with the cat?

4. Why do you think the word *cat* in paragraph 4 has a capital *C*?

3

Illustration: Using Examples

●

INTRODUCTION: USING EXAMPLES TO DEVELOP A PARAGRAPH

This chapter focuses on the use of examples to illustrate a point in a paragraph. Whether you are writing from experience or using facts or research, you often must draw on a number of examples to explain your topic statement.

You may want to write, for example, about how high school taught you about friendship, how your childhood was lonely, or how your older brothers first interested you in sports. In cases like these, you need to use examples representing incidents from your own experience, which will show the reader what led you to your conclusion. Intense sensory details will sharpen the picture for your reader.

But personal experience is not the only kind of supporting material you can use in order to provide examples. Although your own experiences (told through the clear language of the senses) make exciting and informative paragraphs, often you must write about subjects outside your own life. Writing about World War I in history class, about cell reproduction in biology, about the status of Native Americans in sociology—for these assignments you need some source of detail other than your own experience. The information you find in books, in periodicals (magazines and newspapers), or on the TV or movie screen serves well as the basis of support for developing ideas.

For this chapter assignment you will present in a paragraph a number of examples to support a general impression. If you write from your own experiences, you will use concrete sensory detail to help support your general statement. If you write about something you have not experienced firsthand, you can draw on facts that you know or can investigate. You can use expert testimony—what responsible people say or write about a topic. You can quote directly or paraphrase information that you have read or heard from someone else in order to support your idea. When you use a number of examples, you need to move the reader smoothly from one instance to another, and so a review of useful transition words will help you as you write.

● Vocabulary

Step 1. Words for the Past.   In your paragraph of examples you may want to draw on your childhood memories. These words may help you as you write about past experiences. Use a dictionary to check meanings of any words you do not know, and write definitions in your own words on the blank lines.

1. retrospect _____
2. memorable _____
3. reminisce _____
4. evoke _____
5. nostalgia _____

6. recollect _____
7. melancholy _____
8. adolescence _____
9. remembrance _____
10. contemplate _____

Step 2. Trying New Words.   Use a form of an appropriate word from the above list to fill each space in the sentences below.

1. When I _____ about my childhood, I recall all my wonderful birthday parties.

2. For example, my mother's pictures of my sweet-sixteen party give me strong feelings of _____.

3. My tenth birthday was certainly my most _____ one, for my father presented me with a brown-and-white puppy named Skippy.

4. The thought of Skippy licking my face with his hot, wet tongue _____ fond memories.

5. I _____ how hilarious my tenth birthday party was; my school friends tossed balls of whipped cream at each other.

6. During my _____, from my twelfth to my sixteenth year, I thought it was silly and childish to celebrate birthdays.

7. Not surprisingly, I cannot think of my eighteenth birthday party without great _____ because the death of both my parents the year before saddened me.

8. Now that I am thirty, I realize that the _____ of our past is a precious and important part of our lives.

9. Some people find it painful to _____ the past because they are then more aware of the passing of the years.

10. In _____, my past is indeed full of happy, tender memories that I will never forget.

Step 3. Words for Unforgettable Personalities. These words are useful in describing those unforgettable personalities of your youth. Check them in the dictionary and write in definitions.

1. vibrant _____   4. gregarious _____

2. domineering _____   5. volatile _____

3. supportive _____

Step 4. Using New Vocabulary. Fill in each blank with a word from the list in Step 3 so that the sentences make sense.

1. I recall Yau Chun's _____ personality; everywhere she stood, the room throbbed with energy.

2. Her temper was so _____ that she would begin to scream at the slightest disturbance.

3. The _____ politician darted around the room, shaking hands and talking to small clusters of guests.

4. Although I could rarely depend on my father for help, my uncle Vincenzo was much more _____.

5. Donna was so _____ that she allowed her children very little opportunity to make their own decisions about anything important.

● Building Composition Skills

Finding the Topic

Getting Ideas.   Complete any word group below by reading it aloud with your own ending. Then, in a few more sentences, explain what you said by giving two or three examples. Or, if your instructor suggests, write down in a few brief sentences your completion for any of the statements and then read aloud what you have written. Look at the examples.

1. My most important educational experience occurred when _____

   _____

2. Our cities are in trouble because _____

   _____

3. I'm easily embarrassed when _____

   _____

4. To be a safe driver you should _____

   _____

5. To prevent a rise in unemployment we should _____

   _____

6. My family is _____

   _____

7. My childhood was unusual because _____

   _____

8. The major issues facing the earth are _____

   _____

9. Teenagers have many problems like _____

   _____

10. My basic personality trait is _____

   _____

EXAMPLES

   My childhood was unusual because I lived in so many strange places. Because my father was an air force colonel, I lived for a time in Japan and Turkey. One summer I lived on a

houseboat with my uncle and the following winter at a remote radar station complex in
Alaska.

—Karen Youngman

Teenagers have many problems like trying to decide what careers to choose. Competition
is fierce out there. Also, they have to deal with lots of peer pressure. That includes being
influenced to use drugs or alcohol or to do wild things.

—Alfredo Bracco

I'm easily embarrassed when I have to stand up in front of a group to speak. In science class
when I had to make a report on the nervous system, I stammered nervously and felt my knees
shake. And once in high school English I was so nervous that I dropped my note cards to the
floor and had to slip back to my seat without finishing the report.

—Helen Cendrowski

Paragraph Unity: Subtopic Sentences

It is often helpful, especially when you use several examples to support your point, to remind the reader of the topic in several places in the paragraph. A subtopic sentence serves that function.

Here is a topic sentence to introduce a paragraph that uses several instances to support the topic:

When I was seven years old and the family moved from a small village in Puerto
Rico to Manhattan, everyday city occasions frightened me.

This topic will deal with selected events of city life; the writer's opinion is that these events were frightening. The very next sentence would present the first subtopic:

The traffic noises scared me.

The word *scared* repeats the opinion of the topic sentence; *traffic noises* introduce one specific aspect of the topic for discussion. The next three or four sentences would explain how the traffic noises were frightening. Images filled with sensory language in those sentences would support this first unit of thought. After finishing this thought group, the writer would write another subtopic sentence:

I also didn't like the people I saw on the streets.

The words *people I saw on the streets* introduce another part of the topic for the writer to discuss. The words *didn't like* refer back to the opinion in the topic sentence. The next few sentences would illustrate the point of the subtopic with colors and sounds and actions. After this thought unit ends, another subtopic sentence would appear:

And every new thing I saw in Manhattan looked oversized and ugly.

The words *every new thing I saw in Manhattan* refer the reader back to the original topic; the words *oversized and ugly* report the writer's opinion toward the topic discussed in the paragraph. In this way the paragraph achieves unity—all the sentences will build upon the main idea.

Even paragraphs that do not give several incidents can benefit from subtopic sentences. Paragraphs of description (Chapter 1) and narration (Chapter 2) achieve unity too when subtopic sentences introduce major blocks of thought. Each subtopic sentence requires several sentences of support for whatever aspect of the topic the writer introduces. Here a topic sentence introduces a paragraph that narrates:

On a cold December morning I learned how dangerous skiing can be.

Here are two subtopic sentences:

1.   As I rode up the chairlift, the sun reflected off the icy surface of the slope.
2.   Suddenly the hazardous rock loomed in front of me.

What kind of information would you expect to find in the seven or eight sentences after subtopic sentence 1 above? After subtopic sentence 2? What words in each of the subtopic sentences remind the reader of the opinion expressed in the topic sentence?

● Subtopic Sentence Chart ●

Subtopic Sentence	Why
1. Introduces one aspect of the topic you want to discuss	So it's clear to the reader what proof you will use at a given point in the paragraph
	So it's clear to you what part of the topic you are treating at a given point in the paragraph

Subtopic Sentence	Why
2. Uses a word similar to the "opinion" word in the topic sentence	So the reader is reminded of your position on the topic
	So that you remember that you're trying to support only a certain feature about the topic
	So that the details in the sentences that follow the subtopic sentence all try to support the key impression you have given about the topic in the topic sentence

Step 1. Finding Subtopics. Reread "The Gloom Room" on page 23.

1. Copy here the first subtopic sentence, the sentence that introduces the one aspect of the topic that the writer will discuss first.

    _____

    _____

2. Copy the second subtopic sentence.

    _____

    _____

3. What details does Mr. Golden use to support the first subtopic sentence?

    _____

    _____

4. What details does he use to support the second subtopic sentence?

    _____

    _____

Step 2. Writing Subtopic Sentences. For each topic sentence below, write subtopic sentences. The numbers in parentheses tell you how many subtopic sentences to write. Use your own paper.

Hint

Each subtopic sentence:
a. introduces some aspect of the topic that can be discussed in a few sentences
b. may repeat some idea of the opinion word
c. must be followed by supporting details.

EXAMPLE

At Springfield Gardens High School, trouble and I were never far away from each other. (3)

Subtopic sentence 1: *Once I "borrowed" my homeroom teacher's key for a practical joke.*

Subtopic sentence 2: *To protest the awful cafeteria food, I caused a commotion.*

Subtopic sentence 3: *Finally, the Dean of Boys summoned me when he learned I had cut history eighteen times.*

1. Shopping in department stores can be very tiring. (2)
2. My mother's guidance during my adolescence helped me overcome tough problems. (3)
3. The newest models of many cars incorporate several safety features. (3)
4. Traveling by plane has its advantages. (3)
5. My first day as a counselor at Camp Pine Wood was a disaster. (3)
6. My first date was filled with embarrassment. (3)
7. I learned early how to survive in a rough neighborhood. (3)
8. Many cities have developed strong programs to prevent the spread of AIDS. (3)
9. Our senior class tried to reform several school procedures. (3)
10. In our city, there are many things to do on a Saturday afternoon. (3)

> **Hint**
>
> There is no required number of subtopic sentences to use for each paragraph. If you write only two subtopic sentences, each subtopic (thought unit) will need to be developed in greater detail. Write three subtopic sentences, and you will need to use fewer supporting details for each thought unit.

Several Examples without Subtopic Sentences

Sometimes a writer wishes to propose many instances to support the topic sentence in a paragraph. In that case, each instance is not highly developed—it is told in just a sentence or two—and a subtopic sentence to introduce each example is unnecessary. The paragraph below uses several instances to support the attitude in the topic sentence but does not need subtopic sentences. The unity in the paragraph comes from repetition of key words (see pages 68–70).

SOME WORDS TO KNOW BEFORE YOU READ

Downs—an area of low hills in South England

cricket—a popular English game; it is played by two teams, the ball being hit along the ground with a kind of bat

sixpence—an English coin

newt—a salamander, a small lizardlike animal

Memories of Crossgates School

I have good memories of Crossgates, among a horde of bad ones. Sometimes on summer afternoons there were wonderful expeditions across the Downs, or to Beachy Head, where one bathed dangerously among the chalk boulders and came home covered with cuts. And there were still more wonderful midsummer evenings when, as a special treat, we were not driven off to bed as usual but allowed to wander about the grounds in the long twilight, ending up with a plunge into the swimming bath at about nine o'clock. There was the joy of waking early on summer mornings and getting in an hour's undisturbed reading (Ian Hay, Thackeray, Kipling and H. G. Wells were the favourite authors of my boyhood) in the sunlit, sleeping dormitory. There was also cricket, which I was no good at but with which I conducted a sort of hopeless love affair up to the age of about eighteen. And there was the pleasure of keeping caterpillars—the silky green and purple puss-moth, the ghostly green poplar-hawk, the privet hawk, large as one's third finger, specimens of which could be illicitly purchased for sixpence at a shop in the town—and, when one could escape long enough from the master who was "taking the walk," there was the excitement of dredging the dew-ponds on the Downs for enormous newts with orange-coloured bellies. This business of being out for a walk, coming across something of fascinating interest and then being dragged away from it by a yell from the master, like a dog jerked onwards by the leash, is an important feature of school life, and helps to build up the conviction, so strong in many children, that the things you most want to do are always unattainable.

—*George Orwell*

Using Statistics and Cases as Details

An important way to support your position on a topic that you develop through examples is to use statistics or cases as evidence. *Statistics* may be thought of as facts, the numbers and examples revealed through responsible investigation. Statistics make impressive evidence for backing up ideas.

A *case* is a specific incident involving real people and events. It is another kind of factual evidence that writers offer to support topics.

Of course, you must realize that even when presenting facts, writers often weigh the evidence in favor of a particular point of view. Writers who are biased— that is, who have strong opinions about an idea—sometimes do not present complete information; or they may interpret the facts to suit a conclusion they have already reached. Most readers are offended by such practices.

● Guidelines: Statistics and Cases for Strong Details ●

In order to use statistics and cases wisely, make sure that you

1. select them from reliable, unbiased sources; this means that you often must check more than one source for data about the same issue.

2. present them in clear language.

3. give information honestly; do not leave out important records because they do not agree with the point you wish to make.

4. acknowledge your sources—that is, be sure to say where you took your information from.

Statistics and Cases as Supporting Detail.   Read the following excerpt, in which the writer uses statistics and cases to support her point about the earnings of stockbrokers. Answer the questions after you read.

SOME WORDS TO KNOW BEFORE YOU READ

bail out—to leave quickly when conditions become adverse

commodities—economic goods, especially agricultural and mining products

options—the rights to buy or sell securities or commodities

gross—overall total, exclusive of deductions

revenue—income from an investment

generate—to create or bring into existence

commission—a fee paid for transacting business

Selling Stocks and Bonds

For most of the past decade, selling stocks and bonds was a tough way to make a living. After stock prices collapsed from their highs in the late 1960s, investors fled the market, and in many cases their brokers were right on their heels. Between 1969 and 1974, nearly 20,000 registered representatives at New York Stock Exchange member firms—about 35 percent of the total—bailed out of the business.

But for those brokers who managed to ride out the stormy Seventies, 1980 came as a rich and glorious reward. As stock prices rose sharply (Standard & Poor's 500-stock index was up 26 percent for the year), wealthy individual investors returned to the market, and trading volume soared to record highs. The newer lines of retail business, such as commodities and options, were booming too. *Fortune* estimates that the average broker rang up between $140,000 and $150,000 in gross commissions last year. That's about 30 percent better than in 1979, and considerably higher than any year in the Sixties. Since a broker's income is tied to his commission volume, the rise in revenues had a profound effect on take-home pay. Most firms allow their brokers to keep 35 to 40 percent of the commissions they generate. Which means that the average broker pocketed close to $60,000 last year.

The top "producers"—as they are called on Wall Street—did immensely better than that. *Fortune* estimates that over 100 brokers grossed in excess of $1 million last year. Steve Karelitz, 46, pulled in $2.5 million in commissions at Shearson Loeb Rhoade's Boston office, netting himself close to $1 million. A main reason for his success, says Karelitz, is the long list of clients he has built up during 20 years in the business. At last count the list held more than 3,000 names. While many of these customers stayed in the market through the lean times, Karelitz heard last year from scores of customers who hadn't called in years.

In contrast to Karelitz's mass-market approach, Fred Berens, a 38-year-old Cuban émigré in the Miami office of Bache Halsey Stuart Shields, has only about 500 accounts. But many of these are big ones—wealthy individuals in Central and South America who last year found the U.S. securities markets particularly attractive. They helped Berens pull in $1.7 million in commissions, of which he netted well over $600,000. At Morgan Stanley, which caters mostly to very rich clients, roughly a quarter of the 80 retail brokers were above or near the $1 million commission level last year. A better racket than pro sports.

—Linda Hayes

1. Which statistics do you find to be the most impressive or surprising examples?

2. What sources does Hayes cite for the statistics on brokers' earnings? the decline of registered representatives? the rise of stock prices?

3. What cases does the writer present to support her point about brokers' earnings?

4. What is Hayes' main point here? That is, what idea does she attempt to support with statistics and cases as examples?

5. What does the last sentence of the last paragraph tell you about how Hayes wants you to view the data she is presenting?

● Some Pointers for Writing Statistics Correctly ●

1. Use numbers for percent.

   18% or 18 percent

2. Use numbers for dates.

   May 15, 1971

3. To show sums of money:

    a. If you need two words or fewer (*not* counting the word *cents* or *dollars*), write out the words for the numbers.

       three-hundred dollars

       forty-two cents an hour

       eight billion

    b. If you need three or more words, use the numbers.

       $8.76   *$8,487* *$62,908,433*

    c. For a series of numbers, use the figures, not the words.

4. Two-word fractions are written like this:

   seven-tenths of all students

   one-ninth of student drivers

● Hints for Using Cases and Statistics in Your Writing ●

1. When you collect data from charts, graphs, and tables, be sure that you understand what the various figures and numbers mean.

2. Don't just pile up a series of numbers as statistical information, or your reader will lose interest. Make sure that you present your statistics in a clear and honest way. Often an image adds life to a paragraph built upon facts and figures.

3. In using cases, identify as much as possible the people, the events, the specific families or groups whose experiences support your idea.

4. Always select your statistics and cases from reliable sources. Be sure to name whatever sources you use for your information. The chart on page 80 suggests ways for telling the reader what materials you used as the basis for your facts.

5. Make sure that your statistics are not one-sided. By leaving out information or by "loading" evidence to give an incomplete picture, a writer can bias information. See pages 221–224 for other propaganda techniques to avoid.

Quotations and Paraphrase as Details

Another source for supporting topic and subtopic sentences in your paragraph is quoted material from books, magazines, newspapers, radio, and television. By quoting, you use someone else's words and ideas to support your own opinion on a given subject. Of course, if you read something or hear it on the radio, it is not necessarily true; however, by using reliable sources, you can impress your reader with the strength of your position.

If, in your reading or listening, you discover some ideas that you want to use *exactly* as you have read or heard them, you can quote the material just as it was presented by giving the source of your information and by using quotation marks around the material. In that way you tell your reader that somebody else first stated the ideas you are writing about and that they are not original with you.

If you do not wish to use the information exactly as you have read or heard it, you may *paraphrase*—that is, you can use your own words to give an idea of what someone else wrote or said, especially if you want to summarize the idea. You do not need quotation marks, but here too you must identify the source of your information.

Effective Quotations.   Read the following selection (taken from a longer work) that uses quoted material. Answer the questions that appear after it.

SOME WORDS TO KNOW BEFORE YOU READ

propagate—spread a report or an idea from person to person

assertion—an unsupported statement put forward as being true

distortion—a twisting out of shape; misrepresentation

prevalence—widespread or in general use or acceptance

Racism in Education

Since racism is the philosophy of the Establishment and is propagated in the institutions of higher learning and by the mass media which they control through ownership, it is not surprising to observe that "a vast majority of the white population south of the Mason-Dixon Line, and large numbers, probably a majority elsewhere, are firmly of the belief that Negroes are subhuman or only semi-human, despite the positive assertions of biology and anthropology to the contrary." (*The Rich and the Super-Rich,* by Ferdinand Lundberg).

The Black parent knows his child is "educable" in spite of all the funded programs and studies to the contrary. Dishonesty and distortions in intelligence tests are common. The literature on such tests shows that when "two groups of whites differ in their IQ's, the explanation of the difference is immediately sought in schooling, environment, economic position of parents. However, when Blacks and whites differ in precisely the same way the difference is said to be genetic." (*The Study of Race,* by Sherwood L. Washburn). There are other instances which show the prevalence of racism. Trade schools (located in all industrial centers) have a long history of excluding Blacks. However, a Black occasionally slips through the net, after which the net is thoroughly examined to see how it happened. The trustees of these trade schools include the conservative officials of craft unions which exclude Blacks from membership. A classic example involved the Sheet Metal Workers Union Local 28 in New

York. There were 3,300 white members in the union, but no Blacks. Apprenticeship was reserved almost exclusively for relatives of members. Finally, the State Commission on Human Rights found the local union guilty, and the union agreed that "henceforth every applicant for membership would be judged solely on an aptitude test administered by the New York Testing and Advisement Center."

—*Maude White Katz*

1. What is the source of each of the quotations in the above selection?
2. How has the writer used examples to support her point?
3. What *case* does the writer offer to make her point that racism spreads to trade unions? How is the writer's discussion of that case an example of *paraphrase*?
4. Why does the writer talk of a "net" in the second paragraph? How does the word help build an image?
5. What does the writer imply about jobs for minorities as sheet metal workers? Does racism still exist in certain careers? How could you go about finding data to support your belief?

Integrating Testimony into Your Own Writing
(see also pages 268–269, Quoting from Books and Articles)

After you do research on a topic to collect notes that include statistics, exact quotations, and paraphrases, you will have to select from all your information those details that best support the point you want to make in your paper. As you do prewriting and, later, as you prepare your draft, you will be making those selections, choosing one set of dramatic figures over another, or choosing one quotation over others for its clarity and reliability.

Integrating someone else's ideas into your own writing requires special attention.

It is perfectly all right to use someone else's ideas, statements, or conclusions to support your own point in a paragraph or an essay. However, you must always mention the source of your information. Any time you use someone else's words or ideas without giving credit to the person who first presented them, you are guilty of *plagiarism*. Although plagiarism is a serious offense, students often plagiarize merely through oversight or through a misunderstanding of the way to present research findings.

If you use statistics that you have gathered from reading charts, graphs, and tables in books or periodicals, you must state the source of your figures. Often you will see the source named at the bottom of a graph or a table. If no source is named, you can assume that the writer of the book or article that you are using has collected original data. If you cite those data, name the author and the title of the piece as your source. Thus, if you wanted to cite figures from a graph whose source was the Bureau of Labor Statistics, you might do it this way: "According to the Bureau of

Labor Statistics, jobs for professional and technical workers will increase by about two million" or "More than five million jobs will be available to clerical workers in the 1990s reports the Bureau of Labor Statistics."

In Chapter 8, when you develop a short research paper of your own, you will learn more formal ways to cite sources, including a list of works cited.

When you want to quote someone else's words, you must state them exactly, you must put those words in quotations marks, and you must name your source.

Look at this selection from *Overseas Summer Jobs,* by D. J. Woodworth:

> The best opportunities for work in Spain are in hotels, and letters to the recently built hotels could result in an offer of a job. As most of these hotels cater to tourists from Northern Europe, a good knowledge of languages such as German, Dutch, French and English will be a great advantage to foreign workers, for whom there remains a good demand despite high local unemployment.
>
> It should be remembered that hotel workers in Spain work very long hours during the summer months and foreign workers will be required to do likewise. In most cases hotel and restaurant staff work a minimum of 10 hours per day and bar staff may work even longer hours. A 7 day week is regarded as perfectly normal during the summer.

Suppose you were writing a paragraph on summer work in Europe and you wanted to quote from this selection. (Be sure to review pages 400–403 and 391 if you are unsure of how to use quotation marks correctly.) You would have to use quotation marks to separate someone else's ideas from your own, and you would have to cite your source. The trick is to blend your own words and the words of the writer you are quoting to produce a smooth, graceful sentence. Look at these two examples:

1. D. J. Woodworth in *Overseas Summer Jobs* says, "In most cases hotel and restaurant staff work a minimum of 10 hours per day and bar staff may work even longer hours."

2. Workers in resorts overseas have no easy time. "In most cases," writes D. J. Woodworth (*Overseas Summer Jobs,* page 103), "hotel and restaurant staff work a minimum of 10 hours per day and bar staff may work even longer hours."

Notice in the second example above how the writer makes a statement of his own (sentence 1) and then quotes his source. By breaking up the quotation with the words "writes D. J. Woodworth," the writer further weaves his own words into the statement he wants to quote exactly.

If you want to leave out part of the sentence you are quoting because it is too long or because some of the information might not serve your point, use an ellipsis. An *ellipsis* is a punctuation mark made up of three periods with spaces between them. Look at this example:

D. J. Woodworth points out in *Overseas Summer Jobs* that summer restaurant workers in Spain have ten-hour days and that "In most cases . . . bar staff may work even longer hours."

Above, the three spaced periods (the ellipsis) mark the omission of the words "hotel and restaurant staff work a minimum of 10 hours per day and."

If you choose to start your quote with a word that does not begin a sentence in the original, however, you do not need an ellipsis.

In *Overseas Summer Jobs* D. J. Woodworth reminds us "that hotel workers in Spain work very long hours during the summer months. . . ."

In the example above, no ellipsis appears before "that," even though the writer left out the words "It should be remembered." The lower case *t* on "that" tells the reader that the quote is beginning in the middle of a sentence from the original. The four spaced periods after *months*, however, are required. The ellipsis here indicates that the writer left out the words "and foreign workers will be required to do likewise." The fourth period signifies the end of a sentence in the original.

If you wanted to put any of the ideas you read from Woodworth into your own words—that is, if you wanted to *paraphrase* the writer—you would still have to name your source, but you would not need quotation marks. Your paraphrase might look something like this:

According to D. J. Woodworth in *Overseas Summer Jobs* (page 103), hotel workers in Spain work very long hours. A ten-hour day, seven days a week is not at all an unusual schedule for a summer job.

In the paraphrase above, the writer put the sense of Woodworth's paragraph into the writer's own words. None of Woodworth's phrases appears in the new statement: the writer has simply paraphrased the ideas of this source and has acknowledged where they came from.

However, if the writer used any of Woodworth's own phrases, they would require quotation marks.

In *Overseas Summer Jobs,* D. J. Woodworth says that hotel workers put in "a minimum of 10 hours per day" and that it is "perfectly normal during the summer" to work seven days a week.

In the example above, the writer has paraphrased part of Woodworth's sentences, but the quotation marks around exact phrases taken from the original are required to avoid a charge of plagiarism.

Sometimes writers want to quote an authority whom they have interviewed personally or have heard speak. In those cases, the writer usually names the authority and the person's position or credentials.

"We can't afford some top soloists for our subscription season any more," says Harold Lawrence, president and executive director of the Oakland Symphony. "We engage them only for galas with high priced tickets."

Sampson Field, the president of the New York Philharmonic, concurs. "Artists can raise their prices. We can't. We can't price ourselves out of the field or limit ourselves only to the very wealthy."

—*Harold C. Schonberg*

• Quoting and Paraphrasing: Tips and Pointers •

1. Always name your sources if you quote or paraphrase.

   a. Cite the source internally—that is, directly within the sentence you are writing. In Chapter 8 you will learn the more formal internal citation system advanced by the Modern Language Association (MLA) in their guide to doing research and documenting sources.

   b. Name your sources in a list of works cited. A list of works cited is an alphabetical list of all the sources—print and otherwise—that you used in preparing your paper. See pages 264–268.

   c. Cite the source in a footnote directly after quoted or paraphrased material. If your instructor requires footnotes, you must follow an accepted form for writing them. Footnotes are no longer the preferred method of citation.

2. Use quotation marks around all quoted materials, whether you quote full sentences or brief phrases. Review the correct use of quotation marks on pages 400–403 and on page 391.

3. Integrate quotations smoothly into your own writing.

4. Do not load your paragraph with too many quotations or with one quotation that is too long. (If you must use a long quotation, set it off according to the instructions on pages 268–269.) Usually, in paragraphs and essays based upon research, about one-fourth of the writing should be made up of quoted material.

5. Use your own clear language in preference to quoting ordinary material. A sentence or two of your own to summarize a long or complicated point is a good way to offer important information.

6. Always select material from reliable sources.

7. Check unfamiliar words. Be sure that you know the meanings of any words that you quote or paraphrase.

8. Offer your thoughts and opinions based on the data you provide. Readers expect you to evaluate the expert testimony you present. Offer your own insights, but be sure the data support your opinions.

Arrangement of Details by Importance

In telling about an event, you know that the clearest way to present the moment is to give the details in chronological order—the order in which things occur. If you write a paragraph that gives several instances or examples to support the topic sentence, you certainly can write about them in the order in which they occurred. But another method is to tell the details in the order of their importance: tell about the least important thing first and the most important thing last. In this way you build up to the proof that has the most significance.

Suppose you wanted to write a paragraph for this topic sentence:

When I returned to my old neighborhood, I was sad to see how many things had changed.

You could develop these three incidents as illustrations in the paragraph:

1. Mr. Lewis, my old history teacher, had died in a car accident.
2. Mike's Pizzeria, a local hangout, was destroyed in a fire.
3. The park bench where I spent hours reading was gone.

From these incidents, although item 1 might have occurred first in time, because it seems to be the most important it best would be discussed last in the paragraph. Item 3 seems least important so it could be the first event discussed. Of course, only the writer herself could determine which was most or least significant.

Step 1. Making the Order Count. In Column I, jot down three instances you might discuss and expand for each of these topic sentences. In Column II, arrange the details in order of importance.

I

INSTANCES

II

ORDER OF IMPORTANCE

1. I enjoyed many things about working as a summer teller at New City Bank.

    a. _____   1. _____

    b. _____   2. _____

    c. _____   3. _____

2. Working a late-night shift has its disadvantages.

    a. _____   1. _____

    b. _____   2. _____

    c. _____   3. _____

3. Driving an old convertible over country
   back roads invites trouble!

   a. _____   1. _____

   b. _____   2. _____

   c. _____   3. _____

Step 2. Arranging Details by Importance.   Instead of writing in detail about two
or three instances, you can mention seven or eight instances, each in just a sentence
or two. In Column I, list even events that could be written to support the topic
sentence as given. In Column II, arrange the details according to importance as *you*
see it.

I   II

EVENTS   ORDER OF IMPORTANCE

1. Buying the right suit to wear at my sister's
   wedding as tougher than I imagined it
   would be.

   a. _____   1. _____

   b. _____   2. _____

   c. _____   3. _____

   d. _____   4. _____

   e. _____   5. _____

   f. _____   6. _____

   g. _____   7. _____

2. Living in a small town has many advantages over living in a large city.

   a. _____   1. _____

   b. _____   2. _____

   c. _____   3. _____

   d. _____   4. _____

   e. _____   5. _____

3. Children often suffer the consequences of
   their parents' divorce.

   a. _____   1. _____

   b. _____   2. _____

c. _____	3. _____
d. _____	4. _____
e. _____	5. _____
f. _____	6. _____
g. _____	7. _____

Transitions

In Chapter 1 you learned about bridging thoughts through transitions—idea connectors—that move the reader from place to place. But you can also join ideas by means of other types of connecting words.

Connecting through Time

later on	now	former
afterward	some time later	latter
years ago	once	in the first place
earlier	often	in the next place
before	yesterday	further
next	today	furthermore
first	tomorrow	meanwhile
second	then	previously
third	in the past	when
suddenly	thereafter	at last

Hint

These words help refer the reader to the idea that came directly before. The words suggest that the ideas are numbered.

Step 1. Using Time Connectors. Here are several ideas that could be used one after the other in a paragraph. They are not sentences. Using these details, connect the ideas with some of the time transitions above and write complete sentences in a paragraph. Use a separate sheet of paper.

means of effective transportation important to Americans

horses and single riders popular

covered wagons and carriages for more complex travel

go long distance with family's belongings

mass transportation by train important in travel history

bus, ship, airplane development

automobile single most popular form of transportation

relatively inexpensive means of going from one place to another families everywhere consider car necessity

rising costs of oil question auto's continued use

turn to mass transportation

Connecting through Coordinators: *and, but, for, or, nor, yet*

You learned in an earlier chapter that these words could join sentences together. The words also serve to connect ideas in separate sentences. Notice how the sentence on the left below—a correct sentence grammatically—may be written as two sentences, the second of which makes a powerful transition to a new thought group.

Connie tried everything to stop smoking. Yet she refused to give up her morning cigarette.	Connie tried everything to stop smoking, yet she refused to give up her morning cigarette.

Hint

And, but, for, or, nor, or *yet* may be used at the beginning of a sentence. In your early years of school, you were probably warned against doing so because you may have started too many sentences with *and* or *so*. But, used carefully, coordinators open sentences effectively. Make sure a complete thought follows the coordinator. Make sure the sentence before is logically related to the sentence that follows the coordinator. Don't open more than one or two sentences in each paragraph in this way.

Step 2. Coordinators for Transition.   Use a coordinator that make sense as a sentence opener in each blank space below.

1. Many young people live for today. _____ who can tell what tomorrow may bring?

2. She searched for days for her lost puppy. _____ Toby was nowhere to be found.

3. I consider myself an adventurous eater. _____ I can never convince myself to try an oyster.

4. Tom refused to apologize to Michael. _____ Michael was as stubborn as Tom in refusing to settle their argument.

5. We can go to that new dance club tonight. _____, if you are too tired, we can go to the movies.

Hint

See pages 11–14 for explanations of the meaning of coordinators such as *and, but, for, or , nor.*

Connecting through Repetition

Sometimes the repetition of a word or two at the beginning of or within a sentence helps join ideas together. Notice the repetition of the words *who* and *what* in the use of the angry questions below.

Who Are These Men?

Who are these men who defile the grassy borders of our roads and lanes, who pollute our ponds, who spoil the purity of our ocean beaches with the empty vessels of their thirst? Who are the men who make these vessels in millions and then say, "Drink—and discard"? What society is this that can afford to cast away a million tons of metal and to make of wild and fruitful land a garbage heap? What manner of men and women need thirty feet of steel and two hundred horsepower to take them, singly, to their small destinations? Who demand that what they eat is wrapped so that forests are cut down to make the paper that is thrown away, and what they smoke and chew is sealed so that the sealers can be tossed in gutters and caught in twigs and grass?

—*Marya Mannes*

Step 3. Finding Connectors. Read "Memories of Crossgates School" on page 72. Circle the words repeated at the beginning of several sentences, words that help connect ideas through repetition.

Connecting through Pronouns

he	you	its
she	who	our
it	whom	their
we	his	your
they	her	whose

A pronoun takes the place of a noun. When you use a noun in one sentence, a pronoun that appears later on in another sentence automatically refers the reader back to the original noun. In that way, you can move one idea smoothly to another.

Step 4. Pronouns as Connectors. Circle the pronouns that help connect the sentences in this paragraph.

The Tailor Arrives

Almost instantly there was the sound of soft steady footsteps through the open doors, and from the back of the house through the hall following the manservant there came the tailor. He was a tall man, taller than the servant, middle-aged, his face quiet with a sort of closed tranquility. He wore a long robe of faded blue grasscloth, patched neatly at the elbows and very clean. Under his arm he carried a bundle wrapped in a white cloth. He bowed to the two white women and then squatting down put his bundle upon the floor of the veranda and untied its knots. Inside was a worn and frayed fashion book from some American company and a half-finished dress of a spotted blue-and-white silk. This dress he shook out carefully and held up for Mrs. Lowe to see.

—*Pearl S. Buck*

Step 5. A Brief Paragraph with Pronoun Connectors.   Write five sentences to describe the person sitting next to you in class. Mention the person's name in the first sentence. Connect the ideas in each succeeding sentence by using pronouns to bridge each complete thought. Use a separate sheet of paper.

Hint

It must always be clear to the reader just which noun the pronoun replaces. Consider this sentence:

The mother held the baby, and she laughed at her.

We don't know—because the pronouns are unclear—just who did the laughing at whom.

Subordination

In Chapter 1 you learned how to combine sentences using coordination. Another way to join thoughts in paragraphs is to relate the thoughts so that one of the two ideas is stressed more than the other. For example, you can join two short sentences so that one of the thoughts gets more emphasis. Look at these two sentences (from "The Nursery," on page 12), which are then joined, using subordination:

He rests his head on the pillow. I tiptoe quietly to the door.
a. Because he rests his head on the pillow, I tiptoe quietly to the door.

The words *I tiptoe quietly to the door* express a complete thought and, as such, receive the most stress in the sentence.

The words *Because he rests his head on the pillow* are not a complete thought and, therefore, get less emphasis than the rest of the sentence. Those words give "background information": they tell *why* the writer tiptoed quietly to the door. But clearly, it is the tiptoeing to the door that the sentence stresses, and the writer shows that the baby's falling asleep brought about the action of leaving the child's room.

Now look at the sentences joined together in another way:

b. Because I tiptoe quietly to the door, he rests his head on the pillow.

Here, the words *he rests his head on the pillow* are the stressed part of the sentence; they can stand alone as a complete thought.

The words *Because I tiptoe quietly to the door* are not a complete thought. As "background information" they tell *why* the baby fell asleep. But it is the fact that the baby rests his head on the pillow that the sentence stresses. The writer shows that the action of tiptoeing to the door made the baby do what he did.

The technique that gives one part of a sentence more stress than another is *subordination*. Only the writer can decide which part is less or more important. Completely different meanings are achieved by subordinating different words groups: this is clear in sentences *a* and *b* above.

It's obvious that the word *because* is the word that brings about the subordination in sentences *a* and *b*. It is one word among many that are called *subordinators*. Although all subordinators connect the unstressed part of a sentence to the part that gets the emphasis, they explain different things about the emphasized part of the sentence.

If you want to show *why* the stressed part of the sentence occurred, use one of these to subordinate:

as	because	so that
since	in order that	as long as

EXAMPLE

[This tells *why* the lateness occurred.]

Because the train was delayed, I arrived late to work.

[This is the stressed part
of the sentence. It expresses
a complete thought.]

Step 1. Subordination to Tell Why. Make up a correct subordinate part to tell *why* for each of these complete thoughts. Use one of the subordinators in the boxed chart above. Be sure a subject and a verb come after the subordinator.

1. _____, we received no mail yesterday.
2. _____, Mr. Bogan did not go to work.
3. _____, the rain drenched us.
4. _____, Georgette rushed home after school.
5. _____, we wrapped the most tender bushes in burlap.

If you want to show *when* the stressed part of the sentence occurred, use one of these to subordinate.

after	before	whenever	once
as	since	while	provided
as soon as	when	until	

EXAMPLE

[This tells *when* the wish for
   popcorn occurred.]

After the movie began, we decided to have popcorn.

                    [This is the stressed part of the sentence.
                     It expresses a complete thought.]

Step 2. Subordination to Tell When. Make up a correct subordinate part to tell *when* for each of these complete thoughts. Use a subordinator from the chart above. Be sure a subject and verb follow the subordinator.

1. _____, we watched a horror movie on cable TV.
2. _____, the telephone began to ring.
3. _____, Lester laughed so hard he collapsed.
4. _____, I washed his hand with peroxide and bandaged his thumb.
5. _____, she locked the front door and trudged wearily up the stairs.

If you want to show *where* or *how* the stressed part of the sentence occurred, use one of these to subordinate:

wherever	if	as if
where	how	as though

EXAMPLES

[This tells *where* forces of
   good work.]

Wherever evil appears, the forces of good will work against it.

                 [This stressed part of the
            sentence is a complete thought.]

[This tells *how* Susan acted.]

As if she had never seen snow before, Susan dived madly into the drifts.

[The stressed part of the sentence:
it is a complete thought.]

Step 3. Completing Subordinated Sentences.

Write the stressed part of the sentence for each subordinated word group below.

1. Wherever Lil was, _____

2. As though he had not eaten in a week, _____

3. As if he had never written a paper before, _____

4. Where there is smoke, _____

5. If the burgers stay on the grill too long, _____

If you want to show *under what condition* the stressed part of the sentence occurred, use one of these to subordinate:

although	unless
if	provided
though	once

EXAMPLES

[You would not expect a   [This complete thought is
tired person to run.]   what the sentence stresses.]

Although I was tired, I ran the ten blocks home.

[This tells *under what
condition* the bills will be
paid.]

Unless the check comes, I cannot pay my bills.

[This, a complete
thought, is what the
sentence stresses.]

Hint: *Although* introduces an idea that you would not expect to happen because of the information in the stressed part.

Step 4. Subordinators Tell Conditions.

Complete the sentences below by adding a subordinated section that tells under what condition the main part of the sentence occurs. Use the subordinator as indicated.

1. If _____, you must have a valid license.
2. Unless _____, hunger will continue as a major problem in Africa.
3. Although _____, I will not walk home alone at night.
4. Provided _____, we should be in Texas by nightfall.
5. Once _____, the game can begin.

Hint

Use a comma after the subordinate part of the sentence when the subordinate part comes first.

[subordinate part]

As she arrived, we left.

[comma here]

Subordinated portions like the ones you've been writing may also appear at the ends of sentences. You generally do not use a comma before the subordinated section if it comes at the end.

[no comma here]   [subordinated part]

I watched every game of the World Series because I love baseball.

Step 5. Subordinating Your Sentences.   For each topic below, write a sentence that uses subordination at the beginning of the sentence. Use as many different subordinators as you can. Don't forget commas after the subordinated part. Use your own paper.

EXAMPLE

music

After the music stopped, Carol and I sat down for a drink.

1. a recent trip
2. writing a paper
3. a person you admire
4. cooking
5. winter driving

Step 6. Subordination to Join.   Each item in Column I below contains two brief sentences. Subordinate one of the two sentences, and rewrite your new sentence in Column II. Then subordinate the other sentence, and write the new sentence in Column III. Look at the example.

I

II

III

EXAMPLE
I heard the telephone ring.
I unlocked the door.

As I unlocked the door, I heard the telephone ring.

As I heard the telephone ring, I unlocked the door.

1. I was baby-sitting for Gina. She cried all night.

2. Saxophone music played. Lila and I danced slowly across an empty floor.

3. The governor spoke sternly. He stormed out of the auditorium.

4. The saxophone began to wail. We clapped enthusiastically.

5. I wrote a letter to him. He sent a postcard to me.

Hint

If the subordinated part—placed at the end—starts with *though* or *although*, use a comma.
We read the whole book, though we were bored by it.

[comma]

If in the subordinate part of the sentence you want to describe someone or something you have mentioned in the stressed part, use one of these:

who
whose   that
which

[This identifies the
woman.]

1. The woman whose purse was stolen called the police.

[This identifies the book.]

2. We bought the book which had the most pictures.

[This identifies the
man.]

3. The man who enjoys his work does the best job.

4. The Empire State Building, which is in New York, is no longer the tallest building.

Hint: The word *which* never refers to a person, only places and things. Use *who, whom,* and *whose* to refer to people.

Wrong
The people which eat fast will be ill.

Correct
Those people *who* eat fast will be ill. The meat *which* we ate was tasty.

A Hint About Commas: Sentences 1 to 3 above do not use commas with the subordinate part because the subordinating sections identify some subject. Without the words *whose purse was stolen,* we cannot identify the woman. Without *which had the most pictures,* we cannot identify the book in sentence 2. Without *who enjoys his work* we have no idea of which man is being identified. *Because they are essential for proper meaning, subordinate sections that identify the subject don't need commas.*

However, when information is added in subordinate sections to describe further a subject already identified, you need to use commas as in sentence 4 above. This material is *nonessential:* the subordinate section merely adds information about a subject already named. (See pages 302–313 for more information on commas.)

[comma]   [comma]

Professor Barton, who teaches here, is ill.

[This *adds* information:
the person is already
identified.]

The girl who won the contest received $100.

[This identifies the girl:
no commas.]

I admire John Steinbeck's novels, which are full of rich imagery.

[comma]   [This *adds* information; the novels
have already been identified.]

Step 7. Practice with *Who, Whose, Which, That*. Add words to complete the subordinate section in each sentence below. Use commas where necessary.

1. The salesclerk *who* _____ will earn the largest commission.
2. I visited an abandoned town *that* _____.
3. The best crops grow in well-drained fields *which* _____

   _____.
4. The movie star *whose* _____ was no longer popular with the fans.
5. The school years *that* _____ will linger in your memories.

Step 8. Writing Sentences That Subordinate. For each of these subordinate word groups, write a complete sentence that makes sense. Put the subordinated part in the middle or at the end of the sentence; remember to use commas when necessary. Use a separate sheet of paper.

1. who works very hard
2. whose dog is ferocious
3. who cried endlessly
4. that will make you feel better
5. who loves me deeply
6. whose son is a dentist
7. which has never been opened
8. who never forgets my birthday
9. that made me late for work
10. which disturbed our sleep

Step 9. Rewriting Coordinated Sentences. Although coordination is often effective, subordination of ideas allows for much greater sentence variety. Change each coordinated sentence below to a sentence that uses subordination. Use separate paper.

EXAMPLE

I like waterskiing, but the speed frightens me.

Although I like waterskiing, the speed frightens me.

1. Dad parked the car, and we waited outside the restaurant.
2. Nicole knew she would miss her friends, but she was excited to go to Australia for the year.
3. Mr. Wong telephoned for an ambulance, and the three police officers administered first aid.

4. Sue wanted to comfort her sister, but she did not know what to say.

5. You should read your textbook carefully, or you may fail the midterm.

Step 10. Rewriting a Paragraph. On a separate sheet of paper, rewrite the paragraph "The Nursery" that appears on page 12. Use coordination and subordination to vary the sentence length and structure. Use coordination only once; use subordination at least three times.

Word and Sentence Skills: Suggested Topics for Study

Fragments with Subordinators, pages 338–342
Plurals, pages 363–366
Capital Letters, pages 298–302
Abbreviations and Numbers, pages 282–284
Quotations, pages 400–403

● Writing a Paragraph of Illustration

Assignment

Write a paragraph of twelve to fifteen sentences in which you provide examples to demonstrate some general impression about a topic. To develop your paragraph through examples, choose some experiences that you have had. Or use research from other sources as the basis of this written assignment. Express the examples through details of people, places, and actions or by direct quotations or paraphrasing. Try to select examples that fall into a pattern in order to suggest a single impression about the topic. In that case you will develop your paragraph by offering several instances to support your topic sentence.

Suggested Topics

Here are some topics you might wish to write about. If you need other suggestions, reread the sentences on page 67.

1. doing things wrong (right)
2. national pastimes
3. childhood fears
4. government spending
5. dangerous times
6. insecurity: my personality key
7. drugs in sports
8. rules I hated to obey
9. competing with a brother (sister)
10. children of the Vietnam War
11. air or water pollution
12. family trips
13. being independent
14. my fantasies

15. space exploration

16. my handicap

17. experiences dating

18. hunger in our city

19. my friendly disposition

20. the generation gap

Prewriting: Free Association

In free association, you choose a topic and jot down everything and anything about that topic that pops into your head. The ideas may be random and unrelated. The important thing is to let your thoughts run freely. Don't stop to correct the spelling of a word. When you are finished, look over your words and group related ideas together. These ideas can serve as sources of details for your theme. Below is part of one student's attempt at free association. Examine his list of words and answer the questions that follow.

● Prewriting: Free Association ●

Topic: my childhood behavior

sister's appendicitis: threw a tantrum in school

caught smoking in the junior high school bathroom

fishing trip with my father when I was five—I dumped all the bait overboard

happy Sunday mornings at home when I made pancakes and eggs for the whole family (pretty messy!)

bringing home stray parakeet

worm collection in a fish tank

draining a glass of wine from the dining room table (I was seven years old and I couldn't stop laughing)

Halloween fun, howling like ghosts and waking all the neighborhood dogs

learning to swim at Riverhead

collecting money door-to-door for Muscular Dystrophy

sliding down Wilder Hill and knocking out a tooth

eating a whole bag of chocolate kisses.

—Michael D'Angelo

Step 1. Exploring a Student's Free Associations.   Look at the list above to answer these questions:

1. What associations on Mr. D'Angelo's list might you group together because they seem related in some way?

2. What general word or words could you use to describe some of the groups of details? Would you call any of the groups *dangerous? thoughtless? funny?*

3. What central personality thread might Mr. D'Angelo choose to develop on the basis of some of the items on this list?

Step 2. Your Own Free Associations. Select one of the topics on page 94 (or select a topic of your own), and practice prewriting by using free association to shake loose some ideas about the subject. Use separate paper.

Step 3. Associations on Tape. Some writers use a tape recorder for free-association techniques in prewriting. Once you have an idea of the topic you want to write about or have thoroughly researched your topic, speak for about twenty minutes into a tape recorder. Say whatever comes into your mind about the topic. Afterward, with pencil and paper before you, play back the recording of your voice. Try to identify some thread running through your associations. Then play the tape again, listening for those examples that support that central thread. Write down the examples with brief phrases; then try to arrange them in some order.

Student Samples: Drafting and Revising

Use the section called Progress Reminders: A Checklist of Questions on pages 101–102 to guide you as you write and revise your illustration paragraph. Review pages 20–21 on drafting and revising. Also, be sure to study the student samples that appear here and on the following pages.

Step 1. Reading Drafts. Examine the two drafts below for a paragraph of illustration designed to provide a general impression of some feature of the writer's childhood. What changes do you note in the revised draft? Answer the questions after you read.

DRAFT

Early Stages of Embarrassment

I'll never forget my early years of being a teenager because I went through a great deal of embarrassment. I remembered my first year the most because it was the most embarrassing moment. My friends and I decided to celebrate the turn of my thirteenth year in Jones Beach. My friends, two years older, revealed their fully developed bodies through two pieces of cloth. I was persuaded to wear a bright yellow bikini outfit. We ran towards the upcoming waves holding hands. Before I knew

it, the blue ocean enveloped its waves all around me. I struggled to
the surface to grasp for air. Once I caught my breath, I decided to
leave the roaring of the waves behind me. My friends turned red and
yelled, "Go back into the water!" When I wearily looked down, I saw
that my chest was bare to the vast public. The next embarrassment was
on my fourteenth year. I remember how I tried to impress a guy, and
ended up with a sprained ankle. Now he always calls me "Clutzy." He had
jade eyes, which were always surrounded by the giggling of coquettish
girls. In order to impress him, I wore a royal blue dress with white
polka dots and heels which added three inches to my petite height. He
was down on the lower floor. "Just fifteen steps to go," I said to
myself. I lost my balance and stumbled down the steps. From that day on
he called me "Klutzy." I was fifteen when I was invited to the school
dance. I could still hear the loud vibrating sounds of music that was
played. Practically everyone wore tight designer's jean including me.
My flexible body moved and danced with the music's beat. As I bent
down. I felt my skin ripping its force through my jeans. I revealed my
lacy underwear. The laughter crept painfully through my ears. Even
though my early teenage years proved to be a profound embarrassment. I
learned that I was not the only one to have such experiences.

REVISED DRAFT

Embarrassment

　　I'll never forget the embarrassing moments of my teenage years.
When I was thirteen, my friends and I decided to celebrate my birthday
at Jones Beach. My friends, two years older, chose to show off their
bodies in tight, two-piece bathing suits. Despite my immature figure
they persuaded me to wear a bright yellow bikini. At the beach we ran
into the waves with hands clasped tightly to each other. Before I knew
it, the roaring blue ocean enveloped me and pulled me under. Gasping
for air, I struggled to the surface and pushed to the shore. My friends
were shouting, "Go back! Go back into the water!" When I wearily looked
down, I saw that the narrow top of my bikini had slipped to my waist,
and my chest was bare to the public! The next embarrassment occurred
during my fourteenth year. I wanted to impress Miguel, a senior at my
school who lived in my apartment building, and I ended up with a
sprained ankle! Knowing he'd be talking with his friends at the doorway
that afternoon, I dressed up so he'd notice me. I wore a royal blue
dress with polka dots. I put on high-heeled shoes which added 3 inches
to my height. "Just a few more steps to go," I remember saying to
myself as he watched me wobbling down the stairs. Suddenly I lost my
balance and stumbled awkwardly, falling right at Miguel's feet.
Everyone laughed. From that day on he called me "Klutzy." Another
really embarrasing moment took place at our school dance when I was
fifteen. The music vibrated loudly as we danced energetically to a live
band. The style of clothing then was tight designer jeans and everyone,
including me, wore them that night. In one fancy dance step I bent at

the waist and *rrripp*, my pants split clear up the seat. Over the beat of the drums, the laughter of the crowd crept painfully through my ears as I backed out the door and ran all the way home. Although these are experiences I'd like to forget, I'm sure I'll always remember my teenage embarrassments.

—Nydia Gonzales

1. In what ways is the revised draft an improvement on the earlier draft? What additions do you think help make the paragraph clearer? What did the writer leave out? Why?

2. Compare the two opening sentences and the two closing sentences. Which do you prefer? Why? How could the writer improve further upon the closing sentence in the revision?

3. What changes has the writer made in the subtopic sentences?

4. The writer chose a chronological arrangement of details. Does it work effectively? Would you recommend another arrangement? Which? Why?

5. What further changes would you recommend that the writer make in the next draft? Where could the paragraph be made even clearer? Where would more details be helpful?

Step 2. More Student Samples: Examples from Personal Experience. Read the student samples below; pay close attention to the use of subtopic sentences to introduce each new example drawn from personal experience. Then answer the questions that follow.

Childhood Mischief

I will never forget the mischievous things I used to do when my parents were not at home. Sliding across cool beige linoleum on a cushion of talcum was one exciting bit of mischief. I shook baby powder all over my bedroom floor until it looked as if it was covered with snow and was as slick as a sheet of ice. With white socks I became an ice skater gliding gracefully across a frozen pond. Feeling adventurous sometimes, I would run from the hall and slide into my room stopping within a few inches of my wooden dresser, which stands opposite the door. I did another really crazy thing on a night my older sisters babysat for my brother and me. Tired of minding us, Angela and Alethea sent us to bed, but we were not the least bit tired. To make our sisters mad, my brother and I sneaked past them into the kitchen. We each took a little bit of laundry detergent and put it in our noses. Slipping back into bed, we kept sneezing uncontrollably for fifteen minutes. We thought this was funny, and every time a sneeze did not come we laughed. This made my oldest sister Angela very angry. Annoyed, she yelled at us, "You two better stop that sneezing or when Ma comes home I am going to tell her how you were behaving!" From that moment on we had to cover up our sneezes so we would not get into trouble. But the most mischievous thing I did was to throw heavy rocks at passing cars. My friends, my sister Alethea, and I would go to Crotona Park and would climb to the top of a steep, rocky hill that overlooked an exit off the Cross Bronx Expressway. Whenever we hit one of the speeding cars, we would run off somewhere and hide. One day my sister hit a new brown and white Mustang. She did not see a small angry man burst out of his car. All of us ran except Alethea. Cursing in a harsh voice, the man climbed up the hill behind her and almost grabbed her. She darted out of his reach just in time. That was the last time I ever threw rocks! In retrospect, all those mischievous things I did for fun could have caused me trouble not only with my parents but with other innocent people too.

—*Elaine Dawkins*

Horrors and High School Math

I will never forget my math teachers because I disliked most of them throughout my high school years. I remember my eleventh year math teacher vividly. She had a straight nose on which a pair of gold-rimmed glasses sat tightly at the end. Before each lesson began she compelled me, her worst student, to erase long white columns from the chalkboards. Each day she gave pages of homework. I hated those assignments, so I just ignored them. In the end, of course, my reward was a *fifty* in red on my report card. Next, my geometry teacher stands out in my mind. Although Miss Carpenter was twenty-five, she acted like an old witch of a hundred. She wore the same dingy green dress each day. Sloppily, mousy brown hair hung in her eyes, and she scooped strands and curls off her forehead. Her voice, high-pitched, would screech across the classroom and down the hall. "Julius," I can still hear her squeak, her lips pinched in a little pink circle, "if you don't know about diameters, I'll have to fail you." But of all my math teachers, I disliked most the one who taught me algebra. A tall, lanky man, this teacher had an angry temper that kept most of us from asking questions. Once a girl in the last row asked timidly, "Will you explain that again please?" As Mr. Gilian's face grew scarlet, he plunged his hands into his black pants pockets. "Try paying attention," he barked, "and then you won't have to bother me with ridiculous questions." From my past unpleasant experiences with math teachers I have grown to dislike them all automatically; is it any wonder that my math grades never rise above C's and D's?

—*Julius Passero*

1. What is the topic in each paragraph? What is the writer's opinion about the topic in each case?

2. Read aloud the subtopic sentences for each paragraph.

3. How are the details in each case arranged, chronologically or by importance? How do you know?

4. Which details of color, sound, and action do you find most original?

Step 3. Illustrating a Point from Other Sources.   Read this paragraph in which the writer presents examples to make a point about teenage workers. Answer the questions below.

Teenagers as Part-Time Workers

Many teenagers who need money are solving their financial problems by holding one of a variety of part-time jobs. According to the United States Department of Labor's Bureau of Labor Statistics, teenagers say that they work to earn money to meet general expenses or expenses for their education, although many young people do work to get job experience as well. Writing in *A Part-Time Career for a Full Time You,* JoAnne Alter points out that part-time employment can help thirteen- through sixteen-year-olds earn extra money for luxuries like roller skates, new clothing, and records. Among older teenagers, though, students have particular problems. As Alter shows, many of them "must provide at least a portion of their support in addition to attending classes and studying at home." Students continuing their education "must contend with tuition, room and board payments, and the cost of books for classes." Even if the student's parents provide financial support, Alter says, or if the student has found some other source of income, "there is still the matter of everyday living expenses" and "most of those aren't covered by financial grants." Further, the government has cut back sharply on these grants. It should be no surprise then that about four million teenagers, half of them male and half female, worked part-time at different kinds of jobs in a given year. The Bureau of Labor Statistics reports that men worked as dining-room or kitchen staff, as laborers, operatives, and cleaning workers. Women worked as clerks, cashiers, waitresses, household employees, or day-care workers. Of all those teenagers working part-time 16.7% were clerical workers, 14.6% were non-farm laborers and 34.3% were service workers. Half of all food-service workers are teenagers. Next time you place your order at McDonald's or Burger King you might remember that the cheerful teenager who wraps your burger or who salts your French fries may be a student who needs extra money for school.

—*Chris Donovan*

1. What generality has Chris Donovan drawn from the data she examined? Does her topic sentence state the generalization adequately?

2. What sources does she cite in this paragraph?

3. Which examples do you find most impressive? Where has the writer used statistics? paraphrases? direct quotation?

4. Comment on the closing sentence of the paragraph.

5. Does the writer use illustrations successfully here? Explain.

Collaboration: Getting Reader Response

Pair up with one other person, and read each other's drafts. Immediately after you finish reading your partner's paper, write a brief critique about it. (A *critique* is a critical review or commentary.) In your critique, tell the writer how to improve the paragraph. You might want to consider the following ideas:

1. What impressions did you get from the paragraph?

2. What more do you want to know about any of the examples?

3. Do the examples successfully demonstrate the general impression the writer tries to give on the topic? Why or why not?

Return the critique to your partner, along with the essay. Use the critique you have received on your paper to produce your next draft.

Progress Reminders: A Checklist

Follow these guidelines as you write a one-paragraph theme that gives some general impression about your topic and then shows examples to support it. Some of the questions call for a simple yes or no, while others require that you fill in a short answer. Hand in the completed checklist with your final draft. Reread the samples on pages 96–100 before you begin.

1. Did I attempt to use free association as a prewriting method to develop my ideas for this paragraph? _____

2. Did I choose to write (*a*) a paragraph that employs several examples to show something about my topic or (*b*) a paragraph that offers a listing of details without subtopics?

3. Did I write a topic sentence (see pages 5–10) that announces the subject of the paragraph and identifies my attitude or opinion toward the subject? _____

   This is my topic sentence: _____

4. In my rough draft, did all the examples I offered—no matter how many—support the general impression I tried to get across? _____

5. Did I use subtopic sentences where necessary (see pages 68–72) to introduce each new aspect of the topic? _____

   Here is one subtopic sentence: _____

   _____

6. If my examples were based on personal experience, did I show enough details of the scene, including color, sound, touch, and smell? _____

7. If I drew examples from sources other than personal experience, did I use statistics, cases, paraphrases, or direct quotations to illustrate my point? _____

8. Did I use words that show lively actions? _____

9. Have I used effective transitions to tie my sentences together? (See pages 83–86.) _____

10. Have I arranged the details of my paragraph in an appropriate order? _____

11. Have I used some of the vocabulary on page 65? _____

 Here is one of the words I used from those pages: _____

12. Have I opened one sentence with a word that ends in *-ly* (see page 43)? _____

13. Did I start some sentences with different subordinators, explained on pages 86–93? _____

14. Did I use a semicolon correctly in at least one sentence (see page 392)? _____

15. As I proofread my essay, did I look especially for my usual errors? _____

16. After reading my essay, am I satisfied that I have expressed a dominant impression about my topic? _____

 That impression is: _____

17. Does my paragraph have a strong, lively title? _____

• The Professionals Speak

Step 1. Authors Remember Their Youth. The selections below develop topics through the use of examples. Discuss the questions after you read.

Down South

Down South seemed like a dream when I was on the train going back to New York. I saw a lot of things down South that I never saw in my whole life before and most of them I didn't ever want to see again. I saw a great big old burly black man hit a pig in the head with the back of an ax. The pig screamed, oink-oinked a few times, lay down, and started kicking and bleeding . . . and died. When he was real little, I used to chase him, catch him, pick him up, and play catch with him. He was a greedy old pig, but I used to like him. One day when it was real cold, I ate a piece of that pig, and I still liked him. One day I saw Grandma kill a rattlesnake with a hoe. She chopped the snake's head off in the front yard, and I sat on the porch and watched the snake's body keep wiggling till it was nighttime. And I saw an old brown hound dog named Old Joe eat a rat one day, right out in the front yard. He caught the rat in the woodpile and started tearing him open. Old Joe was eating everything in the rat. He ate something that looked like the yellow part in an egg, and I didn't eat eggs for a long time after that. I saw a lady rat have a lot of little baby rats on a pile of tobacco leaves. She had to be a lady, because my first-grade teacher told a girl that ladies don't cry about little things, and the rat had eleven little hairless pink rats, and she didn't even squeak about it.

I made a gun down South out of a piece of wood, some tape, a piece of tire-tube rubber, a nail, some wire, a piece of pipe, and a piece of door hinge. And I saw nothing but blood where my right thumbnail used to be after I shot it for the first time. That nail grew back, little by little, I saw a lot of people who had roots worked on them, but I never saw anybody getting roots worked on them.

Down South sure was a crazy place, and it was good to be going back to New York.

—*Claude Brown*

Boyhood Farm Days

As I have said, I spent some part of every year at the farm until I was twelve or thirteen years old. The life which I led there with my cousins was full of charm, and so is the memory of it yet. I know how the wild blackberries looked, and how they tasted, and the same with the pawpaws, the hazelnuts, and the persimmons; and I can feel the thumping rain, upon my head, of hickory nuts and walnuts when we were out in the frosty dawn to scramble for them with the pigs, and the gusts of wind loosed them and sent them down. I know the stain of blackberries, and how pretty it is, and I know the stain of walnut hulls, and how little it minds soap and water, also what grudged experience it had of either of them. I know the taste of maple sap, and when to gather it, and how to arrange the troughs and the delivery tubes, and how to boil down the juice, and how to hook the sugar after it is made, also how much better hooked sugar tastes than any that is honestly come by, let bigots say what they will. I know how a prize watermelon looks when it is sunning its fat rotundity among pumpkin vines and "simblins"; I know how to tell when it is ripe without "plugging" it; I know how inviting it looks when it is cooling itself in a tub of water under the bed, waiting; I know how it looks when it lies on the table in the sheltered great floor space between house and kitchen, and the children gathered for the sacrifice and their mouths watering; I know the crackling sound it makes when the carving knife enters its end, and I can see the split fly along in front of the blade as the knife cleaves its way to the other end; I can see its halves fall apart and display the rich red meat and the black seeds, and the heart standing up, a luxury fit for the elect; I know how a boy looks behind a yardlong slice of that melon, and I know how he feels; for I have been there. I know the taste of the watermelon which has been honestly come by, and I know the taste of the watermelon which has been acquired by art. Both taste good, but the experienced know which tastes best. I know the look of green apples and peaches and pears on the trees, and I know how entertaining they are when they are inside of a person. I know how ripe ones look when they are piled in pyramids under the trees, and how pretty they are and how vivid their colors. I know how a frozen apple looks, in a barrel down cellar in the wintertime, and how hard it is to bite, and how the frost makes the teeth ache, and yet how good it is, notwithstanding. I know the disposition of elderly people to select the specked apples for the children, and I once knew ways to beat the game. I know the look of an apple that is roasting and sizzling on a hearth on a winter's evening, and I know the comfort that comes of eating it hot, along with some sugar and a drench of cream.

—*Mark Twain*

1. What topic does each writer attempt to support?

2. What examples does he present in order to develop the topic?

3. Which images of action are clearest?

4. What words serve as transitions through repetition in each selection?

Step 2. Reviewing a Professional Sample. Reread "Memories of Crossgates School" (page 72) by George Orwell. What topic does this paragraph develop? What examples does the writer give in order to support his point? Which details are most lively and original?

Step 3. Examples from Research. Read this selection from a college sociology textbook to see how quotations, paraphrases, and cases serve to illustrate the writer's point.

SOME WORDS TO KNOW BEFORE YOU READ

invulnerable—not subject to harm

restrictive—holding back; preventing

entrenched—fixed firmly or securely

abstaining—choosing not to

Men's Gender Role

Boys are socialized to think that they should be invulnerable, fearless, decisive, and even emotionless in some situations (Cicone and Ruble, 1978). These are difficult standards to meet; yet, for boys who do not "measure up," life can be trying. This is especially true for boys who show an interest in activities thought of as feminine (such as cooking) or for those who do not enjoy traditional masculine activities (such as competitive sports). Following are one man's recollections of his childhood, when he disliked sports, dreaded gym classes, and had particular problems with baseball:

> During the game I always played the outfield. Right field. Far right field. And there I would stand in the hot sun wishing I was anyplace else in the world. Every so often a ball looked like it was coming in my direction and I prayed to God that it wouldn't happen. If it did come, I promised God to be good for the next 37 years if he let me catch it—especially if it was a fly ball (Fager et al., 1971:36).

Boys who do not conform to the designated male gender role, like the right fielder quoted above, face constant criticism and even humiliation both from other children and from adults. It can be agonizing to be treated as a "chicken" or a "sissy"—particularly if such remarks come from one's father or brothers. At the same time, boys who successfully adapt to cultural standards of masculinity may grow up to be inexpressive men who cannot share their feelings with others. They remain forceful and tough—but as a result they are also closed and isolated (Balswick and Peek, 1971).

In the last 20 years, inspired in a good part by the contemporary feminist movement (which will be examined later in the chapter), increasing numbers of American men have criticized the restrictive aspects of the traditional male gender role. Yet, after comparing responses by high school students to survey questions posed in 1956 and 1982, educators Miriam Lewin and Lilli Tragos (1987) concluded that teenage males of the 1980s still emphasize both gender-role differentiation and the symbols of male dominance more than their female counterparts do. This study, as well as research by Peter Stein (1984), suggests that young women's views of gender-role issues have undergone a significant change in recent decades, while young men's views have been largely unaffected.

Accounts in the mass media commonly indicate that a "new man" has emerged in the 1980s. Journalist Anthony Astrachan (1986:402) defines this "new man" as:

> . . . one who has abandoned or transcended most traditional male sex roles and the male attempt to monopolize power. He doesn't insist on being the sole or dominant earner of family income and he resists being a slave to his job though he prizes competence and achievement. He believes that men are just as emotional as women and should learn to express their feelings, and he can talk about his own problems and weaknesses. The new man supports women's quest for independence and equality with more than lip service.

However, after an extensive study of American men, Astrachan estimates that only 5 to 10 percent of men come close to (or are moving toward) this ideal definition. Apparently, then, the traditional male gender-role remains well entrenched as an influential element of American culture (see also David and Brannon, 1976; Kimmel, 1987; Lamm, 1977; R. Lewis, 1981; Pleck, 1981, 1985; Snodgrass, 1977).

Despite the persistence of the traditional male gender role in the United States, there has undoubtedly been growing flexibility regarding expected behavior for each sex. Today, few social roles are completely restricted to either women or men within American society. Giving birth is limited to women, but an increasing number are voluntarily abstaining from bearing children (see Chapter 12). Those women who do opt for motherhood are often sharing the moment of birth with their husbands, who assist their wives in the delivery room as coaches. Motherhood is not viewed as the only legitimate occupation for adult women, and family specialists no longer counsel against mothers' working outside the home (Bernard, 1974, 1975:15; Maccoby and Jacklin, 1974:348–374; Schaefer, 1988).

The changing gender roles of American society—as well as the continuing resistance to change—are evident in a story reported by the Olympic swimming champion and television commentator Donna de Varona (1984). Officials of a local basketball tournament in Massachusetts ruled that girls were not welcome on a sixth-grade team from Ashburnham. When the boys on the team heard this decree, they refused to compete without one of their starters: 12-year-old Jennifer Corby.

"I tried out for the one team there is," Jennifer argued. "I practiced very hard and made the team fairly. They can't take that away from me."

Ultimately, they didn't. Bowing to the strong stand taken by Jennifer and her male teammates, tournament officials reversed their ruling. Jennifer played.

—*Richard Schaefer*

1. State the topic of the selection in your own words.

2. Where do the authors use quotations to illustrate a point? Where do they paraphrase?

3. What are the sources used in the article? Writing one sentence for each source, tell how the source helps prove the authors' point.

4. Where do the writers use specific cases to support their point?

CHAPTER

4

Writing Essays

●

INTRODUCTION TO WRITING ESSAYS

In this chapter you will learn some basic approaches to developing an essay, a longer composition made up of four or five paragraphs—or more, if necessary. The basic difference between the theme of one long paragraph (which you practiced in the earlier chapters of this book) and the four- or five-paragraph essay is simply one of length and proportion. An essay allows you to develop your ideas more fully, to use more details, to bring in important information that you might have left out of a single paragraph composition so that it would not be too long.

To give you useful practice in the new elements of essay form and structure presented here, this assignment draws substantially on the paragraph-writing techniques that you learned in Chapters 1 to 3. Return to any of the topics you explored in connection with those chapters and make it the subject of your first essay. Expand your one-paragraph assignment in description, narration, or illustration. To write your essay, describe some unforgettable place, person, or object; or narrate some memorable event in your life; or illustrate your thoughts on some subject by presenting examples drawn from your own experience or from a subject you can support with data and expert testimony. Referring back to the paragraph assignments you developed earlier in the semester will help you see very clearly the connections between a one-paragraph composition and an essay. You can learn some new skills about essay writing as you sharpen your skills in the familiar territory of paragraph development.

And there are many new skills to learn about writing essays. Here you will learn about the various parts of the longer composition. You will see how the various elements in a single-paragraph paper correspond to the elements in a four- or five-paragraph essay. You will learn how to develop a proposal—or thesis— sentence. You will learn how to write introductions and to use transitions between paragraphs comfortably. Also, you will once again practice sharpening your eye for details and conveying your supporting information precisely.

● Vocabulary

The words in this activity will help you present sensory details in specific language.

Step 1. Learning Words for Shape and Size.   Check the words below in a dictionary. Write definitions in the blanks next to the words.

1. colossal   _____   4. spacious   _____

2. minuscule   _____   5. amorphous   _____

3. cramped   _____

Step 2. Sizing It Up.   Write in the blanks the words from the above list that you might use to describe:

1. a one-bedroom apartment
    for four people   _____

2. a flat tire   _____

3. an eighteen-room house   _____

4. a speck of dust   _____

5. the Rocky Mountains   _____

Step 3. More Sensory Language. These words help name sensations of touch and smell. Check their definitions in a dictionary and write them in the blank lines.

SMELL

1. savory   _____
2. acrid   _____
3. dank   _____
4. pungent   _____
5. fetid   _____

TOUCH

6. supple   _____
7. clammy   _____
8. gossamer   _____
9. rigid   _____
10. sinewy   _____

Step 4. Applying New Words. From the vocabulary above, select a word that best describes each of the following:

1. a plant of soft wood   _____
2. vinegar   _____
3. a solid steel door   _____
4. the arm of an athlete   _____
5. sulfuric acid   _____
6. turkey roasting in an oven   _____
7. the feel of perspiration on a cool day   _____
8. a spider's web   _____
9. the cellar of an old house   _____
10. an airless locker room   _____

● Building Composition Skills

Finding the Topic

Explore possible essay topics by discussing them in class. Follow the step below.

Talking It Through. Form groups of three or four students at your teacher's direction. After looking over the various paragraphs you wrote in response to assignments in the earlier chapters of this book, which of your paragraphs do you think you could turn successfully into an essay? Discuss your ideas with the others in your group. Which paragraph could you expand into a longer theme? How could you add details? How would you develop new but related thoughts? What do members of your group think about your plan?

Sharpening Details

In earlier chapters you learned and practiced how to build images with concrete sensory detail and how to use specific words that present a scene exactly. Here are other qualities of words and some techniques for using them that will help you build strong descriptions.

Denotation and Connotation

Words mean more than their dictionary definitions. (The dictionary definition of a word is called its *denotation*.) A word also can suggest meanings to us by appealing to our emotions or by arousing associations we make for that word. (The implied meaning of a word is called its *connotation*.)

Writers who know what words connote can use them to advantage, compelling a reader to respond in exactly the manner the writer wishes.

Look at these sentences:

She lifted the *glass* slowly.

She lifted the *goblet* slowly.

She lifted the *chalice* slowly.

Glasses, goblets, and chalices have very similar denotative meaning—they are vessels to drink from. But the writer who says *goblet* suggests something more elegant about the action than the writer who says *glass*. With the word *chalice,* the writer creates an even more romantic and poetic—even religious—situation: it's not an everyday drink one sips from a fine cup. By using one of these related words, a writer can create essential conditions without having to use too many modifiers.

Step 1. Explaining Connotations. The words in each numbered item have similar denotations but different connotations. Explain what each word in each group connotes. If you need to, use a dictionary.

1. novel, romance, potboiler
2. child, youngster, adolescent, teenager
3. actor, ham, thespian, performer
4. adviser, counselor, psychologist, therapist
5. stone, pebble, boulder, rock

Step 2. Comparing Meanings. For each word below write a denotative definition. Then, explain the possible connotations for the word. Use separate paper.

1. fear
2. pain

3. courage

4. American

5. love

Step 3. Using Exact Meanings.   In the sentences below, the words in parentheses have similar denotations. However, because of what the words connote, only one of the pair is appropriate. Circle the word that suits the meaning of the sentence. Use a dictionary if you need help.

1. "You are (overweight, fat)," the doctor said to me.

2. The fashion designers admired the model's (skinny, trim) figure.

3. Because she did not want her mother to know she was upset, she (wept, bawled) quietly.

4. The (stench, fragrance) from the gymnasium was nauseating.

5. We watched with disgust as he (sipped, guzzled) the drink.

Showing versus Telling

Writers must always resist *telling* a reader how to react when they can better *show* details with strong images. Instead of using words that interpret, writers try to describe clearly by naming colors, sounds, actions, and sensations of touch, smell, and taste. In these two sentences, notice how the first makes a judgment whereas the second compels readers to make their own judgments based upon the detail:

He had an ugly smile.
He smiled a cold, toothless grin.

   With a word like *ugly*—or any such judgmental word, for that matter—the writer is never sure that the reader sees exactly what the writer had intended. After all, what is ugly to one person may not be ugly to another.

Step 4. Showing with Clear Images.   For each item below, write an original image that changes the word in italics into descriptive details. Add other words if necessary. Use separate paper.

EXAMPLE

a *happy* child
a laughing child who shook her rattle playfully

1. a *nice* face

2. a *sad* man

3. a *beautiful* pigeon

4. a *cute* puppy

5. *attractive* eyes

Avoiding Too Many Modifiers

You already know how important it is to select highly specific words in order to build successful images. Using a word like *rose* instead of *flower* or using *pudding* instead of *dessert* helps you avoid using descriptive words you might not need. In general, you should be cautious about using too many modifying words for the objects or people you are trying to describe. A typically weak sentence will pile up a number of descriptive words in front of a noun.

The *tall, dark-haired, blue-eyed* quarterback spoke to his fans.

The modifiers (in italics) smother the noun *quarterback*. The sentence overwhelms the reader with detail; the reader cannot take so much in all at once in this way. By using a modifier after the noun or by expanding a modifier into a word group, the writer achieves a more desired effect.

With *blue eyes* smiling, the *tall, dark-haired* quarterback spoke to his fans.

Removing some modifiers completely is usually one of the best ways to avoid overwhelming your reader with detail.

Step 5. Cutting Down on Modifiers.   Rewrite the sentences below so that the modifiers do not all appear before the words they are describing. In some cases, just shift the modifiers around. In other cases, expand some of them into word groups. In others, simply remove the modifier. All describing words appear in italics.

1. The *tiny, stout, red-haired little* boy smiled a *delighted, dimpled, cheery* smile. _____

    _____

2. Compared to *sedate, charming, gracious* San Francisco, we were shocked by *hectic, smoggy, crowded* Los Angeles. _____

    _____

    _____

3. A *long, black, chauffeur-driven* Cadillac screeched to a stop in front of a *brand-new modern glass and steel* hotel. _____

    _____

4. The *exhausted, frustrated, angry* third-grade teacher reprimanded her *unruly, energetic, noisy* students. _____

_____

5. On a sizzling July afternoon at *approximately twelve* noon, I shoved aboard a *crowded, musty, gray and black graffiti-covered railroad* car and headed south. _____

_____

_____

Essay Form

For every part of the paragraph there is a similar part of the essay. In a one-paragraph theme a *topic sentence* tells the subject and your opinion about that subject. In an essay an *introductory paragraph* gives you more space to build up to the topic you want to discuss. One sentence of this introductory paragraph (often the last sentence) generally announces what the whole essay will be about. This is the *thesis* or *proposal sentence:* it is usually more general than a topic sentence because it must tell what the *whole essay* will deal with.

In a one-paragraph theme the first subtopic sentence introduces one aspect of the topic. In the essay the first subtopic sentence becomes the topic sentence of its own paragraph. It requires a transition to the proposal sentence. You develop the paragraph by using details from your own experience or from what you have read or heard. This second paragraph of your essay is the first *body* paragraph: it is the first paragraph that tries to support some aspect of the topic.

In a one-paragraph theme a *second* subtopic sentence introduces another aspect of the topic. In an essay, the second subtopic sentence becomes the topic sentence of its own paragraph. This topic sentence requires some brief reference to the previous paragraph for an effective transition. You develop the paragraph with the kinds of details that best support your point.

Each subtopic in a one-paragraph composition would correspond to a separate paragraph in a longer essay—depending on the amount of supporting detail the writer presents. Often a writer will develop a couple of subtopics in a single paragraph of an essay.

In a one-paragraph theme you need a closing sentence to tell the reader that you have achieved the purpose of the paragraph. In an essay you need a conclusion, a whole new paragraph that allows you more space to develop an idea related to your dominant impression.

The following chart shows how a one-paragraph theme compares with an essay of several paragraphs.

● From Paragraph to Essay ●

The One-Paragraph Theme	The Essay

The One-Paragraph Theme

Topic Sentence

The Essay

Introduction: A Paragraph

1. Give background to your topic.

2. Make your readers feel that what you are going to say will be of importance and interest to them.

3. Set the stage for the one sentence that will tell the readers what the whole essay will be about (*proposal sentence*).

4. For your own convenience, put the proposal sentence *last* in the introductory paragraph; make sure that the proposal sentence allows you to discuss *two* aspects of the topic.

5. Take as much time with the proposal sentence as you took with the topic sentence.

Subtopic Sentence 1

Topic Sentence of First Body Paragraph

1. Relate this sentence in some way to the proposal (repeat key words, use words that mean the same, use transition words, and so on).

2. Announce the one aspect of the topic that you will discuss in this paragraph.

Supporting Details

Supporting Details

Closing Sentence

Let the reader know you have finished with the subject of this paragraph. Bring all the information together.

Subtopic Sentences 2, 3, etc.

Topic Sentence of Following Body Paragraphs

1. This sentence must relate to the proposal (the last sentence in the introductory paragraph).

2. It must tell the reader the aspect of the proposal that you will discuss in this paragraph.

3. It must also remind the reader of what you discussed in the previous paragraph.

Supporting Details

Supporting Details

Closing Sentence

Let the reader know that this paragraph is finished.

Closing Sentence

Conclusion: A Paragraph

1. Summarize by briefly commenting on your topic (your proposal).

2. Bring in a related idea.

3. Give a dominant impression.

Paragraph to Essay

Reviewing Paragraph and Essay Form.   The first student sample you read in this book—"The Gloom Room" by Harry Golden—appears here for review. An essay on exactly the same topic follows it. These pages should help you see clearly the basic differences between the one-paragraph theme and the essay. Discuss the questions after you read the two pieces.

The Gloom Room

On this dreary October afternoon in my writing class here on the second floor of Boylan Hall at Brooklyn College, a shadow of gloom hangs over the people and things that surround me. The atmosphere is depressing. There is an old brown chair beside the teacher's desk, a mahogany bookcase with a missing shelf, and this ugly desk of mine filled with holes and scratches. As I rub my hands across its surface, there is a feeling of coldness. Even the gray walls and the rumble of thunder outside reflect the atmosphere of seriousness as we write our first theme of the semester. When some air sails through an open window beside me, there is the annoying smell of coffee grounds from a garbage pail not far off. My classmates, too, show the mood of tension. Mary, a slim blonde at my right, chews frantically the inside of her lower lip. Only one or two words in blue ink stand upon her clean white page. David Harris, slouched in his seat in the third row, nibbles each finger of each hand. Then he plays inaudibly with a black collar button that stands open on the top of his red plaid shirt. There is a thump as he uncrosses his legs and his scuffed shoe hits the floor. A painful cough slices the air from behind me. I hear a woman's heels click from the hall beyond the closed door and a car engine whine annoyingly from Bedford Avenue. If a college classroom should be a place of delight and pleasure, that could never be proved by the tension in this room.

—Harry Golden

The Gloom Room

October often looks and feels dreary because school is by then in full swing. Today, a rainy Thursday, is no different. What makes it worse is that I am forced to sit in my writing class on the second floor of Boylan Hall at Brooklyn College and write a theme. It is no wonder that a shadow of gloom hangs over the things and the people that surround me in this room.

[the proposal: it tells what the whole essay will be about]

[the topic sentence (body paragraph 1): it tells what this paragraph will be about]

[As I look around, I see that the surroundings are old and depressing.] There is a broken brown chair beside the teacher's desk; no one will sit in it for fear of leaning back and toppling over onto the floor. There is also a mahogany bookcase with a missing shelf, and all the books are piled on the bottom in a stack of blue and yellow covers, instead of standing in a straight row. This ugly desk of mine is filled with holes and scratches because other impatient students, no doubt, lost their tempers and took out their anger on the wooden surface. As I rub my hand across it, I feel coldness. Even the gray walls and the rumble of thunder outside reflect the atmosphere of seriousness as we write our first theme of the semester. When some air sails through an open window beside me, there is the annoying smell of coffee grounds from a garbage pail not far off. The smell is a perfect indication of our discomfort!

[details: these give concrete sensory language, statistics, cases, quotations, paraphrase, or imagery to illustrate your point]

[closing sentence: it shows you are finished with this paragraph]

[This part of the topic sentence reminds the reader about what you wrote in the last paragraph.]

[Aside from the unattractive surroundings,] ⟨the people around me show this mood of tension and displeasure.⟩ Mary, a slim blonde at my right, chews the inside of her lower lip. I can see by the way her forehead is wrinkled that she is having quite a bit of trouble. Because only one or two words in blue ink stand upon her clean white page, she looks around

[This part of the topic sentence tells the reader what you will discuss in this paragraph.]

[details: these
illustrate the point
of the topic
sentence]

the room fearfully for some new ideas. Slouching in his seat in the third row, David Harris nibbles each finger of each hand. Then he plays with a black collar button that stands open on the top of his red plaid shirt. The tension gets to him too; drops of perspiration run slowly down his cheeks. I hear a thump as he uncrosses his legs and his scuffed shoe hits the floor. A painful cough slices the air from behind me. I hear a woman's heels click from the hall beyond the closed door and a car engine whine annoyingly from Bedford Avenue. All these signs of gloom do not help my mood at all.

These last few painful moments make me wonder if what my friends told me about college was all true. Where are all the beautiful girls I'm supposed to be meeting and talking to in every room? Where are the freedom and relaxed atmosphere my friends bragged about? I'm supposed to be enjoying myself instead of suffering! Everybody seems to have forgotten that college is hard work too. My first days in writing class prove that delight and pleasure often disappear when assignments are due!

—Harry Golden

[conclusion:
1. may summarize
2. makes transition by referring to an idea in the introduction
3. may give a dominant impression
4. may bring in a new—but related—idea]

1. What is the difference between the opening sentence in the one-paragraph theme and the opening paragraph in the essay?

2. How are the proposal sentence in the essay and the topic sentence in the one-paragraph theme alike?

3. How does subtopic sentence 1 in "The Gloom Room" paragraph compare to the topic sentence of paragraph 2 in "The Gloom Room" essay?

4. How do the details coming after subtopic sentence 1 in the one-paragraph composition compare with the details in paragraph 2 of the essay?

5. How does the second subtopic sentence compare with the opening sentence of paragraph 3 in the essay?

6. How do the details after subtopic sentence 2 in his one-paragraph theme compare with the details in the third paragraph of the essay?

7. Read the last sentence of paragraph 2 and that of paragraph 3. Are they effective as closing sentences? Why?

8. What part of the first sentence of the conclusion in the essay refers back to the main idea?

9. Where in the conclusion does the writer bring in a new but related idea?

10. How does the closing sentence of the one-paragraph composition compare with the concluding paragraph of the essay?

Proposal (Thesis) Sentences

The *proposal* (or *thesis*) *sentence*—the sentence in the essay that tells what you propose or intend to discuss in the remaining paragraphs—is the most important sentence in the essay. It controls and limits your entire composition. As a good writer, you will write only about what the proposal *says* you will write about.

• Guidelines for Good Proposals •

1. Make sure your proposal sentence allows you to discuss what you want to discuss. It should announce the topic clearly. It should express an opinion. If you find as you are writing that you no longer are discussing the topic you set for yourself, *go back and change the proposal sentence.*

2. The proposal should allow you to deal with specific aspects of the topic. Notice how Mr. Golden's proposal tells *specifically* the two parts of his topic: the gloom surrounding the people and the gloom surrounding the things in his classroom. Body paragraphs, then, can pick up on each aspect of that topic. In Mr. Golden's essay paragraph 2 focuses on things and paragraph 3 focuses on people.

   But it is not essential to mention in the proposal just what each paragraph will say. An alternate proposal for Mr. Golden's essay might be this:

   It is no wonder that gloominess is everywhere.

   Notice how, in this proposal, the reader has no idea of exactly what kind of treatment Mr. Golden's essay will offer of gloominess. But still, this alternate proposal permits him to develop body paragraphs about the gloomy surroundings and the gloomy people.

3. A proposal sentence may appear anywhere in the introduction, but it is much easier for you if you write it as the *last* sentence of the introduction for several reasons:

   a. You can return to it often if you know exactly where it appears; by reading the proposal often while you write, you can make sure that you are staying on the topic.

   b. You can make the transition between the proposal and the opening sentence of paragraph 2 easily because the idea you must refer back to comes directly above your opening sentence. Mr. Golden's proposal mentions that he is in a room. The first words of paragraph 2 say "As I look around"; and because this looking around takes place in the room mentioned in the previous paragraph, the two paragraphs are thereby connected smoothly.

Step 1. Preparing Proposals. Consider the information below, and write a proposal that you think would serve to develop the ideas suggested by the subject for an essay. Use your own paper.

Hint

You do not need to state in the proposal exactly what each paragraph will illustrate. Just state the main purpose of your essay, the idea your whole essay will be about.

EXAMPLE

This essay intends to show that the writer loves the thrill of skiing although she realizes the dangers that exist.

Although the slopes of Vail, Colorado, present certain dangers, the thrill a skier experiences is worth the risks.

1. This essay points to the steps to take in improving your vocabulary.

2. This essay attempts to show how proper exercise and good nutrition add years to a person's life.

3. This writer will show the pleasures and pains of raising a child.

4. This essay will defend work-study programs in colleges. Its first body paragraphs will discuss the advantages for the student who comes to a college having such a program. The next body paragraphs will illustrate the advantages of such programs to our society.

5. This essay shows the negative effects of alcohol on a person's health.

Step 2. Predicting Body Paragraphs from Proposals. These proposals all come from students' papers. Basing your selection on the topic stated in the proposal, tell briefly what you would discuss in the two body paragraphs.

EXAMPLE

I feel that religion serves two essential functions in our society.

Possible main points of body paragraphs:

Religion binds a family together.

Religion teaches children values.

1. I look forward each year to our family reunion, but I always regret it once I'm there.

Possible main points of body paragraphs:

_____

_____

_____

_____

2. Although the majority of Americans live in big cities, many people are realizing the advantages of living on a farm.

    Possible main points of body paragraphs:

    _____

    _____

    _____

    _____

3. Parents have complained for years about the quality of TV advertising.

    Possible main points of body paragraphs:

    _____

    _____

    _____

    _____

4. The first three years of a person's life strongly influence the sort of adult he or she becomes.

    Possible main points of body paragraphs:

    _____

    _____

    _____

    _____

5. If you are planning a wedding reception, be prepared for anxiety.

    Possible main points of body paragraphs:

    _____

    _____

    _____

    _____

Writing Introductions

Aside from its purpose as the paragraph that starts the essay by stating the topic in the proposal sentence, the introductory paragraph must make readers interested enough in what you have to say to make them want to read on. Any one of the suggestions in the following list can help you write an effective introduction to the proposal statement. Each suggestion is followed by a sample.

Hint

Always write the proposal sentence before you write the introductory paragraph.

1. Tell the reader why your topic is important.

   Sample: For fifteen years I lived on East 92nd Street. I made friends there, earned bloody noses, broke Mrs. Segal's window playing stickball, and nursed back to health a small, frightened sparrow in a shoe box. That block was mother and father to me in a way, presenting a number of unexpected experiences that are so important in the life of someone growing up without "at-home" parents—my father ran away when I was six and my mother worked most of the day. So the block was my teacher, and in several ways the lessons I learned there taught me how to think fast to survive.

2. Give background information on your topic so that readers know when they get to your proposal the ideas and conditions that led you to consider the point you are treating in the essay.

   Sample: Our house was built in 1955, part of a development of small one-family homes in Bellmore, New York, not far from Great South Bay. Two other families lived in this house before us, and the man who sold the place to my father in 1972 was an old eccentric. He had painted all the walls a creamy blue color so that everywhere the vast, empty look of open sky surrounded us. The kitchen was ancient; the garage was a mess of boxes, old tools, and broken furniture; the basement would fill up with water with the slightest rain. This house on Poplar Drive needed lots of work, and I recall two large-scale projects our family undertook together with very amusing results.

3. Show what many people now believe is true if your proposal will attempt to suggest something else.

   Sample: Education is the process by which the young people of today are trained to become functioning members of their society. This process is generally accomplished in schools, where young people become acquainted with all phases of knowledge and, after a few years, are thought ready to accept responsibility as adults. In college the usual picture is a classroom filled with excited, bright-eyed youths soaking up important lessons for living. However, the American school system has failed miserably in trying to accomplish what it sets out to do; our system of higher education does not provide a person with the necessary training to take a rightful place in society.

4. State several points that may contradict, disagree with, or disprove the point you want the rest of the essay to make.

Sample: Working hard from his childhood on, my father has grown into a hard man. He is strict and overprotective, and he screams when I tiptoe into the house at two in the morning on a Saturday. He threatens to disconnect my extension phone so he can get to make a call, but he will never give me the satisfaction of having my own number. I rarely sit down to chat with him because his opinions are so one-sided; besides, when I rush into my room and toss my books on the bed at seven o'clock after my last class, Dad's loud snore already echoes through the house. Despite his difficult qualities, I am still Daddy's little girl and always will be; I am not ashamed that I have grown to love my father very much.

5. Ask questions to arouse the reader's interest.

Sample: Can a black lawyer, a Chinese fashion designer, and a white schoolteacher live happily side by side as neighbors? Can a racially integrated community achieve the dream of brotherhood and understanding? An experiment in a small town in Connecticut is providing some extraordinary answers.

6. Use an interesting quotation that helps you build toward your proposal sentence (see pages 400–403 and page 391 for writing quotations correctly).

Sample: Kahlil Gibran in *A Tear and a Smile* writes, "I looked toward nature . . . and found therein . . . a thing that endures and lives in the spring and comes to fruit in summer days. Therein I found love." This I believe to be true, because people do not "fall in love"; love that lasts is a feeling that must come gradually over a period of time and must develop only with emotional maturity.

Hint

Use quotations from your own reading of newspapers, magazines, and books or from television, radio, or the movies. Books like *Bartlett's Familiar Quotations* and the *Oxford Dictionary of Quotations* have many quotations arranged according to subjects; often you can find a meaningful quotation there to use in your introduction.

7. Tell a brief story—an incident that helps set the stage for your proposal. Make sure that the story suits the purpose of your essay: don't be funny or "cute" unless you expect to deal with matters that are not serious or unless you can work humor into your point.

Sample: A man with one shoe and a face filled with red sores wobbles down the summer morning street cursing to himself. From his back pocket he snatches a paper bag, uncaps the bottle inside, raises it to his lips, and take a long gulp. Then he drops down against a brick wall and, still cursing, closes his eyes. This is skid row, the place of the drunkard, a place of horrors. But urban police are now trying to reach out to these fallen men and women.

8. Tell what each body paragraph (or set of body paragraphs) will deal with.

Sample: Solar energy devices will one day adequately replace our fossil fuels. Wind-driven turbines will also provide us with a reliable, economical source of power. And as safety improves, nuclear energy will further enhance our lives. Together these important resources will meet the future energy needs of America.

Hint

Sentence 1 in the above introduction tells what the writer expects to develop in the first body paragraph (paragraph 2 of the essay). Sentence 2 tells the purpose of the next body paragraph. Sentence 3 tells what the third body paragraph will be about. The writer has divided the topic for the reader.

9. Use a series of images to build up to your proposal.

Sample: Rocks tossed from behind trees; bottles broken on our blacktop driveway; whispering voices behind wrinkled hands at the A&P; taunts of "Kyke" and "There's a Jew" sailing at my back as I march to school alone: a Jew growing up in a small Midwestern town learns how to hate very early in life.

10. Show different aspects of the topic that you will not consider in the essay, as you lead up to the topic you will consider.

Sample: In our society, discrimination has many different forms. There is age discrimination, which prevents a nineteen-year-old from buying a bottle of gin, and racial discrimination, which denies a black youth a job in a labor union. But another form of discrimination that faces many women starting careers today is sexual discrimination.

• Avoiding Pitfalls in Introductions •

1. Don't make your introduction too long. If each of your body paragraphs contains ten or fewer sentences, your introduction usually needs no more than four or five sentences. Longer body paragraphs may justify longer introductions.

2. Don't apologize for what you do not know, for your lack of experience, or for your limited abilities. Even if you do have limitations, to mention them in your paragraph is to make the reader feel that you do not know what you are talking about. Don't make any of these statements:

"Although I am not qualified to discuss this . . . ."

"My knowledge is limited, so . . . ."

"Many people who know more than I do would disagree, but . . . ."

3. Don't think of the reader as someone who is sitting next to you as you write. Don't say "Now I will tell you . . ." or "Now I am going to show you . . . ."

4. Don't talk about the parts of the essay in your composition. Don't say "In my next paragraph, I . . . " or "My introduction and my conclusion will try to show . . . ."

5. Don't write an introduction that wastes words, one that you have just thrown ahead of your body paragraphs to fulfill the requirements of essay form. Your introduction should be an important part of the essay itself.

6. Don't use overworked expressions—trite sayings or quotations that have lost their meaning because of overuse. Don't use quotations or expressions that are too general or that could be applied to hundreds of situations. To say "Too many cooks spoil the broth" in an essay about too many chiefs giving orders in government would not really add anything of significance.

7. Don't say the same thing over and over again. If you don't have much to say by way of introduction, write only the proposal in a clear, well-planned sentence or two of some length.

8. Don't refer to your title in the introduction. A student whose essay title was "How to Save Our National Parks" would be mistaken to start the introduction this way: "It is possible in a number of ways."

Step 1. Writing Introductions to Proposals.   Using any two of the proposal sentences from Step 2 on pages 119–120 write two introductions. Put the proposal sentence last. Try to write a different kind of introduction for each proposal; check the ideas for starting essays on pages 121–123. And make sure you avoid the errors explained above.

Step 2. Reading More Introductions.   Discuss the introductory paragraphs for the essays whose titles and page numbers are listed below. Are the introductions effective? Which of the items on pages 121–123 does each introduction seem to follow? How might you improve each introduction?

1.   "Practice in the High School Gym," pages 142–143

2.   "Uncle Del's Barn," pages 140–141

3.   "Ironing for Food," pages 172–173

4.   "Deprived Children," pages 241–242

5.   "The Growing Demand for Secretaries," pages 141–142

Step 3. Introductions: You Be the Judge.   Decide whether the introductions below would be good first paragraphs for essays. Defend your opinions. Then, make any corrections that you feel will improve the introductory paragraphs. In some cases, you may have to rewrite the paragraph completely. Use separate paper.

1. Swimming is an important activity for a healthy life. I was a swimmer in high school and in college, and I will continue to swim as long as I am physically able. This essay will try to show how important swimming is and how swimmers benefit from swimming.

2. I do not know much about AIDS except what I have heard on TV. Physicians know more about this subject than I do, but I would like to consider the medical facts of the disease and some steps being taken to prevent its spread.

3. Are you fed up with street riots and automobile fumes? Are you trying to escape the summer heat of Newark and the noisy crowds that shove their way across Market Street? Well then pack a tent and a four-burner stove and head for the nearest camping grounds. Outdoor living for summer vacation is a relaxing and unusual way to spend some time with nature.

4. A young boy cowers in the corner whenever he enters a room full of adults. A little girl refuses to talk with her teacher, the school nurse, or the principal. A five-year-old boy refuses assistance from a park attendant as he tries to climb onto the jungle gym. A red-haired, big-eyed seven-year-old girl would rather eat lunch alone than join a group of "grown-ups." Are these children simply cautious? No, they are the fearful victims of child abuse. Fortunately, a national campaign to alert the public about the horrors of child abuse is now under way.

5. In this essay, I will write about my summer vacation house. My first paragraph will show what the house looks like. Then I will tell about our annual Fourth of July party there and how I learned that love makes the world go round.

Step 4. More Work on Introductions.   For any three of the proposals you wrote in Step 1, pages 118–119, write three introductions, using any of the suggestions you studied.

Step 5. Your Own Introductions.   Choose any topic sentence you wrote for any theme assignment in the early chapters of this book, and assume that it is the proposal sentence of an essay. Write a good introduction, following the advice you learned in this chapter.

Step 6. You Judge the Professionals.   Select two introductions to articles by professional writers and bring the introductions to class. One introduction should represent what you consider a good introductory paragraph; the other should represent a poor introduction. Be ready to read them in groups and to point out to others the specifics that support your opinions.

Writing Conclusions

The concluding paragraph of an essay is very much like the closing sentence of a paragraph. It should do all the things you learned about closing sentences in Chapter 1. A good conclusion, therefore, should

- tell the reader that your essay is coming to a close
- give the reader a feeling that you have accomplished what you set out to do

A closing paragraph permits the writer to develop some larger application for the topic. A good conclusion applies the topic of the essay to a broader issue. In a conclusion you can illustrate that the subject you have written about has importance beyond the ideas developed in your body paragraphs. You show that you have used what you have written to help you think about other ideas. This is not an easy chore. You run the risk of sounding too "important" or too philosophical. As a result, the concluding paragraph needs especially careful thought and must often progress through several rewritings, but the finished product is well worth it: it helps the reader see that the narrow topic you developed has relevance in other critical areas. It gives you an opportunity to develop an idea that has an important relation to your topic but is new in the frame of the essay itself.

Let us examine the conclusion of an essay you will read on the next few pages and the relation of the conclusion to the rest of the theme. In the essay "Uncle Del's Barn" (pages 140–141), the writer provides this proposal sentence:

> I had many adventures inside the barn, and I delighted in watching and playing with the animals that made their homes there.

In her second paragraph, the writer shows her adventures in her uncle's barn. The third and fourth paragraphs disclose her memories of the animals living there—the cats and their kittens, the chicks, and the pigs and their treks to the mud. Here is the final paragraph, the conclusion to the essay:

> Even today, I can close my eyes and recall the good times I had playing in the old, weathered barn, the smell of Aunt Annabelle's fragrant spice cake filling the air, Uncle Del's rusty plow sitting on the barn floor, the chicks and kittens and pigs moving freely about. I consider myself fortunate to have experienced a piece of life in decline in America today. Up against high interest rates and soaring costs for equipment, many small farmers (my Uncle Del is no exception) sell out to big businesses with interest only in making money. For Uncle Del and Aunt Annabelle, and for me, too as I now think back, the small Montana farm was a way of life. Even when I knew it, the old barn was past its useful life, but it gave me many joys as a child. I'm sure that barn is long gone now, yet it will always be a symbol in my mind for the carefree, happy, innocent kind of life that is not easy to find these days.

The conclusion points to the disappearance of small-farm life in America. That is *not* an idea clearly part of the proposal sentence:

I had many adventures inside the barn, and I delighted in watching and playing with the animals that made their homes there.

Yet, by bringing in the related idea of the difficulties small farms face in surviving today, the writer offers a new significance for the topic. From the thesis about her past joyous experience on a Montana farm, the writer moves to a larger application: the delights of farm life are vanishing amid economic uncertainties and big business interests. She shows the reader how the ideas she developed in paragraphs 2, 3, and 4 (pleasant memories of life on a small farm) suggest a broader, more general application for the topic (the disappearance of that way of life).

Her new application works effectively in the essay, but it is not the only possibility that she could have chosen. The conclusion—based upon the proposal and the supporting body paragraphs—might have treated any one of these broader issues:

- the value of imaginative play in a child's social development
- the value of a child's being left alone to explore things on her own
- the importance of one's own special place that can provide an escape from the events of everyday life.

This list is not complete, but any of the points, developed with sufficient supporting details, might nicely suggest a wider and more general truth for the ideas proposed in the rest of the essay.

Notice, furthermore, that the first sentence of the conclusion in "Uncle Del's Barn" refers back to the ideas developed in previous paragraphs by mentioning the topic that the writer set out to develop. Look at the two sentences side by side:

PROPOSAL

I had many adventures inside the barn, and I delighted in watching and playing with the animals that made their home there.

FIRST SENTENCE OF CONCLUSION

Even today, I can close my eyes and *recall the good times I had playing in the old, weathered barn,* the smell of Aunt Annabelle's fragrant spice cake filling the air, Uncle Del's rusty plow sitting on the barn floor, the chicks and kittens and pigs moving freely about.

The italicized words in the first sentence of the conclusion act as a transition because they bridge the conclusion to the topic as stated in the proposal. In addition, these words help summarize the topic for the reader who has read two full paragraphs since last seeing the proposal. This device of summary is excellent early in the conclusion because it reminds readers of what the essay set out to do, and permits them to evaluate the writer's success in developing the proposal.

• Writing Strong Conclusions •

For dramatic conclusions, follow these steps:

1. Remind the reader that you have achieved what you set out to do and that your essay is drawing to an end.

2. Strive to establish a new, a larger, a more general application for your topic.

3. Summarize briefly the main point of your essay.

4. Make the conclusion an important part of the essay, not an afterthought you glued on to add more words.

5. Do not
   - start a whole new topic
   - contradict your entire point
   - make obvious or overused statements
   - apologize for your lack of knowledge
   - end suddenly with a one-sentence conclusion such as "That's all I have to say."
   - draw conclusions that are absolute or too general (make sure that you allow for possibilities or exceptions)
   - talk about other parts of your own essay by mentioning words like "my introduction," "so my conclusion is," "my proposal sentence said."

Step 1. Essay Conclusions.   Examine the following essays, paying special attention to the concluding paragraphs. Write in the blank lines below the title the writer's proposal (you may have to restate it in your own words so it is clear when you remove it from the essay). Then, in the blank space alongside, write the broader issue that the writer tries to develop in the conclusion. Study the example.

LARGER APPLICATION (BROADER ISSUE) IN
CONCLUSION

EXAMPLE

"Deprived Children," pages 241–242

Proposal: *Children of working mothers*   *what children left on their own must*

are frequently insecure and unhappy.   *learn*

1. "Practice in the High School Gym," pages 142–143

   Proposal: _____

   _____   _____

   _____   _____

                              _____

2. "Picking Pears," pages 169–171

   Proposal: _____

   _____   _____

   _____   _____

                              _____

3. "Ironing for Food," pages 172–173

   Proposal: _____

   _____   _____

   _____   _____

                              _____

4. "The Growing Demand for Secretaries," pages 141–142

   Proposal: _____

   _____   _____

   _____   _____

                              _____

Step 2. Finding New Areas of Relevance. For any two essays you have read in connection with Step 1 above, suggest some *other* area of importance the writer could have developed in the conclusion. Base your suggestions on the proposal sentence and on the two body paragraphs. Use separate paper.

Step 3. More Conclusions. Look at any of the selections in The Professionals Speak sections of Chapters 1, 2, 3, or 4. Comment on the conclusion you find. Is it appropriate? Does it set a new context? How might you revise the conclusion?

Combining Sentences

In earlier exercises on coordination and subordination (pages 84–86 and 86–93), you learned how combining sentences often helps you relate ideas more closely. Another advantage of combining sentences is that the new word group you have created usually expresses its point more precisely and with fewer words than the original.

When two consecutive sentences discuss the same object and the purpose of one of the two is to describe the object, to identify it, or to add information about it, you can often combine the two sentences into one. Writers have many ways to achieve this effect. Sometimes words like *who, which,* or *that* help join the sentences (see pages 92–93). Sometimes, special verb parts make the combination effective (see pages 44–47).

At other times, a change in punctuation and the removal of some words allow you to put ideas together in a meaningful way. Look at these sets of examples.

A   B

(1) *Henry Chin plays basketball for the county team.* (2) *He is a tall and supple athlete.*

(1) *Across Oakland Drive hobbled an old man.* (2) *He was our former gardener.*

Notice that in example *A* the writer can use fewer words and can bring the descriptive details closer to the person he wants to describe:

[comma]   [comma]

(3) Henry Chin, *a tall and supple athlete,* plays basketball for the county team.

Because the words from sentence (2) now interrupt the main idea of sentence (1), the writer uses commas to signal that interruption (see pages 306–308).

Details from sentence (2) could also be added to the beginning of (1) with slightly different results:

(4) *A tall and supple athlete,* Henry Chin plays basketball for the county team.
[comma]

In example *B* you can put at the end of sentence (1) the words from (2) in order to identify the old man:

[comma]

(5) Across Oakland Drive hobbled an old man, *our former gardener.*

You could write the sentence in this way too:

(6) Across Oakland Drive hobbled our former gardener, *an old man.*

In sentences (4), (5), and (6) a comma sets off the added details from the main idea of the sentence.

Hint

You cannot combine the sentences in examples *A* and *B* simply by removing the period between (1) and (2). That would yield run-on sentences. Why? See pages 313–320.

Practice in Combining Sentences. In each set below, material in one of the two sentences may be incorporated into the other sentence in order to add information about or describe an object or an idea. Using sentences (3), (4), (5), and (6) above as models, combine the two sentences into one, and write your new sentence on the blank lines. Place new material *after* the word you want to describe or identify. Use commas where you need them. Look at the example.

EXAMPLE

The insect repellent works well. It is a white cream.
The insect repellent, a white cream, works well.

1. My sister always was excellent in math. She now wants to become an accountant.

_____

_____

_____

2. The rain beat down steadily on the window panes. Lightening streaked the dark sky.

_____

_____

_____

3. This computer has many special features. It is an instrument that will change your work habits quickly.

_____

_____

_____

4. The instructor stood angrily before the class as he announced the results of our chemistry midterm. The instructor's name is Mr. Hassan.

_____

_____

_____

5. An old hound limped across the dusty road. The dog had sorrowful brown eyes.

_____

_____

_____

Word and Sentence Skills: Suggested Topics for Study

Agreement of Subject and Verb, pages 284–298
Formal and Informal Language, pages 326–329
Mirror Words (Homophones), pages 345–357

● Writing the Essay

Assignment

Write an essay from one of the paragraph assignments you considered in the first three chapters of this book. Or write an essay about any other topic that interests you and that your instructor approves. Remember that good essays rely on supporting details. As a refresher, you might want to refer back to the section called Essay Form (pages 113–117).

Perhaps you want to rethink some memorable place, person, or object that has significance in your life: a room, a friend, a salesperson, a farm, an old stuffed toy, a restaurant, or anything else. Perhaps you want to expand the narrative of an unforgettable moment in your life or perhaps tell two or three narrative moments to support an important point. Perhaps you will expand upon several examples to illustrate your position on a subject that is important to you. In any case, make sure that you can present specific aspects of your subject in the body paragraphs. Make sure that you have a strong-enough feeling about the topic so that you can write an effective proposal sentence. And use your highest level of concrete sensory language for details: color, sound, touch, smell, and images of action will be the essential sources of support for the points you wish to make from your own experience. Quotations, paraphrases, statistics, cases, and facts will help you support interesting topics about which you have no first-hand experience.

Suggested Topics

If you need some topic suggestions for your essay, look at the list below. Also, see Step 1, pages 118–119.

1. solving the transportation nightmare
2. my day in court
3. cleaning up the campus
4. camping in high mountains
5. gun control
6. the homeless in our city
7. late one night

8. chaos at the airports

9. improving our schools

10. my brother to the rescue

11. our dying rivers

12. a run-down neighborhood

13. why study?

14. job opportunities

15. lazy Saturdays

16. the school cafeteria

17. turning to religion

18. the great indoors

19. an electronic-games arcade

20. smoking and health

You remember that the first three chapters of this book introduced some ways that paragraphs may be organized. Essays, since they are composed of paragraphs, may be organized in similar ways, each paragraph following a pattern of organization that suits the topic. Narration, description, several instances to support topic ideas: all these paragraph types (and others) may be extended to the essay itself. The chart below makes suggestions for ways in which you can develop and organize your essay and gives you some sample proposals other students have written for the various developments suggested. But feel free to use any method that you think best suits the topic you are writing about.

POSSIBLE PLAN FOR BODY PARAGRAPHS	PARAGRAPH DEVELOPMENT	SAMPLE PROPOSALS
1. Provide descriptive details to characterize some person, place, or object.	Description through intense sensory language: color, action, sound, smell, touch. Develop related elements of the description in separate body paragraphs.	Our tiny summer cabin on Lake Hope had all the makings of a haunted house. When I attended Public School 40 in Detroit, it was brand-new and had more modern conveniences than any one could imagine. Scholars now have a fairly complete picture of the Globe Theatre in which Shakespeare performed many of his own plays.

2. Tell about two or three special moments related to your subject; develop each moment in a separate paragraph.

Narration through chronology.

I remember two instances when a pair of hand-me-down roller skates brought me good luck and kept me out of trouble.

In the small courtyard of our church I learned essential lessons in humanity that have stayed with me all my life.

Black men and women fought valiantly during the Civil War.

3. One or more paragraphs to show several instances that support one aspect of the subject you are discussing and

Instances arranged through importance.

Instances arranged through chronology.

Listing of instances.

a. another paragraph or two to tell *one specific moment* that illustrates another aspect of your subject, or

Narration through chronology.

In Cook County Hospital not only did I learn that nurses and doctors are really interested in patients, but I also saw that the patients themselves look after one another.

Large urban centers have devised successful programs to prevent teenage suicide epidemics.

b. another paragraph or two *also* to show several instances that support another aspect of the subject you are discussing.

4. Describe the subject fully in one or two paragraphs.

   Tell in the next paragraph or two about a vivid moment.

Description using transitions by place.

Narration through chronology.

The desert near El Paso is a beautiful place, but I know firsthand of its potential dangers.

• Tips for Strong Topics •

1. As you consider the one-paragraph assignments you wrote for the early chapters of this book, select a topic that is important to you, a topic that you feel you can expand successfully into an essay of several paragraphs.

2. If you write from personal experience, make your essay rich in concrete sensory detail. Write about your impressions of the sounds, smells, colors, and actions you associate with the subject. Include bits of dialogue or words spoken by people, if appropriate. By means of details show your reader *why* the subject is special.

3. If you write about a topic for which you have no firsthand experience, draw on facts, statistics, cases, paraphrases, and (or) quotations to enrich your essay with essential details.

4. As you develop your drafts, keep in mind the guidelines you examined in this chapter regarding essay format. Develop a proposal sentence. Link paragraphs with transitions as needed. Keep in mind the proportion of your paragraphs. Generally, the introduction and conclusion should be about the same length, and both of these paragraphs should be shorter (or at least not longer!) than the body paragraphs as well. If you try *generally* for four to six sentences in your introduction and conclusion and six to twelve sentences in each of two or three body paragraphs, you will have set a reasonable and workable goal for yourself.

5. As you write your essay, keep in mind the guidelines you examined in Chapters 1 to 3 of this book regarding description, narration, and illustration as means of developing paragraphs.

Prewriting: Timed Writing

Timed writing is another technique that you can use to stimulate ideas. First, decide on a topic; then without pausing to correct spelling errors or to ponder an idea, write continuously for five minutes. The object is to fill up a page with complete sentences that are related to the topic. Remember, don't stop writing! If you can't think of anything to write, write "I can't think of anything" as many times as you have to. Let your ideas flow naturally. Look at one student's timed-writing exercise below.

● Prewriting: A Timed-Writing Exercise ●

Topic: The IRT Subway

I ride the IRT subway everyday into Manhattan. The people are jammed together like sardines. Everyone reads the morning newspaper, afraid to make eye contact. Some people doze. All types of people ride the trains: drunks, pretty, young secretaries, businessmen in their look-a-like pin-striped suits. I don't know what to write. People look fresh and alert in the morning, but are sweaty and grumpy in the evening. I don't know what to write. I don't know what to write. A man once had a heart attack on the train. His wife was screaming. All the people started to push and shove. I felt trapped. Someone pulled the emergency brake and the train slammed to a stop. The noise was terrible. The air conditioners weren't working; my clothes were soaked with perspiration. I don't know what to write. So many things happen everyday. I hate the trains. They make me feel small and less than human. People get angry at each other for nothing. A guy throws a punch if someone steps on his foot. I remember the black-out in the city. I was trapped in the subway for over three hours. But that was O.K. People were friendly. Everyone helped one another. We shared someone's Coke. Kids played a guitar and we sang songs such as "A Hundred Bottles of Beer." People took turns standing up. The cops did a great job leading us through the black, stinking tunnels to the next station. I was proud to be a New Yorker. Time's almost up. I think I hate most the screeching of the wheels as the train turns and twists under Manhattan. I wish people were more friendly than they are. No one says good morning. They sit in tight little balls as if to say "Don't touch me!"

—Robert Sirola

Step 1. Reviewing Timed Writing.   Answer the questions below based on the preceding paragraph of timed writing.

1. Although many ideas are mentioned in Robert Sirola's timed-writing paragraph, which idea might be suitable to develop in an essay?

2. What are Robert Sirola's feelings about the IRT subway? Which images do you see most clearly?

Step 2. Using Timed Writing.   Choose some place that you see clearly and about which you have strong feelings. Then write continuously about that place for five minutes. Use your own paper.

Student Samples: Drafting and Revising

As you consider your topic and begin writing, study the sections called Suggested Topics, pages 132–135, and Progress Reminders: A Checklist of Questions, pages 144–145. Also, examine the student samples below, and review pages 20–21 on revising your writing.

Step 1. Reading Drafts.   Compare the two drafts of "All Alone," an essay describing an experience the writer had in a hospital room. How does the revision differ from the earlier draft? Answer the questions after you finish reading.

DRAFT

```
                         All Alone

     There I sat all alone in my hard bed at New York University
hospital. This was the place I most definitely did not want to be in.
But because of my rollerskating accident I had no choice. I had to
listen to the doctors and go for the necessary tests. There I layed
stiff and silent in the night listening to the noises outside my room
in the long corridors and watching everything that went on around me.
     As I layed there bundled up in my white sheets and the cold, hard
steel bars of the bed surrounding me I could hear everything that was
happening on my ward. Nurses would pass up and down the corridor with
their white rubber heal shoes squeeking on the white freshly polished
floors. The squeeking would send shrieking chills up my spin. Soft
whispers were heard as doctors and nurses exchanged conversations. If
they only knew how disturbing it was for me to hear these slight
mutters. The most startling noise, though, was when a tray must have
accidentally slipped out of a nurses hand. The clatter of the tray
echoed down the long, endless white corridors setting my nerves on end.
I must have sat there shaking for at least five minutes.
     Watching what was going on outside and inside my room was no picnic
either. In the hall a bright light shown enabling me to view the room
next door. As I was peering out my door, I noticed the little red light
above the opposite door light flash along with a distantly faint
ringing of a bell down the hall. The nurse, in a clean white uniform,
was there in an instant to help the young curly haired girl. With a
sturdy thrust of her hand the nurse pulled the white cloth divider
across the room concealing the two of them in the corner.
     Two other nurses were making their rounds when they noticed I was
```

awake. One was in her mid forties, had brown hair, brown eyes and was slim. The other nurse looked slightly older, taller than the first one, had white streaks throughout her dark hair and was of medium build. The first nurse said to me, "What are you doing up at this hour." I told her I could not sleep. They noticed that I was perspiring and decided to take my temperature. The first nurse left and returned with the thermometer. She placed the cold, thin piece of glass into my warm mouth and put her cool fingers around my wrist to take my pulse. They discovered I had a fever of a hundred and two. The second nurse disappeared this time and returned holding a little silver packet with two tylonal aspirins in it. I took out the two white tablets and swallowed them with water. Every so often until the following morning either one of the nurses would saunter into my room to check on me. All this happened in one night.

Hospital visits can be very frightening. Hospital employees must realize the trauma patients go threw just lying in their beds wondering what will happen to them next. Systems should be devised so that an individual is told what procedures he/she is expected to be involved in. In this way the patient is not surprised at a nurses coming at hm with needles or other such things.

REVISED DRAFT

All Alone

I spent a long, unpleasant weekend in a bed at University Hospital, the result of a bad roller skating accident I had one Saturday afternoon last October. There might be a concussion; there might be broken bones--and so I had no choice but to listen to the doctors and go for necessary tests. Instead of sleeping, there I lay stiff and silent, uncomfortably listening to the noises outside my room off the long hallway and watching everything that happened around me.

Bundled up in my white sheets and surrounded by the cold steel bars of my bed I heard every little sound in my ward all night long. Nurses, their rubber heels squeaking on the freshly polished floors, passed up and down the corridor. I heard soft whispers as one doctor in a green shirt spoke to two orderlies leaning against the wall with their arms folded. Occasionally one of them would laugh and the other two would giggle and say, "Sh! Sh!" If they only knew how disturbing it was for me to hear their muttering! At one point I almost shouted "Would you all get out of here!" but I didn't have the courage, and I pulled the blanket over my head instead. Perhaps the most startling noise, though, was the sound of a tray that must have accidentally slipped out of a nurse's hand far beyond my view. I jumped up as the clatter echoed down the long, endless white corridors, setting my nerves on end. Perspiration streaming down my face, I must have sat there in my bed shaking for at least five minutes.

All the noises aside, watching the activity outside and inside my room disturbed me, too. Across the hall a little red light above the door of the opposite room suddenly flashed on and off. A nurse in a clean white uniform was there in an instant to help a young, curly haired girl twisting and crying on her bed. A bright light in the hall enabled me to see the actions clearly. With a sturdy thrust of her hand the nurse pulled the white cloth divider across the room, concealing the two of them in the corner. However, I saw the nurse's shadow moving up and down, back and forth, until the child quieted down.

Soon after I noted all this, two other nurses making their rounds saw that I was still awake. One, a slim woman in her mid forties with brown eyes, said in a loud voice, "What are you doing up at this hour, dear? It's after two AM." When I said I couldn't sleep, they saw how clammy I was, and the one who spoke to me rushed off for a thermometer. Placing the rigid glass rod in my mouth, she took my pulse with cool fingers at my wrist. "A hundred and two," she said. "Wanda, bring this girl something for her fever." The second nurse disappeared this time and returned holding a silver packet of Tylenol, and I swallowed the pills with water from the drinking glass on my bedstand. Every so often until morning one of the nurses would saunter in, touch my brow, and make cheerful but noisy conversation. I knew they were trying to help, but all this activity did not make me feel any better. It made me feel worse.

Because hospital stays can be very frightening, hospital employees must realize the trauma patients go through just lying in their beds wondering what will happen to them next. The slightest sound, the barest visible action magnifies a million times in a tense person's mind. Couldn't the admitting clerk, a floor nurse, or an intern explain to patients about what to expect at the hospital? I would have liked knowing all about the tests I'd have to go through, but also would have liked knowing not to expect much sleep. If I knew in advance of all the noise and activity I might have relaxed.

—Maria Christoforou

1. Evaluate the proposal sentence in each draft. How does the use of the word *uncomfortably* in the proposal sentence of the revised draft contribute to the essay? What other changes do you note in the introduction?

2. Where in the body paragraphs has the writer used particularly clear images? Where in the revision has the writer created more specific pictures than appear in the early draft? Where would you recommend that the writer eliminate excess adjectives?

3. Where in the revised draft has the writer combined sentences from the earlier draft?

4. Why do you think the writer used the phrase *all the noises aside* to open the third paragraph in the revised draft? Does the addition improve the sentence? Explain. How does the writer open the fourth paragraph in the revision? Why has she created this paragraph, which does not appear in the draft?

5. What is your opinion of the conclusion? How has the writer changed the conclusion in the revised draft? What further changes might you recommend?

Step 2. More Essays. Read the following samples and answer the questions after them.

Uncle Del's Barn

I remember the big, red barn on my Uncle Del's farm in Montana with great fondness. The sight of its sprawling outline etched against the sky was the first thing I'd look for as we pulled into the road leading to my uncle's house. The barn's weathered sides needed painting badly. Once the proud home of cattle and horses, now chickens, cats, equipment, and dust took over as farm life had changed. Cool and dry inside, the barn lit up only occasionally as beams of yellow light from holes in the roof broke the darkness. Sunlight fell in patches on the floor, which was soft and springy from many layers of dust and straw. Walking along, I heard the wind moan through the chinks in the walls and the doors creak on their hinges. I had many adventures inside the barn, and I delighted in watching and playing with the animals that made their homes there.

The barn was an ideal place for a child to find adventure. Filled with junk and old tools, this hideaway offered hours of enjoyment. I would tiptoe between the piles of old harnesses and broken rakes and shovels, ever watchful for the imaginary bandits hiding just out of my sight, waiting to jump me the moment I turned my back. I stalked Billy the Kid, Jesse James, and the Sundance Kid, and I whooped and hollered after them, a toy silver gun in my leather holster. Now I was a brave pioneer, blazing a trail through the wilderness of plows and bales. I hid from attacking Blackfeet and built a homestead out of some loose planks, bits of hay, and an old green horse blanket. At other times I was a big game hunter, capturing lions, tigers, and exotic birds for the big circus across the sea. I pretended that the floor was a river filled with crocodiles and that I had to race across it with a rifle high above my head. Time flowed like molasses as I drifted from one adventure to another, lost in my daydreams.

Sharing in these adventures were the animals who lived in the barn, and they are as much a part of my memories as the barn itself. Hoping that I had a saucer of cream or a scrap of meat for them, barn cats and their new kittens ran to meet me as I opened the heavy wooden door. If I tried to reach out to pet them, they would run away, meowing just outside my reach. Half wild, the kittens trembled and shook those few times I did manage to catch them. As I explored the nooks and crannies and piles of straw, I startled many a chicken guarding her hidden nest. Squawking, with wings flapping, they fluttered off. Peeking at the spot an old hen had abandoned, I saw a pile of straw and feathers with a cluster of creamy-brown eggs. Once in a while, I would see a fluffy, yellow chick only a day or two old, cheeping furiously at his mother's rude departure.

My search through the barn for hidden animal treasures always brought me to the pigs' pen sooner or later, their snuffles and grunts attracting me. I loved to watch them as they lumbered around on their stubby legs. Sniffing at their slop, they would saunter out the door to the creek. After their slow walk they would flop down in its cool, slimy mud. The sight of a hefty porker trying to heave himself out of the goo was enough to send me into gales of laughter. I still crack Uncle Del's tired pig joke when someone says, "Aren't those animals filthy and disgusting?" I say, "What do you think they call them pigs for?"

Even today, I can close my eyes and recall the good times I had playing in the old, weathered barn, the smell of Aunt Annabelle's fragrant spice cake filling the air, Uncle Del's rusty plow sitting on the barn floor, the chicks and kittens and pigs moving freely about. I consider myself fortunate to have experienced a piece of life in decline in America today. Up against high interest rates and soaring costs for equipment, many small farmers (my Uncle Del is no exception) sell out to big businesses with interest only in making money. For Uncle Del and Aunt Annabelle, and for me, too as I now think back, the small Montana farm was a way of life. Even when I knew it, the old barn was past its useful life, but it gave me many joys as a child. I'm sure that barn is long gone now, yet it will always be a symbol in my mind for the carefree, happy, innocent kind of life that is not easy to find these days.

—*Yvonne Wortman*

The Growing Demand for Secretaries

Today's women strive for and can achieve all of the same occupational goals once reserved only for men. It is not uncommon to see female attorneys or computer consultants or major company presidents; and these women, like their male counterparts, are attracted to such jobs by the challenge, the sense of achievement, the glory, and the high salaries. These days the vital role of the secretary is becoming lost in the race for the "top" jobs. Yes, that ever-patient person sitting at the front desk filing, typing, answering phones, mailing letters, and undoubtedly keeping the entire office from succumbing to mass confusion is rapidly becoming rare. Thus, because of growing demand, today's secretaries have exceptional opportunities in the work force.

As the number of available secretaries decreases, the demand for them grows stronger and stronger. The U.S. Department of Labor's Bureau of Labor Statistics believes that the number of secretarial positions will expand to more than 400,000 by the end of the century. Even now, according to *The New York Times*, training schools for secretaries cannot meet business' needs, graduating "only two-thirds of the secretaries needed to fill 305,000 openings each year." A top-level secretary in Detroit makes on the average $641 a week, according to the Bureau of Labor Statistics. That amounts to more than $33,000 a year. Other major cities like Houston and St. Louis are not far behind. Legal secretaries, doing even more highly specialized work with law firms, can earn more. Even lower-level secretarial positions pay as much as $424 weekly in San Francisco.

Along with escalating demands for secretaries, levels of experience and skill also affect the secretaries' salaries. Generally, salaries are directly related to years of experience on the job and speed of typing. The *Times* in a survey of advertised secretarial salaries in the 1980s found that five years' experience brought about $17,000 in annual earnings. A secretary typing from 60–69 words per minute could expect yearly salaries close to $13,000; those typing more than 70 words per minute could find jobs up at $16,900 a year. And now, while the supply of secretaries is so low, experienced secretaries may find themselves virtually choosing where they want to work and earning more money than they expected.

Aside from enjoying the benefits of higher salaries, many of today's secretaries have the possibility of strong upward mobility. Chances for promotion and advancement are numerous. The *Occupational Outlook Handbook (OOH)* indicates that "Many executive secretaries are promoted to management positions because of their extensive knowledge of their employer's operations." Local business schools and colleges as well as the company itself provide courses for self advancement and improvement. Passing a series of exams from the National Secretaries Association, a secretary can earn the title Certified Professional Secretary (CPS). "This designation," says the OOH, "is recognized by a growing number of employers as the mark of achievement in the secretarial field."

As companies become increasingly desperate for good secretaries, they also are realizing the great value that a secretary has. For women—nineteen of every twenty secretaries are women—this means increased status and importance in a job once considered subordinate. And some men are now crossing the once-rigid gender line and becoming secretaries because of the status and benefits. The secretary keeps information moving smoothly and keeps lines of communication open with the office and with other offices or companies. The secretary is someone's "right-hand person," like a physician's assistant or an assistant director of a film or play. Now that people realize the importance of this office job, secretarial positions seem much more desirable. The title of a *Times* article says it all: "Secretaries Have Pick of Jobs: Demand Is Rising, Pulling Up Salaries."

—*Nick Daniello*

Practice in the High School Gym

All my life I have loved baseball. As a little boy I stood at the iron schoolyard gates and watched the ninth graders zip around the bases. I sit glued to the television and suffer with the Mets as their pitchers go limp on the mound. It is easy to understand, then, why when March comes around I look forward to the start of baseball practice in my high school gym. What I liked most about senior practice was the thrill of all my friends around me in the locker room and the activity on the gym floor.

As I dressed in the locker room, I felt the warmth and enjoyment of all my friends who played on the team with me in the previous year. Bob on my left dressed hurriedly to rush out to the gym; as team captain he rapped on the metal lockers and yelled, "Let's get the lead out! Cut the talk and let's move!" Richard on my right stuffed his red flannel shirt and his copy of *Hamlet* into the locker as he dressed, talking continuously about winning a school championship. As I looked around, I saw all the new fellows. Trying out for the team for the first time, they struggled with their uniforms. They were so nervous that they could not even put their bright yellow shirts on straight. Then I saw Coach O'Neill flying out of his office. Even he looked excited for the oncoming season, which would last until June, and the championship games. As he dashed out the door to the gym, he looked at me and smiled as if to say, "Isn't it great to be back with the team again?"

Then, when all the fun in the locker room was over, we charged out onto the shellacked floor of the gym. As we stood waiting for the coach to finish checking the new bats and uniforms, I could not help thinking how I felt like a father to all the new boys on the team. I looked at the brown painted stands halfway pushed out, but before we even got near to sit down, Coach O'Neill grabbed the silver whistle dangling from his neck and blew hard. His gray eyes looked mean as he barked out the drills we had to do. Then we started calisthenics because the coach said they would make us loose. As I did my push-ups to Coach O'Neill's crisp "One-two-three-four," I saw the yellow floor with its black stripes from the basketball court. Blood rushed up to my head, making me feel weak, but I still continued. Next we ran laps around the gym. As I ran I could see the huge panes of glass from the roof of the gym, the sun blinding me every time I looked up. After a loud blast from a whistle, the coach told us to stop running and to take a rest. Five minutes later we ended the workout with wind sprints in the hallway to make room in the gym for the football team on its workout session. These activities in the gym made me feel happy and healthy.

Because I have so much fun in the gym, to me exercise is a wonderful part of living. I was surprised to read in the papers about "Flabby Americans" and of the poor physical condition so many people today are in because of little activity. Maybe some worthwhile exercises and exciting workouts in high school would start more people on physical fitness programs. My friends in public school say that gym teachers leave uninterested students pretty much alone to sit and talk on the sidelines as long as there is no trouble. But I think that this is wrong: physical education teachers should be convincing all those sideline talkers that participating is the greatest part of sports.

—*Thomas Albanese*

1. Put a check next to the proposal sentences in each essay. Is the proposal specific or general?

2. Comment on the introductory paragraphs. Is the introduction effective? Does it reveal the writer's attitude or explain why the topic is important to her?

3. What actions do you see most clearly? Where has the writer appealed to our sense of touch and smell?

4. Underline some of the *-ing* openers. Are they effective? Why?

5. How do the last sentences in paragraph 2, 3, and 4 in each essay serve the context of the paragraphs?

6. What part of the opening sentence of paragraph 3 in each essay tells the topic of that paragraph? What part of the same sentence refers the reader back to paragraph 2? How do the writers connect paragraph 4 with paragraph 3?

7. What is your opinion of the conclusion in each essay? Check the guidelines on pages 126–128.

Collaboration: Getting Reader Response

After you have prepared a draft of your essay, pair up with someone in the class and exchange your work. Read the essay carefully, and then write a paragraph in which you offer advice about what the writer should do to improve the draft. In your critique, try to address these questions, among any others you can think of:

1. Is the topic clearly stated in the proposal?
2. Are the details clear and adequate?
3. Is the logic clear? What parts don't you understand?
4. Do the transitions connect the parts of the essay smoothly?
5. Do the introduction and the conclusion hold your interest? Do they suit the writer's purpose?
6. What single comment can you make to help the writer improve the draft?

Progress Reminders: A Checklist

As you think about this essay and as you plan and write your rough and final drafts, use this questionnaire as a guide. When you have prepared your manuscript, write *yes* or *no* in the blank spaces. If you have two or more no's, you should attempt another revision.

1. Did I think the topic through carefully? Did I follow some   _____
   prewriting activity that works for me, perhaps *timed writing*?
   (See pages 135–137 and above.)   _____

2. Did I prepare a rough draft and any other needed drafts? Did I   _____
   make changes in language and ideas on my rough draft in
   order to make my ideas clearer?   _____

3. After making changes in content, form, and sentence structure, did I check my draft over by proofreading carefully for
   my usual mistakes? Did I check especially for errors in com-   _____
   mas and other punctuation?

4. Am I sure that I understand the way an essay is put together,   _____
   having studied the chart From Paragraph to Essay (pages
   114–115) and the sample essay written from a one-paragraph
   theme (pages 115–117)?

5. Have I prepared carefully a proposal sentence that will let me   _____
   discuss *two* aspects of my topic?

   This is my proposal sentence: _____

   _____

6. Did I write an introduction *after* my proposal was clear to me?   _____
   Did I follow any of the suggestions in the ideas for starting
   essays on pages 121–125?   _____

7. Have I introduced the topic of each body paragraph in the first   _____
   sentence? Have I used transitions in those sentences?
   _____

8. Have I used lively, colorful language in rich sound, smell, touch, and images that use color? Do I name people, places, and times of events specifically?   _____

9. Have I used a variety of sentence patterns?   _____

   a. Do I have several subordinated sentences?   _____

   b. Do I have coordinated sentences?   _____

   c. Have I used a semicolon correctly?   _____

   d. Have I opened some sentences with words that end in *-ing* or *-ly*?   _____

   e. Do I have a quotation sentence using someone's exact words?   _____

10. Did I try to combine sentences (as explained on pages 129–131)?   _____

11. Have I used correctly some of the new vocabulary introduced on pages 108–109 of this chapter?   _____

12. Have I proofread (see pages 28–29) my essay very carefully, looking for the errors that appear most often on my Theme Progress Sheet? Did I check for run-on errors, sentence fragments, spelling mistakes?   _____

13. In rereading my essay, am I satisfied that I have sufficiently supported the opinion I stated in my proposal sentence?   _____

14. Have I written a strong title?   _____

15. Have I written a concluding paragraph?   _____

● The Professionals Speak

Exploring an Essay.   Read the following selection, which describes, in rich detail, a walk down a *towpath*—a path used by animals towing boats along a path or a river—in Maryland. Answer the questions after the selection.

SOME WORDS TO KNOW BEFORE YOU READ

salvage—something extracted as valuable or useful

piecemeal—piece by piece; gradually

obliteration—being wiped out or destroyed

locks—part of a canal closed off by gates and in which a ship or a boat may be raised or lowered by raising or lowering the water level in that part of the canal

coterie—a group whose members associate with each other frequently

culvert—a sewer or drain crossing under a road

catwalk—a narrow platform or pathway

A Walk on the Towpath

I was down in Washington around the middle of March, and smelling spring in the air, I gave myself the pleasure of a walk in the country to meet it. The walk I chose was along the towpath of the derelict Chesapeake & Ohio Canal. Situated on the Maryland bank of the Potomac River, the C. & O. Canal extends from the Georgetown section of Washington to a natural passage in the Appalachians at Cumberland, a distance of a hundred and eighty-four miles. The C. & O. is an old canal—one of the oldest lock and mule-drawn-boat canals in the United States. It is also almost the only one of which more than a trace survives. It was begun in 1828, it was completed in 1850, and it remained in operation until shortly after the First World War. The last boats moved through its locks in 1924. It was then stripped of its salvage and abandoned. The depression saved it from piecemeal sale and certain obliteration, and in 1938, through a freak of chance and charity, it was acquired by the federal government. The oldest section of the canal—some twenty wandering miles between the terminus at Georgetown and a point known as Violet's Lock—is now a part of the Washington park system. Its decline has been arrested, and its several locks and lock tenders' houses have all been fully restored. The rest, though reserved as a national monument, has been left to the wild and the weather, and it was there I chose to walk.

I began my walk by car. There is no other ready way to reach the canal once it emerges from the city. A friend with whom I was staying drove me out on his way to work. We passed for a time through an open countryside of rolling pastures and white paddock fences. Then the fences wheeled away and the fields roughened into brush and woods. We came to the head of a rutted lane that wound down the side of a ridge. My friend pulled over and stopped.

"Here you are," he said, "You'll hit the canal just down around that bend."

I got out. He passed me a lunch that his wife had packed, and a leather-covered flask. I stowed them away in my jacket. "Where am I?" I said.

"Lock 22," he said. "Pennifield's Lock, they call it. Violet's Lock is the next lock up—about three miles from here. Then comes Seneca Creek and Seneca Lock and Aqueduct. That's another mile. After that, it's wilderness all the way to what used to be Edward's Ferry. You won't want to go any farther than that. Edward's Ferry is a good eight miles above Seneca. Maybe more. I'll pick you up there around five." He raised his hand. "Get going," he said, and drove off.

I watched him out of sight, and then headed down the lane. It had rained in the night, and the lane was awash with thin red mud, and puddles stood in the ruts and potholes. It was steep, wet, slippery walking. And cold. Under the trees the morning air had a bite. It felt more like fall than spring. But from what I could see of the sky overhead, the clouds were beginning to break and lift, and there was a hint of a watery sun. I slid down the lane to the foot of the ridge. A coterie of chickadees burst up from a thicket and scattered like a handful of gravel. The lane cut sharply to the left and emerged in a little meadow. At the edge of the meadow stretched the canal. Some fifty feet wide, the color of mud, and flanked by head-high banks, it looked like a sunken road. The towpath followed the farther bank, and beyond it, through a heavy screen of trees, I caught a distant glimpse and murmur of the river. The canal lay as still as a pond. I found a pebble and tossed it in. It sank with a throaty plunk. I guessed the water to be five or six feet deep. About a hundred yards downstream, the canal funneled into a kind of open culvert, which was bridged by a railed catwalk. Facing it, on the towpath side, sat a small white-washed stone house with two stone chimneys and a pitched roof of corrugated iron. That would have been the lock tender's house. The culvert was the lock.

I walked out on the bridge and looked down at the lock. The canal flowed into the lock through a sprung wooden gate just under the bridge. It ran between two narrowly confining walls for about a hundred feet. Then, with a sudden boil and bubble, it broke against another gate, spilled through, and resumed its sluggish course. The walls of the lock were faced with big blocks of rust-red sandstone. Some of the stones were so huge they could have been hoisted into place only with a block and tackle. It was beautiful stone, and it had been beautifully finished and fitted. Time had merely softened it. Here and there along the courses I could even make out the remains of a mason's mark. One device was quite distinct—a double-headed arrow. Another appeared to be two overlapping equilateral triangles. I went on across the bridge to the house. The windows were shuttered and boarded up, and the door was locked. No matter. It was enough just to stand and look at it. It was a lovely house, as beautifully made as the lock, and as firmly designed for function. It gave me a pang to think that there had once been a time when even a lock tender could have so handsome a house. A phoebe called from a sweet-gum tree in the dooryard. Far away, somewhere down by the river, a mourning dove gave an answering sigh. I looked at my watch. It was ten minutes after ten. I started up the towpath.

The sun was still no more than a promise, but the air had lost its chill. It was going to be a spring day after all. The signs of it abounded. Most of the trees that lined the path—sycamore, dogwood, sweet gum, hickory, elm—were coming into bud. Only the oaks still had the wrought-iron look of winter. Some creeping vine—Virginia creeper or honeysuckle—was even in leaf. And everywhere there were birds in sight or sound. Robins hopped and stood and listened at intervals along the way. A woodpecker drummed. A blue jay raced from tree to tree, screaming a wild alarm. There was a flash of cardinal red across the canal. I turned—but too late. It was gone. And so were the lock and the house. They had vanished around a bend. There was nothing behind me but water and woods. It gave me a curious sensation. I felt for the first time completely alone, but I didn't feel lonely. It was an exhilarating loneliness. It was solitude. I took a deep breath and lighted a cigarette. I felt at peace with the world.

—*Berton Roueché*

1. What is the writer's thesis in this selection? Where does he state it most clearly? Which details of sight, sound, color, action, and smell make this scene come alive for you?

2. In the last paragraph of this excerpt, Roueché names particular trees, vines, and birds. Why? What does the naming add to the essay?

3. How has the writer arranged details here? Which transitions help move the reader from one sentence to another? from one paragraph to another?

4. How does the opening paragraph serve the essay? the closing? description? narration? examples (illustration)? Support your response with references to the selections.

SOME WORDS TO KNOW BEFORE YOU READ

inertia—resistance to motion

repugnance—extreme dislike

inhibition—holding back

balderdash—nonsense

unwieldy—clumsy

momentum—the force of movement

ungainly—awkward

laboriously—with hard work

Theme Writing

Scientists tell us it is harder to start a stone moving than to keep it going after it gets started. And every writer can bear witness that the most unyielding stone is mobile as thistledown compared to the inertia of the average human mind confronted with a blank sheet of paper.

It is hard to write. It is infinitely harder to begin to write. Don't I know it? I have been earning my living by my pen for twenty-five years. I shouldn't like to guess how many hundred words I've put on paper, and I have never in my life sat down at my desk and started off without hesitation, repugnance, and wild flounderings. Other authors confess that it is much the same with them. There are exceptions—stories, even novels, where the opening words pop right into one's mind, part of the first conception, but these inspirations are far between.

I set down all this not to discourage those of you who are wondering if perhaps it might not be possible to become an author, still less to add to the gloom of wrestling with the English compositions you all have to write. On the contrary, I hope to encourage you by letting you know that those hopeless moments of inhibition before the blank page, those chewed, balky penholders are only the common lot. There is nothing the matter if you can't start writing without effort. Nobody can.

But perhaps this sounds a little bit like the fortune teller who predicted, "You will have forty years of bad luck and then—then you will be used to it." It is not so bad as that. It is quite true that no one ever learns to write both well and easily. But there are tricks to every trade and some of the most useful of them all are ways of tricking your own rebellious nerves. Perhaps it would help you to know of one that works with most writers. Whenever they have a piece of writing to do, *they begin to write*—to write something, anything. They conquer the inertia of their minds by a spasm of effort, just as a man might give a great heave to a boulder that blocks his way. Grimly, doggedly, they keep on writing. Often what they are setting down is flat, stale balderdash, and they know it. No matter! If they are experienced writers they keep right on, do not stop—not to sharpen a pencil, or get a drink of water, or go to look out of the window, although they yearn to do all these things. They have learned by experience that if they sit and stare at the paper they are lost. The rosy, hazy half-thoughts which flit about the back of the mind always vanish when one tries to think them out. The only way to catch them is to put down on the paper as many of them as possible.

So the struggling author plods ahead, filling page after page with horrible, unwieldy sentences, haphazard, unleavened ideas, and after a time it begins to move more smoothly. Is it because of habit, or because the subconscious mind wakes up, or is it something similar to physical momentum? Nobody knows, but it almost always works. The great boulder begins to roll evenly and more and more in the desired direction. Apter phrases suggest themselves. The whole subject begins to take on shape. Even now it is not good. But there is something there, some stuff which can later be licked into shape. Then comes the moment when the writer realizes that he has said somehow all that was in his mind.

The work is far from being finished, but the hardest part is over. Now comes the mechanical task of breaking up ungainly sentences, cutting out the flat words and phrases, thinking up colorful ones to fill the gaps, shifting related ideas into paragraphs. It is a matter of skill and judgment, only a little harder than correcting grammatical errors—far different from the agony of trying to create, or rather to drag out the raw material from the fringe of consciousness.

It is mechanical work but very necessary. Inexperienced writers don't do enough of it. Very young writers often do not revise at all. Like a hen looking at a chalk line, they are hypnotized by what they have written. "How can it be altered?" they think. "That's the way it was written." Well, it has to be altered. You have to learn how. That is chiefly what English classes can teach you. They can't give you thoughts and material to write about. Only your inherited brain cells and the enriching experience of life as you live it can do that. But you can learn to put what material you have into form. In manual training you wouldn't hand in a lot of sticks and boards bunched together with string, and call it a table. It's no better to hand in a detached bundle of statements, starting nowhere in particular, trailing along a while and then fading out—and call it a theme.

All your first drafts will need revision, but the middle and end of them may not need a great deal. You had steam up when you wrote them; you were commencing to feel what you wanted to say. *But watch your beginning.* That was written when arm and brain were cold. Try as you may to put it into shape, the first page or so is generally hopeless. Then cut it out and begin where the real life begins. You may hate to sacrifice that laboriously written first page, but if it isn't right, can't be made right, it isn't worth keeping. When you wrote it you were only warming up your arm. Do that behind the grand stand, and when you start the game be ready to pitch the real ball.

—*Dorothy Canfield Fisher*

1. How does the first sentence introduce the topic? How does an "unyielding stone" compare to the human mind confronted with a blank sheet of paper?

2. Which sentence states the writer's thesis most clearly.

3. Where does Fisher state the importance of her topic?

4. How and where does paragraph 5 relate to the first sentence of paragraph 1?

5. In the last paragraph, to what does the author compare the writing of the beginning of an essay?

5

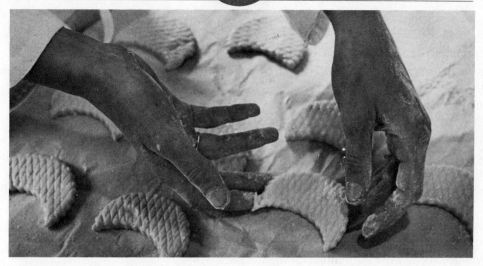

Process Analysis

•

INTRODUCTION TO PROCESS ANALYSIS

One reason for writing is to explain something. Perhaps no explanations are more demanding in terms of clear, precise language than those that give directions.

Of course, each of us has a well of skills and talents that we can draw on to perform tasks knowledgeably and with our own special knack. Chores around the house, activities you do for fun in your spare time, part-time employment (or full-time work)—all these give you skill in how to perform some process. You may know how to clean the garage quickly, how to make sandwiches at a crowded lunch counter, how to run a busy gas station when the boss leaves early. Even if you never

151

have worked in your life, you still have some special interest or ability that someone else could learn from. Or maybe you would like to learn how to do something or how something works so that you can show someone else how to do it.

This essay assignment asks you for a *process analysis*. When you analyze something, you break it down into parts. When you analyze a process, you explain the various steps required to carry it out successfully. Even though the process you want to explain is one you know pretty well, writing about it is a special challenge. Activities on the following pages will help you meet that challenge.

In addition, this chapter will help you practice with degrees of comparison and parallelism.

● **Vocabulary**

Step 1. Words for Explaining Processes. The words below may be helpful as you write an essay that explains a process. In the blank spaces, and using a dictionary if you need one, write definitions for these words:

1. sequential _____
2. routine _____
3. innovate _____
4. outcome _____
5. subsequent _____

6. cyclical _____
7. adjacent _____
8. procedure _____
9. apparatus _____
10. synthesize _____

Step 2. Applying Definitions. In the blank spaces below, write from the above list the word that best suits each meaning.

1. introduce something new _____

2. consequence _____

3. combine separate elements to produce something _____

4. steps taken to do something _____

5. lying next to _____

6. coming afterward in time or order _____

7. equipment used to perform a task _____

8. following an orderly arrangement _____

9. a repeated way of doing something _____

10. happening at regularly repeated time intervals _____

● Building Composition Skills

Finding the Topic

Each of us has enough knowledge about (or enough interest in to find out about) procedures that we can explain to others. Take an inventory of the various processes you might be able to explain.

Step 1. What Do You Know?   On this list of items put a check (✓) next to those you know well enough by firsthand experience to give instructions that someone else could follow. Put an *X* next to any process you might be interested in investigating so that you could understand it sufficiently to explain to others. Discuss your choices with the class.

___	1. how to enlarge a photograph
___	2. how to lose weight
___	3. how to jump-start a car
___	4. how to scuba dive
___	5. how windmills produce electrical current
___	6. how to bake cookies
___	7. how to write a complaint letter
___	8. how to meet a woman (or man) you like but don't know
___	9. how to feed a baby
___	10. how to plant a vegetable garden

Step 2. Finding Out More about the Process.   Form groups of three or four students in the class. Then return to Step 1 and reexamine the items for which you wrote *X* in the blank line. How could you find out more information about those processes? Whom could you talk to? What kinds of books or other resources would you need?

Step 3. Giving and Following Directions: An Experiment.   To understand some of the conditions required for explaining a process that someone else should be able to reproduce, ask someone in the class to give aloud directions that he or she thinks are easy to follow. Ask another person to follow the directions as the first person explains. The person giving directions should bring to class any necessary equipment.

   To make this experiment work, whoever explains the process should face one of the side walls or the back wall as the other volunteer, unseen by the first but visible to the rest of the class, follows instructions. The person following directions must do so *exactly* without taking any steps whatsoever unless specifically instructed.

Here are some possible processes volunteers might like to explain or to follow:

1. how to cover a book
2. how to tie a shoelace
3. how to set a table for a meal
4. how to make a peanut-butter sandwich
5. how to make a paper airplane

As the people in the class watch the joint performance, they should be prepared to evaluate the situation they are observing. Step 4 below will focus on that evaluation.

Step 4. Explaining Processes: Seeing the Problems. If your class is like most others, you have just observed (if you have followed Step 3 according to directions) an exercise in frustration. Even with the simplest of procedures, because there is so much room for misunderstanding, steps must be simply and clearly explained. How would you evaluate the two volunteers? What successes could you point to? When things went wrong, *why* did they go wrong? Use the checklist below and circle your answer to judge the scene you witnessed. (On the checklist, the *instructor* is the person who explained the process; the *performer* is the person who tried to duplicate it.) Discuss your responses with the class.

1. The instructor did not give enough information.　　　　*yes*　　*no*　　*unsure*

2. The instructor's language was too complicated.　　　　*yes*　　*no*　　*unsure*

3. The instructor assumed that the performer knew more about the process than he or she actually did.　　　*yes*　　*no*　　*unsure*

4. The instructor did not have all the materials that were needed to explain the process clearly.　　*yes*　　*no*　　*unsure*

5. The instructor either did not explain steps in the right sequence or did not give all the steps in the sequence.　　*yes*　　*no*　　*unsure*

Including and Arranging Details

In order to write about a process clearly—whether you are giving directions someone can follow or you are giving information about how to do or to make something—you have to include all the important details someone would need to understand what you are trying to explain.

Details in a process essay include, first, the major steps in the procedure you are writing about. People who wanted to follow your directions themselves would need to have every step included. On the other hand, you would not have to offer information with such completeness if you were simply explaining a process readers do not intend to carry out. An essay on how to make an omelet would demand full explanations; an essay on how eggs are produced and gathered could, for most readers, rely more upon general outlines and less upon absolutely complete detail.

Not only must you include all the appropriate steps in the process, but you also must mention any materials involved and any descriptive information that will instruct your readers and will hold their interest. Concrete sensory language (see pages 3–5) can add life to what otherwise might be a boring series of "do this," "do that" instructions. Also, telling readers *why* to perform a certain step keeps their attention with valuable information.

You will discover once you decide which steps to include that arranging details presents no real problems. Usually, a process paper demands a *chronological* arrangement of materials (see pages 42–43). Readers have to know what to do first in time, what to do next, and what to do after that. However, you sometimes have other options.

In explaining how to care for puppies, for example, you might offer the elements of the process in their order of *importance* (pages 81–83)—least important element first, most important element last. Or, similarly, you might first discuss the simplest element to consider in caring for puppies; and you could build to the most difficult element. Finally, you might want to tell the details of the process in order of location—that is, from one point in space to another. You could tell how to care first for the puppies' eyes, then the ears, then the mouth, the digestion, the coat, the limbs and feet. Such an order is called *spatial*.

For the most part, though, a simple ordering of steps and details by chronology works best.

Step 1. An Inventory of Materials.   In explanations of processes, writers must be careful to name all the materials that may be demanded for the task. For two of the following processes, list all the equipment or material someone who wanted to duplicate the process would need. Use separate paper.

1. painting a wooden stool
2. cleaning a garage
3. washing a car
4. repotting a houseplant
5. cooking spaghetti

Step 2. Listing Steps.   For any *one* of the following processes, list all the steps you would mention in an essay that attempted to explain the process. Use separate paper.

1. how to organize your closet
2. how to pitch a baseball
3. how to register for courses
4. how to put up a shelf
5. how to buy a used car

6. how to pick strawberries
7. how to send a large gift in the mail
8. how to dress for skiing
9. how to play poker
10. how to survive rush hour

_____

_____

_____

_____

Step 3. Deciding on an Order.   What method of arrangement would you use to explain the following processes? Explain your choice.

1. how to get from your writing class to the college library
2. how to eat with chopsticks
3. how to form your own band
4. how to catch a fish
5. how to help someone who is choking

Step 4. Checking a Process through Research.   In order to explain a process carefully, you may need to rely on sources outside your own experiences. For the following topics—with the help of your library catalog and your school librarian— write the names of three books or magazine articles that you could use in order to check the steps in the process named below.

1. how a robot works

   a. _____

   b. _____

   c. _____

2. how Freud used hypnosis

   a. _____

   b. _____

   c. _____

3. how to improve your reading speed

   a. _____

   b. _____

   c. _____

4. how to learn how to swim

   a. _____

   b. _____

   c. _____

5. how to grow tomatoes in pots

   a. _____

   b. _____

   c. _____

Audience

Whenever you speak to people—whether they are friends, acquaintances, teachers, fellow workers—you adjust your comments and your language to the situation in which you find yourself. What you sense about the people you are talking to tells you just what topics will interest them. It also tells you how much you must say to be understood, what kinds of words to use, how strongly to make your points. Discussing rock music with your friends who know and love it demands one kind of vocabulary, one kind of talking style; discussing rock music with a neighbor or a teacher who knows little about it demands quite another.

So when you speak, you rely on an already keen sense of audience—the people reacting to your ideas.

Good writers, too, need to have a strong sense of audience. Of course, most of your writing at school is specifically for your instructors or for other people in the class. But it's not a good idea to write expressly and exclusively for them. You want to aim for a more general audience, for a wider range of readers. These would be people smart enough to understand what you are writing about without having to be specialists in your topic. All writers ask themselves as part of their prewriting activity, "Whom do I want to read this? Whom am I writing this for?" The clearer the answer to those questions, the easier it is for a writer to pitch language to readers so that they come away with exactly what the writer wants them to have.

Although a sense of audience is important in any written work, an essay on process demands from writers a very precise idea of whom they are writing for. Just to take one obvious example, you would use completely different approaches if you wrote to explain how to make a chocolate cake to a class of newlyweds or to a group of master bakers.

Knowing your audience is critical. The box below suggests questions to ask yourself in order to identify the precise audience you are writing for in your process paper.

● Identifying Audience: Questions to Ask for the Process Theme ●

1. Whom am I trying to explain the process to?

2. Will my readers know the technical vocabulary I may have to use? Or, will I have to define new or difficult terms?

3. Do I expect my readers to be able to perform the process I am writing about? If so, what steps can I assume that they already know? (Be careful. It's easy to assume that readers know more than they actually do. Without talking down to your audience, it's always best—when in doubt—to think of your readers as having almost *no* knowledge of your subject.)

4. What purpose do my readers have in reading my essay? Do they want only to be informed, or do they expect also to be amused or inspired or moved to action?

Step 1. Seeing Different Audiences.   For each of the following processes, name two or three different kinds of audiences that might be interested in reading about the process. Discuss your responses with the class. What demands would each type of audience place upon the writer? Look at the example.

PROCESS

1. how to fix flat tires on bicycles

2. how to make a speech

3. how to cook a gourmet meal in half an hour

4. how to pack efficiently

5. how to write an essay

KINDS OF AUDIENCES

a. young teenagers

b. bicycle repair shop owners

c. people who sell tires to bicycle manufacturers

_____

_____

_____

_____

_____

_____

_____

_____

_____

_____

_____

_____

_____

_____

_____

_____

Step 2. Assessing Vocabulary.   Column I below names a process. Column II names the readers the writer is aiming for. Column III offers several technical words required in explanation. Considering the process and its intended audience, check only those terms you think the writer would have to define in his or her essay (or would have to replace with simpler words). Defend your choices. Look at the example.

I	II	III
PROCESS	INTENDED AUDIENCE	VOCABULARY
1. how to stir-fry Chinese vegetables	beginning cooks	✔ bok choy ✔ wok ✔ soy sauce tablespoon ✔ peanut oil

2. how to read a newspaper | a class of fourth-graders | print
headline
column
pages
editorial
ads

3. how to relax through yoga | an out-of-shape business executive | meditation
tension
lotus position
complete breath

4. how to light a wood stove | a ski-resort vacationer from the city | seasoned hardwood
flue
chimney
kindling
asbestos mitt

5. how to register for classes in college | entering college students | prerequisites
program
bursar
registrar
baccalaureate

6. how to paint a picture | beginning artist | canvas
brush
linseed oil
acrylics
palate

Essay Transitions

Using transitions effectively in an essay helps you connect your paragraphs smoothly. The following essay transition signboards suggest key places for transitions. Before you examine the charts, review pages 113–115 on the parts of the essay.

Review Hints: Remembering the Proposal Sentence

1. It must tell the reader the purpose of the essay
2. It should allow you to discuss two aspects of your topic. It can state both aspects quite specifically, or it can merely suggest what these aspects are.
3. It is conveniently placed as the last sentence of the introduction.

Hint

See pages 118–120 for more about proposal sentences.

• Essay Transition Signboard I: First Sentence of Paragraph 2 •

What to Do	**Why**
1. Tell what part of the proposal you want to discuss in paragraph 2 by	
a. repeating one of the points you want to write about if you have mentioned them clearly in your proposal	These steps help show your reader that you are moving logically from your proposal sentence to the first part of your topic.
OR	
b. stating (for the first time) the point you want to write about, a point based upon the suggestion made in the proposal.	
2. Use transition words (page 11, pages 83–85, pages 187–189) to help you connect the opening sentence of this paragraph with the proposal.	This makes the move from the proposal to the next paragraph smooth and not too sudden.

Step 1. Analyzing Transitions in Paragraph 2.   Column I states a proposal. Decide whether or not you think the sentence alongside it in Column II would be effective as the opening sentence of the second paragraph, and explain your reasons. Base your ideas on Essay Transition Signboard I. Use separate paper.

I

1. Clipping the wings of a pet parakeet requires great caution.

2. To make a deluxe superburger requires imagination and planning.

3. Fall foliage season in Vermont is extremely important to the state's economy.

4. Going camping for the first time can be a very frustrating experience.

5. My memories of Callahan Beach include busy, joyful summer moments and the sudden changes autumn always brings.

II

You must first spend time in calming the bird so it feels relaxed.

Not everybody likes hamburgers.

From the top of Mount Equinox, you can see five states.

Pitching a tent is the first major challenge.

In July, our beach buzzes with activity.

Step 2. More on Paragraph 2 Transitions. Comment on the opening sentence of paragraph 2 in the student essays on pages 169–173.

Step 3. Your Own Opener for Paragraph 2. For any three proposals in Step 1, page 153, write your own opening sentence for the paragraph of an essay.

● Essay Transition Signboard II: First Sentence of Body Paragraphs After Paragraph 2 ●

What to Do	**Why**
1. Refer to the main idea of the previous paragraph	to show that the new paragraph grows logically from the previous paragraph
OR	OR
refer to the last event, instance, or detail you discussed in the previous paragraph.	to tie together the body paragraphs, which develop your proposal
2. Tell what part of the proposal you intend to discuss in the paragraph by	to remind the reader of the whole topic of the essay
a. repeating another aspect of the topic that you may have mentioned in the proposal, or	to let the reader know exactly what the body paragraph will contain
b. stating for the first time—based upon the suggestion you made in the proposal—the part of the topic you want to discuss in this body paragraph.	to remind you, the writer, to stick to the topic that you stated in the proposal

Hint: 1. Coordination (pages 84–86) and subordination (pages 86–94) are especially effective in opening sentences of paragraph 3.
2. Use transitional expressions (page 11, pages 83–84, and pages 187–190) as needed.

Step 4. Openers for Paragraph 3. Read the opening sentence of body paragraphs after paragraph 2 in each of the essays on pages 169–173. Which part of the sentence refers to the previous paragraph? Which part announces the topic of the paragraph to follow?

Step 5. Opening Sentences for Paragraphs 2, 3, and 4. Each of the following sentences is a proposal sentence for an essay. In the spaces below, write opening sentences for the body paragraphs that would develop logically from the proposal.

1.   Retirement does not need to be a boring or purposeless time of life.

paragraph 2: _____

paragraph 3: _____

paragraph 4: _____

2. My father has always been a friend to me.

   paragraph 2: _____

   paragraph 3: _____

   paragraph 4: _____

3. My friend Darius really knows how to prepare an elaborate dinner without too much work.

   paragraph 2: _____

   paragraph 3: _____

   paragraph 4: _____

• Essay Transition Signboard III: First Sentence of the Conclusion •

What to Do

1. Make some reference to the main idea of the previous paragraph, or refer back to the last event, instance, or detail you discussed in the previous paragraph.

2. Refer to something you wrote in the introduction (see pages 126–128).

   a. Pick up the idea of the proposal.

   b. Pick up a point from the background material you may have given.

   c. Repeat why you felt your subject was important.

   d. Refer to any questions you may have asked.

   e. Refer to any quotation you may have used.

   f. Pick up the idea of the story you may have told in the introduction.

   g. Refer to your title.

Why

to show that the conclusion grows logically from the last body paragraph

to tie the last body paragraph more closely to the conclusion you will start to develop

to remind the reader about how your whole idea started

to help you begin writing the conclusion, which may be based upon one of the suggestions you made in the introduction

to help you make sure that the introduction is an important part of your essay

Step 6. First Sentence in Conclusion. Read and discuss the opening sentence of the conclusion in each of the essays named below.

1. "The Gloom Room," pages 116–117
2. "Practice in the High School Gym," pages 142–143
3. "Uncle Del's Barn," pages 140–141

Expanding Sentences and Changing Word Order

The words in the chart below are *prepositions*. They all help show relations between ideas and objects in sentences. Each word can introduce a word group that tells where, when, or how things happen.

● Words That Show Where, When, and How (Prepositions) ●

about	except	within	between
by	under	beside	upon
beneath	onto	since	by means of
inside	across	as to	through
above	on	toward	along with
for	near	beyond	because of
over	into	up	by way of
outside	after	before	on account of
along	to	like	in spite of
among	with	below	in front of
of			

In this sentence:

An old man hobbled away.

Notice how the following word groups in italics expand its meaning.

A

An old man hobbled away *down the street*.	The words *down the street* show *where* the old man hobbled.
An old man hobbled away *on shaking legs*.	The words *on shaking legs* tell *how* he hobbled.
An old man hobbled away *before noon*.	The words *before noon* tell *when* he hobbled.

Using word groups that tell *where, when,* or *how* in various sentence positions helps you vary your sentences. You can shift the word group from the end to the beginning of the sentence.

B

Down the street an old man hobbled away.

On shaking legs an old man hobbled away.

Before noon an old man hobbled away.

You can also use the word group *within* the sentence.

C

An old man *down the street* hobbled away.

An old man *on shaking legs* hobbled away.

An old man *before noon* hobbled away.

You can use two or more word groups to expand meaning even further.

D

Down the street an old man hobbled away *on shaking legs.*

Before noon an old man *on shaking legs* hobbled away *down the street.*

Of course, you cannot simply insert the word group just anywhere in the sentence. It might not make sense, or it might not sound right to you. Also, by shifting a word group you might be changing even very slightly the meaning you had intended. For example, the first sentence in A, above, says that the man hobbled down the street. In C, the first sentence says that the man was already down the street when he hobbled away. In B, you could argue that either of those two meanings worked in the first sentence. The differences are minor, certainly; but there are differences.

Step 1. Expanding Sentences.   Select word groups from among the following, and use them to expand the sentences below sensibly. Use the word groups in sentence positions that you think work best for the intended meaning. Look at the example.

in the hotel   with glowing eyes

behind the mountaintops   in great pain

in the restaurant   at once

beside the highway
with great passion
in a sad voice
beyond the pines

with a bright smile
by five o'clock
with great courage
through a darkened tunnel

EXAMPLE
The sky glowed brilliant reds, oranges, and purples.

By five o'clock, the sky glowed brilliant reds, oranges, and purples behind the mountaintops.

1. A cat slunk across the roadway.

   _____

2. Suddenly she addressed the crowd.

   _____

3. She leaped overboard and saved the crying infant.

   _____

4. A frightening boom echoed.

   _____

5. Groaning softly, he climbed the stairs.

   _____

Step 2. Changing Word Order. Rewrite the expanded sentences you wrote in Step 1 above so that you shift the word group that tells *where, when,* or *how* to different sentence positions. Try for at least two new sentences for each. Look at the example. Use your own paper.

EXAMPLE

By five o'clock, the sky behind the mountaintops glowed brilliant reds, oranges, and purples.

By five o'clock behind the mountaintops, the sky glowed brilliant reds, oranges, and purples.

Word and Sentence Skills: Suggested Topics for Study

Punctuation Guidelines, pages 389–400
Commas, pages 302–313
Showing Possession, pages 367–374

● Writing a Process Essay

Assignment

Select some process that you can command, and explain it in a clear essay that takes into account the principles you have been exploring in this chapter.

Suggested Topics

You might find these possible topic ideas helpful as you consider various processes and how to approach them during your prewriting. More suggested topics appear on pages 156–157.

1. how to baby-sit
2. how pretzels are made
3. how to plan a party
4. how to groom a horse
5. how to take notes in Professor _____'s class
6. how to find a job
7. how to brighten a dull room
8. how your governor was elected
9. how a steam engine works
10. how to pick up a woman (man)
11. how to combat alcoholism
12. how to make money
13. how to reduce stress
14. how beer is made
15. how to wait on tables
16. how to surf
17. how to make tacos
18. how to draw cartoons
19. how to adopt a child
20. how to raise tropical fish

Prewriting: Making a List

Because completeness and sequence of steps are so important in a process paper, a helpful prewriting activity calls for making a list. Simply write down all the possible steps you can think of, steps required in the process you want to write about. Don't worry about whether you are repeating yourself or whether or not you have put in things that don't belong or have left out things that do belong. Just keep writing and letting thoughts develop. The point here is to get down on paper, before you attempt a draft, as much raw material as possible. And don't worry about spelling or other errors in mechanics. At this stage they are unimportant.

Once you have your list, look it over. If you've left lots of space between entries, you'll have room to add any steps or details you may have left out. You might want to rearrange some steps or to group some together logically. Little by little, the shape of your essay will suggest itself. Certain steps you'll describe in the first body paragraph because they fit together there sensibly. Other steps you will develop in the second body paragraph. Using your list and the changes you've made with it, you can then move on to your rough draft.

Look at the list below, prepared for an essay on growing roses.

```
                 Topic: planting a rose garden

 1. piece of earth 15' x 5'
 2. turn soil and rake it (tell them to watch out for rocks)
 3. have 8-10 different rose bushes (point about variety)
 4. treat soil with peat or compost or manure--lime too
 5. work soil to depth of 2'
 6. dig hole 1-1/2 times as big as root ball (watch out for bud and root
    joint: DEFINE!)
 7. cover roots with soil and water right away
 8. pine bark mulch keeps weeds away
 9. prevent diseases with early treatment for aphids and black spot
10. spray or dust weekly during growing season ·
11. feed every four weeks
12. stop feeding in mid-August
13. to protect plants against cold weather let rose flowers mature into
    hips
14. mulch base of plant heavily in fall
15. prune only in early spring--not fall
```
--Lee Bowen

Step 1. Understanding the List.   Discuss the answers to these questions about Lee Bowen's list. Or, write your responses on separate paper as your instructor suggests.

1.   The announced topic is "planting a rose garden," but all the points Lee Bowen has written on his list suggest a more expanded topic. How might you restate his topic so that it allows him to deal with most of the steps he states on his list? What thesis sentence might you write as a result of that topic? On the other hand, if the writer wanted to stay with his announced topic, "planting a rose garden," what steps would you suggest he leave out?

2.   Notice the little note the writer made for himself in item 2 on the list. How will the note help him expand details? What other messages has he written to himself?

3.   In item 6 the writer reminds himself to define "bud and root joint." Why does Lee Bowen want to define this term? How does his wish to define it suggest the

audience he wants to write for? What other words do you think he should define for that audience?

4. The items on the rough list suggest one possible grouping of steps into three categories: readying the soil, planting the bushes, caring for the new plants. If you were rewriting this list before you did your first draft, which points would you group in each of these categories? How could the grouping help you plan the body paragraphs of the essay?

Step 2. Prewriting: Making Your Own Rough List.   Select a topic you think you could develop into an essay that explains a process. Then, using Lee Bowen's list as an example, on separate paper prepare your own rough list of steps that the process suggests. List everything that comes to mind. Skip lines between items. Later, go back to add steps or take them away. You might want to group steps together in broad categories, as in question 4 in Step 1 above.

Student Samples: Drafting and Revising

Using your prewriting effort as a starting point, draft and revise an essay on process. Be sure to read the samples below and to refer to the section called Progress Reminders for Your Process Essay: A Checklist. Review pages 20–21 on drafting and revising.

Step 1. Examining Drafts.   Read these two drafts of "Picking Pears," and note the changes in the revision. Where do you think the writer has made substantial improvements? What further changes would you recommend? Answer the questions after you read.

DRAFT

                         Picking Pears

     When I wake up at four in the morning I know that today is the day
for picking pears at Kibbutz Ein Zurim, an Israeli commune on which I
am working this summer.
     I fumble around in the dark until I get to my closet. I snatch my
clothing from the hangers and then dress expectantly at my bed. I slide
open the front door and go to meet my companions to start the day's
work. In Israel everyone works equally. Both regular commune members
and volunteers like me plant the fields and harvest crops, even the
leaders work with us. As I pass the bungalows of other workers crickets
murmur their sounds. Two lizards chase each other while the sun makes
its way over the desert sky. As I get onto the old bus hooked up to a
tractor, its mustiness makes me cough. Around me my companions are
sitting on the hard wooden seats, resting weary heads on the window
sills in last minute efforts at sleep.

When we reach the fields everyone is fully awake. We get off the bus. Each of us receive a sturdy bucket with a steel hook. We also get a ladder and a small wooden square with a circle in it. Danny tells us in Hebrew which trees to pick. Renee repeats his instructions in English. I follow the group to the fifth row and directly against a tree I place my ladder so its legs hit the dirt sturdily. I climb up among the massive trees with my bucket and square. Pulling one of the leafy branches downward. I hang the bucket on it with the hook. With my left hand I grab another branch full of pears and pull it closer to me. Raising my right hand, I try to slip a pear through the hole in the wooden square. The pear doesn't fit; that means it is big enough for picking. I give this test to each pear. If it ripe enough, I grasp it by the bottom, lift it upward, and give it a sharp snap. If I do not do it this way, the pear might break at the bottom of the stem, and that would make the fruit unsalable. To avoid bruises further, I do not drop it into the bucket; instead, I place the pear down very carefully.

When my bucket fills up, I take it off the branch and get off the ladder. A few feet away I tenderly place the pears in a huge wooden crate. When I return to my ladder, I see that all the pears on my tree have been picked. I grasp the ladder on both sides, tilt it horizontal, lift it and lean it on my shoulder. There is another tree to pick and I dig the legs of my ladder into the dirt close to the truck. I do again what I did before, and everyone around me does likewise.

Working in groups helps us stand this job. We sing or talk to our friends. During our every two hours break we rest together on crates as we joke or gulp down drinks. I have a wonderful feeling of pride in this work, a feeling that comes from my playing a part in a large and important task.

REVISED DRAFT

Picking Pears

The day starts when I rise at four in the morning. Dawn has not yet broken over Kibbutz Ein Zurim. Still, the members of this Israeli commune are beginning their tasks for the day. Today, the picking of pears awaits me; inexperienced, I am both excited and worried about the job.

Preparing for it takes some time. I fumble in the darkness, finding my closet. The door creaks as I open it, and I grab my yellow T-shirt, my gray socks and slacks, and my blue sunhat. Sitting back on my bed, I dress expectantly. As I slide open the front door to go outside, the hall light stings my eyes. Then into the chill morning I stroll, ready to meet my companions and to start the day's work. I pass the bungalows of other workers as crickets murmur their sounds. Two lizards chase each other while the sun makes its way over the desert sky. As I hop onto the old bus hooked up to a tractor, its mustiness makes me cough. Around me my companions slump on the hard leather seats, resting weary heads on the window sills in last minute efforts at sleep. But the sudden, grinding sound of the tractor ends the morning's silence as we make our way down bumpy dirt roads to the pear field and our coming chores.

By the time we reach it, everyone is fully awake for pear picking. We leave the bus and each of us receives a sturdy plastic bucket with a steel hook on the handle, a steel or a wooden ladder, and a small wooden square with a circle cut out in the middle. Our leader Danny instructs the group in Hebrew on which pear trees to pick. "We are to pick the fifth row of pears and when we are finished to go on to the sixth," Renee repeats in English. I follow the group to the fifth row and directly against a tree I place my ladder so its legs hit the dirt sturdily. I climb up among the massive trees with my bucket and square. Pulling one of the leafy branches downward, I hang the bucket on it with the hook. With my left hand I grab another branch full of pears and pull it closer to me. Raising my right hand, I try to slip a pear through the hole in the wooden square. If the pear does not fit, that means it is big enough for picking. I give this test to each pear. If it is ripe enough, I grasp it by the bottom, lift it upward, and give it a sharp snap. Otherwise, the pear might break at the bottom of the stem, and that would make the fruit unsalable. To avoid further bruises, I do not drop it into the bucket; instead, I place the pear down very carefully.

When my bucket is filled with the pears I've picked, I remove it from the branch and step down the ladder. A few feet away I tenderly place the pears in a huge wooden crate. I note that someone will seal these crates, and the pears will find their way to supermarkets all over the world. When I return to my ladder, I see that my tree has no more ripe pears. I grasp the ladder on both sides, tilt it horizontally, lift it, and lean it on my shoulder. Not far away, another tree needs picking, and I dig the legs of my ladder into the dirt close to the trunk. Once again I climb up to repeat the procedure.

For Kibbutz life in Israel everyone works equally. Both regular commune members and volunteers like me plant the fields and harvest the crops. Even the leaders work with us, the sun beating down on all our backs together. This group effort helps us tolerate our job. We join in songs, or we talk to our neighbors on nearby ladders. At breaks, given every two hours, we rest together on crates as we joke, gulp down water, brush off the dust on our clothing. I have a wonderful feeling of pride in this work, a feeling that comes from my playing a part in a large and important task. Too often we look at the work we do as single efforts involving ourselves alone, but I am learning that when there is a strong spirit among people, it is easy to accomplish even the most unpleasant chores.

--Myra Grossman

1. How is the introduction in the revised draft an improvement over the introduction in the earlier draft?

2. What words and phrases appear in the revision that add concrete sensory detail to the essay? Where else might you recommend the use of color, sound, smell, action, or touch?

3. What sentences from the second paragraph in the early draft appear in the last paragraph of the revision? Do you approve of the change? Why or why not? What other changes do you like in the last paragraph of the revised draft?

4. How has the writer connected the body paragraphs? What details in paragraph 4 of the revision do not appear in the draft?

5. Is the process clear enough for you to understand? What might help you see it more clearly?

Step 2. Another Student Sample.   Read the essay below, and answer the questions after it.

Ironing for Food

I have never doubted the usefulness of an iron. It presses crisp pleats into my jeans and eliminates networks of tiny wrinkles in blouses I have jammed into my closet. Since coming to Penn State, however, I found that an iron is not only useful as a piece of laundry equipment but also as a fantastic cooking appliance for a dormitory room. University regulations prohibit the use of hot plates, ovens, or grills. So, when one of my cravings aroused me, I decided to experiment with my iron. Since that time I have become an expert at "iron cooking," my specialty being toasted cheese sandwiches.

When the urge for one of them strikes me, I convert my dorm room into a kitchen. I dig through the shoes and boxes at the bottom of my closet and resurrect my iron. Since I do not own a portable ironing board, I improvise. I drag my footlocker out from under my bed and place it in the center of the floor. My white bath towel serves as the cover. At the bathroom sink I fill the steam chamber of the iron with water. Examining the battered cord for exposed wires, I plug it into the outlet closest to my makeshift ironing board and turn the small black dial on the handle to the wool setting. Laying the iron down on the towel to heat, I gather ingredients for my sandwich. From our refrigerator I collect the cheese slices, bread, and pats of butter that my roommate and I smuggled out of Redifer Dining Hall. I grab a knife and a roll of aluminum foil out of my bolster cupboard and spread the supplies out on my desk.

Preliminary preparations over, I concoct my special toasted cheese sandwich. I select two slices of bread, and butter both sides of them lightly, careful not to tear holes in the bread with the knife. Melted cheese drips out of any holes in the finished sandwich and makes a gooey mess. Once I butter the bread, I tear off about one foot from the roll of foil and place it shiny side down on the top of my desk. On the foil I lay one slice of buttered bread, then two slices of cheese on it, topping these with the second piece of bread. Then, I wrap the sandwich in the foil. Crimping its edges tightly, I tear off another piece of foil and cover my sandwich with it. Secured between two shields of armor, my creation awaits the iron. I put the sandwich gently on my ironing board, and with one smooth motion I pick up the iron and touch it to the foil. Steam pours out and hisses angrily as I move the iron back and forth without pressure. (Too much pressure crushes the bread.) It takes only three minutes to grill one side; afterwards I remove the iron and wait for the steam to clear. With a washcloth potholder I flip the sandwich over and iron the other side. When the foil cools slightly, I peel it away, always burning my fingers despite my potholder. The aroma of melted cheese and warm bread pours into the room. Beneath the crisp toast, melted cheese peeks out. For me, heaven is seconds away.

Using my iron, I can prepare delicious sandwiches in fewer than ten minutes, and I can satisfy my late night cravings or can escape dining hall meals with my simple technique. But, more important, here in the midst of my college education where my teachers are cramming acres of information into my brain, I have learned a little something on my own to meet my needs at the moment. I do not expect to make a career of "iron cooking"; and I am sure that my knowledge and skill will have no long-range benefits for humanity. Still, learning takes place in unexpected ways. A professor's formal lectures, as important as they are, can never replace good old necessity as the best teacher.

—Stacy Kissinger

1. What process, according to the proposal sentences, does this essay intend to show?

2. Which words in the opening sentence of paragraph 2 help make a transition from paragraph 1? Which words in the opening sentence of paragraph 3 help connect it to paragraph 2?

3. Which details in the essay do you find most original and most clear? Find appeals to the sense of sight (color and action), sound, touch, and smell.

4. For what audience do you think the writer intends this process essay? How can you tell?

5. How does the conclusion serve as a fit ending for the essay? How does it relate to the proposal?

Collaboration: Getting Reader Response

In a "how-to" paper, you must be careful to include *all* the steps of the process. Team up with three other students and pass your papers down the line so that everyone has a chance to read the others' process paper. As you get each paper, note on a separate sheet where omitted instructions would make it difficult for you either to understand the process or to perform the task yourself. Such responses from other readers will help you revise your draft so that you explain the process fully.

Progress Reminders: A Checklist

As you prepare your list and do other prewriting, as you do your first and later drafts, and before you write your final copy, use this checklist so that you follow as many of the suggestions as possible. After you prepare your manuscript to hand in to your instructor, fill in the checklist and submit it with your theme.

1. Did I spend time considering the topic? Did I follow some prewriting activity that works well for me? (See pages 19–20.)   _____ _____

2. Did I make a list of the steps in the process and then change and regroup the steps in the list?   _____

3. Did I write a rough draft and any other needed drafts before making my final copy? Did I make changes in my rough drafts so that I expressed thoughts clearly and smoothly?   _____ _____

4. Did I write a proposal sentence that defines my topic clearly and that allows me to develop different aspects of it, one in each of my body paragraphs? (See pages 118–120.)   _____

5. Does my introduction provide a strong beginning for my essay? Does my conclusion close off my point successfully?   _____

6. Did I use transitions to tie paragraphs together?   _____

7. Did I use adequate detail? If I wrote from personal experience, did I use images of color, sound, action, smell, and touch? Or, did I use statistics, cases, quotations, or paraphrases as supporting detail?   _____ _____

8. Did I experiment with sentence structure? Did I try for one or two sentences with changed word order like those explained in this chapter? (See pages 164–166.)   _____ _____

9. Did I define my audience as clearly and as precisely as I could? The audience I intend this essay for is

_____

10. Did I try to use words from the new vocabulary on page 152?   _____

11. Did I take care to include all the steps my audience needs to understand the process? Did I leave out any unnecessary steps? Did I pay special attention to the sequence of steps, making sure that I discussed them in the right order?   _____ _____

12. After making changes in my drafts for clarity and smoothness, did I check my draft over by proofreading for my usual mistakes?   _____

13. Did I write a strong concluding paragraph?

14. Did I write an effective title?   _____

15. Did I read the sample themes on pages 169–173 to help me see how other students explained processes clearly?   _____

● The Professionals Speak

Step 1. Reading a "How-to" Essay. Among the more popular articles currently found in magazines and journals are the "how-to" pieces, essays by professionals who tell you how to accomplish everything from improving your lifestyle to flattening your stomach. Read the essay below from *Blair & Ketchum's Country Journal*. In this piece, a specialist in how to grow and care for plants explains the steps in making a terrarium—a closed, see-through container in which small plants are grown. How does the selection reflect some of the principles you've been exploring in this chapter? Answer the questions after you read.

SOME WORDS TO KNOW BEFORE YOU READ

devotee—an enthusiast; a supporter

lichens—small plants made up of an alga and a fungus

transparent—clear enough to see through

brandy snifter—pear-shaped goblet

tamper—something that packs down materials

drainage—a system for water to run off through

waterlogging—excessively filling up with water

sterilized—made free from germs

topography—the form and features of a place

romantische Landschaft—German for *romantic landscape*

ecosystem—a self-contained environment functioning in nature

How to Make a Terrarium

If you need an excuse for a walk in the woods, make a terrarium. Gathering terrarium ingredients sharpens one's appreciation of the rich variety of life at boot level. Terrarium makers see the world in fine. No detail escapes their attention. A confirmed devotee could probably wander in a redwood grove with gaze fixed on the ground—looking for moss of just the right texture, tiny seedling trees, interesting bark chips. After I made my first terrarium, I found myself gathering tiny plants, lichens, and pebbles on every walk—and mentally collecting when I was not walking our own land.

Woodland plants are perfect for the terrarium. Most things that grow on the forest floor thrive in cool, moist, partly shady situations, which are easy to provide under glass. Many house plants adapt equally well to life in a terrarium. You can grow exotics like the Venus flytrap, which requires warmth and moisture and gets along on soil nutrients when no flies happen by.

Whether you gather the makings of your miniature landscape on the trail, in a greenhouse, or from among your houseplants, the procedure for assembling the terrarium is the same. First, you need a container. Any kind of transparent, waterproof, easily covered container may be used to house a terrarium. Some of the more popular enclosures for these self-contained gardens include brandy snifters, apothecary jars, fish bowls, rectangular aquarium cases, and large glass carboys. Wine jugs, large test tubes, butter jars, mason jars, gallon mayonnaise jars (from restaurants), and even baby-food jars may also be used. Jean Hersey, the authority on wildflowers, once constructed a terrarium in the globe of a 150-watt light bulb with the threaded end broken off.

Wide-mouthed containers are easiest to plant by hand; those with narrow necks are tricky but by no means impossible. You need a few tools—a planter made of a length of wire coat hanger straightened out, with a loop on one end to hold the plant; a tamper, which could be a dowel stuck into a cork, or whatever you can improvise from materials at hand; a digger, a long-handled spoon, or any kind of long, thin poker capable of making a hole in loose soil. A long-handled tweezers is also useful. Use a rolled-up newspaper as a funnel to direct the soil to the bottom of the jug.

Begin by putting down a base composed of several layers, as follows, remembering that each layer serves a purpose. First, put down a mat of moss to absorb moisture and form an attractive lining. Then pour a layer of sand or fine gravel over the moss to promote drainage and prevent waterlogging. Next scatter a handful of charcoal pieces over the gravel to prevent souring of the soil.

Now add the final layer—soil. Bagged sterilized soil is fine, but if you want to mix your own, aim for the following proportions.

2 parts topsoil
1 part sand
1 part leafmold or compost

Put in a thin layer, just covering the charcoal. Then set the plants in place and firm the remainder of the soil around their roots. Much of this soil will later settle lower around the roots.

Arranging the topography of the terrarium is a matter of taste. You might keep in mind that a variety of leaf textures is usually pleasing, and that plants of different heights and shapes—pyramidal, tall and spiky, short and shrubby, trailing—make the scenery interesting. If your container is large enough you can even make a small hill or a path within its bounded wildness. Color may be provided by including partridge berries, mushrooms, lichens, and stones. No well-made terrarium needs a plastic deer or china bird, but the woods are full of props that can add local color to your small scene: mossy twigs, weathered pieces of wood, scraps of textured bark, squirrel-gnawed nutshells. A weird craggy stone may be just the boulder you need for a classic gothic scene—a *romantische Landschaft* in miniature.

The pleasure of terrarium building, though, has more to do with the freedom to improvise, collect, seed, play with your materials, arrange a world as *you* would have it, than with conformity to a form. Do with it what you wish. Arrange and rearrange the plants until you are happy with the way they look.

When all the plants are in place, water the soil lightly, using less water than you think you'll need. You can always add more but you can't remove it. Overwatering encourages rot, mold, and fungus.

Covering the terrarium makes it a self-contained system, with its own weather: water vapor condenses on the walls and returns to the soil. Use the cover provided with the vessel or simply place a circle of glass over the top. (Plastic wrap is a more temporary but nonetheless practical cover.) Since each terrarium is a different ecosystem with its own water balance, it is impossible to formulate definite schedules for watering. Observation is the key. If the glass is misty, or if you notice mold anywhere within it, or water pooling on the bottom, the terrarium needs to be ventilated. Uncover it for about a day. Some people ventilate their terrariums routinely once a week.

When should you add water? Seldom, if at all. If the terrarium is too dry, the soil will be lighter in color and the whole thing will feel lighter than normal when you pick it up. Use an eye dropper to add water—you'll be less likely to overwater.

Terrarium plants need some light, but direct sun will cook them. Indirect light on a table or light from a north window should suit most plant populations. If leaves turn brown, the terrarium is probably too hot. Try putting it in a cooler place.

Those of us accustomed to fertilizing houseplants may tend to include the terrarium in that routine, but it is best to keep terrarium soil on the lean side, lest the plants outgrow the container. Choice of plants influences the length of their stay too, of course. Our first house—a mid-nineteenth-century Philadelphia weaver's cottage—is now guarded by a pine that spent its first two years in a terrarium. When its top hit the cover we planted it in front of the loom shed. Now, twenty years later, it towers over the house. The loom shed is gone, but pine needles fall around its foundation. Everything lasts, we think as we drive by—just in a different form, sometimes.

—Nancy Bubel

1. What is Bubel's purpose in writing the essay? Why do you think that she does not state the purpose in a proposal (or a thesis) sentence?

2. Make a list of the general steps to follow in making a terrarium.

3. What details does the writer provide to help readers understand the process? Which words in paragraph 8 paint especially clear pictures that rely on sensory detail?

4. What audience do you think Bubel is aiming for? How do her language and sentence structure serve that audience?

5. What order does the writer use in explaining the process? What transitions are used to connect ideas within paragraphs and to connect one paragraph with another?

6. How does the introduction serve to involve the reader? In what way does the last sentence in the closing paragraph establish a new frame of reference?

Step 2. An Essay on Making a Speech.   Read this essay by George Plimpton about steps to take in improving your speech-making skills.

SOME WORDS TO KNOW BEFORE YOU READ

uninitiated—those who have never tried a particular activity

convulses—shakes violently and uncontrollably

exhortation—a forceful urging or warning

ad-lib—improvise

brevity—shortness of duration

dais—a raised platform

notion—idea; concept

How to Make a Speech

One of life's terrors for the uninitiated is to be asked to make a speech.

"Why me?" will probably be your first reaction. "I don't have anything to say." It should be reassuring (though it rarely is) that since you were asked, somebody must think you do. The fact is that each one of us has a store of material which should be of interest to others. There is no reason why it should not be adapted to a speech.

Scary as it is, it's important for anyone to be able to speak in front of others, whether twenty around a conference table or a hall filled with a thousand faces.

Being able to speak can mean better grades in any class. It can mean talking the town council out of increasing your property taxes. It can mean talking top management into buying your plan.

You were probably asked to speak in the first place in the hope that you would be able to articulate a topic that you know something about. Still, it helps to find out about your audience first. Who are they? Why are they there? What are they interested in? How much do they already know about your subject? One kind of talk would be appropriate for the Women's Club of Columbus, Ohio, and quite another for the guests at the Vince Lombardi dinner.

Here is where you must do your homework.

The more you sweat in advance, the less you'll have to sweat once you appear on stage. Research your topic thoroughly. Check the library for facts, quotes, books and timely magazine and newspaper articles on your subject. Get in touch with experts. Write to them, make phone calls, get interviews to help round out your material.

In short, gather—and learn— far more than you'll ever use. You can't imagine how much confidence that knowledge will inspire.

Now start organizing and writing. Most authorities suggest that a good speech breaks down into three basic parts—an introduction, the body of the speech, and the summation.

Introduction: An audience makes up its mind very quickly. Once the mood of an audience is set, it is difficult to change it, which is why introductions are important. If the speech is to be lighthearted in tone, the speaker can start off by telling a good-natured story about the subject or himself.

But be careful of jokes, especially the shaggy-dog variety. For some reason, the joke that convulses guests in a living room tends to suffer as it emerges through the amplifying system into a public gathering place.

Main body: There are four main intents in the body of the well-made speech. These are (1) to entertain, which is probably the hardest; (2) to instruct, which is the easiest, if the speaker has done the research and knows the subject; (3) to persuade, which one does at a sales presentation, a political rally, or a town meeting; and finally, (4) to inspire, which is what the speaker emphasizes at a sales meeting, in a sermon, or at a pep rally. (Hurry-Up Yost, the onetime Michigan football coach, gave such an inspiration-filled halftime talk that he got carried away and at the final exhortation led his team on the run through the wrong locker room door into the swimming pool.)

Summation: This is where you should "ask for the order." An ending should probably incorporate a sentence or two which sounds like an ending—a short summary of the main points of the speech, perhaps, or the repeat of a phrase that most embodies what the speaker has hoped to convey. It is valuable to think of the last sentence or two as something which might produce applause. Phrases which are perfectly appropriate to signal this are "In closing . . . " or "I have one last thing to say . . ."

Once done—fully written, or the main points set down on 3" x 5" index cards—the next problem is the actual presentation of the speech. Ideally, a speech should not be read. At least it should never appear or sound as if you are reading it. An audience is dismayed to see a speaker peering down at a thick sheaf of papers on the lectern, wetting his thumb to turn to the next page.

The best speakers are those who make their words sound spontaneous even if memorized. I've found it's best to learn a speech point by point, not word for word. Careful preparation and a great deal of practicing are required to make it come together smoothly and easily. Mark Twain once said, "It takes three weeks to prepare a good ad-lib speech."

Don't be fooled when you rehearse. It takes longer to deliver a speech than to read it. Most speakers peg along at about 100 words a minute.

A sensible plan, if you have been asked to speak to an exact limit, is to talk your speech into a mirror, and stop at your allotted time; then cut the speech accordingly. The more familiar you become with your speech, the more confidently you can deliver it.

As anyone who listens to speeches knows, brevity is an asset. Twenty minutes are ideal. An hour is the limit an audience can listen comfortably.

In mentioning brevity, it is worth mentioning that the shortest inaugural address was George Washington's—just 135 words. The longest was William Henry Harrison's in 1841. He delivered a two-hour 9,000-word speech into the teeth of a freezing northeast wind. He came down with a cold the following day, and a month later he died of pneumonia.

Consult a dictionary for proper meanings and pronunciations. Your audience won't know if you're a bad speller, but they will know if you use or pronounce a word improperly. In my first remarks on the dais, I used to thank people for their "fulsome introduction," until I discovered to my dismay that "fulsome" means *offensive* and *insincere*.

It helps one's nerves to pick out three or four people in the audience—preferably in different sectors so that the speaker is apparently giving his attention to the entire room—on whom to focus. Pick out people who seem to be having a good time.

A question period at the end of a speech is a good notion. One would not ask questions following a tribute to the company treasurer on his retirement, say, but a technical talk or an informative speech can be enlivened with a question period.

The larger the crowd, the easier it is to speak, because the response is multiplied and increased. Most people do not believe this. They peek out from behind the curtain and if the auditorium is filled to the rafters they begin to moan softly in the back of their throats.

Very few speakers escape the so-called "butterflies." There does not seem to be any cure for them, except to realize that they are beneficial rather than harmful, and never fatal. The tension usually means that the speaker, being keyed up, will do a better job. Edward R. Murrow called stage fright "the sweat of perfection." Mark Twain once comforted a fright-frozen friend about to speak: "Just remember they don't expect much." My own feeling is that with thought, preparation and faith in your ideas, *you* can go out there and expect a pleasant surprise.

And what a sensation it is—to hear applause. Invariably after it dies away, the speaker searches out the program chairman—just to make it known that he's available for next month's meeting.

—*George Plimpton*

1. Is the process explained thoroughly and clearly? Are any steps missing? Explain your answer.

2. In what kind of order does the author arrange the steps in making a speech?

3. Who is the audience, and how do you know?

4. What reasons does Plimpton give for the need for an introduction and a summation?

5. How does the author incorporate humor in this essay?

6. What does Plimpton suggest about most first-time speakers in the last paragraph?

CHAPTER

Comparison and Contrast

•

INTRODUCTION TO COMPARISON AND CONTRAST

One of the best ways we have to analyze, understand, and evaluate is through
comparison and contrast. It is second nature for us to compare related experiences,
ideas, and issues in order to see points of resemblance and difference. In writing,
such a process adds force to your presentation; the reader comes to understand the
value of your experiences as you yourself weave together the strands of comparison or contrast.

A good way to begin is to choose two objects that may seem alike and to show
how they are different or to choose two things that appear very different but are
actually similar. For example, you could illustrate how swimming in a pool and
swimming in a lake or ocean are very different experiences, though one might

think they are similar. Or you could write about how your house is very much like a zoo, though these appear to be quite different places. This kind of comparison makes for an interesting paper.

Strictly speaking, *compare* means "show likenesses" and *contrast* means "show differences," but the meanings do overlap. Unless your instructor tells you otherwise, you should feel comfortable dealing with both similarities and opposites. Many writers decide to treat both likenesses and differences in their essays; others choose to illustrate either likenesses or differences; both of these options are acceptable and are open to you when you write your comparison-contrast essay.

In this chapter, you will examine a number of strategies for making thoughtful comparisons in your essays. You will learn several ways to organize information in a comparison-contrast essay. A number of transitions can help show relations between similar and different ideas, and you will explore them here too. As usual, many student examples will help you see how others before you have responded to the chapter assignment

● Vocabulary

Step 1. Words for Opposite Qualities. The words in each numbered set below are opposites and may be useful in contrasting subjects. In the blanks write definitions for the opposite—or nearly opposite—words in each set. Use a dictionary for assistance.

1. *a.* dexterous   _____   *b.* awkward   _____
2. *a.* genteel   _____   *b.* boorish   _____
3. *a.* rotund   _____   *b.* slender   _____
4. *a.* conventional _____   *b.* rebellious   _____
5. *a.* superficial _____   *b.* sincere   _____

Step 2. Applying Meanings. From the words above select one to describe a person who

1. is rude_____
2. challenges rules _____
3. does things in accepted ways _____
4. is honest and truthful _____
5. is gracefully thin _____
6. is clumsy _____

7. is not genuine _____
8. has a plump shape _____
9. is mannerly _____
10. is skillful in the use of body or mind
    _____

Step 3. Words for Contrasting Moods.   Check the definitions of these words to describe moods. Write definitions that you understand in the blank spaces (see Appendix A).

"UP" MOODS   "DOWN" MOODS

1. elated   _____   6. irate   _____

2. confident   _____   7. listless   _____

3. affectionate _____   8. anxious   _____

4. serene   _____   9. egotistic   _____

5. energetic   _____   10. despondent _____

Step 4. Listening In on Moods.   Each statement made below identifies a mood named in Step 3. Identify the mood that the person who speaks seems to be experiencing.

_____   1. "I feel that I can do the job right."

_____   2. "I'm wide awake and ready for a day of fun and activity."

_____   3. "Let me kiss you again. I love to hold you."

_____   4. "If I get my hands on him, I'll kill him. I'll tear him limb from limb."

_____   5. "I'm so worried about everything, especially the test tomorrow."

_____   6. "I'm too worn out to do anything."

_____   7. "I am the smartest and most thoughtful person in this class."

_____   8. "I feel so calm and peaceful."

_____   9. "I'm delighted at being alive. What a beautiful, wonderful, sunny day!"

_____   10. "I never felt so rotten in all my life."

● Building Composition Skills

Finding the Topic

Step 1. Talking It Over.   Using the suggestions below, speak for a minute or two about two items or ideas that are similar to or different from each other. Show how your specific experiences illustrate your point as Thomas Baim does in his talk below.

1. two jobs you had (or have)
2. high school cafeterias versus college cafeterias
3. two different boyfriends (girlfriends)
4. how water skiing and snow skiing compare
5. how your weekdays and weekends are different
6. two very different restaurants
7. two cars you have had
8. a teacher who lectures as opposed to a teacher who guides class discussion
9. a book and the film made from that book: likenesses and differences
10. your son (daughter) at one age compared with the same child at another age

To me lectures are worthless; group discussions make much better and more interesting class sessions. Mr. Goldman, my junior history teacher at Park Lane High, lectured to us all the time. Even though he had a lively booming voice and a good knowledge of his subject, after thirty minutes, feet would shuffle on the floor, pencils would drop, students would whisper and yawn as the teacher turned his back to write on the board. I loved history, but I found myself staring out the window at the sky or the clouds. But Mr. Rudnicki, my psychology teacher here at State, never lectures. Sure, he contributes information to our discussions—sometimes he talks for ten minutes straight—but lots of other people talk as well. It's much more exciting to hear different voices and different opinions. We all sit around with our chairs in a circle and usually more than half the class talks at each session. I know it's much harder to learn in this kind of class because you never really know what's "right" since there is often no definite information. But I find I'm always thinking about what went on in my psych class, and I can't wait to forget what I scribbled in my notebook during a lecture!

—*Thomas Baim*

Figures of Speech

One way to improve your written expression is to make comparisons so that the reader sees clearly some picture you are describing. Notice how the picture in Column I below takes on new life in Column II by means of a comparison.

I	II
Her blue eyes sparkled.	Her eyes sparkled *like small blue circles of ice*.

By using the word *like* (or, often, *as*) in II above, the writer compares *eyes* to *small blue circles of ice.* Such a comparison, using *like* or *as*, is called a *simile.*

A *metaphor* is a comparison that leaves out the comparing word *like* or *as:*

Her eyes were *small blue circles of ice.*

This kind of comparison is often very forceful because it shows that the object is so much like the thing to which it is being compared that it almost becomes that thing. Look again at the difference.

Her eyes were *like small blue circles of ice.*	Her eyes *were small blue circles of ice.*
Here, a woman's eyes are compared to circles of ice, and there are two distinct features of the comparison, *eyes* and *blue circles of ice.*	Here, the woman's eyes are said to *be* those *blue circles of ice.* It is as if the eyes and the icy blue circles were one and the same; the eyes take on all the qualities of the ice.

Sometimes, to add liveliness, a writer can give some nonhuman object living qualities. The comparison between a nonhuman object and a living thing is called *personification:*

The hot day dragged its weary feet into the evening.

In this sentence, the *day,* a nonhuman object, is given the qualities of a person who is tired: the words *dragged its weary feet* express the human quality.

Step 1. Reading Lively Comparisons. Read aloud these comparisons by professional writers. Explain the meaning of each one. Which sentence lets you see most clearly what the writer had in mind? Which comparison is most original?

1. If dreams die, life is a broken-winged bird that cannot fly.
    —*Langston Hughes*
2. A sickly light, like yellow tinfoil, was slanting over the high walls into the jail yard.
    —*George Orwell*
3. The town hung like a bird's nest in the cliff, looking into the box canyon below, and beyond into the wide valley we call Cow Canyon, facing an ocean of clear air.
    —*Willa Cather*
4. His face was white as pie-dough and his arms were lank and white as peeled sticks.
    —*Robert Smith*

5. The mysterious East faced me, perfumed like a flower, silent like death, dark like a grave.

—Joseph Conrad

Step 2. Comparisons of Your Own.

Select word groups below and, on separate paper, write sentences that make a comparison in a vivid picture. Strive for originality, humor, beauty, clarity. Use any of the three types of comparisons you have learned so far—simile, metaphor, personification.

EXAMPLE

rain

The rain hissed on the hot cabin roof, then slithered down the window in streams like transparent snakes.

—Gerald Hull

1. wheat fields
2. cafeteria
3. a friend's smile
4. clouds
5. a skyscraper
6. a garden
7. a street after the rain
8. an alleyway
9. crowds
10. an empty beach

Step 3. Metaphors for Abstract Words.

Try to explain your view of some hard-to-define emotion, idea, or concept in a metaphor rich in sensory detail. Select a word such as *hope, love, fear, power, war, hate, hunger, life, sorrow, joy, death,* or any other abstract term. Look at the student samples below. Use your own paper.

Life is a rosebush growing in my garden, full of thorns but fragrant and lovely.
—Alayne Finkelstein

Fear is sitting in a creaking dentist's chair and seeing only the top of Dr. Rifkin's bald head as his trembling hand tries to zero in on a cavity.
—Janet Hunter

Life is an elusive, black fly buzzing through cool air, slipping past the blue-eyed youngster stalking him with a fly swatter.
—Terry Sanders

Step 4. Avoiding Trite Comparisons.

When a comparison appears too frequently in language, it loses its originality. Any statement or expression that is overused is called *trite* or *hackneyed*. Such expressions appear numbered from 1 to 9 below. For each one, rewrite the comparison to strengthen it. Use separate paper.

EXAMPLE

quiet as a mouse

quiet as a school yard early on Sunday morning

1. red as a beet
2. white as a ghost *or* white as a sheet
3. fresh as a daisy
4. so hungry I could eat a horse
5. wise as an owl

6. different as night and day
7. busy as a bee
8. sweet as sugar
9. pretty as a picture

Transitions

As you may recall, certain words help one idea in a paragraph flow smoothly into the next idea. The *transition* words below, cementing together ideas so that the thoughts are related clearly, show relationships you might want to indicate in your paragraph.

TRANSITION WORDS THAT ADD ONE THOUGHT TO ANOTHER		TRANSITION WORDS TO COMPARE IDEAS (TO SHOW LIKENESSES)
in addition	furthermore	in the same way
moreover	likewise	similarly
and	nor	likewise
and then	further	resembling
besides	next	alike
again	last	like
too	also	

TRANSITION WORDS TO CONTRAST IDEAS OR TO ADMIT A POINT (TO SHOW DIFFERENCES)

but	although	dissimilar
still	on the other hand	unlike
however	in contrast	differ(s) from
nevertheless	otherwise	difference
on the contrary	conversely	different
after all	while this may be true	
notwithstanding	yet	
even though	granted	
though	in spite of	

TRANSITION WORDS TO SHOW THAT ONE IDEA RESULTS FROM ANOTHER

as a result	accordingly
thus	therefore
because	consequently
since	then
hence	

Step 1. Transitions to Show Relationships. In this paragraph, fill in each blank with a transition word that will help move one idea smoothly into the next. The information at the right tells what kinds of transition words you need. Be sure that the word you select makes sense in the blank.

The True Musician

_____ Plato believed that music played a strong part in a man's education, he did not ignore other areas of learning. Music, through rhythm [contrast]

and harmony, could bring grace to the soul _____ a man educated in [add]

music could develop a true sense of judgment; _thus_ he would be able [result]

to recognize quality in art and nature and could respond with praise for good

things. _____ a man who knew music could, without having to think [compare]

too long, give blame to any bad artistic works. __But__ any man who [contrast]

devoted his life only to music risked the chance of becoming too softened and

soothed. _____ such a man would be a feeble warrior and of little use [result]

to the Greeks. Someone who practiced gymnastics, _however_, could fill [contrast]

himself with pride and could become twice the man that he was. _____ [compare]

he could develop courage for battle. _____ athletics made an essential [admit point]

part of the educated man, Plato also knew that too much focus on physical

training could make a man excessively violent and fierce. _____ he [add]

might come to hate philosophy and the art of persuasion in preference to

battle. _____ such a man would live in ignorance and would not be [compare]

civilized. _____ Plato showed that the man who learned music and [result]

athletics in good balance was best; "He who mingles music with gymnastics

in the fairest proportions . . . may be rightly called the true musician. . . . "

TRANSITION WORDS THAT SUMMARIZE

therefore	consequently
in conclusion	thus

finally	to sum up
as a result	accordingly
in short	in brief
as I have [shown]	in other words
	[said] all in all
	[stated]

TRANSITION WORDS THAT EMPHASIZE

surely	indeed
certainly	truly
to be sure	in fact
undoubtedly	without a doubt

TRANSITION WORDS THAT TELL THAT AN EXAMPLE WILL FOLLOW

for example	specifically
for instance	as an illustration
as proof	to illustrate

Step 2. Example, Summary, Emphasis: Transitions.   From the three lists of transition words, select one word that will fit in the blank as a good transition. The words at the right tell the kinds of transition words you need.

1. Environmental pollution has become a great concern in recent years. _____, many people are now realizing the importance of cleaning up the air and water.   [emphasis]

2. Recently many popular magazines have addressed the topic of nuclear war. _____, it is no longer an issue people are evading.   [summary]

3. _____, the desire to be better educated is represented in the increase in community college enrollments.   [example]

4. I try a different kind of community service each year. _____, last summer I read books to blind children.   [example]

5. He failed his driving test three times. _____, he could not use the family car all summer long.   [summary]

6. _____, there are many different ways to interpret a painting.   [emphasis]

    _____, lowering the thermostat drops oil consumption remarkably.   [example]

7. _____, she became even more bitter as the evening went on.   [emphasis]

8. He watched a total of six hours of television _____.   [summary]

Step 3. Checking More Transitions. Read "The Two Willies," pages 192–193. Circle the transition words that add, compare, contrast, show result, summarize, or indicate example.

Expanding Quotation Sentences

A sentence in which you tell the exact words someone is saying adds life to a paragraph. Often you can expand a quotation sentence by using sensory language in order to paint a vivid picture of the speaker or the circumstances under which the speaking is done. By adding action words and appeals to color, smell, touch, or sound, you can create a full and satisfying image for your reader.

HOW TO BUILD A QUOTATION SENTENCE

1. Start with a lively, realistic quotation:

   "You took that turn too fast, son."

2. Tell who talks:

   "You took that turn too fast, son," the trooper drawled.

3. Tell how, when, or where the words were spoken:

   "You took that turn too fast, son," the trooper drawled softly.
   "You took that turn too fast, son," the trooper drawled yesterday at dusk.

4. Add a detail to describe some action or movement:

   Leaning against the door of my old Ford, the trooper drawled softly, "You took that turn too fast, son."

5. Describe the speaker's face. Add a detail of color or touch or sound.

   His lips curled in a tight smile, the trooper leaned against the door of my old blue Ford and drawled softly, "You took that turn too fast, son."

   Hint
   Review the correct punctuation of quotations on pages 400–403.

Step 1. Expanding Quotation Sentences. Expand each of these quotations by adding details in several steps like those described above. Use separate paper.

1. "Have a good time."

2. "Close the door because it's freezing in here."

3. "I just don't care anymore!"

4. "I'll meet you for lunch at noon."

5. "We're never on time for anything."

6. "What do you mean by that?"

7. "Call your son immediately!"

8. "I'm going to miss you."

Comparison and Contrast: Three Essay Patterns

An important method of paragraph and essay development involves comparison and contrast. *Comparison* means showing how things are alike, and *contrast* means showing how things are different. If you are asked to *compare* two things, you usually need to *contrast* them as well. The patterns below will help you strengthen your comparison-contrast essay.

LIKENESSES OR DIFFERENCES: THE BLOCK METHOD

In this kind of essay, first you discuss one of the two subjects, then you discuss the other. You "block out" each feature of the topic for discussion in its own body paragraphs. After you treat one feature, then you treat the next feature.

You can single out one basic way in which the two objects are alike or different in order to limit your topic effectively. For example, you might decide to compare two people at work by discussing the way they do their jobs. The introductory paragraph would contain your thesis, telling the reader what your essay will be about. The first body paragraphs of the essay would show something about one person's approach to work; the following body paragraphs would show something about the other person's approach. In the concluding paragraph, you would briefly summarize the topic and give a dominant impression about the similarities and (or) differences in the two workers' approaches to their jobs.

However, instead of deciding on one basic way by which to compare the two things, you can choose to discuss a *few* points or ideas about the first object in the first body paragraphs; then you can discuss a *few* points or ideas about the second in the following paragraphs. Here you do not use a single focus of comparison. For example, in an essay comparing running and swimming as exercises for today's busy, health-conscious people, you might want to discuss these points:

1. the equipment necessary

2. the physical benefits

3. the mental benefits

First, you would discuss all those ideas in regard to *one* exercise; then you would discuss the same points in regard to the other exercise. The number of body paragraphs you need would depend on how fully you developed each of the points for each of the activities.

Some Hints about Block Comparisons

If you decide on a basic focus of comparison:

1. A topic sentence for each body paragraph (see pages 113–115) will help you introduce the basic difference for each object.
2. You might wish to illustrate your point with *a specific instance* about one feature of the topic and *a specific instance* about the other. Drawn from your own experience, each instance would be a dramatic moment expanded by means of sensory language.
3. If you want to use more than one instance to illustrate each part of your point, you can use sensory language as well. True, you will not be able to go into great detail for each instance, but you need to make the details as clear as possible.
4. You might wish to combine hints 2 and 3: state briefly several instances that illustrate your point about the first feature of the topic, then focus on the dramatic moment that illustrates your point about the second feature of the topic.

If you decide to discuss a few points about each object:

1. Each body paragraph's topic sentence can help you introduce appropriate features of the topic.
2. You will not be able to go into great detail for each of the points. However, make sure that you can support each point with some kind of illustration.
3. You risk writing a dull paragraph because each point is usually stated twice, once for each object. Lively illustrations and varied vocabulary can help overcome dullness.

Step 1. A Student's Theme. Read the student sample below. Answer the questions after the paragraph.

The Two Willies

Only five years old, my son Willie tickles the family with opposite sides to his behavior. In some instances he is very shy and he will not utter a word. But at other times he is a noisy, mischievous little boy.

Willie's quiet, shy side usually shows when he is with strangers. Last month I had to drag him up the steps at Presbyterian Nursery School for his first day in class. Willie clutched at my leg in silent terror as we stood at the doorway to his room. Two little boys sat at a table near the window and played with green clay as they giggled to each other. Nearby a boy and girl dressed and undressed two rag dolls. "Well, so this is Willie," said his teacher, Miss Natalie, with a bright smile. "Come, let's say hello to the rest of the class." But she had to pry his fingers one by one off my skirt as he stared without a sound. When Miss Natalie led Willie from child to child, saying his name, Willie never breathed a word. Though his teacher says that he is coming along quite well now, he is still the quietest boy in the class.

Yet, when I watch Willie's behavior at home, I can hardly believe that he is ever quiet. Just let him loose in the backyard of our house and he turns into a wild man! Yesterday, a warm fall afternoon, he hung by his ankles from a limb of our elm as my heart pounded. Calling like a monkey and beating his chest, he swung back and forth. Leaping down, he raced to the gray wooden fence and barked through it at my neighbor's German shepherd, who howled and rattled his pen. Then like a squirrel Willie dug a dozen holes in the lawn and buried whatever he could find, bottle caps, pieces of glass, leaves, cigarette butts, broken twigs. He's never quiet or shy! He chased flies, snorting through his nose. Off key he sang the Sesame Street song as he poked a pink worm with a rock. When Charlotte, my next-door neighbor's four-year old came to play, Willie screeched at her like a plane about to crash and pushed her to the grass. She cried miserably, but Willie showed no mercy. I had to yell at him a half dozen times to behave himself and calm down, but he ignored me completely.

Willie's loud, rebellious side is so different from his timid behavior with strangers. Sometimes I wonder how one person can act so differently at different times. Since Willie is my first child, I'm still getting used to the mysterious ways of children. I worry about even the silliest things because I want to be sure my son grows up to be a stable, happy person, and I know that childhood experiences and behavior can influence the life of the adult. Fortunately, my psychology teacher assures me that my son is perfectly normal for his age, even though he is not at all easy to understand.

—*Mollie Boone*

1. What is the basic focus to show the different qualities of Mollie Boone's son Willie?
2. What two moments does she use to illustrate her point?
3. Which, in your opinion, are the liveliest images of action? What details name sounds? Where is color used effectively?
4. Read the topic sentence in each of the two body paragraphs. How do they connect with the proposal in the introduction?

Step 2. Another Comparison-Contrast Essay. Read the selection below. How does the writer use comparison and contrast strategies? Answer the questions when you finish reading the essay.

In the Swim

The jogging craze is sweeping the country. In fancy jogging suits or in simple jeans and T-shirts, men and women everywhere jog to build stamina, tone muscles, take off unwanted pounds, strengthen the heart, and just to feel good. Yet jogging is probably the worst form of self-torture a person can inflict upon the body. Swimming, on the other hand, provides physical and mental well-being without the unnecessary hazards of running.

Although running is popular for its improvement of muscle strength and endurance, there are many negative points to consider. First, running concentrates on the lower body, helping people develop strong leg muscles but ignoring the upper body, our arms and chests, the parts important for what we do most. Another disadvantage is that runners frequently strain muscles and pull ligaments in their legs, which are painful and can keep a person off his or her feet for days. Also, running on hard surfaces like cement and asphalt has devastating effects on the knees, ankles, and back. For people recovering from illness, running is simply too vigorous an activity. Those requiring exercise after a heart attack, stroke, or surgery are in no shape to start running—it is just too strenuous. Running also causes breath to grow short quickly, which could bring on an asthma attack for people who suffer from this illness. Finally, despite some of its other benefits, running is a much more intense, straining exercise than swimming. Feet pound on the pavement, jarring all the internal organs. One could hardly call running a relaxing exercise.

Swimming, on the other hand, puts much less strain on the body, while still improving fitness. Swimming—like running—improves muscle strength, muscular endurance, stamina, balance, digestion, and sleep and aids in weight loss. Yet research shows that swimming increases flexibility much more than running does. In addition, swimming improves upper body strength as well as lower body strength, and suspension of the body in the water supports the back. The even strokes of the arms gliding over the water's smooth surface eliminate the intense physical jarring that running causes. Swimming is also the best exercise for building stamina among the ill or recovering. Warm water improves circulation and relaxation, and cool water reduces swelling and decreases the pain of strains and bruises. Many doctors say that swimming is an ideal exercise for pregnant women. Finally, another important benefit of swimming is its proven effect on mental relaxation. One researcher showed that the water and the rhythmical breathing and movement of swimming are extremely soothing and help people relax easily. The water muffles sound, producing a stillness, a calm, with no distractions, as the body is suspended. The water also cools body temperature, which is in itself relaxing. Thus a person is free to allow the mind to wander instead of having to focus complete attention on exercise.

All of this positive information about swimming may seem heaven-sent to anyone who adds him or herself to the list of "I-hate-to-run" people. With all the facts we now have about the direct correlation between regular exercise and the prevention of heart diseases and cancer, more and more people are exercising. Inactivity is out, fitness is in. People play tennis and racquetball, run, jump rope, do aerobics, bicycle ride, swim, and find many other ways to become physically active. Yet the many positive effects of swimming on the body and mind may soon make it the most popular exercise in the country.

—*Carey Byer*

1. What is the thesis in this paper?
2. What details support the writer's beliefs about running? swimming?

3. What transitions connect elements within the body paragraphs? between paragraphs?
4. How does the conclusion attempt to set a new frame of reference?
5. How would you improve this paper? What changes would you recommend for the next draft?

Step 3. Using a Focus for Comparison. Assume that you would develop each topic in Column I in a comparison-contrast essay where you would use a single focus of comparison. In Column II, write down the basic way in which the two ideas are either alike or dissimilar. In Column III, name two specific moments you might use to illustrate each object. Look at the example.

I	II	III
TOPICS TO COMPARE	BASIC FOCUS OF COMPARISON	TWO ILLUSTRATIONS
EXAMPLE	*level of excitement*	*a. time I sat through an*
baseball and football	*(baseball: dull; football:*	*eleven inning no hitter.*
	exciting)	*b. time I watched the Jets*
		and Packers at Shea
		Stadium.
1. spring and fall		
2. a blind date compared with a date I chose myself		
3. two local shopkeepers		

Step 4. Understanding Another Approach. Assume that you would develop each topic in Column I in a comparison-contrast essay where there is no basic focus but where, instead, a few points are discussed for each object. In Column II, list three significant points you might use to illustrate each part of the topic. Look at the example.

I

TOPIC FOR COMPARISON

EXAMPLE

city and country winters

II

DISCUSSION POINTS

a. *transportation*
b. *ways of having fun*
c. *landscape*

1. riding a bicycle and riding a motorcycle

   a. _____
   b. _____
   c. _____

2. dressing casually and dressing up

   a. _____
   b. _____
   c. _____

3. high school and college clubs or other extracurricular activities

   a. _____
   b. _____
   c. _____

LIKENESSES OR DIFFERENCES: THE POINT-BY-POINT METHOD

This pattern does not separate the two objects you are discussing. Instead, it treats both objects together as you present each point of comparison.

For example, in a paragraph comparing high school and college, let's assume that a writer wants to discuss these three points:

1. the physical appearance
2. the way people look
3. the way time passes

After mentioning each point, the writer would discuss both the high school and college in relation to that point. He or she would illustrate how high school and college compare in physical appearance, then illustrate student freedom at both places, and finally compare friendliness at the two schools.

Step 5. A Point-by-Point Comparison. Read the student essay below, developed by means of the point-by-point method. Answer the questions that come after it.

High School and College: Some Differences

Schools seem on the surface to have many similar qualities. Everyone knows them: corridors, rooms, chalkboards, chalk, teachers. Nevertheless, institutions of learning can vary greatly in many ways. After my first year in college, I see many differences between my high school, Mater Christi, and LaGuardia Community College, my current school. From physical appearance to free-time activities these places differ greatly, and it amazes me that two schools standing within three miles of each other can have so little in common.

The buildings and neighborhoods of Mater Christi and LaGuardia are far from similar. Oak trees, brick homes, and a hill surround Mater Christi High School; LaGuardia is set within smoke-puffing buildings where the sharp smell of acetone and other chemicals from nearby factories sickens me. The free open spaces of the grounds around the high school and its ample track make LaGuardia feel a little closed in, although high skylights do bring the sun into the main hallway and some of the open lounges. Windows made it possible to stare from Mater Christi at the flow of miniature cars on the Triborough Bridge or to watch a sleek train ascend a nearby hill of tracks. Here at college, many rooms do not have windows; all we get to see is a dusty green chalkboard or perhaps a wall painted bright orange.

Besides the physical setting, the people at the two schools look different too. For example, no nuns dressed in modern habits scurry about the corridors of the college. At LaGuardia male and female teachers alike saunter down the halls, a leather briefcase or a book in one hand and a cup of steaming, aromatic coffee in the other. Neither does one see sitting in one room at the college thirty-five identical green skirts, green vests and starched white blouses. A dress code at LaGuardia does not exist, so people wear what they wish without fear of an "Out of Uniform" pass. What a relief for me to sit in a classroom in faded jeans and an old black sweatshirt and to look around at the patches of brown and blue and swirls of red and yellow, all students dressed according to their tastes. In fact, another difference that distinguishes people at LaGuardia from those at Mater Christi is the appearance of males in the rooms. In high school no female student dared even step into the left side of the building because it belonged to the boys. Even now when I hear Cliff's deep voice sound out in English class, I jump with surprise!

Another interesting difference between the two schools is the way time passes. In high school forty minute periods, eight periods a day ticked away slowly, especially on Friday afternoons when heartbeats raced quicker than the sweephand on a watch. Each period dragged on even more slowly than the one before it, and there was barely enough time to rush from one class to the next before the dreaded bell rang. At college, although classes last for seventy minutes, time glides along smoothly and painlessly. I have no more than three classes a day and with the free time between sessions I can relax over a coke in the cafeteria or read my psychology book at a new brown table in the library, or listen to rock music at one of the student lounges. At Mater Christi a free period meant the horrors of the study hall. In the auditorium on hard backed chairs the students sat tall, scribbling in their loose leaf books, not daring to breathe a word under fear of detention.

Thus, considering only its appearance, one might conclude that Mater Christi was more pleasant than LaGuardia because the physical surroundings are so much more appealing. However, the high school's many regulations make it almost unbearable. Some students decide not to continue with college which is just a short walk from my high school, because they are tired of following strict rules, and they think that the same rules will exist in college. They do not know that college students have much more freedom than high school students. If they did realize this, I think that they would find this college much more pleasant than high school, in spite of its unattractive surroundings.

—Patricia Logan

1. What is the proposal sentence? How does the introduction serve to build toward the proposal?
2. Which details let you see bits of the college setting? of the high school?
3. What differences does Patricia Logan see among the people? What details best illustrate the differences?
4. How does the writer compare the way time passes at each place?
5. How many body paragraphs does the writer use? Why? What transitions connect the body paragraphs together?

Some Hints about Point-by-Point Comparisons

1. Ordering details by importance (see pp. 81–83) is often the best plan for this pattern. You may wish, therefore, to discuss in less detail your first point or points so that you can concentrate more fully on the last point, the one that is most important to you.
2. The opening sentence of each paragraph helps you introduce each new point of comparison and connect it to the previous point.
3. Transitions help you move easily from one point to the next.
4. The number of points you treat and the extent of the details you use will determine the number of body paragraphs you need.

LIKENESSES AND DIFFERENCES

In this type comparison and contrast essay, you discuss both likenesses *and* differences. You can decide on *one basic way* in which the two objects may be compared, or you can discuss a number of points for the two objects without naming some central focus. The idea here is that both similarities *and* dissimilarities appear in the paragraph. Of course, you will have to illustrate just *how* these two objects have some similar features and how they have different features. If you think the differences are more important, discuss the *similarities* first so that you can give the reader the most important idea *last* (see pages 81–83 for order of details). If you think the similarities are more important, discuss the differences first.

Let us assume that you want to compare two of your relatives and that you select *the way they disciplined you as a child* as the one basic point of comparison. Let's also assume that the differences in these methods of disciplining are what you think are most important. The first few paragraphs could illustrate through vivid details one or more of these similarities:

1. your relatives' concern for your welfare
2. their strictness
3. their little speeches after you did something wrong

Then, you might focus on one or more of these differences:

1. the way the two relatives looked when they were angry
2. what they actually did to you
3. how long it took them to get over their anger

Determine the number of points you want to discuss by the nature of the details you wish to use. One dramatic, expanded illustration for one of the points would mean that fewer points would be treated in the paragraph.

• Hints about Addressing Likenesses and Differences •

1. The proposal (or introduction) should indicate that your essay will treat *both* similarities and differences. You may be able to use coordination or subordination effectively in your proposal sentence.

   [subordinator]

   Although my mother and father shared similar outlooks in rearing children and in disciplining them, mom took her responsibilities more seriously.

   [coordinator]

   Both my parents were very liberal in the way they reared their children, but my father's sudden loss of temper in moments of anger always scared me.

2. Remember, if differences are more important to you, discuss similarities first; if likenesses are more important, talk first about differences. Thesis sentence I below stresses the major area of difference; thesis sentence II stresses the major areas of likeness. The sentences deal with similar topics.

I	II
Although my mother and my grand-mother supported strict rules in rearing young children, I could always count on grandma's understanding when I got in trouble at school.	*Despite their different ways of showing approval or disapproval for my behav-ior, my mother and my grandmother supported strict rules in rearing chil-dren.*
This essay will stress the differences in the degree of understanding the rela-tives showed toward school problems.	This essay will stress the similarities in the support shown by the two relatives for strictness in raising children.

3. Sometimes you do not need to explain both similarities and differences, even though you wish to make the point that likenesses and differences exist. You can assume that the reader understands, appreciates, or agrees with the part that you do not wish to explain. In this way you can use the essay to develop the more important element of your comparison. For example, in proposal sentence I above, the writer could assume that readers would accept this part of the sentence: "my mother and my grandmother supported strict rules in rearing young children." The writer would not have to discuss these strict rules but could move right on to illustrate the differences as she sees them.

Step 6. Understanding the Pattern. For each subject of comparison or contrast in Column I list in Column II two or three similarities that might be expanded with details in an essay. In Column III list two or three differences between the two objects, differences that might also be expanded with details in the essay. Look at the example.

I	II	III
TOPIC FOR COMPARISON	SOME SIMILARITIES	SOME DIFFERENCES
EXAMPLE		
cats and dogs as pets	*a. companionship*	*a. cats are very easy to care*
	b. owners develop a sense of	*for*
	responsibility	*b. cats often get in trouble*
	c. amusement	*c. cats are moody and*
		unpredictable

1. ice skaters and roller
   skaters

   _____ _____

   _____ _____

   _____ _____

2. city children and rural
   children

   _____ _____

   _____ _____

   _____ _____

3. being the driver and being the passenger

   _____ _____

   _____ _____

   _____ _____

Step 7. Comparison and Contrast. Likenesses and Differences: A Student Model. Read the student's essay below, which discusses likenesses and differences in two people who are close friends. In the margins are explanations of the various parts of the essay. Answer the questions that appear after Stacy Kissenger's theme.

Birds of a Feather?

People generally tend to get along with those with whom they have the most in common. In that way, they can enjoy their mutual interests together. For example, those who love sports play together, those who enjoy the same music attend concerts together, those who like to stay up far into the night keep each other company. Many people have difficulty tolerating differences. However, my friends Tammy Smith and Laurie Potter are one exception. Despite their close relationship, these two friends provide striking contrasts in their dispositions. I am often amazed at how well they get along. Although they do have some similarities, their differences in personality are far more noticeable.

[topic sentence of introductory paragraph
1. tells that similarities and differences will be discussed
2. tells that the *differences* are more important]

Granted there are many ways in which these friends are similar. Both born on farms, Tammy and Laurie prefer fields of corn to busy city streets. Their love for farming unites them as together they lecture their city slicker friends like me about Guernseys and Holsteins or about the uses of cultivators. Both girls also share an interest in athletics. The two of them played on the high school basketball team and by their senior year had developed the flawless "Smith-Potter" rebound method, which included elbowing and stomping on anyone separating them and the ball. Off the basketball court, their fun-loving natures further reinforce each other. They tease and joke, often to the dismay of those around them. Once they convinced the shop teacher's daughter that rubber crowbars and metric screwdrivers really existed.

[topic sentence of first body paragraph: tells that discussion of likenesses will follow]

[one similarity and instances to illustrate it]

[another similarity (note transition "also" and reference to topic sentence with "Both girls share an interest") and a supporting example]

[more points to finish discussion on similarities]

[topic sentence of second body paragraph: tells that discussion of differences will follow]

But the personality differences between these two friends are much more outstanding than the likenesses. Laurie is carefree and easygoing with a well of cheerfulness within her. Her sapphire eyes twinkle brightly and the corners of her lips curl upward into a smile as she chats with her friends in the college hallways. When I am feeling miserable, she jokes and giggles to chase away the depression. Her own anger rarely surfaces. When everyone else rages, Laurie rarely shows hostility, except perhaps in her face. Angry, she retreats within herself. Her chatter ceases as the twinkle disappears from her eyes. Her jaw locks tightly, and every muscle tenses. The soft brown crop of curls and the light sprinkling of freckles across her nose suddenly make her face look sharp. But the anger passes quickly, and Laurie again radiates warmth and excitement.

[details to show qualities for one person]

[topic sentence of third body paragraph and contrasting details to show qualities for other person]

Tammy, in contrast, is much less even-tempered than Laurie. Though she is a warm and generous person, Tammy's moods often change drastically. Frequently she grows depressed and sulks for days at a time. Her forehead wrinkles with anxiety; her hazel eyes glare disgustedly, even at best friends. If Laurie or I try to find out why she is so angry, she growls, "Just leave me alone!" and stalks away. Once I watched her face flush with crimson as she snatched a phone book and hurled it, its pages flapping before it thudded against the floor like a dead bird. At another time I saw her kick the wall beside her bed, leaving a black heel mark just above her pillow. Neither people nor things are safe when one of her famous moods transforms Tammy into a monster!

(note transition "in contrast" and reminder of the differences between the two girls with "much less even-tempered")

[closing paragraph
1. uses transition "then"
2. restates main idea that two friends are alike yet have distinct personality differences

Despite some likenesses, then, these two contrasting personalities have convinced me that being birds of a feather is not essential for friendship or for mutual understanding. This makes me hopeful for the future. If two people with such different dispositions can be best friends, then people from different cultures who have grown up with very different backgrounds should be able to get along. People can overlook their differences and concentrate on learning from each other. Maybe they would even find that they have some unexpected things in common.

—*Stacy Kissenger*

3. introduces a new but related idea: people do not have to have similar personalities in order to be close friends (see pages 126–129 for information on conclusions)]

1. What is the basic feature of contrast between the two friends?

2. In what two ways are the girls alike? What details does Stacy Kissenger offer to support those likenesses?

3. How does she illustrate the major difference she sees between the two people she is discussing? Do you find her illustrations effective? Why or why not?

4. Discuss the images in the essay. Which pictures best use color and sound?

Word and Sentence Skills: Suggested Topics for Study

Verb Tense, pages 407–419
Degrees of Comparison, pages 323–326

● Writing a Comparison-Contrast Essay

Assignment

Write an essay that compares and (or) contrasts two people, ideas, objects, places, or issues that interest you. When you compare and contrast, you show likenesses and differences. Use the patterns discussed on pages 119–202 as models for your paper. Remember that complete details and examples will make your essay more vivid and particular.

Of course, any two subjects may be contrasted in some way. To say that two subjects are different is not really saying much. To emphasize contrasts in a paper, present two subjects that do not *seem* dissimilar and then make a case for their differences. In like manner, in a comparison paper select two subjects that do not seem to be alike and then make a case for their similarities. Also, you must make clear to your reader the reason for the comparison and contrast, and you must balance your presentation by giving equal time to each element in your topic.

Read the student themes on pages 192–194 and 197–202 in order to review the approaches you might use for your own comparison-contrast essay. Look at the suggested topic ideas below and at the ideas on page 184 to help you along.

Suggested Topics

Use any topic of your own, of course, but in case you are stuck for ideas, you might find one of these titles helpful as you think about comparing or contrasting two objects, people, ideas, or issues.

1. Grandma (Grandpa) and Me: Comparing Childhoods
2. Political Opponents: Two Different Campaigns
3. City Summer and Country Summer
4. Two Teaching Styles
5. A Book and the Film Made from It
6. Puppy Love Versus Lasting Love
7. The City versus the Suburbs
8. High School and College
9. My Son (Daughter): Two Different Moods
10. Jogging and Swimming
11. Travel: By Train and by Car
12. Germany (or any country): Then and Now

13. Two Leaders: A Contrast in Style

14. Selling through Advertising: Adult Ads versus Children's Ads

15. Store-bought and Homemade Christmas Gifts

16. Two Newspapers (or magazines)

17. My Education: Mother's Views, Father's Views

18. Coworkers: Same Office, Different Styles

19. Computers or Pencils: The Best Way to Write an Essay

20. Poverty: Yesterday and Today

Prewriting: Informal Outlines

As a way of exploring and grouping information on a topic, the *informal outline* (sometimes called a rough or a scratch outline) can be helpful before you prepare your first draft. With an informal outline you lay out in groups or categories various thoughts you intend to develop in your paper. Under each group or category you jot down a few words or phrases that will help you expand ideas into sentences. For extensive assignments or for complicated topics outlines can be very helpful.

Preparing an outline is not a prewriting activity like list making or brainstorming or free association. Those help you to uncover ideas about topics and to discover what you know or what you need to find out when you are stuck for ideas. Outlining, however, demands that you already know in some detail what you want to write about. Of course, an outline should be highly flexible so that you can eliminate idea groups or can add to them as you write your first draft.

Because a comparison-contrast theme usually involves balanced parts that can be separated easily—you deal with one object, then another; or you deal with one point as it relates to two objects before you go on to another point about the objects—informal outlines can help you, once you have stated and limited your topic. Look at this informal outline. Notice how the writer uses numbers (1, 2, 3) and letters (a, b, c) to organize her material easily. Although numbers and letters are not *required* in a scratch outline, many writers find them convenient.

• Prewriting: A Scratch Outline •

```
Topic: Contrasts between High School and College

Mater Christi High School and LaGuardia College
1. passage of time
   a. Mater Christi
      eight forty-minute periods
      classes go slowly
      little time between periods
      study halls in auditorium
```

```
      b. LaGuardia
         seventy-minute classes
         time goes faster
         three classes a day
         free time to relax or study in cafeteria, library, or lounge
   2. people
      a. LaGuardia
         male and female teachers
         students in bright clothes
         no dress code
         males in the room
      b. Mater Christi
         nuns
         girls in uniform
         boys only on left side of building
   3. physical settings
      a. M.C.--oaks, hill, brick homes, windows, open space
      b. LaG.--factory smells, skylights, no windows
                                            --Patricia Logan
```

Step 1. Comparing Essay to Outline.   Reread "High School and College: Some Differences" on pages 197–198. Comparing it to the outline above, answer these questions. Use separate paper.

1. How does the topic sentence compare with the statement of topic in the outline?

2. What new order does the writer present in her essay for the thought groups numbered 1, 2, and 3 in the outline? Why do you think she has made the change?

3. The outline is not consistent in the order of discussion of the two objects. Under 1, Mater Christi comes first; under 2, LaGuardia comes first. Why has Patricia Logan changed this situation in the essay so that she discusses the same subject, Mater Christi, first each time?

Step 2. Practice with Informal Outlines.   Look at the topics you developed in Step 3 or 4 on pages 195–196. On a separate page, prepare a scratch outline for any of the topics and their accompanying illustrations or discussion points. Be sure to include in your outline some details you might use to develop the thought groups.

Step 3. An Outline for Your Essay.   If your instructor requests it, prepare an informal outline after you have decided on your own comparison and contrast topic and before you write your first draft. Use separate paper, and hand in your outline when you hand in your theme for evaluation. Use Patricia Logan's outline (pages 204–205) as a model, but take whatever liberties you need with it so that the outline works for you. Remember, this is a *rough* outline. Its main purpose is to help you write your paper successfully.

Student Samples: Drafting and Revising

As you think about and write your own drafts of a comparison-contrast essay, study the section called Progress Reminders: A Checklist, on pages 209–210. Review the section called Drafting and Revising on pages 20–21.

Reading Drafts.   Examine the two drafts below. How does the revised draft improve upon the earlier one? What further changes would you recommend for the next draft? When you finish reading, answer the questions.

DRAFT

```
                      Double Trouble

     When looking at my twin sons, Paul and Michael, it's hard to
believe two identical beings could be so different. Everytime I walk
down the street and a passerby comments about how much alike my sons
are, I tell them "You should only know how different my boys really
are."
     Paul and Michael both have platinum blonde hair and hazel eyes;
they each weigh fifty pounds and stand forty-eight inches tall.
Everyone who meets them have much difficulty telling them apart because
their appearances are so similar, but that is where the similarity
ends.
     For instance Michael is a very spirited child. As an infant when
Michael soiled his diaper, he had to be changed that instant. His face
would turn beet red, and he would send a chill up my spine with his
loud scretching clamor. He would kick his scrawny legs vigorously as I
tried to change his diaper. As soon as I finished changing him, he
would calm down, and his eyes would sparkle, and he would give me an
enormous smirk. Paul, on the other hand, would not make it obvious like
Michael when his diaper was wet. When I would unsnap his terry stretch
outfit to change his diaper, he would lay very cooperativly. He would
gurgle and smile at me as I approached him. Changing Paul's diaper was
such a pleasure compared to Michael's.
     As toddlers their temperaments were so amazingly different.
Feeding time was always an adventure. Their oak wood high chairs were
placed side to side against the stark white walls of the kitchen. Their
menu for this particular evening was strained chicken, mashed squash,
sweet peas and apple sauce for dessert. Paulie would sit straight up in
his chair, and with his silver spoon neatly eat his dinner. Michael, on
the other hand, never did quite like eating with a spoon; he was more
comfortable eating with his hands. He enjoyed smearing his mashed peas
```

all over the wall as well as all over his brothers high chair. He was never fond of eating peas or any other vegetable. I would scold him sternly and he would give me this devilish grin, and I would have to smile back.

Ironically, as they grew a little older their roles changed; suddenly Paul was the livily child. Michael was content sitting on the sofa with me, and watching Sesame Street or Mr. Roger's Neighborhood on television. He loved hearing Mr. Roger's sing "It's a beautiful day in the Neighborhood." He would sit hypnotized gazzing at the television. He loved singing along with the characters from Sesame Street and Mr. Rogers Neighborhood. Meanwhile, Paul would be in his bedroom pulling all his clothes out of his dresser drawers and scattering them all over his bedroom. Next he would wander into the kitchen and take out the pots and pans from the lower cabinet and thump on them as if he was playing the drums. I guess you never have a dull moment when you have twin sons.

REVISED DRAFT

My Boys

When looking at my twin sons, Paul and Michael, I find it hard to believe two physically identical beings could be so different. Paul and Michael both have blond hair and hazel eyes; they each weigh fifty pounds and stand forty-eight inches tall. Everyone who meets them struggles to tell them apart because they look so much alike. But that is where the similarity ends.

Michael and Paul have always had very different dispositions. For instance, Michael is a very spirited child. As an infant when Michael soiled his pamper, he cried unless I changed him instantly. His face would turn red as a strawberry, and he would make me shiver with his loud screeching clamor. As soon as I finished changing him, he would calm down, his eyes would sparkle, and he would give me an enormous smirk. Paul, on the other hand, would not make it obvious when his diaper was wet. When I would unsnap his terry stretch outfit to change him, he would lie still, very cooperatively, gurgling and smiling at me. Changing Paul's diaper was such a pleasure, compared to changing Michael's!

Even as toddlers my sons' temperaments were amazingly different. Feeding time was always an adventure. Their oak wood high chairs stood side by side against the white walls of the kitchen. Their menu for one memorable evening was strained chicken, mashed squash, sweet peas, and apple sauce for dessert. Paulie would sit straight up in his chair, and with his silver spoon neatly eat his dinner. Michael, on the other hand, never did quite like eating with a spoon; he was more comfortable eating with his hands. He enjoyed smearing mashed peas all over the wall as well as all over his brother's high chair! "You'd better eat those peas and squash," I would scold him firmly, but he would throw me a devilish grin, and I would have to smile back.

Ironically, as they grew a little older, their roles changed;

suddenly Paul was the lively child. Michael was content sitting on the sofa with me and watching <u>Sesame Street</u> or <u>Mr. Rogers' Neighborhood</u> on television. He would sit hypnotized, gazing at the television, and loved singing along in a squeaky little voice with the characters from his two favorite shows. Meanwhile, Paul would be in his bedroom pulling socks, undershirts, and pajamas out of his dresser drawers and scattering them all over his bedroom. Next he would wander into the kitchen, take out the pots and pans from the lower cabinet, and thump on them as if he were playing the drums.

There is never a dull moment when you have twin sons. But I am glad my sons are developing their own personalities. They don't wear identical shirts and pants, nor do they have all the same toys. Too often, parents assume that their children are alike, when the fact is that despite similar appearances, they are individuals. I believe that mothers and fathers should nurture the differences in their youngsters, twins or no. In that way each child becomes special and a person in his or her own right. Every time a passerby on my street comments about how much alike my sons are, I mumble under my breath, "You should only know how different these kids really are."

--Marie Mikulka

1. Which pattern does the writer use here—the block or the point-by-point? Does it suit her purposes well? Do the transitions move you smoothly from one part of the paper to another?

2. What changes has the writer made in the title and the topic sentence? In your opinion are these changes improvements?

3. What words or phrases in the early draft do not appear in the revision? What additions appear in the revision? Are you generally satisfied with the changes? Why or why not?

4. Find two or three errors that Marie Mikulka corrected in the revised draft. What other corrections must she still make?

5. What further changes would you recommend in this essay?

Collaboration: Getting Reader Response

After you write your first draft, pair up with one other student in the class and read his or her essay carefully a couple of times until you understand it well. Then prepare a simple outline of that essay as it is written. The outline should show the balanced parts of the work as they appear to you. Use numbers and letters to organize the material you have read. (You might want to review pages 204–205 in this chapter.) Using this outline, write a few sentences of suggestions that can help the writer produce the next draft.

When your classmate returns the outline of your essay and the suggestions, use them to write your next draft. Are there any inconsistencies between your essay and the outline? Does the outline indicate any lapses in logic—things you thought were clear but which the reader did not understand? Do the parts of your essay balance, or do you have to add details or remove any?

Progress Reminders: A Checklist

While preparing your outline and your first and later drafts, but before writing your final copy, use this checklist for your essay so that you will follow as many of the suggestions as possible. After you prepare your final copy, fill in the checklist and submit it to your instructor along with your theme.

1. Did I spend time thinking about the topic in some prewriting   _____
   activity that works well for me? (See pages 19–20.) Did I try to
   use a scratch outline to help me organize ideas?   _____

2. Did I write a rough draft and any other needed drafts before   _____
   making my final copy? Did I make changes in my rough drafts
   so that I expressed thoughts clearly and smoothly? Does my   _____
   final copy follow correct manuscript form?
                                                                     _____

3. Did I write a proposal sentence that makes clear what I want   _____
   my essay to deal with and that states some dominant impression I have about the subject? (See pages 118–120.)

   Here is my proposal sentence:

   _____

   _____

4. Did I use topic sentences and transitional expressions in each   _____
   body paragraph to help the ideas move smoothly from one to
   the other? (See pages 68–72 and pages 187–190.) Here are two
   transitional expressions that appear in my theme:

   a. _____

   b. _____

5. Does my essay contain several word pictures that use sound,   _____
   color, smell, and touch? Here is one image that uses sound:

   _____

6. Did I use figures of speech (see pages 184–187) in my essay?   _____

7. Did I follow one of the methods of comparison outlined on
   pages 191–202? The pattern that I followed most closely was

   _____

8. Does my essay distinctly stress either similarities or differ-   _____
   ences between my subjects? It stresses

   _____

9. If I stressed differences, have I included any similarities for a _____
balanced essay (or, if I stressed similarities, did I include
differences)?

10. Is there a clear enough *reason* or *basis* for my comparison or _____
contrast?

11. Did I try to use words from the new vocabulary on pages 182– _____
183? Here is one word I used:

_____

12. After making changes in my drafts for clarity and smoothness, _____
did I check my Theme Progress Sheet (page 454) and proofread the draft before my final draft? Did I proofread again _____
before I submitted my final draft?

13. Did I check a dictionary for any words that troubled me as I _____
spelled them?

14. Did I use a variety of sentence types: subordination; coordina- _____
tion; sentences that open with words that end in *-ly*?

15. Did I try to write one expanded quotation sentence that _____
through strong images includes details of the speaker? (See
pages 190–191.)

● The Professionals Speak

Step 1. An Essay about Farm Life.   Read the essay below. It describes the
writer's feelings about a Massachusetts farm he recalls from his youth. Notice how
the contrasting personalities of his parents emerge in this essay. Answer the
questions after the selection.

SOME WORDS TO KNOW BEFORE YOU READ

hand-hewn—made or cut by hand, as with an ax

cavernous—vast, like a cavern

irascible—easily angered

varmints—undesirable birds or animals

whimsy—odd or fanciful idea

railed—to condemn in bitter language

solace—confront in sorrow or distress

intangible—not touchable

The Family Farm

Two years ago, my sister and I sold our family farm, 100 acres in western Massachusetts. It was a glorious piece of land, with rolling meadows leading to sweeping views of the Berkshire hills, a brook that glistened through a hemlock forest and a rambling 19th-century farmhouse with slanting floors and hand-hewn rafters. My wife and friends told me I was crazy to want to get rid of the place. I kept four acres, not because of their remarks but for another reason that, I have only recently come to understand, is closely related to a mother's influence over a son.

Our mother and father bought the farm when I was 3 years old and my sister 7. It was a working farm, and my father was a dirt farmer. He was my childhood hero. I was in his constant tow—milking cows, erecting fences, hauling hay bales from field to barn, collecting eggs from clucking hens. He cut a dramatic figure. He attacked the fields with a roaring tractor. He furrowed the earth into great brown snakes and cut crisp swaths of moist hay. He dug cavernous holes for foundations and built a barn over them. He squeezed milk from cows and pulled broken engines apart.

With this kind of excitement at hand, my awareness of my mother was dim. To this day, my memories of her are not clearly defined—only a lingering awareness of her quiet and concentrated appreciation of the place. She tried to help my father run the farm, but when she got into the driver's seat of the irascible old truck or when she cleaned freshly killed chickens, even my young eyes could see her mind travel away from her work, invariably stopping when she hit upon an object of natural beauty. She stared at clouds racing across long-grassed fields, at Queen Anne's lace waving in the meadows and especially at the mountainside that rose from the valley below the farm and towered above us.

A little meadow high up on the mountain was visible from our house. She often wondered who had cleared it. She told me a story. Long ago, the man who had built our house went hunting on the mountain and shot a deer. He brought it back to the house and hung it on a tree. The next morning he found an Indian in the kitchen. The Indian told him that he had killed the deer on *his* mountain and he wanted *his* deer back

I cannot recall that she taught me anything specific, certainly not the way my father did. She did not know the names of the trees or the flowers or even when they blossomed. She must have taught me, though, how to observe. We took long walks through the fields and along the brook, she pointing out the nuances of nature. My father mocked what he considered to be her misty-eyed appreciation. To him the wildflowers that blanketed the fields took up space in which sweet grass could grow for his cows. Woodchucks were not designers of intricate underground passages. They were varmints whose holes were booby traps for tractor wheels. I thrilled when he threw smoke bombs into their dens and quickly shoveled dirt over the openings to trap the animals in smoky death.

I was too much in awe of his gruff power to take in my mother's gentle whimsy. Still, he forced me at last to grow away from him. One incident, especially, increased the distance. My father was cutting hay and I, as usual, was riding on the rear fender of the tractor. A highpitched scream came from the long grass near the blade. We found a young rabbit with its four legs cleanly severed. My father said nothing, but carried the poor animal to a stone wall. The thing was in shock; it did not even try to hobble away on its stumps. My father picked up a rock and brought it down on the rabbit's head with such force that the head vanished, smashed into blood and fur. The body flipflopped up and down like a shirt on a clothesline. Not a word from my father; not a glance at me, a 10-year-old boy as stunned into silence as had been the rabbit

The farm eventually wore him out. He tried for 15 years to bend the land to his will, but the land beat him. He gave up the farm, confused and embittered.

The barn began to sag; wildflowers crept closer to the house; the unpruned branches of the apple trees split from their trunks. He railed against my mother as if the land and she had been allies working against him.

He took his anger out on me, too, but, like my sister, I escaped—first to college and then to the big city. I no longer thought much about the farm. I paid dutiful visits there to a father who had become distant and to a mother who now depended on her communication with the land for solace. I began to respect her long staring at the mountainside.

After my father died, my mother continued to live on the farm alone, taking solemn joy in her wanderings through the broken apple orchard and among the seedling white pines that sprouted where clover had grown. At last no one ridiculed the treasures she brought back—blossoming boughs, a cluster of silvery marsh grass or an assortment of berries.

When my mother was stricken with a disease that forced my sister and me to move her to a nursing home, I wanted to get rid of the farm. I talked to my sister about it, thinking, perhaps hoping, that she would protest. But she agreed with a shrug, as if to say, "Sure, I couldn't care less." Her response stung me. The pain made me realize that to discard the place like a used car would betray a love of something intangible that my mother had given me—the smell of freshly cut alfalfa, the springtime chorus of peepers in the brook, the cry of red-winged blackbirds in the meadows. My mother's passive caressing of the land had penetrated me far more than my father's energetic shaping of it.

The little corner of the farm that I decided to keep is far away from the rotting buildings that remind me of my childhood. I was glad to sell those and the surrounding land to a stranger. My four acres are a lovely meadow slanting toward the mountain, a testimony to my mother's steadfastness. From it, the little pasture up above is just visible, though it is less manicured now, as nature reclaims it. That is fine with me. The years have dissolved any desire to beat back natural growth. Now my heart races when I feel the tangled orchard grass and wildflower stems underfoot. I like them just as they are.

—*Christopher Hallowell*

1. What is the main point of this essay? Why does the farm have such significance for the writer? How does his sister shock him?

2. How are the writer's mother and father alike? How are they different? What does each one teach him? How does the incident with the rabbit increase the distance between father and son?

3. Which images do you find clearest and most satisfying? Where does the writer appeal to color? sound? action? Which details of the father best show his character?

4. How does the conclusion serve the rest of the essay? How does the conclusion relate to the main point? the body paragraphs?

Step 2. Thin People, Fat People.   Note the comparison and contrast strategies in this essay comparing thin and fat people. Answer the questions after the selection.

SOME WORDS TO KNOW BEFORE YOU READ

condescending—acting as though talking down to someone; acting superior

inert—unable to move

nebulous—lacing definite form or limits

rutabagas—edible root of a kind of plant

expound—explain; interpret

prognose—predict

guffaw—hearty burst of laughter

gluttonous—tending to eat in huge amounts

That Lean and Hungry Look

Caesar was right. Thin people need watching. I've been watching them for most of my adult life, and I don't like what I see. When these narrow fellows spring at me, I quiver to my toes. Thin people come in all personalities, most of them menacing. You've got your "together" thin person, your mechanical thin person, your condescending thin person, your tsk-tsk thin person, your efficiency-expert thin person. All of them are dangerous.

In the first place, thin people aren't fun. They don't know how to goof off, at least in the best, fat sense of the word. They've always got to be adoing. Give them a coffee break, and they'll jog around the block. Supply them with a quiet evening at home, and they'll fix the screen door and lick S&H green stamps. They say things like "there aren't enough hours in the day." Fat people never say that. Fat people think the day is too damn long already.

Thin people make me tired. They've got speedy little metabolisms that cause them to bustle briskly. They're forever rubbing their bony hands together and cycing ncw problems to "tackle." I like to surround myself with sluggish, inert, easygoing fat people, the kind who believe that if you clean it up today, it'll just get dirty again tomorrow.

Some people say the business about the jolly fat person is a myth, that all of us chubbies are neurotic, sick, sad people. I disagree. Fat people may not be chortling all day long, but they're a hell of a lot *nicer* than the wizened and shriveled. Thin people turn surly, mean and hard at a young age because they never learn the value of a hot-fudge sundae for easing tension. Thin people don't like gooey soft things because they themselves are neither gooey nor soft. They are crunchy and dull, like carrots. They go straight to the heart of the matter while fat people let things stay all blurry and hazy and vague, the way things actually are. Thin people want to face the truth. Fat people know there is no truth. One of my thin friends is always staring at complex, unsolvable problems and saying, "The key thing is . . ." Fat people never say that. They know there isn't any such thing as the key thing about anything.

Thin people believe in logic. Fat people see all sides. The sides fat people see are rounded blobs, usually gray, always nebulous and truly not worth worrying about. But the thin person persists. "If you consume more calories than you burn," says one of my thin friends, "you will gain weight. It's that simple." Fat people always grin when they hear statements like that. They know better.

Fat people realize that life is illogical and unfair. They know very well that God is not in his heaven and all is not right with the world. If God was up there, fat people could have two doughnuts and a big orange drink anytime they wanted it.

Thin people have a long list of logical things they are always spouting off to me. They hold up one finger at a time as they reel off these things, so I won't lose track. They speak slowly as if to a young child. The list is long and full of holes. It contains tidbits like "get a grip on yourself," "cigarettes kill," "cholesterol clogs," "fit as a fiddle," "ducks in a row," "organize" and "sound fiscal management." Phrases like that.

They think these 2,000-point plans lead to happiness. Fat people know happiness is elusive at best and even if they could get the kind thin people talk about, they wouldn't want it. Wisely, fat people see that such programs are too dull, too hard, too off the mark. They are never better than a whole cheesecake.

Fat people know all about the mystery of life. They are the ones acquainted with the night, with luck, with fate, with playing it by ear. One thin person I know once suggested that we arrange all the parts of a jigsaw puzzle into groups according to size, shape and color. He figured this would cut the time needed to complete the puzzle by at least 50 per cent. I said I wouldn't do it. One, I like to muddle through. Two, what good would it do to finish early? Three, the jigsaw puzzle isn't the important thing. The important thing is the fun of four people (one thin person included) sitting around a card table, working a jigsaw puzzle. My thin friend had no use for my list. Instead of joining us, he went outside and mulched the boxwoods. The three remaining fat people finished the puzzle and made chocolate, double-fudged brownies to celebrate.

The main problem with thin people is they oppress. Their good intentions, bony torsos, tight ships, neat corners, cerebral machinations and pat solutions loom like dark clouds over the loose, comfortable, spread-out, soft world of the fat. Long after fat people have removed their coats and shoes and put their feet up on the coffee table, thin people are still sitting on the edge of the sofa, looking neat as a pin, discussing rutabagas. Fat people are heavily into fits of laughter, slapping their thighs and whooping it up, while thin people are still politely waiting for the punch line.

Thin people are downers. They like math and morality and reasoned evaluation of the limitations of human beings. They have their skinny little acts together. They expound, prognose, probe and prick.

Fat people are convivial. They will like you even if you're irregular and have acne. They will come up with a good reason why you never wrote the great American novel. They will cry in your beer with you. They will put your name in the pot. They will let you off the hook. Fat people will gab, giggle, guffaw, gallumph, gyrate and gossip. They are generous, giving and gallant. They are gluttonous and goodly and great. What you want when you're down is soft and jiggly, not muscled and stable. Fat people know this. Fat people have plenty of room. Fat people will take you in.

—Suzanne Britt

1. In your own words, state the topic of the essay and the writer's attitude toward the topic. Is this clear in the opening paragraph?

2. In paragraphs 2 through 5 and 8 through 10, which pattern of comparison and contrast does the writer use? Which does she use in paragraphs 6, 7, 11, and 12? Which do you find more effective? Why?

3. What is the writer's objection to thin people's using phrases like "get a grip on yourself," "cigarettes kill," and the others in paragraph 7?

4. List the words the author uses in paragraphs 11 and 12 to describe thin people and fat people. Which words are more positive words?

5. Comment on the conclusion. How does it support the thesis?

C H A P T E R

Argumentation

●

INTRODUCTION TO THE USE OF ARGUMENT

Another important strategy for writers is knowing how to build arguments, and this chapter explains a number of techniques to help you develop your arguing skill. When you argue, you try to convince someone to accept your opinion on an issue. It is important to note that the true test of an opinion is the way in which you make it convincing and believable. Anyone can scream a point of view angrily, make fun of people who disagree, or resort to emotional appeals. But most educated people require solid reasons before accepting opinions, and you should always keep your point clearly in mind so that you can provide valid evidence for your beliefs.

When writing an argumentative paper, you must be well informed about your subject before you begin. You can draw on many different subjects to develop an argument simply by writing about the issues that affect you deeply. Your own strong beliefs will help you convince others that your position is the right one. But your argument will be convincing to readers only if you know enough about the subject to win them over on all points. You may believe, for example, that laws should require public officials to be tested for drugs. You may feel that religion is an essential human need, that television educates children poorly, or that recycling is not as beneficial in protecting the environment as some people believe.

Whatever your impressions, you can convince someone about them only by presenting adequate supporting detail. You can illustrate your impressions through dramatic experiences in your own personal life. Or you can try to support your opinions with information that you gather from other sources. With either approach, you will have to learn how to present your points logically and in an orderly manner and to avoid the faults in reasoning that inexperienced writers sometimes show when they write essays to argue a particular position. You will be able to draw on other writing strategies that you learned in previous chapters—description, narration, illustration, process analysis, comparison and contrast—to help you develop your points effectively.

● Vocabulary

Step 1. Words to Use When Arguing Your Point.   The following words may prove useful in a paper arguing some point. Using your dictionary, write definitions for them.

1. advocate   _____   6. resolute   _____

2. dispute   _____   7. unconvincing   _____

3. endorse   _____   8. persuade   _____

4. adversary   _____   9. contradict   _____

5. controversy   _____   10. invalidate   _____

Step 2. Matching Meanings.   From the list of words in Step 1, write on the blank line the word whose meaning appears alongside.

_____ 1. dispute between sides with opposing views

_____ 2. convince by argument or reasoning

_____ 3. opponent; enemy

_____ 4. argue or debate

_____ 5. determined

_____ 6. destroy effectiveness; nullify

_____ 7. express the opposite of a statement

_____ 8. person who argues for a cause; supporter

_____ 9. not believable

_____ 10. approve or support

Step 3. Words in Your Own Sentences. On separate paper, write sentences using the ten words you have learned in this chapter.

● Building Composition Skills

Finding the Topic

Step 1. A Questionnaire on Issues. The statements below examine your attitudes on key issues of interest today.

If you agree with the statement completely, put the number 1 in the blank space.

If you agree with the statement to some degree, put the number 2 in the blank space.

If you completely disagree with the statement, put the number 3 in the blank space.

If you have no idea or feeling at all about the statement, put the number 4 in the blank space.

_____ 1. Women should not hold a position of great responsibility because they are much more emotional than men.

_____ 2. Foreign cars are much better made than American cars.

_____ 3. The drinking age should be eighteen instead of twenty-one.

_____ 4. The SATs are unfair for many women, minorities, and people not in society's middle class.

_____ 5. The death penalty will discourage criminals and is a suitable punishment for murderers and rapists.

_____ 6. The right of abortion is one that all women should be able to use if they want to.

_____ 7. Marriage is an outdated way of labeling a relationship.

_____ 8. Americans do not care enough about nature and wildlife.

_____ 9. Every city should provide special transportation for the elderly and the handicapped.

_____ 10. Today's doctors are neither trustworthy nor reliable.

Step 2. Illustrating Opinions. Select any statement from the above questionnaire for which you have written a 1 or a 3 in the margin. Discuss your reasons for believing what you do by giving an illustration from your own experience or from something you have heard or read.

Step 3. Examining Opinions. These statements drawn from people in our time and in the past express strong opinions. Discuss with the class the one that you think most interesting. How would you argue in favor of the opinion? against it?

1. Money is like an arm or a leg—use it or lose it.

    —*Henry Ford*

2. There is no fortress so strong that money cannot take it.

    —*Cicero*

3. Science robs men of wisdom and usually converts them into phantom beings loaded up with facts.

    —*Miguel de Unamuno*

4. Injustice anywhere is a threat to justice everywhere.

    —*M. L. King, Jr.*

5. The death of democracy is not likely to be an assassination from ambush. It will be a slow extinction from apathy, indifference, and undernourishment.

    —*Robert Maynard Hutchins*

6. Public instruction should be the first object of government.

    —*Napoleon Bonaparte*

7. Those who cannot remember the past are condemned to repeat it.

    —*George Santayana*

8. There are only two or three human stories and they go on repeating themselves as fiercely as if they had never happened before.

    —*Willa Cather*

9. Man's best possession is a loving wife.

    —*Robert Burton*

10. The great question that has never been answered, and which I have not yet been able to answer despite my thirty years of research into the feminine soul, is: What does a woman want?

    —*Sigmund Freud*

Interview Techniques

For a topic of argument, a topic that interests a wide range of people, you may wish to gather ideas and details by interviewing. An interview gives you firsthand experience in collecting and comparing data; by talking to several people, you can broaden your sense of an issue. Further, if you have taken notes carefully, you have lots of raw material upon which to draw as you plan and write your essay.

● The Interview: Tips for Good Techniques ●

1. Write down questions about the general idea you are investigating. If you choose to interview people about whether or not women should serve in high political offices, you might prepare a list like this one:

   • Should women get preferred treatment in political offices?

   • What special qualities, if any, can women bring to high-pressure jobs?

   • Would a woman make a good president of the United States?

   • What women in politics do you admire? dislike?

   • Are there any sex-related qualities that make men or women better suited for certain political jobs? What are those qualities?

2. Good questioning is a skill. Try to make your questions draw out the answers you want to know.

3. Listen carefully to what people say. Take notes as they speak, eliminating any information that is not important. Be careful to get as much important material as you can as accurately as you can. If someone says "sometimes" or "maybe," make sure that you do not change those remarks into "always" or "definitely."

4. Ask everyone the same questions. That gives you a basis for comparing any differences of opinion.

5. Identify the people who agree to give information to you. Be specific so that in your essay you are able to quote somebody's exact words accurately. Say "Charles Davidson, a freshman at Fairleigh Dickinson, said '. . . .' " If you want to present interviewing results statistically in your essay, you do not need to identify every person you interview. You can say, "Seven out of the ten people I spoke to agreed that . . . ."

6. Write down exact quotations where you can. This requires very careful listening and quick writing. But often the interviewee says something so unusual or so important that you want it down exactly as it is said; then when you write up your findings in an essay, the quote can add liveliness and interest to your own work.

7. If the person you are interviewing is important, take down some details of his or her character and appearance to spark your own presentation of the person's ideas.

Practice Interviewing.   Select some current issue that interests you, and conduct at least five interviews with people in your school or home community. Your instructor may suggest that the class break down into groups so that students can ask each other questions. Follow the tips for good techniques included in the chart above.

Logical Arguments

When you relate from your personal experience some moment about a given topic or subject, you are not attempting to *prove* your idea. You are merely demonstrating your point. When you seek to argue by giving *proofs*, however, you often need more than just a single instance from your life. To try to prove that women are competent as doctors by basing your argument upon one experience you had with one good woman doctor would be unconvincing. For readers to agree with your point of view, you need material that is solid and plentiful, evidence that is believable, reasoning that is not faulty.

   The fifteen types of poor reasoning below show some of the more familiar kinds of incorrect evidence students frequently use in essays. Each logic trap is followed by an example and an explanation alongside.

FIFTEEN FAULTS TO FAIL THE ARGUMENT

1. *Don't* give too few instances to prove a point.

EXAMPLE

Women cannot be trusted to make decisions when the pressure gets rough. My wife cries as soon as some high-pressure situation arises.

One instance cannot adequately support the point.

2. *Don't* use famous people's names as the sole proof of your point.

EXAMPLE

Whitney Lewis, the actor, advertises that camera, so I'm sure it's good.

How does mentioning the name prove that the product is good?

3. *Don't* praise or blame the *people* who state a proof you cite—and then ignore the idea.

EXAMPLES

She's such a brilliant scholar that any candidate she supports has to be good.

Praising the woman's intelligence does not prove that the candidate is a good one.

He's an atheist. As a candidate, therefore, he has to be weak.

Attacking the man's religious beliefs does not prove that the candidate is a poor one.

4. *Don't* try to prove something by showing that people always believed in a certain thing.

EXAMPLE

Women over the centuries have not been allowed to compete with men in professional sports. Why should we allow it now?

People may have believed one thing a long time ago. But they can change their minds.

5. *Don't* try to prove something by showing that everyone is doing it.

EXAMPLE

Young people all over the world are using marijuana without harm. And many middle-aged people too are joining the drug culture. How harmful can marijuana be?

So what if everyone does it? How does that prove it is not harmful?

6. *Don't* try to prove something by saying the point over and over again.

EXAMPLE

Women should have the same rights as men. Women's rights are just as important as men's rights, and women should receive the same treatment as men. After all, women have rights, too.

There is no proof here at all, just the same point made again and again.

7. *Don't* use a source to back up an idea unless the source is reliable and an authority.

EXAMPLES

My brother Jerry says politicians are liars and cheats, and I have always trusted his judgment.

What makes Jerry an authority on politicians?

The president of Apco, a leading oil company, believes that lead in automobile gasoline is really not a polluting agent.

An oil company that has to remove lead from its fuel may have to spend large sums of money. It might be expected to try to disprove lead as a polluter.

8. *Don't* make a comparison that is weak or not true.

EXAMPLE

I know I can drive a motorcycle. I can ride a bicycle can't I?	The writer fails to realize that there are many differences between bicycles and motorcycles.

9. *Don't* appeal to a person's prejudices or unreasonable emotions.

EXAMPLES

Foreign-born people should not be allowed to work at all kinds of jobs. If they are, Americans will be squeezed out of work, and you and I will be out of employment.	This writer tries to arouse the reader by appealing to personal involvement. Where is the proof that readers will lose their jobs to others?
Anyone who opposes Governor Badley's reelection is anti-American!	This writer uses a word intended to fire up emotions unreasonably. Instead of real proof, he uses a name that is designed to arouse feelings.

10. *Don't* draw conclusions that do not follow from previous information.

EXAMPLES

When Astor was president of the union we really made progress. Now that Alterman has taken over, workers are losing jobs and getting less and less overtime.	The writer doesn't take into account other factors. There is no proof here that the loss of jobs has anything to do with the new president.
When I went to college, I got all A's and B's. Anyone who wants to can get good grades.	The second sentence doesn't follow from the first because the writer does not take into account individual learning abilities.

11. *Don't* try to prove that someone or something is good or bad only because of associations with other "good" or "bad" things.

EXAMPLES

How could he be a criminal? He goes to work in the morning, has dinner out with his family on Sundays, and is best friends with the mayor and the principal of our high school.	This proof of innocence is built by trying to associate a person with good and solid qualities of citizenship. But it does not prove the man is no criminal. If he deals in drugs, what would his friendship with the mayor prove?

Since the dean was found guilty of robbing city funds, surely the president herself must have some illegal dealings too.

This is "guilt by association": The president is not guilty of crimes because one associate is guilty.

12. *Don't* generalize—that is, don't make one fact the source of a broad conclusion. *Don't* state the proof so strongly as to admit no possibilities of exceptions; always leave room for a margin of error.

EXAMPLE

Women drivers are the worst drivers on the road.

It may be true that some women—like some men—are poor drivers, but this certainly is not true of all of them.

13. *Don't* try to show that if something happened *after* an event, that thing is necessarily a *result* of the event.

EXAMPLE

Five convicted killers said that when they were younger, they enjoyed watching programs of violence on television. This proves that watching violent actions on the screen can lead to murder.

Did the killers murder *because* they watched violence on television? This might be a contributing factor, but as a proof alone, it is not very solid.

14. *Don't* state your proof in *either-or* terms.

EXAMPLE

It is no wonder that he failed so many courses. College students go to school or they work; they certainly cannot do both.

What about the people who work only an hour a day, or those who work weekends or summers? This writer suggests that there are only two alternatives when there are many.

15. *Don't* ignore information that contradicts the point you wish to make.

EXAMPLE

Investigations suggest that legalizing heroin would be a positive step toward controlling drug abuse.

On such a controversial issue, the writer should mention studies that disagree with the statement. Much material is available on the failure of parts of the British system in which drugs have been legalized.

Step 1. Finding Foggy Thinking.   Each statement below contains some error in argument such as the ones described above. Discuss the errors the writers make. Then tell how you would correct the statement.

1. Samuel Taylor Coleridge and Edgar Allan Poe both used drugs and still created great works of art. Writers should use some drug if they need stimulation for their work.

2. You're kidding! You're twenty-three years old and you don't drink?

3. My aunt, who owns a chain of stores selling fur coats, says that none of the animals for the coats is killed painfully.

4. Cashiers are so stupid. Yesterday, the cashier at Foodwise Market charged me twenty dollars too much.

5. How could anyone who keeps his hair so long and who wears jeans and sandals all the time know anything about conservative politics?

6. The murdered man's wife refused to talk to the media. She must be guilty of killing him.

7. That family does not go to church. They must all be atheists.

8. If we don't stop the revolutionaries in the Middle East, they'll be at our doorstep soon enough.

9. Ovens are now useless. My mother cooks everything in the microwave.

10. That actor played the role of Fidel Castro so convincingly, he must believe that Castro is a good man.

Step 2. Straight Thinking, Strong Proofs.   How would you go about proving or disproving each statement below? Discuss your answers, making sure to avoid the faults in argument that you just learned about.

1. The courts continue to give custody of children to mothers, not fathers, in divorce cases.

2. Small cars are more efficient than large cars.

3. The attitude of single young women toward marriage has not changed in the last ten years.

4. Alcoholism has always been one of the most common causes of teenage deaths.

5. College graduates now have more trouble finding jobs than ever before.

Step 3. Proof for Attitudes.   Return to the questionnaire in Step 1, page 218. Select any item for which you have written the number 1 or 3, and in the blank lines below explain how you would attempt to prove your opinion.

Hint

This time do not use personal experience as proof. Plan on using other kinds of details. See crucial questions 2 to 4 on page 245.

_____

_____

_____

_____

_____

Using Opposing Arguments

If you are trying to support an idea that you know not everybody agrees on, you can defend your point of view with details of personal experience, statistics, or quotations. But you should not ignore the issues raised on the other side of the argument. What the opposition (those who disagree with you) believes can give you the content of a solid paragraph.

● Why to Mention Opposite Opinions ●

1. Your reference to opposite opinions shows that you know what others are saying.

2. It shows that you are not purposely overlooking points in order to make your own ideas look stronger.

3. It shows that you are fair and that you do not see things in black and white terms only, that you are willing to consider points that do not agree with yours.

4. It gives you more to write about: you can go on to attack the ideas others have, if you wish.

Step 1. Seeking the Opposition.   Assume that the proposal in Column I is one that you would try to support in an essay. Write three *opposing* arguments that others might raise against your point of view. Use your own paper.

I

EXAMPLE

A woman's place is at home with her family.

II

1. *Women are efficient workers.*

2. *Women are creative on the job.*

3. *Some women are psychologically unfit for the dullness of housework.*

1. Automobiles are the best means of transportation.
2. A dog is the best pet to own.
3. Elderly people belong in nursing homes.

Opposing Arguments: Where to Place Them

You can mention the points of view that oppose yours in your introduction. Using the ideas that do not go along with your own, you can build to a proposal sentence that states what you believe in and what you will try to prove.

In the introduction below from the essay "In the Swim" on pages 193–194, notice how the writer discusses opposing arguments. The effect here comes, of course, when the reader finally reaches the proposal sentence. It is apparent only there that the writer's position is opposite to all the points made so far.

> The jogging craze is sweeping the country. Before dawn, at noon, after dusk, men and women everywhere take to the trails and to the streets; in fancy jogging suits or in simple jeans and T-shirts these people are running to improve their health and fitness. Jogging tones the muscles, helps the heart work more efficiently, takes off unwanted pounds. Psychologically runners boast a relaxed life-style, a sense of peace with themselves. But this exercise is probably the worst form of self-torture any human being can inflict upon mind and body.

There are other places in the essay to explore your opposition.

If you know sound arguments that are raised in opposition to your proposal, you can build one body paragraph around those opposing arguments. Paragraph 2 of your essay can mention a few of the points made by people who disagree with you, and you might show with solid details the evidence these people give for believing what they do. Another possibility, if there are many arguments on the opposition's side, is to state in the second paragraph of your essay as many of the most effective arguments against your position as you possibly can. Then you can write paragraph 3 in one of two ways.

- Try to disprove the arguments of the opposition. Give details to convince your reader that you are right and that "they" are wrong.

- Say that the points the opposition raises are good, but that you believe differently. Give details to convince the reader that your points are just as good as the points made by those who oppose you.

On pages 239–240, you can see how opposing arguments serve in a body paragraph.

Step 2. Paragraph Practice: The Opposition in Introductions. Select any proposal and opposing ideas from Step 1 on pages 226–227. Write a brief introduction that mentions the opposition's points as it builds to the proposal statement. You may change the proposal somewhat. Use separate paper.

Hint

Transitional expressions like *however, but, on the other hand* will help you introduce the proposal.

Step 3. Paragraph Practice: The Opposition in a Body Paragraph. Select any proposal from Step 1 on page 218 as the proposal of an essay, and write a brief first body paragraph in which you show what arguments could be used against your proposal. Develop just a few arguments with specific details, or mention a number of arguments that are frequently used against the proposal. Use your own paper.

Hint

In this paragraph, do not try to prove that the opposition is wrong.

Combining Sentences: Changing Verb Forms to Expand Sentences

You remember from exercises in another chapter how verb parts as sentence openers help you vary your style. You can use verb parts in other positions, too, to connect logically elements in one sentence to another nearby. In some cases, eliminating all or part of a verb helps you unite thoughts. Looking over your early drafts, then, you can tighten sentence structure by manipulating verbs.

Look at this group of sentences:

(A) Charlene slumped in the driver's seat. (B) She gripped the wheel tightly. (C) Her neck was tense. (D) Her eyes were red. (E) She stared angrily through the windshield.

1. You could combine sentences A and B by changing one of the underlined verbs into an *-ing* form and by using it to open a new sentence:

    Slumping in the driver's seat, Charlene gripped the wheel tightly.
    or
    Gripping the wheel tightly, Charlene slumped in the driver's seat.

2. In another kind of combination you could keep the verb in its *-ed* form and combine A and B in this way:

    Slumped in the driver's seat, Charlene gripped the wheel tightly.

3. Sometimes you can drop the verb or part of it and can join what's left of the sentence to a sentence nearby. If you took out the verb *was* from sentence C look at how the rest of it combines with B or A or E:

<u>Her neck tense</u>, she gripped the wheel tightly.
<u>Her neck tense</u>, Charlene slumped in the driver's seat.
She stared angrily through the windshield, <u>her neck tense.</u>

The steps numbered 1, 2, and 3 are especially helpful in allowing you to transform—transform means to change into something else—a series of complete thoughts into one sentence that combines the ideas of the several sentences. Of course, you have to decide which ideas you want to stress so that your new sentence structure emphasizes them. The kind of transformation you do depends upon the meaning you are aiming for. But transforming sentences is valuable because it means, first, that a writer can often use fewer words than otherwise necessary to make a point and, next, that a writer has more options for varying sentence structure.

By using the techniques explained in 1, 2, and 3 to combine a whole series of sentences connected in meaning like those in sentences A through E above, look at just two of the possibilities you have for expanded sentences:

Slumping in the driver's seat (A) *and staring angrily through the windshield* (E), *Charlene gripped the wheel tightly* (B), *her neck tense* (C), *her eyes red* (D).

Her neck tense (C), *her eyes red* (D), *slumped in the driver's seat* (A) *and gripping the wheel tightly* (B), *Charlene stared angrily through the windshield* (E).

In each case, before you combine you need to decide which sentence in the group you think is most important, which sentence you want to emphasize. Keep that as the base sentence and use the other sentences, which you change by transforming their verbs, to expand and to modify it.

Hint

Be sure that the verb part you use stands close enough to the word it modifies so that you avoid illogical sentences. Instructions about verb-part *openers* on pages 320–323 go for verb parts used in any sentence positions.

Combining Sentences by Transforming Verbs. Create one complete sentence by combining the sentences in each group. Transform the verb into another form as you saw in the previous examples. You may have to change a noun subject into a pronoun, or vice versa.

Hint

Decide which sentence will be your base sentence; transform the verbs in the surrounding sentences only.

1. A crow sat on the branch of an oak tree. He cawed at the wind. He hopped from branch to branch. His feathers were black as tar. His eyes were small and beady.

   _____

   _____

   _____

2. Cindy waited for her turn to audition. She tapped her foot nervously. She stared straight ahead. Her stomach was queasy. Her heart thumped rapidly.

   _____

   _____

   _____

3. The defense lawyer gave his closing speech. He spoke passionately to the jurors. He had tears in his eyes. He paced around the courtroom.

   _____

   _____

   _____

4. Child actors work very hard. They must go to school. They must do homework. They study their parts for long hours. They rehearse strenuously.

   _____

   _____

   _____

5. Feminism works for all people. It encourages equality among the sexes. It is an important political philosophy for today. It brings people together on the strength of their abilities.

   _____

   _____

   _____

Word and Sentence Skills: Suggested Topics for Study

Pronouns as Subjects, pages 374–377
Pronouns as Objects, pages 377–383

• Writing an Essay of Argument

> **Assignment**
>
> Write an essay in which you explain and defend a strong opinion you have about some issue. As you write your various drafts, be sure that you have avoided faults that will fail in your argument (see pages 221–224), that you have successfully dealt with the opposition (see pages 226–228), and that you have written a conclusion that sets a new frame of reference (see pages 126–128).

Think about some point of view that you hold about today's world—perhaps something suggested in the early pages of this chapter or in the list of suggested topics on this page. Use some prewriting techniques (see pages 19–20) that work successfully for you. You might try the *subject tree*, explained in this chapter on pages 235–236.

Suggested Topics

If you need help in finding a topic, here are some possibilities for this theme assignment.

1. child custody: always with the mother?
2. day care: how does it affect the child?
3. saving energy
4. nuclear disarmament
5. should there be national skills tests?
6. racial or gender discrimination on the job
7. advertising: is it true to the consumer?
8. politicians of the 90s
9. drug testing in sports
10. the nutrition craze
11. ecology in an age of pollution
12. censorship in the media: how far will it go?
13. choosing a career: enjoyment versus salary
14. pornography: degrading the modern woman
15. exercise and the modern worker

You may wish to challenge one of the statements in Step 3 on page 219. You may wish to write about a topic suggested in the questionnaire on page 218.

Suggestions for Thinking It Through

Once you think you know what topic you want to write about, and once you can prepare a proposal that states what your essay will discuss, your concern is then with details: how can you illustrate your point to the reader? If you ask yourself these questions before you begin the essay, you will know before you write just what source of supporting details you might be able to use.

● On the Hunt for Details: Four Crucial Questions to Ask Yourself ●

1. What moments have I experienced in my own life that can help me illustrate my reasons for believing what I do about the topic?

2. What have I read recently in books, newspapers, or magazines—or what can I read quickly and easily before I write—that can help me support my reasons for believing what I do about the topic?

3. What have I learned from the television, the movies, or the radio that can help me support my reasons for believing what I do about the topic?

4. What have I learned from reliable friends, parents, relatives or teachers that can help me support my reasons for believing what I do about the topic?

Suppose, for example, you believe that despite assertions to the contrary, women are excellent automobile drivers. And you can remember two specific moments in your life that will illustrate to readers why you feel the way you do, moments that might even persuade them to believe what you believe. After your introduction (see pages 121–125), you might show in each body paragraph one of those moments expanded with concrete sensory details. You will not have *proved* that women are excellent drivers or that they are better drivers than men; but you will have *illustrated* to the readers how your own experiences explain the opinion you hold. That is a very effective way to build an essay.

But you may want to use several reasons to back up your opinion. Make a list. Eliminate any ideas you think would be hard to illustrate or prove. Then perhaps your list will look something like this:

- Women think very quickly in times of danger.
- Women are very cautious on the road.
- Women are courteous drivers.
- Women are particularly familiar with safety regulations.

- Women rarely drink before they drive, so they have fewer fatal accidents than men.

- Women have fewer accidents, in general, than men.

Consult now the Four Crucial Questions cited in the box above. Did you live through incidents that could illustrate any of these reasons? Did you, on the other hand, see important statistics about women drivers and their safety record? Did you read an article about women drivers (and could you quote or paraphrase accurately from this article)? Did you hear on one of the radio or television talk shows an interview in which you learned about the driving patterns of women and the effects of these patterns on insurance rates? Of course, you will have to decide how to arrange the details effectively.

Whatever points you decide to develop, your essay should have some kind of support. If you feel that you have a great deal of support to offer for a few of the reasons above, fine. Forget about the others. Discuss one or two points in the first body paragraph (paragraph 2 of the essay), using support you think convincing. Discuss the other points in the next paragraphs. There too, you need to use as many details as you think will convince the reader that you are right.

But perhaps you want to discuss in your essay *all* the reasons listed above. First try to pick out the reason for which you have the most solid and convincing support. Save that one until last. In the paragraphs that come after the introduction, discuss all the *other* reasons, giving brief support for each that you mention. In the paragraphs before your conclusion, discuss the one most important reason you have. By saving the most important reason for last, you impress the reader with your most striking evidence.

Perhaps you want to show in the paragraphs after the introduction the arguments many people give when they say women are *not* good drivers (see pages 226–227). Then, in subsequent paragraphs, you can try to show why all those reasons are, in your opinion, wrong. You would support the points you made with some strong details. Or you can say that you think there is some truth to what others say; and then you can go on to develop your own reasons for believing what you do about women drivers.

These are only suggestions: *you* decide what you want to include in each paragraph, how many points you want to discuss, and whether you want to stress certain ideas more than others. You will need to think about the various ways of developing ideas (explained in the earlier chapters of this book) so that you can figure out which method will be best for your essay. You might wish to describe, narrate, compare and contrast, or explain a process. With any approach you must provide answers to one or more of the crucial questions on page 245 so that you will know just what details to use before you write and so that you will not run out of things to say. Everyone has opinions (you have hundreds of your own), but the details that illustrate your opinions are what will convince readers that you know what you are talking about.

● Handy Pages for Reviewing Details ●

1. Imagery and Sensory Language   pages 3–5, 184–187

2. Using Statistics and Cases   pages 72–75

3. How to Paraphrase   pages 75–77

4. How to Use Quotations   pages 400–403, 190–191

Practice Planning for the Essay. Read the proposal sentences below. Consult the list of Four Crucial Questions. In the spaces provided tell briefly what you might discuss in the body paragraphs and what kinds of details you would use. Study the example.

EXAMPLE

Even in the field of hard physical labor, women should not be over- looked.

Discussion of women laborers in Russia. (Statistics from New York Times Almanac.) American women overlooked for jobs of hard physical labor. Paraphrase of TV interviews with feminist leaders. More statistics from Labor Department.

1. Children who do not eat properly will not perform as well as those who eat well.

2. Every family should know what to do in the event of a fire at home.

3. There is no proven connection between violence on TV and actual violence.

_____
_____
_____
_____

4. Young people who listen to music at very high volumes will have hearing problems later on.

_____
_____
_____
_____

5. Police should not waste their time giving speeding tickets and should concentrate on catching killers, thieves, and rapists.

_____
_____
_____
_____

Prewriting: Making a Subject Tree

The subject tree is a prewriting technique that helps you move from one level of thought to another as your mind considers the topic. In this way you follow your thoughts as they develop into higher and higher levels of specificity. The final product looks like a tree with branches reaching out toward possibilities for focused writing. After you consider what your tree includes, any one branch can serve as a starting point for the development of other ideas, for expanding and grouping details, and ultimately for writing a first draft. Look at the following example. The general topic, "Women in the Work Force," appears on the next page.

Step 1. Examining a Subject Tree.

1. What are the three general topic ideas Maria Montalvo uses as the basis for branching into specific areas?

2. If she chose to write about the psychological advantages of work, according to her subject tree what kinds of details might she use? How do you know? If she chose to deal with working mothers, what kinds of details might she use?

3. Select any one of the topic ideas on her subject tree. What proposal sentence could you develop for it? How might some people argue against the topic? What points could you make in each of the body paragraphs?

● Prewriting: A Subject Tree ●

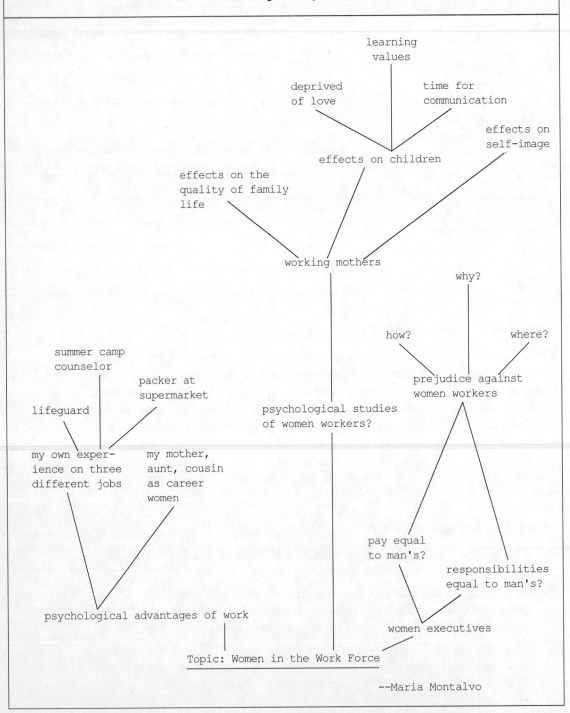

learning
values

deprived
of love

time for
communication

effects on
self-image

effects on children

effects on the
quality of family
life

working mothers

why?

how?

where?

summer camp
counselor

packer at
supermarket

prejudice against
women workers

lifeguard

psychological studies
of women workers?

my own exper-
ience on three
different jobs

my mother,
aunt, cousin
as career
women

pay equal
to man's?

responsibilities
equal to man's?

psychological advantages of work

women executives

Topic: Women in the Work Force

--Maria Montalvo

Step 2. Your Own Subject Tree.   Using a topic from the list on page 231 or one of your own, develop a subject tree in which you explore by branching a number of different possibilities for your basic idea.

● Prewriting: Brainstorming in Groups

You saw in a previous chapter (pages 51–53) how to brainstorm on your own. Brainstorming is also very useful when you work in small groups of people discussing the same idea or issue. You have a chance to share your impressions, to talk through any thoughts that develop in conversation, and to see how other people are thinking about the topic. Group collaboration can help you when you are developing an argument by giving you a chance to test your points with an audience before you write your paper formally. Questions people raise in discussing your points can help you see what questions *readers* might have if you wrote those points in a paper. Thus, discussion groups are testing grounds for your own developing ideas, ideas that group conversation can influence, shape, and direct. And, if each small group reports back to the larger group—your class, for example—you get a chance to hear many different points of view and to see how other writers in the class are developing their arguments.

When you brainstorm in groups, you can discuss a topic in a variety of ways. Have an open-ended discussion—that is, let everyone say whatever comes to mind about the topic—and allow free interaction among group members who may raise questions or may interrupt with fresh insights. Or, structure the discussion in advance with a set of questions everyone will try to answer. With either approach, it's always valuable to ask each group member to *write* down ideas for a few minutes before discussion begins.

● Guidelines for Brainstorming in Group Settings ●

1. Select someone to act as recorder. This person should summarize the main issues that arose in the group and should report back to the class on those issues.

2. Require each person to write for a few minutes before discussion begins.

3. Limit the size of the group to three to five members. Larger groups discourage everyone from talking, and some people will not have a chance to contribute.

4. Limit discussion time. Fifteen or twenty minutes is enough time for developing useful insights on a topic.

5. Decide on a format:

   Prepare a list of questions or guidelines.
   Run an open-ended discussion.

Collaborating in Groups.   Divide the class into groups of no more than five people each, and ask each group member to share his or her argument topic with the others. Also, ask each group member to suggest some of the points being considered to support the argument. Ask questions freely. Do not censor any relevant thoughts or ideas.

Student Samples: Drafting and Revising

As you consider your topic and begin writing, study the sections called Suggestions for Thinking It Through, pages 232–234, and Progress Reminders: A Checklist, pages 245–246. Also, study the student samples below.

Step 1. Reading Drafts.   Examine these two drafts of an argumentative essay on pornography. How has the writer improved the essay in the revised draft?

DRAFT

Pornography and Women

Pornography is the depiction of erotic behavior. Pornography is intended to cause sexual excitement. We observe pornography in various forms such as novels, pictures, triple-X rated movies and magazines. Is pornography degrading women of our society?

It is easy to see why many people feel that pornography isn't degrading. Some people feel that women can do whatever they want with their bodies and that acting in porno movies is an expression of their freedom. The pornographic industry is a million dollar industry. Various young women in this field do it for the money involved. Easy money seems to be an inspiration for many people living in a profit-motive economy. Such magazines as Playboy, Playgirl, Hustler and Penthouse don't feel that using nude women in their magazines is "wrong" or degrading. Marilyn Monroe, the great movie queen, displayed her body in nude photos that millions of people saw. To give another example. I was watching Good Morning America and they interviewed a young women who appeared in pornographic films. When asked if she thought she was doing anything wrong she replied, "I'm not ashamed of my body and I have nothing to hide." Nevertheless, pornography still is a fact of life.

Although pornography is considered just another "business," I and the majority of people in society feel that it is wrong and extremely degrading! There are many classic examples of women police officers who posed in nude pictures. As a result of posing the women were either suspended or fired. Normal people do not tolerate this kind of behavior from people in respectable positions in our society. The case that will probably remain in my mind for awhile is the Vanessa Williams story. She is the former Miss America. Because she posed in nude pictures before she had the title of Miss America, she was stripped of her crown. The Miss America position represents honor, self-respect and dignity. No woman who poses nude could have those values. Perhaps Miss

Williams liked the idea of men being stimulated by her body (or maybe she just needed extra cash). But she should have learned to overcome the old chovanistic saying "A woman's place is in the kitchen and the bedroom." Penthouse Magazine has a title called "Pet" of the month. Women who receive these positions show off their bodies. Personally, I think they're crazy to consider the term "Pet" an honor. I feel that it is perfectly normal for a woman to share her body, but with her HUSBAND and not the world.

In spite of all the money women and "glamour" in the pornography industry, there are many broken hearts that go along as a result of some of the crimes associated with it. There are perverts and rapists who get a kick out of using pornographic materials. There are sexual crimes against children as a result of this insane practice. Young, teen-aged, female runaways often turn to this as a form of security and money. I think the people in our society should get their lustful minds out of the gutter and concentrate on making the world a better place to live.

REVISED DRAFT

Pornography and Women

Pornography intends to cause sexual excitement through the depiction of erotic behavior. We observe pornography in various forms, such as novels, magazines, photographs, and triple-x-rated movies. By its very nature, pornographic material completely degrades the women of our society.

It is easy to see, however, why many people feel that pornography is not degrading. Pornography is a million dollar industry, and young women choose it for easy money, which seems to be an inspiration for many people living in a profit-motive economy. Such magazines as Playboy, Hustler, and Penthouse do not believe that using nude women in their magazines is "wrong" or degrading. After all, in now classic "nudie" photographs, Marilyn Monroe, the great movie queen, displayed her body to millions. On the television talk show Good Morning America, to take another example, one of the reporters interviewed a young woman who appeared in pornographic films. When asked if she thought she was doing anything wrong, she replied, "I'm not ashamed of my body and I have nothing to hide." In fact, some feminists and their supporters believe that women should be able to do whatever they want with their bodies and that the choice to show sexual activity in public is the ultimate act of freedom. From the enormous numbers of people who purchase pornographic material, not many think the degradation of women is an issue worth considering.

Although there is a lack of concern for women in pornography by a portion of our society, most civilized people feel that pornography is extremely degrading. Pornographers are considered outcasts. In a well-publicized case a few years back, for example, women police officers posed for nude pictures. As a result, the women were either suspended or fired from their jobs. Normal citizens have little respect for such women and do not tolerate this kind of behavior from people in respectable positions in our society. The case that will probably remain in the public's mind for a while is the case of Vanessa Williams, the former Miss America of 1983. Because she posed in nude pictures before she won the title, she was stripped of her crown. The Miss America position represents honor, self-respect and dignity; no woman who takes her clothes off for public viewing could reflect those values. Perhaps Williams was flattered to think that her naked body would stimulate men all over the country. Yet she was misled by the idea still held by many male chauvanists that, aside from the kitchen, a woman's place is in the bedroom. Penthouse Magazine gives the title "Pet of the Month" to a woman who will share her nude body in erotic photographs for male readers. Such women are crazy to consider the term "Pet" an honor. It is perfectly normal for a woman to share her body, but with her husband and not the whole world!

In spite of all the money, supposed thrills, and "glamour" in the pornography industry, it is a dangerous business for society. Many crimes are associated with pornography. There are perverts and rapists who enact on unwilling women in the streets what they see in X-rated movies or snapshots. There are sexual crimes against children, who are forced to pose before cameras. Young female runaways, drug addicts, prostitutes, and mentally ill women often turn to pornography for security and money. Our whole culture is affected negatively when we accept the sexual exploitation of women because we pay for the violence and crime attached to it. If pornography is freedom for the individual, that freedom makes a prison for the rest of the society!

--Rhonda McCullough

1. What changes has the writer made in the introduction? Do you like the way she combined the first two sentences? Why or why not? Do you prefer the original proposal sentence, stated as a question, or do you prefer the proposal sentence in the revised draft? Why?

2. The writer made a major change in the organization of material in paragraph 2. Why do you think she made the change? What other changes or additions do you note in paragraph 2 in the revised draft? Does the writer convincingly argue from the opposition's point of view in that paragraph?

3. Paragraph 3 presents the writer's view of pornography as degrading to women. How has she improved the quality of that paragraph in the revision?

4. Was there a point at which you felt you needed more information, data, or examples? Where?

5. What changes did the writer make in the conclusion? What is the new frame of reference she is attempting to set? Is she successful?

Step 2. More Essays. Read the following student essays and answer the questions that follow each one.

Deprived Children

An untrained observer watching a group of children at play may see no real difference between them. The child sitting in the sand pile looks similar to the one squealing happily down the sliding pond. Yet a closer look might reveal many differences. Each child has her own physical appearance; each has her own mental abilities; each has a home life that may not resemble the others'. A few people do notice, however, that some children appear insecure and unhappy; I believe that these are frequently the children of working mothers.

Children of working mothers are deprived of the security of a healthy and loving environment. As a young child with a working mother, I felt her absence deeply. On my first day in third grade, for example, a violent storm shook the streets of Brooklyn. Happy at the idea of a new teacher and new friends, the class grew even more excited by the trees whipping back and forth across from our first floor windows and the sound of September rain pounding against the glass.

However, this happiness soon wore off when streets flooded and winds of sixty miles an hour soaked the sidewalks. All the classes moved to the basement, and the principal, Mr. Greenwalder, announced that only children whose parents came for them could go home. Nervously hugging my new notebook to my thin jacket, I prayed somehow my mother would get to me. A slow line of mothers holding yellow raincoats and black umbrellas and boots trudged in to pick up their nervous children while I stared at a speck on the floor. The hours unfolded gradually, and soon I stood in the midst of the huge gray basement, alone except for my faithful teacher, Mrs. Timmins. The fear of a trip home in the hurricane disappeared in the pain and shame I felt that day by not having a mother at home like everyone else. As a child of a working mother I often felt that sense of loss and shame.

The results of such feelings in the children of a working mother can be very serious as the example of my brother Richie clearly illustrates. My older brother, younger sister, and I grew up in the care of indifferent housekeepers. At eleven years old, Richie often left the house for hours at a time with no excuses or explanations of his absences. No one really knew his friends, and my mother's own daily battle with tiredness after work kept her from questioning Richie's activities. As we grew older, Mother's continued absence became an accepted part of our family life, and neither my sister nor I could detect the gradual change in our brother. Richie grew into a sullen, moody, overweight teen-ager. He failed miserably in school, finally dropping out. He rarely spoke to anyone in the house.

Although these signs all pointed to tragedy, I was too busy with my own problems to pay any attention—and Mother just was not around. One night a call from a far off hospital told us that Richie's condition was fair after a drug overdose. My mother's eyes looked confused as if to say, "How did it happen?" when we sped to the hospital, but through the shock I knew the cause. Richie survived and is now in the midst of costly psychiatric care. But in my opinion, this whole tragedy might have been avoided through the presence and guidance of a mother. My mother was never there.

In many cases, then, a working mother's child is under great stress. She must become independent early in life and must learn to accept the loss of a parent. She can easily fall under bad influences and must be strong enough to resist if she wants to stay out of trouble. At a very young age she must learn the difference between right and wrong and must often face the difficult chore of choosing alone. These tasks present a challenge to the child of a working mother, and one can only hope that the child will succeed in mastering them.

—Phyllis Gold

1. What, according to the proposal sentence, does the essay try to illustrate? How does the purpose of paragraphs 2 and 3 differ from the purpose of paragraphs 3 and 4?

2. Has the writer convinced you that what she believes is true? If she has, what kinds of details has she used to do so? Which images do you find most appealing?

3. Do you find any examples of the kinds of poor reasoning described on pages 221–224? Where?

Developing Reading Skills in Preschool Children

Reading skills instruction belongs only in the schools. It is a teacher's job to teach children to read. Preschoolers are too young to learn how to read. These are some of the thoughts of people who argue that helping a child learn to read is a complicated process that only elementary school teachers should take on. Yet parents who become actively involved in their children's reading, starting when their children are still young, will find that this involvement is certainly rewarding.

An excellent and simple approach to preschool reading is to enroll three- and four-year-old children in special schools such as the Whitby School in Whitby, Connecticut, where reading instruction is part of the curriculum. Nursery school teachers aim to teach reading skills enjoyably and without stress. For example, they use special instructional aids. These include vowel shapes cut from light-colored sandpaper mounted on dark cards and consonants and groups of letters cut out of black sandpaper mounted on white cards. Afterwards, the children select words, and eventually phrases and sentences, from baskets. Enthusiastically, they translate the words into sounds and carry out the actions that they read. Not only private schools but now also many public schools with preschool programs are teaching little children reading skills.

Aside from these highly structured school programs, many educators now advise parents to help their children learn to read at home before the children reach the first grade. Commercially produced materials for home use are available at book stores, department stores, and specialty shops for children. One set of reading tools, for example, calls upon scientifically designed materials that are easy to use. Explanatory guides help parents plan a home program. The child examines large red lower-case letters as the visual pathway matures. Systematically, the child learns to differentiate between simple words such as "mommy" and "daddy." Later the child assimilates "self" and "home" vocabulary. And following that, "sentence structure vocabulary" develops in the context of "structural phrases and sentences." Because the alphabet is such an abstract concept, it is taught last.

Parents do not have to go it alone; they can learn how to help their youngsters by joining special support groups. Many parents along with their children, are enrolling in home-based projects that lead directly to success in reading. Mothers and fathers learn how to read aloud and how to hold a book so that the child can see and participate. The parents also learn how to follow reading with informal conversation, how to question the child, and how to stimulate the child's interest. The Preschool Readiness Outreach Program (PROP), for example, emphasizes the importance of a child's preschool years to later reading success. In PROP, parents construct educational games to develop their children's talking, listening, and observing skills. The more actively the parents participate in the program, the greater are their children's gains.

Parents should work with teachers in developing children's reading abilities. The great number of illiterate and reading disabled Americans aged sixteen and over and the large increase in remedial education at all educational levels provide enough evidence for us to reexamine our teaching methods. Preschoolers who have some reading ability will be a step ahead of their peers when they enter elementary school, and with parental involvement and the right program selected for each child, our future school-aged children should be able to bring essential skills with them when they reach the classroom.

—Muriel Guba

1. In her thesis, what two statements is the writer asserting about developing reading skills in children?

2. How does the writer use the opposition's arguments to make her essay stronger? Where does she recognize these arguments?

3. How does the writer move smoothly from paragraph 2 to paragraph 3? Are her other transitions as polished?

4. How does the conclusion bring in the importance of teaching young children to read?

Working Mothers

"Toward the end of World War II," reports economist Dr. Eli Ginzberg, "large numbers of wives and mothers entered the labor force, but the experts were sure that when peace came, the mothers would return to their traditional ways, leaving the work force to devote themselves exclusively to child-rearing, homemaking, and volunteer activities." Time proved the experts wrong. The percentage of working wives and mothers kept on accelerating through the 50's, 60's, and 70's. "Today," he says, "about two out of every five women with a child under six is working at an outside job." Those are strong figures. Millions of mothers are pushing their way into the job market, and are dealing successfully with responsibilities as parents, workers, and homemakers.

It is easy, however, to understand the feelings of many mothers who refuse to work, mothers who quit their jobs to stay at home and devote their full time to raising children. In a special issue on working mothers by *Parents' Magazine,* Ellie Brock explained that it is her sole responsibility as wife and mother to take care of her three-year-old daughter Lauren, her husband Richard, and their home in Arlington, Virginia. An attorney, Richard is busy all week and unable to help. No paid housekeeper or sitter, Ellie is convinced, could devote more time and energy than she herself could. No longer teaching high school students, she is less tired and, therefore, she feels, more interesting to her husband.

Many working women like the freedom being at home offers. They can do things they had no time for when they worked, reading for an hour on a living room chair, taking courses in yoga or tennis or dance at the neighborhood health club, tinkering around the kitchen with a chocolate cream pie or a Caesar's salad. My own mother, a "floor lady" in a pocketbook factory for thirteen years, quit her job twenty years ago for the coming birth of her first child, my older brother Salvatore. Three more babies came in the next seven years, and Mom feels that her staying at home all this time kept the family strong.

Although many women choose to stay home and care for their families, increasing numbers of working mothers have made new lives for themselves outside the home. In the same issue of *Parents' Magazine* Eleanor Seale, mother of three-year-old Archie, tells of a life filled with active, money-making work. During the day she is secretary to Justices Thomas Dickens and Clifford A. Scott of the New York State Supreme Court. Between eight and ten at night she keeps the books, does ordering and inventory work, and serves customers at the Seales' new, family-owned store. "We weren't born with silver spoons in our mouths," she says. "We want certain things for our family and we have to struggle to achieve them."

Women like Eleanor feel that their jobs make them more attractive and more interesting to their husbands. With the money earned by a working mother the family enjoys things they otherwise could not: a shiny new sedan, perhaps, a summer vacation on the West Coast, an assured college education for the children. These mothers believe that carefully selected day-care centers, nursery schools or at-home sitters enrich the child's life with experiences no parents alone can offer. Perhaps children have much less time with a working mother than they do with a mother close by all day long; but the quality of the time is what is important. In a single hour a thoughtful working mother can give to her child as much love and attention as a mother at home all the time can give to her child in a full day.

Because of the attention to women's rights, many mothers who in the past might have felt trapped in their homes have seized opportunities to use their energy and potential in stimulating careers. Yet there are women at home who see their work there as more important than anything. The point in all this, as I see it, is that the society must be made to tolerate choices so that no one is locked into a hateful life simply because someone expects him or her to behave in a required way. People must be free to choose the lives they believe are best for themselves and must have enough opportunities to change their minds if they make mistakes.

—Carmelyn Martini

1. What is the proposal of this essay? How does the introduction build to the proposal?

2. Where does Carmelyn Martini argue against her own point? What supporting details does she provide for her opposition's argument? What supporting detail does the writer then offer for her own point?

3. What transitions help the writer move from paragraph to paragraph?

Collaboration: Getting Reader Response

After you write your draft, form groups. Each group member should read his or her paper aloud as the others in the group take notes. Discuss each paper in regard to the following pointers in particular:

1. Is the thesis stated clearly in the introduction?

2. Do details (sensory, statistics, cases, quotations, or paraphrases) support the topic?

3. Does the writer treat opposing arguments fairly?

4. Are facts presented accurately and logically?

5. Are transitions within and between paragraphs clear?

Use comments made after you read your paper to help you produce your next draft.

Progress Reminders: A Checklist

As you prepare a subject tree or do other prewriting for your essay, as you do your first and later drafts, and before you write your final copy, use this checklist so that you can follow as many of the suggestions as possible. After you prepare your manuscript to hand in, fill in the checklist and submit it with your theme.

1. Did I consider the topic carefully before writing anything? Did _____ I use some prewriting activities that work particularly well for _____ me?

2. Did I write a rough draft and any other needed drafts before _____ making my final copy? Did I make changes in my rough drafts _____ so that I expressed thoughts clearly and smoothly?

3. Is my proposal clearly stated? _____

Here is my proposal:

_____

_____

4. Did I use smooth transitions as explained in the Essay Transition Signboards I, II, and III on pages 161–163? _____

5. Did I avoid the traps in logic and clear reasoning by studying the Fifteen Faults to Fail the Argument on pages 221–224? _____

6. Did I sufficiently consider the opposition's arguments and include some of them in my essay? (See pages 226–228.) _____

7. Did I consider carefully the types of details I want to use in my essay by asking myself the Five Crucial Questions explained on page 245? Do I know the difference between *illustrating* my opinion and *proving* that my opinion is correct? _____

8. Did I use a variety of sentence patterns: coordination and subordination, sentences with verb-part openers, sentences joined by transforming verbs? _____

9. Did I try to use strong verbs, clear expressions, and images that appeal to the senses? _____

10. If I used statistics, cases, or opinions expressed by others, have I mentioned the source of my information? Have I used reliable sources? _____

11. Did I read carefully the themes on pages 238–244 to help me see how other students presented their ideas? _____

12. After making changes in my drafts for clarity and smoothness, did I reread my essay, looking for errors in the use of verb tense and for other errors I tend to make? Did I examine my own Progress Sheet? _____

13. Did I try to use some of the new vocabulary listed in this chapter? _____

Here, from my theme, is a sentence that uses one of those words: _____

_____

14. Did I write a convincing conclusion to my essay? _____

15. Did I use a title that will attract the reader's attention? _____

16. Did I ask others to read my drafts and to tell me if they were convinced by my argument? _____

● The Professionals Speak

Step 1. "Uncaring Women's Health Care."   Read this essay in which Leonard Abramson argues strongly about the quality of health care for women.

SOME WORDS TO KNOW BEFORE YOU READ

coronary—anything relating to the heart

disparity—inequality

disproportionate—out of proportion

inadequate—not enough; not good

fulcrum—center of support

succumb—give in

Uncaring Women's Health Care

A woman visits her doctor for a yearly checkup. Aware of heart trouble in her family's history, and knowing that heart disease is the number one killer of women, she asks the doctor whether she should begin taking one aspirin a day, as her husband does, to decrease the risk of heart attack.

What does the physician advise? If the doctor is honest, he will admit that he doesn't know. Most of the research on the protective qualities of aspirin was performed on 22,071 men and, like so many medical studies, *no* women. And a study measuring the links between high cholesterol, lack of exercise, smoking and heart disease likewise featured 12,866 men—and no women.

Researchers argue that members of a sample group must be as alike as possible to test the hypothesis. But if only one sex is to be used, why not use women?

Recently in Los Angeles, a team of doctors found that women who need heart bypass surgery usually exhibit more severe symptoms of coronary disease than men before doctors take their condition seriously. As a result, many women who undergo bypass surgery face a greater risk of dying from it.

This disparity in research and treatment—the National Institutes of Health reported that, in 1987, they spent only 13.5 percent of their research budget on women's health—is important for its own sake and also as a symbol of the larger neglect of women in our health care delivery system. Women spend more on health care than men, and yet a disproportionate amount of medical attention goes to men.

Consider that every day, tourists stream past the Vietnam veterans' memorial in Washington, remembering a war that cost 58,000 American lives. Yet breast cancer takes 40,000 American lives every year, a tragic and unnecessary toll that is increasing steadily.

Almost a fifth of those deaths are preventable by the simple expedient of a timely mammogram. Yet, according to the Centers for Disease Control, as many as 9 out of 10 doctors do not follow the American Cancer Society's guidelines on recommending mammograms.

Nor can doctors assure women that other threats are guarded against adequately. Studies have shown that Pap smears, which test for cervical cancer, are inconclusive almost half the time because of poor sampling and interpretation methods. And, scandalously, it was just discovered in New York City that the Department of Health has a year's backlog of 2,000 unanalyzed Pap tests. Untold numbers of women who relied on the city's health care services now may die from a treatable disease.

Our nation's health care system must move to redress the inadequate attention paid to women's health concerns. There is no better way, I believe, to practice true "family medicine," for women are often the fulcrum of family life.

It is impossible to estimate the annual cost of poor prenatal care for women. Premature and low-birth-weight babies put immense pressure on the health care system; the care of one such baby costs as much as $1 million in the first year of life. And children who are inadequately nourished during pregnancy are known to have greater developmental difficulties than well-nourished babies—difficulties that can persist throughout life.

Studies also show that women are undergoing more Caesarean sections and other procedures than are medically appropriate. There is a need for an aggressive monitoring program to prevent unnecessary hysterectomies, a continuing problem in many regions of the country.

Medicine is not a perfect science, by any means. But when thousands of American women are dying from diseases we *can* treat, when thousands more succumb to diseases that more research might prevent, and when thousands of babies are born with unnecessary handicaps because their mothers' medical care was inadequate, then something is deeply wrong.

Women are reaching equality in earnings, in education and in employment. They must achieve equality in health care.

—Leonard Abramson

1. What is the thesis of this essay? Where is it stated most clearly?

2. What is the nature of the argument here?

3. List several examples given in the article that support the writer's belief about women's health care.

4. Does Abramson rely on illustrations of personal experience or does he use other sources to back up his argument? Explain your answer.

Step 2. Another Essay of Argument. Read the essay below and answer the questions after it.

SOME WORDS TO KNOW BEFORE YOU READ

litigation—legal action

mesmerized—hypnotized

subliminal—beneath conscious awareness

covert—hidden

truncated—cut short

legion—in large numbers

remorseless—without sorrow

culprit—guilty one

absolution—forgiveness for sin

Suicide Solution

It was two days before Christmas when Jay Vance blew the bottom of his face off with a shotgun still slippery with his best friend's blood. He went second. Ray Belknap went first. Ray died and Jay lived, and people said that when you looked at Jay's face afterward it was hard to tell which of them got the worst of the deal. "He just had no luck," Ray's mother would later say of her son to a writer from Rolling Stone, which was a considerable understatement.

Jay and Ray are both dead now. They might be only two of an endless number of American teen-agers in concert T-shirts who drop out of school and live from album to album and beer to beer, except for two things. The first was that they decided to kill themselves as 1985 drew to a close.

The second is that their parents decided to blame it on rock-and-roll.

When it was first filed in Nevada, the lawsuit brought by the families of Jay Vance and Ray Belknap against the members of the English band Judas Priest and their record company was said to be heavy metal on trial. I would love to convict heavy metal of almost anything—I would rather be locked in a room with 100 accordion players than listen to Metallica—but music has little to do with this litigation. It is a sad attempt by grieving grown-ups to say, in a public forum, what their lost boys had been saying privately for years: someone's to blame for my failures, but it can't be me.

The product liability suit, which sought $6.2 million in damages, contended that the boys were "mesmerized" by subliminal suicide messages on a Judas Priest album. The most famous subliminal before this case came to trial was the section of a Beatles song that fans believed hinted at the death of Paul McCartney. The enormous interest that surrounded this seems terribly silly now, when Paul McCartney, far from being dead, has become the oldest living cute boy in the world.

There is nothing silly about the Judas Priest case, only something infinitely sad. Ray Belknap was 18. His parents split up before he was born. His mother has been married four times. Her last husband beat Ray with a belt and, according to police, once threatened her with a gun while Ray watched. Like Jay Vance, Ray had a police record and had quit high school after two years. Like Jay, he liked guns and beer and used marijuana, hallucinogens and cocaine.

Jay Vance, who died three years after the suicide attempt, his face a reconstructed Halloween mask, had a comparable coming of age. His mother was 17 when he was born. When he was a child, she beat him often. As he got older, he beat her back. Once, checking himself into a detox center, he was asked "What is your favorite leisure time activity?" He answered "Doing drugs." Jay is said to have consumed two six-packs of beer a day. There's a suicide note if I ever heard one.

It is difficult to understand how anyone could blame covert musical mumbling for what happened to these boys. On paper they had little to live for. But the truth is that their lives were not unlike the lives of many kids who live for their stereos and their beer buzz, who open the door to the corridor of the next 40 years and see a future as empty and truncated as a closet. "Get a life," they say to one another. In the responsibility department, no one is home.

They are legion. Young men kill someone for a handful of coins, then are remorseless, even casual: hey man, things happen. And their parents nab the culprit—it was the city, the cops, the system, the crowd, the music. Anyone but him. Anyone but me. There's a new product on the market I call Parent In A Can. You can wipe a piece of paper on something in your kid's room and then spray the paper with this chemical. Cocaine traces, and the paper will turn turquoise. Marijuana, reddish brown. So easy to use—and no messy heart-to-heart talks, no constant Parental presence. Only $44.95 plus $5 shipping and handling to do in a minute what you should have been doing for years.

In the Judas Priest lawsuit, it's easy to see how kids get the idea that they are not responsible for their actions. They inherit it. Heavy metal music is filled with violence, but Jay and Ray got plenty of that even with the stereo unplugged. The trial judge ruled that the band was not responsible for the suicides, but the families are pressing ahead with an appeal, looking for absolution for the horrible deaths of their sons. Heavy metal made them do it—not the revolving fathers, the beatings, the alcohol, the drugs, a failure of will or of nurturing. Someone's to blame. Someone else. Always someone else.

—Anna Quindlen

1. What is Quindlen's proposal, or thesis, here? State it in your own words.

2. What kinds of details does the writer use to support her argument? Which details do you find most impressive?

3. Comment on the first three paragraphs. How do they work together as an introduction to the essay? What is your reaction to the one-sentence paragraph?

4. Where has the writer used transitions to connect ideas within paragraphs? Between them?

5. Explain the last three sentences. Why does Quindlen repeat the basic idea? How do the last three sentences make for a powerful conclusion?

8

Writing a Brief Research Essay

●

INTRODUCTION TO THE SHORT RESEARCH PAPER

A research paper grows out of careful investigation of books, periodicals, and other library materials to support a thesis. In other chapters you used expert testimony, data, statistics, and cases to back up your points, so that you now have some rudimentary experience in research. But in a formal research project your objective is to examine a variety of sources in depth, to use these sources to help you shape an opinion about some significant topic, and to cite the sources carefully in a written essay. A research paper also requires documentation of all sources at the end of the paper. In addition, your instructor may require an outline.

In this chapter you'll learn the fundamentals of research including how to limit a topic, find and record books and periodicals dealing with your topic, and take notes on your readings. You'll learn how to prepare a list of works cited to indicate your sources. In addition, you'll learn how to develop an essay by drawing on concrete supporting details from reliable sources.

● Vocabulary

Step 1. Terms Related to Research. The words below are useful in writing that draws on research. Determine the meaning of the word from the way it is used in the sentence. Circle the letter next to the best definition.

1. Though no one knew what had happened to the child, the social worker studied all the evidence and presented her own *hypothesis*.

   a. set of questions   *b.* educated guess
   c. research   *d.* schedule

2. To learn more about leukemia, I will interview Dr. Kim, who is an *authority* on the many kinds of cancer.

   a. author of books   *b.* surgeon
   c. expert   *d.* speaker

3. The students studied the *demographics* of post-World War II Europe to see how the war affected the size, growth, and distribution of populations there.

   a. graphs   *b.* certain areas on maps
   c. war reports   *d.* characteristics of populations

4. Before reaching a decision, the jury evaluated all the *data* they had from the physical evidence, the witness testimony, and the presentation of each case.

   a. opinions   *b.* information
   c. clues   *d.* confusion

5. Although books and newspapers like the *Boston Globe* were helpful in my research, *periodicals* like *Popular Science* and *Discover* contained much more interesting information.

   a. nondaily publications   *b.* specialized reading material
   c. publications about time periods   *d.* magazines

6. *Statistics* show that a frighteningly large number of young Americans know little or no geography.

   a. media reports   *b.* people who conduct polls

   c. charts   *d.* facts based on numbers

7. The teacher will *substantiate* her belief that Silas is a neglected child by showing the principal pictures of his neglected physical appearance and by producing reports of his poor schoolwork.

   a. convince someone of   *b.* reverse

   c. form   *d.* prove

8. You must *abridge* this lengthy report if you expect me to read it today.

   a. shorten in length   *b.* proofread the content

   c. explain   *d.* expand

9. Our company will *analyze* charts on consumer preferences so that we can learn to make our products more desirable to the buyers.

   a. invest in   *b.* introduce to the public

   c. examine the parts of   *d.* find out about

10. In his oral presentation, the student will *cite* several quotes from U.S. presidents.

    a. look for   *b.* study closely

    c. recite from memory   *d.* identify the source of

Step 2. Writing Sentences with New Words.   Write an original sentence using the words listed below.

1. demographics _____

   _____

2. statistics _____

   _____

3. data _____

   _____

4. analysis _____

   _____

5. citations _____

_____

6. substantiate _____

_____

7. hypothesis _____

_____

8. abridge _____

_____

9. periodicals _____

_____

10. authorities _____

_____

● Building Composition Skills

Finding the Topic

Sharing Ideas.   Here are several statements about different topics that you may wish to research. Pick out one or two remarks with which you strongly agree or disagree, and discuss your opinions briefly, giving reasons to support your point of view.

1. Freedom of speech is constantly under attack in the United States.
2. The number of AIDS patients will increase before it begins to decrease.
3. Most laboratory testing involving animals is inhumane.
4. People belonging to minority groups often have trouble getting good jobs.
5. Many children in American schools get poor instruction in reading.
6. Child abuse is a serious problem in American families.
7. Advertisers try to trick consumers.
8. Programs for the gifted place unnecessary burdens and stress on children.
9. College graduates tend to earn more money later in their lives than those who did not attend college.
10. State governments should spend more money to support day-care centers.
11. Overweight people are often burdened with many medical problems.
12. Childhood traumas can cause problems in adulthood.

13. The public schools are not doing enough for the physically disabled student.

14. Nuclear power is harmless when correctly used.

15. Public schoolchildren should take sex education courses.

Starting Research: Browsing

Any of the statements you discussed in Step 1 on pages 254–255 might help you identify one of your interests. But your topic might not yet be clearly formed in your mind; and you don't really know yet whether or not there is adequate material for you to research. You'll want to do some preliminary browsing in the library, therefore. When you *browse*, you inspect, informally, books and articles in your general area of interest. Your purpose in reading materials at this stage is not research. Instead, you're trying to limit your topic and to think about ways of developing it and ways to organize your research.

These pointers will help you browse about the library as you explore a topic idea:

● Starting Your Research ●

- Look in the library reference section at encyclopedias, almanacs, and other reference books for an overview of your area of interest.

- Check the library catalog under the subject that interests you. The library catalog helps you to see some possible subtopics under a large topic that you are exploring; it also helps you see the range of books written about your topic. Simply by examining titles of books, you can see many possibilities for topics to write about. The library catalog, which names all the books contained in the library, will probably be a *card catalog* arranged alphabetically in drawers. Many libraries now use an Automated Library System in which catalog information may appear on computers, microfilm, or microfische. Check with your librarian.

- Using the call numbers for books named in the catalog, go to the shelves that contain several of the titles you've identified. Examine them and other books on those shelves. Because library classification systems group near each other all books on similar topics, you have at your fingertips many approaches to your topic. Flip through the books; look at the table of contents, the index, the glossary, or the appendixes. Read the preface or the introduction. Read the first paragraph of a chapter or two. Practices like these can give you excellent ideas for shaping a topic.

- Examine indexes to periodicals. A *periodical index* is an alphabetical listing (usually annual) of authors, titles, and subjects of articles in magazines, journals, or newspapers. An index like the *Readers' Guide to Periodical Literature* has entries for popular magazines like *Time, Newsweek,* and *The Atlantic. The New York Times Index* lists articles and stories that appeared in *The New York Times.* There are many other indexes, some highly specialized, about particular subjects or writers.

    Like a library catalog, an index shows you at a glance the kinds of subtopics current writers have addressed as parts of larger topics. Reading over the titles of current articles, you can see a variety of approaches to a topic that interests you.

- Do a computer search. Automated Library Systems make it easy for researchers to call up extensive information from data bases (electronic reference lists). Using key words, called *descriptors*, you can signal a topic and find hundreds of bibliographic references.

- Talk to the librarians. Often they can direct you to appropriate reference materials that can help you develop a topic.

Browsing in the Library. For any topic you've already limited somewhat, browse in the library by following the pointers above. Then answer these questions. Use your own paper.

1. Which encyclopedias or other reference tools did you use? On which pages did you find information that may help you develop your topic?

2. From the library catalog, list three book titles (and their authors) that you feel may help you with your topic.

3. Remove from the library shelf any book you listed in 2, or any other book nearby that deals with your general topic. Look through the index, and write down the names of three or four entries you find there that might help you with your topic.

4. Check under a subject heading in last year's or this year's *Readers' Guide to Periodical Literature.* Name two or three articles that you might want to examine for information on your topic. Also, name the authors and the magazine in which the article appears.

Limiting the Topic

One of the most important goals in doing research is limiting the topic. Especially when you face very broad topics, you must consider carefully how to narrow the subject down so that you are not overwhelmed with reading. Even when you think that you have selected some reasonable area within a large topic idea, you can no doubt shave the subject down even more. The chart shows how to narrow down a topic in a series of steps.

● Narrowing the Topic ●

Too General	Still Broad	Less Broad	Narrow Enough
teaching	teaching number concepts	teaching number concepts to children	teaching number concepts at home to children under five
religion	religious customs	ancient religious customs in North America	Anasazi religious customs in America's Midwest
pollution	fighting air pollution	fighting air pollution in California	the government's role in fighting air pollution in Los Angeles
World War II	effects on WWII	effects on WWII in the United States	economic effects of WWII in Detroit

---

Step 1. Limiting the Topic.   How would you narrow the following topics down into reasonable areas for research?

1. computers _____

2. the crime rate _____

3. advertising and young children _____

4. nursing homes _____

After your first effort to limit your topic as a result of browsing and of some preliminary thinking, you should expect to limit your topic even further. Later on, as you read and think about what you've read, you'll discover new ways of looking at your subject.

Step 2. Limiting Your Own Topic.   After you browse about the library and after you select some topic that interests you, limit it, using methods similar to those explained above.

Step 3. Getting Feedback.   Read your chosen topic aloud as other students evaluate it, using the criteria established on pages 232–234. Or, your instructor may ask you to write your tentative topic down and submit it so that he or she can offer comments about it.

Making Bibliography Cards

Once you've identified resources to help you investigate your topic, you'll have to return regularly to the books and periodicals you have chosen.

Because you'll be reading information from more than one source, you'll want to keep track of the sources you use in order to prepare a list of works cited (see pages 264–266). Most students use *bibliography cards,* 3 × 5 inch index cards, on which the researcher copies basic bibliographic information about books or articles consulted in research.

Sample bibliography card (a book)

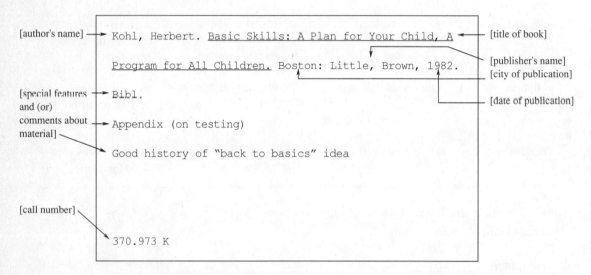

[author's name] → Kohl, Herbert. <u>Basic Skills: A Plan for Your Child, A</u> ← [title of book]

<u>Program for All Children.</u> Boston: Little, Brown, 1982. → [publisher's name] / [city of publication]

[special features and (or) comments about material] → Bibl.

Appendix (on testing) → [date of publication]

Good history of "back to basics" idea

[call number] → 370.973 K

Sample bibliography card (a magazine)

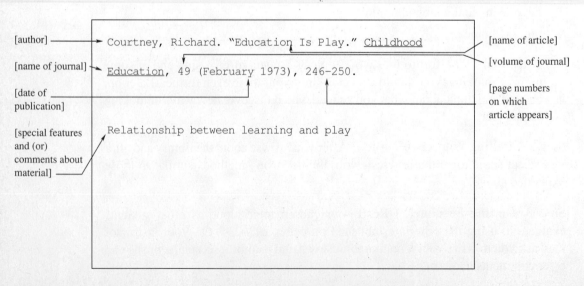

[author] → Courtney, Richard. "Education Is Play." <u>Childhood</u> → [name of article] / [volume of journal]

[name of journal] → <u>Education,</u> 49 (February 1973), 246–250.

[date of publication]

[page numbers on which article appears]

[special features and (or) comments about material] → Relationship between learning and play

Bibliography cards are useful because

- You have an accurate record of all the sources you consulted with all the critical information about them.
- If you are required to do so, you can prepare a list of works cited (see pages 264–266) from the data on the bibliography cards.
- Since all bibliographies are alphabetical, you can arrange the cards in alphabetical order by moving them about easily. You can use the cards to prepare your list of works cited (see pages 265–266).
- Notations to yourself about your first impressions of the materials help you decide later whether to return to the source for closer study.

Although your first sources of information for your bibliography cards are the library catalog and periodical indexes like the *Readers' Guide to Periodical Literature,* you must check all information against the books and articles themselves.

Preparing accurate bibliography cards saves you time later on. For example, with the call number of the book written on your card, you do not have to waste time returning to the card catalog each time that you must consult your book. With magazine titles and page numbers written down for articles, you can go directly to the periodical without having to check in the index again.

Preparing Your Bibliography Cards.   For the topic you have limited, prepare at least six bibliography cards for books and periodical articles related to your topic. Of the six, at least two should be from magazines or newspapers.

Making Note Cards

Most researchers find it useful to take notes on 4 × 6 inch cards. As you read about your topic in books or periodicals, you have to record important information that you can use to write your essay later on. Because a good research essay relies upon exact quotes drawn from other writers, you should record whatever information you select accurately.

On your note cards, copy, word for word, any passages of importance to your topic. (Use an *ellipsis,* three spaced dots, to indicate words you decide to leave out. See page 260.) Copy only one piece of information on a card; this will help you organize your thoughts later on. In order to keep track of your resources, record, on each card, the last name of the author, the name of the book or article, and the page number you've copied from.

From a note card like the one on the next page, you could choose words, phrases, or sentences from *Freedom and Beyond* to use in your own essay. Also, you might decide to paraphrase some of this material, that is, to put it into your own words (see pages 75–80), but you would have at your fingertips the writer's exact comments from which to work.

However, copying only exact quotes on everything you read can be exhausting and time-consuming. Therefore, many researchers paraphrase rather than quote information directly on their note cards. Or they will combine quotations and paraphrases in taking notes. Paraphrasing compels you to think carefully about what you read so that you can express it in your own words.

1. Sample Note Card: Exact Quote

```
"In his first years, before he gets to school, the
child lives his life, as he should, all in one piece.
His work, his play, and his learning are not separated
from each other. What is even more important, they are
not separated from him . . . . But in school . . . the
child is taught to think that his work, his play, and
his learning are separate from each other, and all
separate from him . . . ."
                                    —Holt, Freedom and
                                      Beyond, p. 254.
```

The risk in preparing note cards of paraphrase is that when you write your own essay from such cards, you no longer have the writer's exact words. Should you later decide that a quote rather than a paraphrase would suit your point better, you will have to return to the source. With note cards that combine quotations and paraphrases, you must be certain that you can tell your own words from the words of the writer whose idea you are recording.

In the note card directly below, the student paraphrases information from the book. The words "all in one piece" are quoted exactly as a reminder to enclose them in quotations if the student decides to use them in the paper. Notice, too, how an asterisk (*) comes before and after the student's own thoughts. Asterisks (or some such symbols) can help you separate the words and ideas of your source from any ideas of your own that your reading stimulates.

2. Sample Note Card: Paraphrase

```
In early years, child lives "all in one piece." Work,

play, and learning are connected to each other. In

school, however, child believes that all those are

separate and that all are apart from himself. *Check

against Holt's How Children Learn. Use in intro?*

                              --Holt, Freedom and

                                 Beyond, p. 254
```

Sometimes you write a note card merely to remind you of the content of pages you have read. This kind of card is especially useful when you have the book physically available to work from as you draft your essay. Thus, you can return to the text if you need to select a quote. (Unfortunately, much research is done from resources that must remain in the library, and fuller note cards like 1 and 2 above are more the rule.)

3. Sample Note Card: Reminder Card

```
Good discussion of how children's attitudes toward

learning (reading especially) change for the worse

because of values set by the schools (Holt, Freedom and

Beyond, pp. 254-256). Compare with How Children Learn

(Holt) and Hooked on Books (Fader). Use in intro?
```

The note card above signals the student to return to selected pages in the book *Freedom and Beyond* and, possibly, to use a quotation from those pages in the introduction of the student's research essay.

When you are preparing a draft of your essay and you select data or quotes from your note cards, you must be sure to cite your sources according to your instructor's directions. You can review internal citations and footnotes as possible formats for such citations on pages 266–268.

Making Note Cards.   For whatever readings you have singled out as pertinent to your topic—a chapter (or a few pages) from a book, an article in a magazine, or a newspaper—prepare note cards. Remember that if you quote or paraphrase you should put *only one* piece of information on each card.

If your instructor requests it, submit a set of note cards on one or more of your readings for comments and suggestions.

Developing a Proposal (Thesis)

As you read material on your topic, you should start developing ideas for a proposal (or thesis). Your proposal, as you recall, should make some assertion about your subject. That is, the proposal should state a limited topic and give your opinion about it. (Be sure to reread pages 118–120 to review guidelines for good proposals.)

But don't think of your proposal as anything fixed or permanent at this stage. As your research continues, you'll want to change your proposal, modifying it to address new ideas you learn as you read. The student who developed the limited topic below read books and articles that helped her formulate the proposal on the right.

TOPIC	PROPOSAL
teaching number concepts at home to children under five	Parents can teach important number concepts to five-year-olds at home.

The student's research convinced her that parents do play a role in helping children learn about numbers at home; and so, after some initial reading, she formulated the proposal above. As she examined more and more books and periodicals, she changed her proposal a few times until she produced the following, which she finally used in her essay.

Using simple techniques and easy-to-find materials in the home, preschool children can have fun exploring number concepts with a parent's guidance.

The new proposal changes the writer's focus. Now the essay will deal essentially with what the *child* can do; the first proposal stressed the parent. There is also more specific attention to the actual techniques that can be used. Next, the writer injected an opinion, "fun," and readers can expect details to support the notion of enjoyment. Any techniques explained in the essay will have to demonstrate the element of fun in this kind of home learning.

You should be ready to revise your proposal as often as necessary both during your research and during your writing of early drafts.

Step 1. Writing Proposals.   For each topic in the box on page 257, write a draft of a proposal sentence.

Step 2. Your Own Proposal.   Write a proposal sentence based upon the research you have done up to this point. Submit your proposal for your instructor's comments, or discuss your proposal in small groups in class.

Organizing Notes

By the time you finish reading, no doubt you'll have quite a stack of note cards. You'll want to organize them so that you can write your essay using the cards to provide data.

First, collect all your cards, and number them consecutively. Next, reread them carefully, looking for similar subject groups related to your proposal. Several of your readings will undoubtedly address the same issues, and you will find it useful to identify easily all the cards that pertain to the same subtopics. If you prepare a summary of your note cards by listing the major issues you noticed as you read over your cards, you can then write the number of the pertinent note card alongside the issues you've listed. Look at the following example:

ISSUE	CARD NUMBER
mathematics toys and games for preschoolers	6, 12, 13, 14, 15, 16, 28, 52, 53
child's attitudes toward numbers	1, 2, 3, 19, 20, 26, 30, 31, 54
counting objects at home	4, 5, 7, 8, 9, 11, 24, 29, 33
writing numbers	10, 17, 18, 21, 22, 23
drawing and pasting for number concepts	25, 27, 36, 37, 38, 39, 40

A summary like the one above allows you to arrange your cards in groups according to general headings. Since each card is numbered and contains the name of the author and the title of the book or article, you won't confuse your sources. With this method of organization, you can try different grouping patterns, and you can shift around the order of the issues you may address in your essay before you actually write about them. Also, if your instructor requires an outline (see pages 204–206), you can prepare one by using the card summary as a guide.

Summarizing Your Note Cards.   Gather together your note cards, and number them consecutively. Read them over, looking for subtopics related to the proposal you developed in Step 2, page 263. Now prepare a guide like the one above.

Developing a List of Works Cited

Writers of research papers always provide their readers with a list of names of the sources used in writing the paper. A *list of works cited* is an alphabetical listing of books, articles, films, recordings, interviews, or other sources that you referred to in presenting your research. With a list of works cited, you can abbreviate considerably any references to the sources you name in your essay. That is, because the list of works cited contains full information about the source, you can key citations to that list and can shorten the entries you'd otherwise need to expand fully (see pages 266–267, Making Citations in Your Essay).

Using the information you copy carefully on to your bibliography cards, prepare your list of works cited according to the following suggestions and models, which have been developed from guidelines established by the Modern Language Association for writers of research papers.

1. The list of works cited appears on a separate page at the end of the paper (see page 269 for a sample).
2. Do not number the entries. List then alphabetically according to the author's last name.
3. Write author's last name first, then first and middle name.
4. List alphabetically according to title other works by the same author, directly under the first entry for the author's name.
5. For works by more than one author, list the entry under the last name of the first author, giving other writers' names in regular order (first name, middle, last).
6. List works with no authors alphabetically, according to the first important word in the title.
7. Do not give pages for books. Do give pages on which essays and articles in periodicals, encyclopedias, and newspapers appear.
8. The first line of each bibliography entry starts at the left-hand margin. Indent all other lines.
9. Double-space all entries. Separate one entry from another by triple spacing.
10. Place the title "Works Cited" about an inch from the top of the page. (Do not use quotation marks; do not underline.)

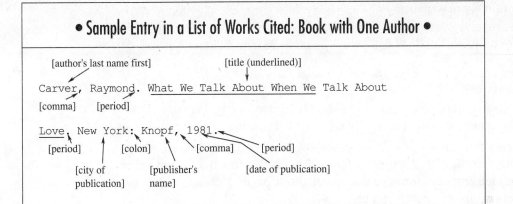

● Sample Entry in a List of Works Cited: Book with One Author ●

[author's last name first]   [title (underlined)]

Carver, Raymond. What We Talk About When We Talk About
[comma]   [period]

Love, New York: Knopf, 1981.
  [period]   [colon]   [comma]   [period]

    [city of   [publisher's   [date of publication]
    publication]   name]

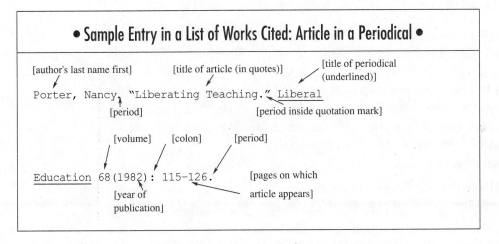

● Sample Entry in a List of Works Cited: Article in a Periodical ●

[author's last name first]   [title of article (in quotes)]   [title of periodical
                                                                     (underlined)]

Porter, Nancy, "Liberating Teaching." Liberal
               [period]   [period inside quotation mark]

          [volume]   [colon]   [period]

Education 68(1982): 115–126.   [pages on which
          [year of   article appears]
          publication]

OTHER ENTRY MODELS

An article in a journal that numbers pages separately in each issue:

Skerl, Jennie. "Training Writing Lab Tutors." WPA: Writing Program Administra-
    tion 3.3(1980): 15–18.
[This entry includes both the volume number and the issue number (3.3). A period separates them.]

An article in a monthly magazine:

Williams, Joy. "The Killing Game." Esquire Oct. 1990: 112–128.
[This entry includes the month that the periodical appeared, here abbreviated as *Oct.* for *October*.]

An article in a daily newspaper:

"Faculty Strike Clouds Future at Bridgeport." The New York Times 19 Sept. 1990.
    B1.
[This entry names the date (19 Sept. 1990) and the section and page number (B1).]

For other special entries, consult the 1984 *MLA Handbook for Writers of Research Papers* or some other documentation style book recommended by your instructor.

Writing Sample Entries.   Prepare a list of works cited for the three items below. Be sure that each entry conforms to the guidelines of pages 265–266 and that the list itself follows the ten pointers on page 264.

1.   A book called *Summerhill: A Radical Approach to Child Rearing* by A. S. Neill, published in 1960 in New York by the Hart Publishing Company.

2.   An article in *Technology Review* by Gar Alperovitz. Printed on pages 22–34 in the August 1990 issue, the article is called "Why the United States Dropped the Bomb."

3.   In a journal called *College Composition and Communication,* an article in the December 1979 issue (volume 30). The article is called "Sexism in Five Leading Collegiate Dictionaries"; it was written by Maxine S. Rose at the University of Alabama; it appears on pages 375–379.

Making Citations in Your Essay

In a research paper, your list of works cited gives full publishing information for all your sources; but every time you quote or paraphrase those sources, you must tell your readers directly in your essay just where you took your information from. In the past, writers used footnotes or end notes to serve this purpose. However, writers now use a simpler and more efficient system of internal documentation based on the MLA guidelines. You practiced a variety of internal documentation techniques in Chapter 3, and with a few minor changes and additions, you can learn the new method easily.

Continue to cite all sources directly in your essay. In each citation, be sure to include the author's last name and the page number on which you found the ideas to which you are referring. Other information about the author or the book or article is unnecessary because it all appears in the list of works cited.

● Sample of Internal Documentation ●

[quotation mark to open quote]

"To liberate teaching and for teaching to be liberating, we will need first to free the learner in ourselves" (Porter 116). [period at end of sentence]

[quotation mark to end quote] [author's last name] [closing parentheses]

[opening parentheses] [page number of text]

A reader who wanted to know full publishing data for the quote from Porter would check the list of works cited. (You can see the complete entry for Porter's work on page 265.)

The sample above is only one possibility. The key to an effective internal citation is to integrate it smoothly with your own writing. For example, you might want to name the author directly in your sentence and not in parentheses, as shown below:

Porter writes, "To liberate teaching . . . we will need first to free the learner in ourselves" (116).

"To liberate teaching," Porter points out correctly, "and for teaching to be liberating, we will need first to free the learner in ourselves" (116).

Porter says that for teaching to be liberated, teachers must first liberate their own abilities to learn (116).

Practicing with Citations.   On separate paper, write an original sentence that quotes, paraphrases, or summarizes any part of the passage below. Use internal citation to acknowledge your source. Use the samples above to help you construct your sentence.

The passage comes from page 306 of A. S. Neill's famous book *Summerhill: A Radical Approach to Child Rearing*. The book was published in 1960 by the Hart Publishing Company of New York.

Often the spoiled child is the only child. Having no one of his own age to play with or to measure himself against, he naturally identifies himself with his parents: he wants to do what they do. Since his parents consider him the world's wonder, they encourage this apparent precociousness, because they fear to lose his love if they thwart him in even the slightest way.

Quoting from Books and Articles

As you think through the draft of your research paper and look through your note cards, you will want to use the ideas and words of some of your sources. You can paraphrase, summarize, or quote directly. Be sure to name any sources you use; otherwise you may be guilty of plagiarism. Your note cards are valuable resources at this point.

When you quote or paraphrase, integrate smoothly the words of your source with your own words. These pointers may be useful as you use your note cards to produce a draft of your brief research essay. (See also pages 77–80, Integrating Testimony into Your Own Writing.)

- If the passage you select to quote has fewer than one-hundred words, work the quotation smoothly into your own sentences. Use a colon or a comma before the quotation. Use quotation marks at the beginning and at the end of the statement you are quoting (example *a* below).

- If you quote a longer passage (three or more typed lines or more than one-hundred words), block the quotation off from the rest of the text by leaving several spaces from the margin on each side. If you type, this longer quotation should be single-spaced (the rest of the paragraph or essay is double-spaced). Do not use quotation marks when you set off this longer passage (example *b* below).

- If you want to leave out any words of a sentence in the selection you are quoting, use three dots (. . .). If a complete sentence precedes the omission, use four dots (. . . .).

Here is part of a student's paragraph on understanding reading problems. Note the correct use of quotations.

```
Every teacher and psychologist knows that emotional factors play an

important part in the way a child reads; but specialists are still

unsure of how emotional problems really affect reading skills. No one

knows whether or not the problems are there to prevent the child from

reading properly or come after the child sees that he cannot learn the
```

[quotation mark]

way others do. One teacher of reading says, "Some writers have gathered

[comma]

evidence to support the view that emotional upsets are perhaps caused

[quotation mark]

by reading failure" (Karlin 29). Failure affects the way we all regard

a.

ourselves, and reading failure would have an emotional effect on a

student (Karlin 29-30). Even if this is true, however, there does not

seem to be any pattern in how personality affects reading competence.

Analyzing the findings in some recent studies, Jack A. Holmes, a

leading specialist, concludes:

[colon]

[no quotation mark]

> If one hopes for consistent grade-to-grade findings in these
> results one is bound to be disappointed. However . . . if one takes
> a developmental approach, one discovers that relationships between
> [single-spaced] reading and personality . . . found at the primary level become
> inconsistent at the intermediate and junior high school grades, and
> so far as the evidence is concerned, seem completely to disappear
> at the high school and college levels. Of course, there may be many
> possible explanations, such as the increased selectivity of
> students, the unreliability and use of different types of tests,
> etc. (112).

b.

[no quotation mark]

But no matter how these factors work in the reading process, no one can

disagree with Karlin that "Students who are . . . disturbed by major

c.

fears and anxieties should be referred to persons qualified to help

them . . ." (29).

--Steve Lederman

Works Cited

Holmes, Jack A. "Personality Characteristics of the

Disabled Reader." Journal of Developmental Reading

4 (1961): 111-112.

Karlin, Robert. Teaching Reading in High School. In-

dianapolis: Bobbs, 1964.

[list of works
cited, on separate
page, for full
information on
sources]

Transforming Sentences: Active-Voice Verbs for Strong Meanings

Many verbs can express the same thought in two different ways. Which of these sentences do you prefer?

1. The tired employee locked the office door.
2. The office door was locked by the tired employee.

If you selected sentence 1, you probably realized, correctly, that the extra words needed to make sentence 2 really added nothing of importance to the sentence. Why take more words to say exactly what you could say with fewer words?

Notice further that in sentence 1, the subject (*the tired employee*) performs the action of the verb. (It is he who *locked the office door*.)

But in sentence 2, the subject (*the office door*) does not do anything. In fact, something happens to it (it *was locked by the tired employee*).

Because the subject of sentence 1 actively performs the action of the verb, we say the verb is in the *active voice*.

Because the subject of sentence 2 is acted upon by the verb, we say the verb is in the *passive voice*.

Hint

In most cases, choose the active voice over the passive.

It is easy to transform passive-voice sentences to active ones. Just remember these pointers:

1. Passive-voice sentences always use some form of *to be* in combination with the verb. Look for word groups like *is seen, will be observed, can be cleaned, was done, should have been bought, would have been eaten*. You will have to remove the *to be* part to write an active-voice sentence.
2. Decide who performs the action of the verb. Usually the performer appears after the word *by*. Make that word the subject.

Passive	Active
	┌─[*was* is removed.]
The pencil was sharpened *by* Harriet.	Harriet sharpened the pencil.
[This is a clue to who performs the action.] [This is who performs the action of the verb *sharpen*.]	[The person who performs the action is now the subject of the verb.]

Passive into Active. In the spaces provided, change the passive-voice sentences into active-voice ones.

> **Hint**
>
> Sometimes the person who performs the action is not mentioned in the passive-voice sentences. You will have to determine the performer of the action before you write the active-voice sentence. Study the example.

EXAMPLE

The two employees were quickly brought to the manager.
(Here we do not know who actually brought them to the manager. Decide who you think performs the action, and then rewrite.)

The guards quickly brought the two employees to the manager.

1. The new buses were ordered by the transportation agency chief.

   _____

2. The dripping faucets in the apartment were finally fixed.

   _____

3. A college diploma is needed by many students who want jobs in management.

   _____

4. The iceberg was rammed by the ship.

   _____

5. Three freshmen were chosen by Coach Andros to be on the baseball team.

   _____

6. We were looked at with suspicion in every store in town.

   _____

7. The blazing Montana sunset can be seen from Len Anderson's ranch.

   _____

8. Reelection campaigns are often launched years before the election takes place.

   _____

9. The plants must be watered every day.

   _____

10. Roses were delivered to Susan Wo Tan at five o'clock in the afternoon.

   _____

Word and Sentence Skills: Suggested Topics for Study

Parallelism, pages 360–363

● Writing a Brief Research Essay

Assignment

Write an essay in which you present research on some vital issue. In order to support your ideas, draw upon statistics, cases, and quoted material you have chosen from your readings. Your readings should include a minimum of three sources, at least one of them a periodical. Cite your sources directly in the text of your essay, following the guidelines on pages 266–269. Also, prepare a list of works cited (see pages 264–269).

Suggested Topics

You might want to choose one of these suggested topics to develop in an essay that relies upon research. Some of the topics are quite specific; others require narrowing before they can lead to productive essays. (Review pages 256–257.)

1. ghetto health conditions
2. computers and learning to read
3. black schools in a southern city
4. mental illness in America
5. dishonesty in politics
6. prison conditions in your city
7. student dropouts
8. an endangered animal species
9. coal mines and working conditions
10. saving oil
11. teenage pregnancies
12. the divorce rate
13. the gifted child
14. services and facilities for the mentally retarded
15. the "greenhouse effect"
16. teenagers and suicide
17. curing AIDS
18. early-childhood sex education
19. automobile safety
20. illegal adoption services

Prewriting: Advance Planning

For research-based assignments that require a number of activities before you can produce a rough draft, you will find it useful to plan a schedule of deadlines in advance. In that way, you can set a realistic program of deadlines for yourself based upon the date that your final manuscript is due. Without such a plan, you may postpone some of the steps required to produce your paper and, as a result, you may discover suddenly that not enough time remains to complete your work success-fully. If your instructor plans to examine work you do at various stages, you'll need to build your schedule around the due dates announced to the class. Instructors who collect your materials will return them in time for you to move to the next stage.

The form below will help you to produce your own plan.

RESEARCH ESSAY: SCHEDULE OF DATES

ACTIVITY   TO BE COMPLETED BY

1. Browsing to identify topic   _____
2. Development of limited topic and discussion (or submis-   _____
   sion) for evaluation by instructor or classmates
3. Preparation and discussion (or submission) of bibliography _____
   cards
4. Preparation and discussion (or submission) of note cards on _____
   two readings
5. Preparation and discussion (or submission) of remaining   _____
   note cards
6. Preparation and discussion (or submission) of written pro-   _____
   posal sentence for the essay
7. Preparation and discussion (or submission) of note-card   _____
   summary guide
8. Preparation and discussion (or submission) of outline   _____
9. Preparation and discussion (or submission) of tentative   _____
   introductory paragraph with revised proposal
10. Preparation and discussion (or submission) of rough draft   _____
11. Preparation and discussion (or submission) of list works   _____
    cited
12. Preparation and submission of final draft   _____

Planning a Schedule.   Using the form above or a form developed with your instructor's guidance, write out a plan for your research-based theme.

Student Samples: Drafting and Revising

The section called Progress Reminders: A Checklist will help you keep in mind the various steps in preparing your brief research essay. As you write your drafts, consult the checklist on pages 279–280.

Step 1. Reading Drafts.   Read the two drafts of "Adolescent Pregnancy." How has the writer improved upon the early draft? What further changes would you recommend? When you finish reading, answer the questions.

DRAFT

Adolescent Pregnancy

"Each year close to 1.1 million adolescents in the age range of fifteen to nineteen become pregnant. More than one out of every ten girls become pregnant" (Berman 133). The majority of teenage pregnancies are unplanned and unwanted. According to Bode, Planned Parenthood officials report that when it comes to unmarried teens as few as ten percent of pregnancies are intential (15). For the million of American teenage girls who experience unwanted pregnancies about half abort their fetus. Teenage pregnancy and childbirth are problems that concern the emotional and physical well being of young expectant mothers.

When a girl discovers she is pregnant, she doesn't have many choices. The pregnant adolescent can have an abortion, or carry the fetus to term. Today teenagers have access to cars, and with a car comes privacy and temptation. Also many parents work, and with no adult supervision at home will-power dimishes. Along with these factors pregnant teenagers contribute their pregnancy to feelings of loneliness, peer pressure, parental abuse, and signs sent out by society. "Many females feel that they are persuaded or even coerced by males to have sex" (Bode 24). Furstenberg states "that most pregnant girls want to marry the father of their child only if and when they thought he would be capable of running a family" (193).

This enforces the fact that the pregnant adolescent is in need of security and balance in her life. If she can't get this from her parents or the father of her child, she will keep on searching. Another major contributing factor of teenage pregnancy is that youngsters lack information about their bodies. This is when parental guidance should be demonstrated, however often it is not. Many parents feel that if they avoid the issue of sex with their children, their children won't figure out it exists. Parents must talk with their children about sex. They should discuss the responsibility a person takes on when they become sexually active.

Bode introduces "there are a combination of factors that contribute to the world wide increase of teen sexual activity and pregnancy. Missed menstrual period, nausea, appetite loss, or craving for a particular food, tender or enlarged breasts are definite signs of pregnancy, which many pregnant teenagers try to ignore. However the teenager may very well be harming herself and her fetus by denying her pregnancy." Britt says that about a third of pregnant teens will have abortions. Berman points out that "although most teenagers choose abortion, among unmarried teens there are still three live births for every five abortions. And 96 percent of those who do give birth now choose to keep their babies: children having chidren" (134). The risks are great both to adolescent mothers who choose to have their babies and to those who choose abortion.

In conclusion to this problem of adolescent pregnancy, I would stress that society must become more aware of this growing epidemic. Society must inform and guide adolescents about sex and its consequences. Maybe if sex education is required in all the states, the dropout level in school, due to teenage pregnancy, would decrease. Billions of dollars every year are spent on programs for women who give birth as teenagers. Wouldn't it be much wiser and more economical to provide more programs for adolescents before they are faced with pregnancy? Adolescent pregnancy wouldn't be such a dilema today if clinics provided all the facts about sex with understanding and true concern.

--Kathy Clementi

REVISED DRAFT

Adolescent Pregnancy

Every year about a million adolescents between fifteen and nineteen become pregnant--"More than one out of every ten girls" (Berman 133)--and most of these pregnancies are unplanned and unwanted. According to Bode, Planned Parenthood officials report that when it comes to unmarried teens as few as ten percent of pregnancies are intentional (15). Millions of American teenage girls with unwanted pregnancies abort the fetus. Researchers offer a variety of causes for teenage pregnancy and childbirth; yet they remain serious problems that concern the well-being of young girls.

Many conditions in today's society seem to encourage early pregnancies. Today teenagers have access to cars, and with cars come privacy and temptation. Also, many parents work, and with little supervision at home will-power diminishes. In addition to these factors, pregnant teenagers attribute their pregnancy to loneliness, peer pressure, parental abuse, and signals sent out by society (Bode 24). Also, they long for security and balance in their lives. Furstenberg states that "most pregnant girls would marry the father of their child only if and when they thought he would be capable of running a family" (193). But few teens with children do marry, and the single mother finds little security either from her parents or from the father of her child.

Another major factor contributing to teenage pregnancy is that youngsters lack information: "They don't know basic facts about their bodies, as when conception is likely to occur, and they are afraid of asking questions for fear of appearing dumb" (Berman 133). Parents should provide guidance; however, often they do not. Many parents feel that if they avoid the issue of sex with their children, their children will not learn that it exists! But parents should discuss the responsibility a young person takes on when she (or he) becomes sexually active. "Young people must be taught responsibility," Berman insists. "We expect kids to be responsible, but we don't make them act responsible." (133)

But none of the reasons to explain teen pregnancies reduces the terrible risk for pregnant teenagers and their babies. First many girls deliberately ignore the signs of pregnancy, like missed menstrual periods, nausea, loss of appetite, craving for a particular food, or tender or enlarged breasts. The teenager may very well be harming herself and her fetus by denying her condition. "The younger you are the greater the risks for the child," Menken writes. "Young mothers have a higher frequency of giving birth before the nine month gestation is completed. Premature babies have low birth weights, which can contribute to congenital defects such as epilepsy, retardation, blindness, and deafness" (167). These are serious illnesses; considering that "among unmarried teens . . . 96 percent of those who do give birth now choose to keep their babies" (Berman 134), many infants face lives of pain and suffering.

The other side of the problem is just as serious. Britt writes that "One third of pregnant teenagers, about 300,000, have abortions. About one half of all the adolescents who obtain abortions are eighteen or nineteen years old. Forty-five percent are between fourteen and seventeen, and five percent are fourteen or younger" (44). Even under good hospital conditions, abortions are not without serious health risks for young girls. Besides, politically active "right-to-life groups" and threats to abortion clinics are sure to make abortion a difficult choice, and we are faced with a future with even more "children having children" (Berman 134).

Society must become more aware of the growing epidemic of teenage pregnancy. We must inform and guide adolescents about sex and its consequences. Of course, parents should play a major role here in educating their children, but parents are not the only solution. Unfortunately only a few states like Maryland, New Jersey, and Kentucky now require sex education programs in school. Maybe if sex education is required in all the states, the dropout level because of teenage pregnancy would decrease in the nation's schools. We spend billions of dollars every year on programs for women who give birth as teenagers. Would it not be much wiser and more economical to offer more programs for adolescents before they are faced with pregnancy? Adolescent pregnancy would not be such a dilemma today if clinics and more counseling programs provided all the facts about sex with understanding and true concern.

--Kathy Clementi

Works Cited

Berman, Claire. "When Children Bear Children." Reader's Digest May

1983: 132-136.

Bode, Janet. Kids Having Kids: The Unwed Teenage Parent. New York:

Franklin Watts, 1980.

Britt, Maj. "Why Are There So Many Teenage Pregnancies?" Mademoiselle

Oct. 1983: 44-45.

Furstenberg, Frank F., Jr. "The Social Consequences of Teenage

Parenthood." Teenage Sexuality, Pregnancy, and Childbearing. Ed.

Frank F. Furstenberg, Jr., Richard Lincoln, and Jane Menken.

Philadelphia, University of Pennsylvania Press, 1981. 184-210.

1. How is the introduction in the revised draft an improvement upon the introduction in the early draft? How has the writer sharpened the proposal sentence?

2. The writer has cut several sentences from paragraph 2 in the early draft and has rewritten the opening sentence in that paragraph. What is your opinion of the changes? How do they improve the essay?

3. Where has the writer added quotations or paraphrases in the revision in order to make her points more convincingly?

4. What is your opinion of the conclusion? Which version of the conclusion do you prefer, the one in the early draft or in the revised draft? Explain.

5. What further recommendations for change would you make?

Step 2. Another Student Sample.   Read the research essay below. Pay special attention to the use of quotes and paraphrases as supporting details. Answer the questions after the selection.

The Advantages of Attending Kindergarten

With increasing attention to improving our country's schools, many educators are supporting expanded programs for pre-school and early school age youngsters. Our past history, however, does not suggest that we will move quickly in this important area. In 1970, 3,024,398 American children attended kindergarten (Grant 42). This number is very disappointing: Hymes, writing about conditions only twenty years ago, points out that "only about 60% of our five-year-olds go to any kind of kindergarten: public, private, church-sponsored. About 40% go to no school at all" (6). Hymes also gives one of the main reasons for the low rate of attendance: "Only 29 states provide state aid for kindergartens, 21 do not. And most of the 29 provide only half aid . . .'' (6). It is unfortunate that kindergarten is so low a national priority because kindergarten is one of the essential educational experiences for children.

It improves the child's long-range learning skills. David Mindess states that "children who have attended kindergarten . . . show less tendency to reverse and confuse letters, have more positive work habits, are able to work independently as well as in groups, and do more accurate work" (17). Mindess reports on a four-year study by researcher Loretta McHugh. Involving 709 kindergarten and 620 non-kindergarten children, the study concludes "that the verbal abilities, quantitative reasoning and phonetic abilities of the kindergarten children were superior to those of the non-kindergarten group. In the third grade the kindergarten group was markedly superior in total achievement and seemed to have made more satisfactory school adjustment" (18). Certainly, sound early childhood programs allow children "to gain in language, to expand their store of knowledge, to grow in curiosity and in problem solving and in creativity, to stretch their attention spans" (Hymes 3).

But the kindergartner develops not only learning skills but also social skills. Kindergarten stresses play, allowing the child freedom of expression during a large part of the school day with classmates. "Play is the . . . way the small child discovers how to use the world for his own purposes, to manipulate it. He does so by imagining in his head . . . and then externalizing those imaginings in his play" (Courtney 246). Kindergarten is also the child's first opportunity to learn from television with the aid of a teacher, and this, too, is part of an important socializing process. Palmer makes the following observations about two classes using television: "One class gave the program its entire attention. Down the hall a class of children the same age was only partially attentive. . . . The explanation seems to be found in the different attitudes of the two teachers. One teacher is indifferent . . . . Her colleague down the hall socializes the attitude in the opposite direction. When the program hour draws near, she enthusiastically announces, 'It is *Sesame Street* time' " (19-20). She then gets the children's attention and encourages a positive attitude toward the program. Improved perception and social awareness are achievements of kindergarten programs that provide a fruitful learning experience for a child.

That is what kindergarten really is, a fruitful learning experience. For all the talk about improving early childhood opportunities for children, it will be very hard to reverse years of neglect very soon. Low budgets will probably continue to prevent many five- and six-year-olds from attending kindergarten programs. Although high costs for education are a problem everywhere, we should try to take advantage of unpaid volunteers who might be interested in helping young children. Senior citizens who are retired or who are out of work, for example, could help many states expand limited educational programs. With some simple training, volunteers could assist in providing important skills for early school-age children throughout the country. And, such a program would help bring meaning to the lives of many old people who have little to do but waste time. Early learning experiences are essential for children, and to assure a strong society we must provide the means for educating kindergartners in social and intellectual skills.

—April Wynn

Works Cited

Courtney, Richard. "Education Is Play." <u>Childhood Education</u> 49(1973): 246–250.

Grant, Vance W., and C. George Lind. <u>Digest of Education Statistics</u>. Washington: GPO, 1975.

Hymes, James L., Jr. <u>Teaching the Child Under Six</u>. Columbus: Merrill, 1968.

Mindess, David, and Mary Mindess. Guide to an Effective Kindergarten Program. West Nyack, N.Y.: Parker, 1972.

Palmer, Edward L. "Sesame Street: Shaping Broadcast Television to the Needs of the Pre-schooler." Educational Technology 11(1971): 18–22.

1. How does April Wynn's introduction set the stage for her proposal?

2. What two basic features of kindergarten does she support in her essay?

3. What statistics or cases do you find most impressive? Which quotation is most dramatic in supporting the writer's point? The statistics do not come from recent sources and do not refer to current figures. How do you feel about that? Would more up-to-date data have made points more strongly?

4. What new context does the writer set in her conclusion? Has she made a convincing point? Explain your reasons.

5. Comment on the first sentences of paragraphs 2 and 3. How does each serve as a transition in the essay?

Collaboration: Getting Reader Response

After you write a draft of your introduction and first body paragraph, divide the class into groups of three. Let each person read his or her paper aloud while the other group members take notes. After each paper is read, answer the following questions:

1. Does the proposal sentence inform the reader of the writer's main purpose in the essay?

2. Does the introduction capture and hold the reader's interest?

3. Does the writer make a smooth transition from the introduction to the next paragraph?

4. Are there sufficient details drawn from reliable sources?

5. Are there citations? Are the citations named correctly?

Progress Reminders: A Checklist

As you plan and write your various drafts, use these questions to check on your progress in preparing your research essay. Fill in responses to the questions and submit this checklist with your essay.

1. Did I think carefully about the topic, using whatever prewriting techniques work for me? Did I plan a realistic work schedule? _____ _____

2. Did I check several library resources, including books and periodicals? _____

3. Did I limit my topic sufficiently? _____

4. Did I prepare bibliography cards and note cards? _____

5. Did I write a proposal sentence that asserts the topic clearly _____
   and allows me to develop two aspects of it, one in each of my
   body paragraphs? (See pages 118–120.) Did I revise the pro- _____
   posal sentence, if necessary, to reflect changes in my thinking _____
   as my research and writing progressed?

   Here is my proposal sentence: _____

   _____

6. Did I organize my research notes with a note-card summary or _____
   some other plan? Did I write an outline if my teacher required
   one? (See pages 204–205.) _____

7. Did I write a rough draft and subsequent drafts changing _____
   language and sentence structure for clarity and correctness?
   Does my final draft follow correct manuscript form? _____

8. Did I use adequate detail—statistics, cases, quotations, con- _____
   crete sensory images, or a combination of these? Did I write
   quotations and paraphrases correctly, and did I cite my sources _____
   according to the instructions on pages 265–268? Did I include
   a list of works cited?

9. Did I read the student themes on pages 274–279 as models for _____
   my essay?

10. Did I use transitions to connect ideas smoothly and logically, _____
    both within paragraphs and from one paragraph to another?

11. Did I write an introduction that stimulates the reader's interest? _____
    (See pages 121–124.)

12. Does my conclusion bring to a successful closing the points I _____
    made in the essay?

13. Did I use a variety of sentence types? Did I open sentences _____
    with subordinators (pages 86–94); *-ing* words, infinitives,
    and other verb parts (pages 44–48); and one or two *-ly* words _____
    (page 43)?

14. Did I proofread my paper carefully both before and after I _____
    prepared my final draft? Did I check my Theme Progress
    Sheet (page 454) in advance so that I could look for my own
    usual errors? _____

15. Did I write a title for my essay? _____

Word and Sentence Skills

● Abbreviations and Numbers

When you take notes, it's often convenient to use some sign or shortened form of a word to save time. But in formal writing, you should avoid abbreviated forms of words.

WHAT NOT TO USE	WHAT TO USE INSTEAD
& or ∻ or Ɛ	and
Feb., Apr., Wed.	February, April, Wednesday Write out the word for the day or month.
bio, psych, eco	biology, psychology, economics Write out the word for all school subjects.
thru, tho, boro, nite, lite, brite	through, though, borough, night, light, brite Don't leave off the ends of words or make up short forms.
st., h'way., ave., blvd., rd., co.	street, highway, avenue, boulevard, road, company, } Always write these out.
ch., p., pp.	chapter page pages } Write these out, except in footnotes or bibliography.
lbs., oz., ft., in.	pounds, ounces, feet, inches } Measurements are spelled out
L.A., Ill., Calif., Rocky Mts.	Los Angeles Illinois California Rocky Mountains } Names of states, countries, cities, geographical places are not abbreviated. (For addresses on envelopes, however, established post office abbreviations are preferred.)
e.g.	for example
no., #	number
and etc., or ect.	etc. This is the abbreviation for *et cetera*. Do not use *ect.* or *and etc.*

Hint

Use *etc.* very infrequently.

• When You Can Use Shortened Forms •

1. &, *&*, Co., Inc.	1. only when part of an official name: *A&P, Tiffany & Co.*
2. Mr., Mrs., Dr.	2. only immediately before someone's name
3. Jr., Sr.	3. only immediately after someone's name
4. Ph.D., M.D., M.A.	4. only immediately after someone's name
5. FBI, NAACP, UN	5. Some organizations and government departments are usually referred to by initials. No periods are necessary after the letters.
6. A.M., P.M. (or a.m., p.m.)	6. when numbers appear directly before: 8:15 P.M.
	Hint: If you use the word *o'clock*, write out the number: ten o'clock *not* 10 o'clock.
7. $, No.	7. when numbers come after: *$5.00, Booth No. 6*

Hint

1. Abbreviations usually require periods.
2. If you don't know what an abbreviation means, consult any dictionary.
3. It's better, in general, not to use abbreviations.

• Do's and Don'ts about Numbers •

Don't use the number if you can write it out in one or two words.

fifty	*not*	50		nineteenth	*not*	19th
three hundred	*not*	300		eightieth	*not*	80th
eighty-eight	*not*	88				

Do use the number if more than two words are needed to write it out.

654   *not*   six hundred and fifty-four

Do use the number for the year and day of a date.

February 2, 1971

> **Hint:** Don't use *-st, -th, -nd, -rd* after any number in a date.

Do use numbers if you need to mention a series of numbers.

On the rack hung *50* red dresses, *340* skirts, and *15* vests.

Do use the number for percentages and decimals.

Of the students, *45* percent were boys.
The paper measures *8.73* inches in length.

Do use the number for items in street addresses.

480 Rockaway Parkway
1874 Ninth Avenue

> **Hint:** If the street itself is named by a number, write the word out if the number is below ten. Otherwise, use the number, *without -st, -th, -nd, -rd* at the end.

251 East *91* Street
1880 *18* Street
37 *Fifth* Avenue

Do use the number for parts of a book.

On page *18*, the author presents a graph to illustrate his point.

Don't start a sentence with a number.

Nine parents attended (not 9 parents attended).
The room held 350 seats (not 350 seats were in the room).

Step 1. Correcting Errors. In each sentence below, correct whatever errors you find in the numbers and abbreviations. The numbers in parentheses tell how many errors there are.

1. After so many yrs., you still can buy clothing cheaply on 2nd Ave. on N.Y.'s E. Side. (5)
2. On the 2nd Thurs. nite of every month, I take bio & soc classes at Drs. Hospital, located on Madison H'way. (8)
3. Getting thru eco 101 is my #1 concern in school this yr. (6)
4. 1,000,000 people turned out for the antinuclear rally in LA last Oct. 11th, tho the newspapers reported much fewer. (5)
5. On April 6, 1975, 5 children earned grades of forty-five percent on their arith. tests; but Mark's bro, 8 years old, missed only No. 4. (6)

● Agreement of Subject and Verb

You probably know already that a verb can tell time, so to speak, because it indicates whether an action has already happened, will happen soon, or is in the process of happening.

The girl spoke *in a loud voice* shows, through the verb *spoke,* that the action happened in the *past.*

The girl will speak *in a loud voice* shows, through the verb *will speak,* that the action is going to occur sometime in the *future.*

The girl speaks in a loud voice shows, through the verb *speaks,* that the action is happening at *present.*

The time-telling quality of verbs is called *tense:* past, future, and present are three of the main tenses in the English language. In using the present tense, you must be sure that the verb agrees with the subject. (See A Sentence Review, pages 403–407.)

• Agreement Defined •

When a subject is singular, the verb must be singular.
When a subject is plural, the verb must be plural.

The girl speaks in a loud voice
[singular   [singular verb
(no -*s*   (-*s* ending)]
ending)]

The girls speak in a loud voice.
[plural   [plural verb
subject   (no -*s* ending)]
(-*s* ending)]

Hint: The letter *s* is often a clue to proper agreement.

(1) Singular Subjects	Singular Verbs	(2) Plural Subjects	Plural Verbs
(which usually do not end in **s**) { *go with* }	(which usually do end in **s**)	(which usually do end in **s**) { *go with* }	(which usually do not end in **s**)

A dog howls at the moon.
　　[no *s* to show
　　singular subject]

Dogs howl at the moon.
　　[no *s* to show
　　plural verb]

A safe driver moves carefully.
　　[no *s* to show
　　singular subject]

Safe drivers move carefully.
　　[no *s* to show
　　plural verb]

Remember: Some subjects form plurals in ways other than adding an -*s* (*children, men, mice*). See pages 363–366.

Step 1. Verb and Subject in Agreement. Select a subject from Column I and a verb that agrees with that subject from Column II. Write the words in Column III. In Column IV, tell whether the subject and verb are singular or plural. Then, on separate paper, write a sentence with each subject-verb combination below. Look at the example.

I	II	III		IV
		SUBJECT	VERB	
EXAMPLE		*daisies*	*grow*	*plural*
women	grow			
telephones	laughs			
glass	breaks			
daisies	barks			
blood	learn			
students	ring			
eggs	flows			
puppy	crack			
	study			
	work			

EXAMPLE

White daisies grow wild along Harden Creek.

● Pronouns and Agreement Problems ●

A singular pronoun works with a singular verb.
A plural pronoun works with a plural verb.

Pronouns used as subjects do not end in *s*, so the letter *s* cannot serve as a clue to agreement as far as the subject is concerned. But because a singular *verb* in the present tense usually ends in *s*, look for an *s* at the end of the verb used with a singular pronoun subject.

Singular Pronoun Subjects		**Plural Pronoun Subjects**	
I	it	we	you
he	you	they	
she	who		

He dances smoothly.
[singular   [*s* ending on verb]
pronoun]

They dance smoothly.
[plural   [no *s*]
pronoun]

Exceptions

1. *I,* even though it is singular, is always used with a verb that does NOT have the singular *s* at the end.

   I sing   NOT   *I sings*
   I run   NOT   *I runs*

2. *You,* even though it can be used as singular or plural, is always followed by a verb that does NOT have the singular *s* at the end.

   You sing   NOT   *You sings*
   You run   NOT   *You runs*

Step 2. Plural to Singular.   Rewrite each sentence below, changing the plural subject to a singular pronoun subject. In most cases you will have to change the verb too so that it agrees with the new subject. *Do not add* -ed *to the verb:* that will *avoid* the agreement error by shifting into the past tense where there are few problems in agreement! Study the example. All subjects and verbs are underlined.

EXAMPLE

Children watch too much TV.

She watches too much TV.

1. Those cashiers work the late shift.

   _____

2. Romance novels help readers escape.

   _____

3. Tropical storms scare the people of Puerto Rico.

   _____

4. Falcons fly high in the sky.

   _____

5. For car repairs, my friends use Anthony's Service Station.

   _____

6. Some dogs eat food right from the table.

   _____

7. Computers save time.

   _____

8. My <u>brothers</u> <u>take</u> the bus to school every morning.

_____

9. The <u>lakes</u> <u>ripple</u> when the <u>boys</u> <u>cast</u> the fishing lines.

_____

10. The harvesting <u>machines</u> <u>roar</u> from morning to night during October.

_____

Step 3. Verbs That Work with Pronouns.   Draw a line through any verb that does not work correctly with the pronoun in each group below. Look at the example.

EXAMPLE

They

~~sings~~   laugh   speak   ~~listens~~   ~~votes~~   complain   ~~jumps~~

1. She
   runs   talk   hikes   draw   laugh   spell   spill   have
2. He
   gardens   read   acts   decide   appear   go   does
3. I
   study   tries   work   plan   decides   asks   has   walks
4. We
   jump   eats   remain   swims   attends   want   does   dances
5. It
   break   sparkles   cut   squeaks   shine   falls   slice   wave
6. You
   explain   drives   try   work   does   remembers   goes   suffer
7. Who
   speaks   lose   know   reads   smoke   leaves   kisses   write

Step 4. Sentences with Correct Verbs and Pronouns.   For any _five_ correct combinations of pronoun subject and verb that appear in Step 3 above, write an original sentence. Use separate paper.

EXAMPLE

They complain whenever the temperature drops below seventy degrees.

Some Special Pronouns and Agreement

Even though they may seem plural to you, some pronouns, when used as subjects, are singular and always go with singular verbs. Although people do not usually keep to this rule when they speak, formal writing still requires that you use singular verbs with these subjects.

SINGULAR PRONOUNS

anybody	somebody	neither
anyone	everybody	either
nobody	someone	everything
no one	everyone	nothing
none	each	something

EXAMPLES

[singular verb (*s* ending)]

Singular   Anybody believes a sincere speaker.
Subject   Everyone tries hard.

[singular verb (*s* ending)]

Step 5. In the following sentences, fill in the correct form of the verb in parentheses.

1. Neither child (to know) _____ what to do in the event of a fire.
2. Everyone (to want) _____ to believe the dean's speeches, but no one ever (to do) _____.
3. Each (to believe) _____ that the test was unfair.
4. Everything (to go) _____ wrong just before closing time.
5. Somebody (to phone) _____ me every night at midnight.

Step 6. Sentences of Your Own. On a separate sheet of paper, write a sentence for each singular pronoun listed in Step 4. Be sure that the verb is singular (check for the *s* ending) and that the tense is present (don't add *-ed*).

EXAMPLES

Each of the boys drifts off on his own.

Everyone buys a newspaper.

● Four Troublesome Verbs ●

I. To Be

Singular Forms

am: Use with *I* only.
is: Use with all singular subjects (except *you*).

I *am* tired today.
It *is* late.
The wind *is* blowing.

Plural Form

are: Use with all plural subjects and with *you.*

You *are* attractive.
The students *are* busy.
They *are* all outside.

Hint: Do not use *be* with any subject.

It *is* late.   NOT   It *be* late.

They *are* at the movies.
        NOT
They *be* at the movies.

This verb has agreement problems in the past tense as well.

Past Singular

was: Use with all singular subjects (including *I*) except *you*.

I *was* awake early.

        NOT

I *were* awake early.
He *was* seated in the rear.

        NOT

He *were* seated in the rear.

Past Plural

were: Use with all plural subjects and with *you*.

They *were* singing.

        NOT

They *was* singing.
You *were* lucky to miss being drafted.

        NOT

You *was* lucky to miss being drafted.

II. To Have

Singular Form

has: Use with all singular subjects except *I* and *you*.

He *has* a cold.
The book *has* a torn page.
It *has* a bright red cover.

Plural Form

have: Use with all plural subjects and *I* and *you*.

I *have* five dollars.
You *have* a cold.
The women *have* new cars.

Hint: If the subject is singular, the verb usually ends in *s*. If the subject is plural, the verb usually does not end in *s*.

III. To Go

Singular Form

goes: Use with all singular subjects except *I* and *you*.

She *goes* to sleep early.
The dog *goes* out before dinner.
It *goes* to its favorite tree.

Plural Form

go: Use with all plural subjects and *I* and *you*.

I *go* to the garage daily.
The men *go* this way.
You *go* too far when you drive.

Hint: If the subject is singular, the verb usually ends in *s*. If the subject is plural, the verb usually does not end in *s*.

IV. To Do

Singular Form	**Plural Form**

does: Use with all singular subjects except *I* and *you*.

do: Use with all plural subjects and *I* and *you.*

She *does* important work.
It *does* not look right.

You *do* the work!
I *do* too much driving.

Hint: If the subject is singular, the verb usually ends in *s*. If the subject is plural, the verb usually does not end in *s*.

Another Hint: Although you should usually avoid contractions in formal writing, contractions with some of these verbs and the word *not* can cause many agreement problems. To select the correct form of the verb, separate the contraction into two words.

doesn't: does not   Use with singular.

> He doesn't work.
>   (does not)

don't: do not   Use with plurals, *I*, and *you*.

> They don't work.
>   (do not)

wasn't: was not   Use with singular (and *I*).

> The doctor wasn't in.
>   (was not)

weren't: were not   Use with plurals and *you*.

> You weren't ill.
>   (were not)

Step 7. Picking Correct Verbs.   Circle the correct forms of the verbs in each sentence on the right. Then write the subjects and the verbs in the appropriate columns on the left.

SUBJECT   VERB

1. _____   1. _____   1. When she (be, am, is) tired, she (go, goes) right to
    _____   _____   bed or she (have, has) a headache all the next day.

SUBJECT	VERB	
2. _____ _____ _____	2. _____ _____ _____	2. I (be, am, is) practicing each day, but even if I (do, does), it (have, has) no noticeable effect on my tennis game.
3. _____ _____ _____	3. _____ _____ _____	3. Although they (were, was) best friends, she (don't, doesn't) even nod when he (go, goes) by.
4. _____ _____ _____	4. _____ _____ _____	4. When she (go, goes) on a construction job, she (does, do) the work quickly; when her assistant takes over, though, he (doesn't, don't) ever work fast.
5. _____ _____ _____	5. _____ _____ _____	5. He (don't, doesn't) work after school, because his tutor (comes, come) every day at four.
6. _____ _____ _____	6. _____ _____ _____	6. They (was, were) very lucky; the fire (weren't, wasn't) very serious.

• More Than One Subject (compound subjects) •

[Subject is plural.]   [plural verb]

A desk and an old lamp stand in the room.

    Since *desk* and *lamp* both make up the subject, the subject is plural; therefore the sentence requires a plural verb.

When
> either . . . or
> neither . . . nor
> or
> nor
> not only . . . but also

join subjects, the verb agrees with the subject that stands closer to the verb.

Either the manufacturers or the <u>driver is</u> at fault.

         [closer subject: [verb: singular]
         singular]

Either the manufacturer or the <u>drivers are</u> at fault.

         [closer subject: [verb: plural]
         plural]

Step 8. More Than One Subject.   Use the expressions indicated to open each sentence. Then use the correct form of the verb in parentheses to finish a sentence of your own. *Do not use the past tense:* use only the present. Use your own paper.

EXAMPLE

The TV or the radio (to play)
The TV or the radio plays in my house most of the day.

1. The TV and the computer (to work)
2. Not only my sisters but also my cousins (to be)
3. Air pollution and water pollution (to destroy)
4. A hot dog and a coke (to make)
5. Neither my Father nor my sister (to know)
6. Not only Marissa but also her sisters (to have)
7. Either the children or their grandmother (to do)
8. An oak tree and some wooden benches (to stand)
9. The boy and his puppy (to play)
10. Neither that article nor those books (to explain)

● *Is, Are, Was,* and *Were* with *It, Here, Where,* and *There* ●

To start a sentence correctly with *Here is, There is,* or *Where is,* remember that *here, there,* and *where* are not subjects: subjects in these sentences always come after the verb.

[not the subject]   [subject (singular)]

Here is an old maple tree.
         [verb: singular]

[not the subject]   [subject (plural)]

There are dead lilacs on the lawn.
           [verb: plural]

It is followed by a singular verb, *is,* even when the word it refers to is plural.

It is an important idea.
                [singular]

It is ideas like these that we need.
           [plural]

Step 9. Special Openers.   Use the words given below as the subject for each sentence. Open each sentence with *it, here, where,* or *there* and the verb that agrees with the subject: *is, are, was,* or *were.* Use your own paper.

EXAMPLE

two open doors   *There were two open doors in the hallway.*

1. a bad dream   _____
2. ice skates   _____
3. a paper clip   _____
4. paper clips   _____
5. horses   _____

• Words That Get in the Way •

Don't be confused by singular or plural words that appear between the subject and the verb in a sentence.

[Although this word is plural and close
to the verb, it is *not* the subject.]

The rain (on the rooftops) is causing trouble.
[singular subject]   [singular verb]

[Although this word is plural and close
to the verb, it is *not* the subject.]

A group (of students) was here before you.
[singular subject]   [singular verb]

Don't be confused by certain words that join with the subject: *together with, as well as, in addition to, along with* do not affect the subject.

[These words do not affect the subject.]

The banker, (together with his partners), was arrested for theft.
[singular verb]

Step 10. Verbs That Agree.   Circle the correct form of the verb.

1. A set of fine glasses (look, looks) lovely on the shelf.
2. Presents for your son (is, are) under the tree.
3. Nancy, as well as her twin, (take, takes) evening classes.

4. The best groomed of the horses (were, was) awarded first prize.

5. Mr. Pinto, with all his cats, (look, looks) ridiculous.

6. Creativity, together with technical training, (make, makes) a good photographer.

7. The pieces of chocolate cake (has, have) icing.

8. Maria, as well as her children, (was, were) caught in the rain.

9. One of your roses (is, are) dying.

10. The chief, along with the fire fighters, (goes, go) to the annual conference in Chicago.

• Plural Words That Act as Singular •

Some words, though they look plural, always take singular verbs:

physics	Amounts of weight, height or length, time, and money:
economics	
civics	Three ounces *is* a small amount.
mathematics	Six feet *is* very tall.
news	Three hours *was* not enough time.
measles	Five dollars *is* what I am paid each day.

Economics *is* difficult.
Measles *is* a childhood disease.

Titles, though they may be plural, take singular verbs.

Ghosts is a play by Ibsen.

Hint: These words are always plural and take plural verbs:

scissors	trousers
glasses	means
riches	pants

The scissors *are* on the table.

• Words Both Singular and Plural •

Words like *committee, group, team, family,* and *class,* when referring to an action by the group as a whole, take singular verbs.

When you want to stress that each individual in the group does something, use a plural verb.

The committee *are* leaving the work until to-morrow. [The plural verb *are* stresses individuals leaving the work.]	The committee *is* leaving the work until to-morrow. [Here you are showing that the committee acts as a whole in leaving the work.]

Step 11. Singular or Plural Verbs? Write the correct form of the verb in parentheses.

(to need)   1. My pants _____ cleaning.

(to buy)   2. Five dollars _____ very little these days.

(to encourage) 3. Mathematics _____ creative thinking.

(to practice)   4. Our singing group _____ every other day.

(to fly)   5. Two hours _____ quickly when you are happy.

(to seem)   6. The news _____ hopeful.

(to look)   7. My reading glasses _____ cloudy.

(to be)   8. *Star Wars* _____ still a very popular film.

(to practice)   9. The team _____ on the parade ground every Saturday morning.

• Agreement with Who, That, Which •

The words *who, that,* and *which* are singular *or* plural depending on the words they refer to.

The boy who finds the money keeps it.
[*Who* is singular   [singular because
because it refers   *who* is singular]
to *boy,* a
singular word.]

One of the pages that appear in the text looked badly torn.
[*That* is plural   [plural because *that*
because it refers   is plural]
to *pages,* a
plural word.]

Step 12. Agreement with *Who, That Which*. Circle the correct form of the verb.

1. He is one of those physicians who always (pays, pay) attention to your questions.
2. One of the men who (is painting, are painting) my house broke his arm.
3. Aspirin is one of the drugs that (require, requires) careful use.
4. Betsy Leung is one of those women who (work, works) while others play.
5. One of the bananas that (grow, grows) on that tree fell on the grass.

Step 13. Reviewing Agreement Problems. Finish each incomplete sentence below so that agreement is correct. Use the verbs in the columns.

is	go	speak
are	goes	speaks
was	do	stand
were	does	stands
looks	have	sit
look	has	sits
taste	bring	feel
tastes	brings	feels
want	speed	throw
wants	speeds	throws

EXAMPLE

A cup and saucer *sits on the table*.

1. Three weeks _____
2. One of my neighbors _____
3. Physics _____
4. Speakers who _____
5. Connie, along with her sisters, _____
6. One of the elevators _____
7. Either the mayor or the governor _____
8. Neither books nor TV _____
9. Twenty-five cents _____
10. The committee _____

Step 14. More Review. Circle the correct form of the verb.

1. At night she (does, do) her homework.
2. One of the children (has, have) a cold.

3. A jar of green jellybeans (sit, sits) on her desk.

4. A nest of bees (causes, cause) problems.

5. Here (is, are) the ten dollars you asked for.

6. Neither the bread nor the milk (is, be, are) fresh.

7. He (doesn't, don't) know his uncle's address.

8. The team (travel, travels) by bus to all their games.

9. The team (sleep, sleeps) in separate hotels.

10. The scissors (seem, seems) too dull.

11. In high school, economics (was, were) my best subject.

12. Fifty pounds (is, are) too much weight to lose.

13. One of the teachers (wear, wears) purple-tinted sunglasses.

14. One of the old posters, which (hang, hangs) in the bedroom, (is, are) torn.

15. Somebody always (help, helps) me when I ask for directions.

● Capital Letters

Step 1. What Do You Remember?   Write a *full* sentence response to each question below.

1. If you were writing a job application letter to someone named Jeanne Gilbert, how would you open the letter? How would you close it?

   _____

2. What cities would you most like to visit?

   _____

3. What are three subjects you enjoy at college?

   _____

4. Which flower has the sweetest scent?

   _____

5. If you could board a plane and fly anywhere, in which direction would you go?

   _____

6. What kinds of animals would you most like to have as pets?

   _____

7. What high school did you attend? (Write the words *high school* as part of your answer.)

   _____

8. Which mountain range is in your state or in a neighboring state?

_____

9. Which president do you think did the most for our country?

_____

10. What is the name of your favorite book, and who is its author?

_____

If you could not make up your mind about the use of capitals in some of your answers, study the reference chart on capital letters on pages 300–301.

Step 2. Making Sense with Capitals.   In each of the following sentences, the first letter of several words is omitted. Decide whether you need a capital or a small letter, and then fill in the blank spaces.

1. My ___ _a_ unt left her job at the ___ _U_ nion ___ _S_ avings and ___ _L_ oan ___ _C_ ompany to attend ___ _H_ arvard ___ _L_ aw ___ _S_ chool this ___ _f_ all.

2. On ___ _N_ ew ___ _Y_ ear's ___ _D_ ay, I went with ___ _U_ ncle Joe and my ___ _M_ om for a drive out ___ _E_ ast.

3. A ___ _C_ row fluttered from one ___ _E_ lm ___ _t_ ree to the other, occasionally dropping to the ground to play with a ___ _d_ andelion or to caw at a lazy ___ _c_ at sleeping under the ___ _p_ ark bench.

4. The ___ _S_ hopwell ___ _S_ upermarket, located on ___ _R_ iverside ___ _D_ rive between ___ _T_ enth and ___ _O_ ak ___ _S_ treets, is the busiest ___ _s_ tore in our ___ _t_ own.

5. When I took a class in ___ _A_ merican ___ _h_ istory, I learned a great deal about the ___ _C_ ivil ___ _W_ ar and about the differences between a ___ _R_ epublican ___ _g_ overnment and a ___ _D_ emocratic ___ _g_ overnment.

6. When writing ___ _b_ usiness letters, I prefer to see "___ _D_ ear ___ _M_ iss ___ _J_ ones" rather than "___ _M_ y ___ _d_ ear ___ _M_ iss ___ _J_ ones"; in closing, I use a simple "___ _Y_ ours ___ _t_ ruly."

7. It is not true that science— ___ _b_ iology, ___ _c_ hemistry, ___ _p_ hysics, ___ _p_ sychology—denies the existence of ___ _G_ od; it is possible to believe, for example, in ___ _F_ reudian ideas and the ___ _B_ ible as well.

8. On ___ _S_ aturday, ___ _J_ ean Fuller and her husband, who is a ___ _F_ rench

_P_rofessor, attended a _C_onvention for _t_eachers in _M_assachusetts, held at the _M_arriott _H_otel in _B_oston.

9. Television _S_oap _O_peras like _O_ne _L_ife _t_o _L_ive have loyal _a_udiences on the _E_ast _C_oast.

10. The _M_ayor was late for the dinner given by the _U_rban _L_eague because her car broke down at the old _E_ndicott- _J_ohnson _S_hoe _F_actory.

● Quick Reference Charts: When and When Not to Capitalize ●

School Things

La Guardia Community
  College
     BUT
a new **college**

Mohawk High School
     BUT
our old **high school**

Coleman Junior High
  School
     BUT
a **junior high school**

English, Spanish, French
     BUT
American **history**
economics, **biology**,
  business

Hint: Languages are always capitalized. Other subjects are not, except when specific courses (usually indicated by numbers) are meant.

Economics 13.2
History 64

a **sophomore** in **college**
the senior **class**

Writing Letters

Opening. Capitals for first word and any names.

Dear Mr. Stevenson:
My dear Miss Trumball:
Dear Jerry,

Closing: First word only:

Sincerely yours,
Yours truly,
Very truly yours,

Areas and Directions

Lower East Side
East-West relations
Far East
Midwest
lives in the West
  but not for
  directions

New York is six miles east
  of here.
They drove **north** across
  the bridge.

No Capitals for Plants, Animals, Games

daisies	a vicious lion
sycamore tree	baseball
an old oak	football
bananas	swimming
a bluebird	monkeys
six sparrows	apple

Geography

Russian River
Rocky Mountains

> BUT

a tall **m**ountain

Salt Lake City

> BUT

our **c**ity

Yellowstone National Park
Market Street

> BUT

a noisy **s**treet

Historical Occurrences, Names, and Writings

Tonkin Resolution
Revolutionary War
Seward's Folly
Fifth Amendment
the Constitution

The Family

I get along with Mom.

> OR

I get along with mom.
This is Aunt Celia.

No capitals to show relationship.

That is my **s**ister.
Our **u**ncle is generous.
My **a**unt is very helpful.

Buildings and Organizations

Dime Savings Bank
Sears, Roebuck and Company
Brookdale Hospital
Pathmark Supermarket
Republican Party
San Francisco Giants
Girl Scouts

The Word "I"

Always capitalize the word *I*:

When *I* saw her, *I* was
delighted.

Days, Months, Seasons, Celebrations

Monday
April

> **not seasons**

spring, summer, **f**all,
autumn, **w**inter

Election Day
Festival of Lights
New Year's Eve

Religion, Race, Nationality

God, Lord
Bible, Genesis
New Testament
bless His Name
the Egyptian gods
Catholicism
the Jewish religion
Protestant beliefs
Negro, Indian
Dutch Reformed Church

Titles
Books, Stories, Shows, Poems

"Oh Captain, My Captain"
Love Story
A Tale of Two Cities

> BUT

a **b**ook by Dickens

The Washington Post
All in the Family
"The Legend of Sleepy
  Hollow"

Titles
People

President Carter
Judge Black
Dr. Bracken
He is the president of the
  company.
Mr. Davis, President of the
  company

> OR

Mr. Davis, president of the
  company
Harriet Parsons, Ph.D.

> BUT

a **t**eacher, a **l**awyer, a
  professor

Hint: If the title takes the place
of a person's name, use a capital.

The Mayor arrived late.
The **m**ayor's job is difficult.

Step 3. Correcting Your Errors. Return to Step 1, pages 298–299. Make corrections in what you wrote, based upon the reference chart on pages 300–301.

Step 4. Finding Mistakes with Capitals. Each sentence below has the number of errors with capitals indicated in parentheses. Make the corrections directly on the page.

1. My house is just 10 miles East of detroit, but i have never visited uncle Mario, who lives near the Museum. (5)

2. my Dear ms. stromberg,
   I would like you to know that I received dr. weber's offer of a Teaching Position in the english department to teach three sections of creative writing 127. I accept with pleasure.

   Sincerely Yours,
   tess carver, ph.D. (16)

3. i would like to play Baseball for the chicago white sox, but my Father insists that I become a Lawyer and work for the law firm of davis and rutter in seattle. (10)

4. The hartville city council will consider a plan for a new High School for the study of Art, Philosophy, and Humanities. (8)

5. when i saw the President of First National bank at a Baseball game in Shea Stadium one hot august day, i was surprised because i thought he was visiting his Daughter in the midwest. (11).

● **Commas**

Commas have two basic functions within our punctuation signal system. First, they separate main sentence parts. Second, they enclose interrupters within the sentence. The following seven sections on commas illustrate those two basic functions.

● I. To Separate Items in a Series ●

A. We bought eggs, bread, and cereal.

B. My mother rushed to the garage, to the car, and then to the library.

C. Larry bought a Mustang, Gina bought an old Pontiac, but Andrew bought a sleek new motorcycle.

         1   2   3

D. He was a tall, handsome, and hardworking man.

Words 1, 2, and 3 above describe "man." Since they are equally important, can be written in any order, and would make sense if the word *and* appeared between them (He was a tall *and* handsome *and* hardworking man), you need to use commas.

$$1 \quad 2 \quad 3$$

However, in this sentence, *Steve ate four small chocolate candies,* commas are not needed. You could not reverse the order of the describing words, nor could you make sense if you used *and* between the words (Steve ate four *and* small *and* chocolate candies).

Hints:

1. Each item can be either one word (as in A above) or a group of words (as in B or C above).
2. There must be at least three items in the series.
3. The comma before *and* or *but* is *NOT* required.
4. To determine whether you need commas between describing words:
   a. Try to reverse their order in the sentence.
   b. Try to use *and* between the describing words.
   If you can do *a* and *b*, use commas.

Step 1. Commas and Series.   Use commas where they belong. If a sentence is correct, mark it *C*.

1. Broccoli cauliflower and carrots are high in fiber.
2. The radiator transmission and fuel pump all have to be fixed on my old Ford.
3. If I want to have a party, I must vacuum the rug dust the furniture and wipe the windows.
4. It is best to read through your essay once to put it aside for a while and then to reread it thoroughly for errors.
5. Down the dark wooden staircase through the empty hallways past the musty living room the old man hobbled with his cane.

● II. To Set Off a Direct Quotation (see page 400) ●

I said, "Sit down!"

"I'm not tired," she replied.

"But a person needs rest," I said, "even if she's not tired."

Hint: If you use a question mark or an exclamation point after a quotation, do not use a comma too.

"Where were you?" he asked.

"Stand up!" she screamed.

Step 2. Commas and Quotations. Use commas correctly in these sentences. If the sentence is already correct, mark it *C*.

1. Sadly, Senator Davis announced "I will not run for a third term."

2. "Chicago is lovely this time of year" he admitted "but I miss the serenity of the country."

3. "Why is the tray so late?"

4. "Pull over" commanded the police officer "and show me your license."

5. "I wish" Mom complained "that you would clean up your room."

● III. To Set Off Introductory Sections ●

A. Certain Transitions as Openers
(one word or several words)

[comma]

Nevertheless, try to speak in a loud voice.

In other words, be careful!
   [comma]

B. Certain Conversational Words
(to set off *yes, not, oh well, why,* and *now* used in conversation)

[comma]   [comma]   [comma]

Yes, he will be there. *Why,* how did that happen? *Oh,* that is awful!

C. -*ing* Word or Other Verb-Part Openers
(see pages 320–323)

[-*ing*   *Sailing along the lake*, I felt peace and contentment.
opener]   [comma]

[verb-part   *To reach the top of the shelf*, the child stood on a chair.
opener]   [comma]

     Scribbled quickly, the note was hard to read.
                   [comma]

D. Subordinated Word Groups as Openers

[subordinator]

Although the moon hung in the sky, the sun still shone.
                      [comma]

Because the vocabulary confused us, we used a dictionary to check definitions.
   [subordinator]   [comma]

Hint: Brief opening-word groups not covered in A, B, and C above usually do not have commas after them.

[no comma]

In a few months I will be twenty.

[no comma]

Beyond the tree stands a small house.

If the introductory subordinated word group is brief, you may omit the comma.

When he sang I left the room.

[no comma]

Step 3. Commas After Openers. Put in commas where they belong. Mark the sentence *C* if it requires no commas.

1. Beyond the black clouds a sleek jet soared noisily.
2. Illustrating the effects of the drought the chart compares countries in the third world.
3. On the other hand I do love Japanese food.
4. Without a substantial increase in salary very shortly John will quit his job.
5. However a tax increase is rarely a popular strategy.

● IV. To Help Separate Two Complete Thoughts When a Coordinator ● Is Expressed (see pages 12–15)

Hint 1: Coordinators are *and, or, nor, but, for.*

[comma]

Many people believe that Memphis is a large city, but it has few problems of traffic congestion.

[comma]

Just turn the key, and you will see when the engine starts that this car is like no other you have ever driven.

Hint 2: The comma may be left out when the two complete thoughts are very brief.

[no comma]

We ate and they drank.

They flew but we drove there.

[no comma]

Step 4. Commas and Coordinators. Select a sentence from Column I and coordinate it sensibly on separate paper with a sentence in Column II, using one of the five coordinators. Use a comma when necessary.

I	II
1. You should always eat breakfast.	1. My mother was born in Vietnam.
2. I enjoy a good cry.	2. You can write it by hand.
3. Fred bought a very expensive shirt.	3. It saves me time.
4. My father was born in China.	4. Its colors faded after the third washing.
5. You can type your essay.	5. It provides you with energy for the rest of the day.

V. To Separate Words or Word Groups That Interrupt the Main Idea of the Sentence

A. Transition Words to Interrupt

We felt, however, that whitewall tires were unnecessary.

[commas here]

But the kangaroo, to be sure, is an unusual animal.

B. Subordinating Word Groups to Interrupt

That old truck, which has ignition trouble, is hard to start.

[commas here]

Mr. Davis, who drives to work, always complains about the traffic.

[commas]

Caroline, whose voice is soft, is really charming.

The subordinated word groups do not give information to identify the subject, and they could be removed from the sentences without changing the meaning. We know which truck is hard to start (*that old one*) without the interrputer. We know who complains about traffic (*Mr. Davis*) without the interrupter. We know who is charming (*Caroline*) without the interrupter. Therefore, commas are needed to set off the added information.

But if the subordinating word group is needed to identify the subject, commas are not required.

[no comma]   [no comma]

A truck that has ignition trouble is hard to start.

[These words identify the truck.
Without these words, we don't
know which truck is hard to
start.]

[no comma]   [no comma]

People who drive to work always complain about the traffic.

[Without these words, it
would seem that all
people complain about
the traffic.]

[no comma]   [no comma]

A girl whose voice is soft is speaking on the telephone.

[Without these words,
we don't know which
girl is speaking.]

Hint: If *that* opens the subordinating word group, you usually do not need commas.

C. Interrupters That Describe

1. *-ing* word groups to interrupt

                  [commas here]

A shaky station wagon, laboring up the hill, backfired in a crash.

         [commas]

The puppy, trembling, drew close to its mother.

2. Interrupters starting with *-ed* words or other verb parts

[comma]   [verb part]   [comma]

Miss Kelly, *dressed* in red, ran for the bus.

[comma]   [verb part (infinitive)]   [comma]

The dog, *to get* his food, barked wildly.

[comma]   [verb part]   [comma]

A mirror, *broken* in small pieces, lay on the street.

Hint: The interrupting words in 1 and 2 just add information about the subject. They could be left out of the sentence without disturbing the meaning. Therefore, commas are needed. However, when interrupting word groups like those above identify the subject, commas are not used.

[Not just any wagon backfires: this word groups identifies the wagon and is essential to the meaning of the sentence.]

A wagon *laboring up a hill* can backfire.
[no commas]

[It is only the woman dressed in red who is attractive according to this sentence. This word group identifies the subject.]

The woman *dressed in red* is attractive.
[no commas]

3. Other describing words

[These words describe the driver. They could be left out of the sentence.]

The driver, a doctor, was not injured.
[commas]

The Mustang, a new white convertible, crashed into a pole.

[These words describe the car, which has already been identified. The words could be left out of the sentence.]

Step 5. Commas for Interrupters.   Select from Column II an interrupter that could be used sensibly within each complete thought in Column I. Decide whether or not commas are needed. Then, write each new sentence on separate paper.

EXAMPLE

A student who doesn't study will fail.

I	II
A student will fail.	despite her nervousness
My history textbook is unpleasant to read.	a chef
	which contains sexist ideas
A news story is unprofessional.	that contains the reporter's opinion
My father just retired.	
My girlfriend is learning to drive.	who doesn't study
A city is heartless.	that will not help its poor

• VI. Seven Familiar Places for Commas •

1. In dates, after everything but the month

   On April 7, 1980, my life began.
         [commas]

   On Saturday, May 7, 1981, Alexander's Department Store had a sale on men's suits. [commas]

2. In an address

   [comma]

   A snowstorm occurred in Brooklyn, New York.

   Atlanta, Georgia, has many qualities of Northern big cities.
         [commas]

3. Before and after someone's title if the title comes after the name

   [commas]

   Carl Berkson, Ph.D., practices psychology in Los Angeles.

   [no comma]

   Dr. Smithers has retired.

4. To set off someone's name, if that person is being spoken to in the sentence

   Carol, why don't you do your assignment?
            [commas].

   I understand, Mr. Harrington, that you cannot pay this last installment.

5. In informal letters, after the opening words and the words before the signature

   Dear Martin,
   Dear Carl,   [comma]
   Yours sincerely,
   Very truly yours,

   Hint: In a formal letter, use a colon after the salutation.

   Dear Mr. Porter:
   Dear Senator Byrd:

6. To indicate that words are left out.

   [Comma here shows that the words *man owns* are omitted.]

   The older man owns the sedan; the younger, the convertible.

7. To set off a variety of numbers

   [comma]

   volume four, page eighteen

   [comma]

   six feet, three inches

   19, 385 students
      [comma]

Step 6. Using Commas in Seven Ways. Fill in the commas where they are needed.

1. Sun Jae Luck Ph.D. was born on April 7 1940 at 9181 East Street in San Francisco California.

2. Henry Davis the superintendent lives in building four apartment 12A.

3. "Would you explain Mr. Kingsley what 2 meters 50 centimeters is equal to in American feet and inches?

4. Dear Mr. Evans

    The information you asked for is in volume 3 page 8 paragraph 6.

                                        Sincerely

                                        Jerry

5. Jose please call your mother to the phone.

● VII. Three Places Not to Use Commas ●

Excessive use of commas distracts the reader, especially when the writer places commas incorrectly.

1. *Do not* use commas to separate subject and verb.

    Incorrect: A small violet, grew beneath the elm.

    Correct: A small violet grew beneath the elm.

2. *Do not* use commas after short word groups, even if they are introductory, unless they are transitional words like *in fact, for example, however* or unless confusion might otherwise result.

    Incorrect: Beside the fence, a calf stood grazing under a blue sky.

    Correct: Beside the fence a calf stood grazing under a blue sky.

    Correct: In fact, the child arrived after noon.

    Correct: From the ceiling, light bits of plaster fell.
    [Without the comma, readers would read *ceiling light*.]

3. *Do not* use commas before coordinators when the subject of the following complete sentence is not stated.

    Incorrect: She dug a deep hole, and planted a fir tree.
                                        [no subject here]

    Correct: She dug a deep hole, and she planted a fir tree.

                   She dug a deep hole and planted a fir tree.

Step 7. Avoiding Excess Commas. Correct any errors with commas in the following sentences. Mark correct sentences *C*.

1. We saw the accident, and called the police.

2. Amanda, and most of her friends, went out to lunch.

3. Playing soccer, always makes him hungry.

4. Rosa took down the license-plate number, and tried to remember the model and make of the car.

5. That tall, graceful man, is my husband, but I am not surprised that you did not recognize him.

6. In any case, our new compact discs, sound great, and are easy to dance to at a party.

7. We brought Dennis a cake, for his birthday, but forgot to buy candles.

8. Breathing heavily, she whispered sweet nothings into his ear.

9. For example many grocery stores, now use laser beams to detect price codes.

10. Twelve noisy children played beside a park bench.

Step 8. Comma Review. Here are some sentences written by professional writers. All the commas have been left out. Put in the commas where you think they belong. In each blank space, write the number of the review chart on pages 302–309 that tells why the comma (or commas) is needed.

_____ 1. The drama like the symphony does not teach anything.

            —John Millington Synge

_____ 2. I have said for example that I am as much a stranger in this village today as I was the first summer I arrived but this is not quite true.

            —James Baldwin

_____ 3. To be sure in all ages people have been afraid of loneliness and have tried to escape it.

            —Rollo May

_____ 4. All words grouping themselves round the concepts of liberty and equality for instance were contained in the single word *crimethink* while all words grouping themselves round the concepts of objectivity and rationalism were contained in the single word *oldthink*.

            —George Orwell

_____ 5. She drove up over a rise and suddenly looming out of the mist the deer was there.

            —Jayne Anne Phillips

_____ 6. "The aim of biography" said Sir Sidney Lee who had perhaps read and written more lives than any man of his time "is the truthful transmission of personality" and no single sentence could more neatly split up into two parts the whole problem of biography as it presents itself to us today.

—*Virginia Woolf*

_____ 7. In a way I suppose that the little I recall of my early childhood in Russia my first eight years sums up my beginnings what now are called the formative years.

—*Golda Meir*

_____ 8. I have now spoken of the education of the scholar by nature by books and by action.

—*Ralph Waldo Emerson*

_____ 9. On that bleak hill top the earth was hard with a black frost and the air made me shiver through every limb.

—*Emily Brontë*

_____ 10. It reasons that the present is undefined the future has no other reality than as present hope and the past is no more than present memory.

—*Jorge Luis Borges*

Step 9. More Comma Review.   Follow directions. Use separate paper.

1. Write a sentence that you heard someone speak last night. Identify the speaker at the beginning of the sentence.

2. Write a complete sentence that tells your street address, your city, and your state.

3. Write a sentence that tells the name of some important artist or performer. Use the words *an important artist* after the person's name.

4. Write two *complete* sentences about a busy place that you visit regularly. Use the words *and* or *but* to separate the sentences.

5. Write a complete sentence that lists your *three* favorite ice cream flavors. Use the word *and* only once.

6. Write a complete sentence about your boyfriend or girlfriend, your husband or wife. Use the words *who I love* somewhere in the sentence.

7. Write a quotation sentence about something you argued about recently. Use the words *I said* in the middle of the sentence.

8. Write a sentence about life in a small town. Use the word *although, when, if, while,* or *because* at the beginning of the sentence.

9. Write a sentence of advice to someone who is just starting to attend college. Start your sentence with either of these word groups: *Going to college* or *To go to college.*

10. Use the word *however, nevertheless, on the other hand,* or *besides* in the middle of a sentence that describes how you feel about the current administration in Washington.

● Comma Splices and Run-on Sentences

Every sentence must have a subject and a verb to be complete. (See A Sentence Review, pages 403–407.) Run-on sentences are word groups that mistakenly push two or more sentences together as one. Find the "sentence collisions" in the following example:

I ran to the door my sister stormed in suddenly she burst into tears.

● How to Fix Run-on Errors ●

---

1. The easiest way to fix a run-on is to use a correct end mark between sentences: a period, a question mark, or an exclamation point. *A comma is not an end mark. It does not separate complete sentences.* If you read aloud the run-on sentence above, listen to the sound of your own voice. Where your voice stops and drops, use a period.

     [capital letter]   [capital letter]

    I ran to the door. My sister stormed in. Suddenly she burst into tears.

         [period]

Of course, you need to use a capital letter to start each new sentence. If you had used a comma after *door* or *in* in the sentences above, you would have incorrectly separated two sentences (the subjects and verbs are underlined for you to help you see how the standards for completeness are met). A comma is too weak a punctuation mark to separate complete thoughts. Some instructors like to call the run-on error that uses a comma to separate complete thoughts *a coma splice.* A *comma splice* is merely two or more sentences run together with a comma between them.

2. When two run-on word groups, each complete with subject and verb, are very closely related in meaning, these words groups may be separated by a semicolon. A semicolon, which includes both a period and a comma in its structure, indicates a stronger pause than a comma. The semicolon can separate complete thoughts. If you choose to use a semicolon, always begin the word group after the semicolon with a small letter.

             [small letter]

    I ran to the door. My sister stormed in; suddenly she burst into tears.

         [semicolon]

Hint: A subject and a verb must come both before and after the semicolon. The structure of the sentence looks like this: *Complete thought; complete thought.*

3. Instead of keeping complete word groups apart, you may join them together with suitable joining words (*conjunctions*) and proper punctuation.

  a. When the two sentences have equal importance in your mind, use one of these joining words: *and, but, or, for, nor.* Use a comma before the conjunction. (You learned about combining sentences in this way—called *coordination*—on pages 12–15.)

  [conjunction]
  ↓
  I ran to the door, and my sister stormed in. Suddenly she burst into tears.
  ↑
  [comma]

  [conjunction]
  ↙
  I ran to the door. My sister stormed in, and suddenly she burst into tears.
  ↗
  [comma]

  b. You may also join the run-on sentences by making one complete word group less important than the other (see pages 86–94). Many different conjunctions perform that function. Here are a few: *because, while, although, since, when, if, as.* Use a comma after you complete the word group that begins with one of these joining words. Sometimes you need to add a new word or two, to take away words, or to change the position of words when you correct the run-on with one of these conjunctions.

  [less important
  word group]
  ⌒
  As I ran to the door, my sister stormed in. Suddenly she burst into tears.
  ↑
  [comma]

  [less important word group]   [word *suddenly* left out]
  ⌒   ⌒
  I ran to the door. When my sister stormed in, she burst into tears.
  ↑
  [comma]

Step 1. One Error, Five Corrections.   Here are two complete sentences run on as one:

The music grew louder I felt my heart pounding.

Fix the run-on error on the blank lines below. The words and punctuation will tell you which methods to use.

1. The music grew louder ; _____

    _____

2. As _____ , _____

    _____

3. The music grew louder. _____

    _____

4. The music grew louder, _____

    _____

5. Because the music grew louder, _____

    _____

Step 2. One Error, Five Corrections.   Here are two complete thoughts joined by a comma. On separate paper, correct the comma splice in at least three different ways.

The sun blazed in the sky, we felt hot and tired.

HOW TO FIND RUN-ON ERRORS

Repairing the run-on mistake is easy, once your instructor points out the error by writing in the margin of your paper "RO" for run-on or "CS" for comma splice. The trick is, of course, to find the run-on errors yourself.

1. Here are some simple hints to help you find run-on sentences:
    a. Read your paragraph aloud. When your voice stops and drops, use a period.
    b. Read your paragraph from the last sentence to the first sentence. That will help you keep apart complete thoughts.
    c. Count your sentences. In this way, you will be looking for end marks, and you will be aware that a small number of sentences probably means run-ons in your paragraph.
2. The best way to recognize the run-on is to learn carefully two groups of *run-on stop signs*. These words, used at the start of complete-thought word groups, mean trouble to you because they, more than any other words, frequently cause run-on errors. Each time you use one of the words in either group, you must stop to think of the possibility that you may be writing a run-on sentence.

• Run-on Stop Signs: Group I •

then	there	consequently
now		moreover
finally		therefore
suddenly		however

Hint: These words are not conjunctions. They do *not* join sentences correctly. If they open complete-thought word groups, they must be preceded by a period or a semicolon. At times, a conjunction and a comma work as well.

In this word group, the run-on stop sign starts a complete-thought word group and must have either a semicolon or a period before it:

[run-on
stop sign]
↓

We drove for a long time. However, we rested afterward.
We drove for a long time; however, we rested afterward.

In the word group below, the run-on stop sign is used correctly in the middle of the sentence; *however* does not start a complete-thought word group here:

We drove, however, for a long time.

Step 1. Correct Punctuation for Run-ons.   Correct the run-on errors below by inserting correct punctuation or by changing incorrect punctuation. Two sentences are already correct.

Hint

If you have doubts about where your voice stops and drops, check for subjects and verbs to test sentence completeness.

1. We ran into the rain half naked, then we threw wet mud at each other from a nearby creek.
2. I love to wander through rows of corn there is a peacefulness that I enjoy.
3. By the time the Ramos family arrived, the steak was all gone, consequently they ate only chicken.

4. The plumbers finished their work, now we can run the faucets again.

5. Their team scored three runs in the second inning, however, they did not win the game.

6. Alyson is a textbook editor, however, she has always wanted to be a pilot.

7. A good diet, therefore, consists of fatty fish like salmon and tuna.

8. Mr. Child's eyes opened slowly; suddenly, he bolted out of bed.

9. Always wipe food-preparation counters dry, there is less chance of having roaches.

10. The President is holding a news conference, therefore, regular TV programming is suspended.

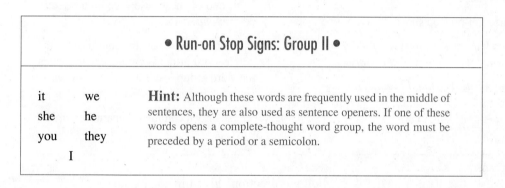

● Run-on Stop Signs: Group II ●

it	we	**Hint:** Although these words are frequently used in the middle of sentences, they are also used as sentence openers. If one of these words opens a complete-thought word group, the word must be preceded by a period or a semicolon.
she	he
you	they
I	

Step 2. Rewriting the Run-on. Using your own paper, fix the run-on errors below by rewriting the word groups correctly. Use any of the methods explained on pages 313–314. All the run-on mistakes are caused by Group II stop signs. Write the letter *C* if the sentence is correct.

1. Despite the bomb threat, flight 451 left Paris on time.

2. We waited for the train all afternoon it arrived at seven o'clock after a three-hour delay in Boston.

3. Professor Kent entered the classroom frowning he held the final exams in his hand.

4. When José raises his voice, we stop everything fast.

5. Sean told us the news we could not believe it.

Use the run-on review chart on the next page to help you complete Steps 3 to 5 correctly.

• Run-on Review Chart •

Run-on Finder

1. Read word groups aloud. At stop and drop of voice, use a period.

2. Read word groups from the last complete thought to the first complete thought. Look for subject and verb to test completeness.

3. Count sentences.

   Recognize run-on stop signs:

   a. Group I: *then, now, however, finally, there, consequently, moreover, therefore.*

   b. Group II: *it, she, you, I, we, he, they.*

Run-on Fixer

1. Use end marks between complete sentences. Use capital letter for next word after period.

2. Use a semicolon. Start next word with small letter.

3. Use a conjunction

   a. With one of these, use a comma directly before: *and, or, nor, but, for.*

   b. With one of these, use the comma after the whole word group is completed and when the word group opens a sentence: *because, since, while, although, as, when.*

4. Never use only a comma to separate complete sentences.

Step 3. Avoiding the Run-on Mistake. Follow directions given in each statement below. Use separate paper.

1. Write two sentences about eating a late breakfast on Sunday mornings. Start the second sentence with the word *it*.

2. Write two complete thoughts about your best friend, separating them with a semicolon. Open the second thought with the word *however*.

3. Write two sentences about your favorite TV personality. Begin the second sentence with the word *I*.

4. Write a pair of sentences about travel, opening the second sentence with the word *there* or *now*.

5. Write two complete-thought word groups about a job you once had. Join the two thoughts with the word *but*.

Step 4. Stop-Sign Words in Sentences. Use correctly in the blank space the *stop sign* that appears in parentheses before each set of word groups. Use correct punctuation and capitals when needed.

(however) 1. The lawyer _____ tried to influence the jury unfairly.

(then) 2. The dark clouds collected in the sky _____ it began to pour.

(we) 3. Skiing is our favorite sport _____ go to Mount Snow every February.

(there) 4. The living room felt like an icebox _____ were no heating ducts in that part of the house.

(however) 5. The pond was completely dried up _____ the ducks still returned every summer.

(finally) 6. Lynn tried for days to find a baby-sitter _____ she canceled her appointment.

(there) 7. Cutting wheat properly is not easy _____ are several steps to follow.

(now) 8. Before the accident, André drove to school each day _____ he takes a bus.

(I) 9. As I began to write, my thoughts came more easily _____ realized writing was easy!

(therefore) 10. The theater had only one projector _____ we had a five-minute wait between reels.

Step 5. Correcting Sentence Errors.   In the blank lines after these run-on errors, rewrite the sentences correctly in any way you wish. Write *C* if the sentence is already correct.

1. I watch the stars from my bedroom window it's such a peaceful sight. _____

   _____

2. She was not a famous actress she was just an understudy. _____

   _____

3. I called the fire department immediately, however, the flames destroyed most of our house. _____

   _____

4. The turnips are inedible. The radishes, however, are sweet and firm. _____

   _____

5. My sister spent her junior year traveling then she returned to Boston to finish her degree. _____

   _____

6. Some children are poorly motivated to read, consequently, problems such as illiteracy arise. _____

   _____

7. James loves to paint, but he rarely has time he works two jobs. _____

   _____

8. We got closer and closer to the fence, finally Fudge jumped I held on for dear

   life. _____

   _____

9. I brought her to the pound myself there was one problem, I couldn't bear to see

   her die. _____

   _____

10. It was no longer a feeling of friendship that was inside me, it was a feeling of

    love, I adored Ellen. _____

    _____

Step 6. Run-ons in a Paragraph. Correct the run-on errors and comma faults by changing some of the punctuation in the paragraph below. Capitalize the first letter of any word that starts a sentence. You may add words if you wish. Study the charts on pages 316–318 for review.

My Uncle's Den

It's a dark and rainy afternoon as I sit in my uncle's drafty den and consider the somberness of this room it has a dreary white ceiling and oversized books plaster the walls. Faded black letters announce *The New International Dictionary*. Two worn paperbacks, *Moby Dick* and *Animal Farm* lie sloppily beside it, the smell of mildew seeps up from the floor planks. The room is very dimly lit, as a result I feel sad sitting at Uncle Tom's Victorian desk. Gazing at a painting of grapes, apples, and plums, I can hear outside the constant dripping of rain into the aluminum gutters. The room grows dimmer as the hours slip by finally I switch on a fluorescent desk lamp it casts a shadow on the green inkbottle before me. I continue to glance around and feel totally isolated as I see only darkness beyond the arched doorway. I get up and as I step across the room, I trip over a tin wastepaper basket it clatters to the floor, and I feel a tingling go right through me. I turn and out of the corner of my eye I notice the mahogany grandfather clock beaming from the corner. I inspect its pitted brass face, the dull black hands creep sluggishly around its roman numerals. As I flounder about this eerie room, the clock chimes five times, then I realize that I've spent two hours here. What a depressing place! I need a more jovial and spirited atmosphere. As I pull the door closed I hear the latch click a dark cloud leaves me.

—*Kathy Clementi*

Dangling Modifiers: Errors with Verb-Part Openers

When you use verb-part openers, you must remember to name the correct subject (the person or thing that performs the action of the verb part) in the first few words after the opening word group. Whether or not it is intended, the first noun or pronoun after the verb-part opener is automatically the subject; this often yields strange and humorous sentences. Look at the columns below.

I	II
CORRECT	INCORRECT

1. While dressed in a new overcoat,
   [This tells who was dressed in an overcoat.]

   I brushed against a bus and soiled my sleeve.

2. Feeling fine, the little old man
   [This tells that the man was feeling fine.]

   smiled at the trees and flowers.

1. While dressed in a new overcoat,
   [This shows that the bus was dressed in an overcoat.]

   a bus brushed against me and soiled my sleeve.

2. Feeling fine, the trees and flowers
   [These words tell that the trees and flowers felt fine.]

   made the little old man smile.

It is obvious that the sentences in Column II do not say what the writer wants them to say (a *bus* dressed in an overcoat? *trees* feeling fine?).

• To Correct the Error Made with Verb-Part Openers •

1. Ask *who* or *what* is performing the action indicated by the verb part.

   Who is dressed in a new overcoat?

   Who is feeling fine?

   If necessary, rewrite the sentence so that the words that answer that question appear within the first few words after the verb-part opener.

2. Rewrite the sentence so that the subject is included in the opening word group. You will have to add a word to make a complete verb.
   Sentence I in Column II could be rewritten in this way:

   [added word to make a verb]

   While I was dressed in a new overcoat, a bus brushed against me and soiled my
   [subject now included in opening word group]

   sleeve.

Sentence 2 in Column II could be written in this way:

[added word to
make a verb]

Since the little old man was feeling fine, the trees and flowers made him smile.

[subject now included in
opening word group]

Although this second option helps you correct errors, it also removes the *-ing* structure from the beginning of the sentence. Because *-ing* words are valuable in varying your style, try to keep them by naming the subject right after the verb-part opener, as explained in Column I on page 321.

Step 7. Making Sense with *-ing* Words. For each item below, draw an arrow from the verb part to the person or thing that the *sentence says* is the subject. Then, rewrite the sentence so that it makes sense. If the sentence is already correct, mark it *C*.

EXAMPLE

After failing the final exam, her father scolded her. *After she failed the final exam, her father scolded her.* ●

1. Sprinting the last few yards of a 5-mile race, my nose detected the scent of fresh-brewed coffee. _____

   _____

2. Gazing at the sky, the stars twinkled like sequins on a black velvet cloth.

   _____

   _____

3. While biting my nails nervously, the judge called my name. _____

   _____

4. While waiting for the train to Cheyenne, I read my textbook from cover to cover. _____

   _____

5. Dreaming about my math test the next day, my mother unexpectedly called me.

   _____

   _____

6. While shopping for Christmas presents, the fire engines raced down the street.

   _____

   _____

7. After undressing completely, the doctor examined me. _____

   _____

8. Attempting to improve educational programs, many tests for students are required by school administrators. _____

   _____

9. After waiting impatiently for two hours, my desire to see Cathy increased greatly. _____

   _____

Step 8. Checking Your Sentences. Examine the sentences you wrote in Steps 1 through 7 on the previous pages. Have you made any errors with verb-part openers? Does the sentence state clearly the subject you intended for the verb part? Correct any problems you find.

● **Degrees of Comparison**

When we use describing words, we can often compare one thing with another merely by changing word endings.

EXAMPLE

One boy is tall. Another boy is tall*er*. Parker is the tall*est* boy at the party.

You have to be careful, however, to use the correct ending.

Use *-er* at the end of a word if you want to compare only two items.
Use *-est* at the end of a word if you want to compare three or more items.

One Person or Thing Is	Of Two People or Things, One Is	Among Three or More People or Things, One Is
short	shorter	shortest
smart	smarter	smartest
silly	sillier	silliest

If the word you are using to compare has *three or more* syllables:

Use *more* in front of the word if you want to compare only two items.

Use *most* in front of the word if you want to compare three or more items.

Hint

If you are not sure how to make the correct form of the word, use your dictionary.

One Person or Thing Is	Of Two People or Things, One Is	Among Three or More People or Things, One Is
beautiful	more beautiful	most beautiful
enormous	more enormous	most enormous

Some words do not form comparisons in the usual way; these you have to memorize because they are irregular.

One Person or Thing Is	Of Two People or Things, One Is	Among Three or More People or Things, One Is
bad	worse	worst
done badly	done worse	done worst
good	better	best
done well	done better	done best
little	less	least
many	more	most
much	more	most

Some words may not be compared at all because their meanings do not allow for degrees in comparison.

unique   empty

perfect   full

Step 1. Correct Comparison. Fill in the spaces in the two columns below. The word you write must make sense in the blank line that appears in the sentence on top of the column. Look at the example.

Hint

For some words you have the choice of either adding an ending (*-er* or *-est*) or of using *more* or *most*. But remember, use one or the other—not both.

Wrong: She is more thriftier than her friend.
Right: She is more thrifty than her friend.

OR

She is thriftier than her friend.

	Between Professor Merryl and Professor Grace, Professor Grace is *more interesting*	Of all the teachers I have had, Professor Grace is *the most* *interesting*
1. interesting		
2. friendly	_____	_____
3. stylish	_____	_____
4. busy	_____	_____
5. strict	_____	_____
6. slim	_____	_____

Hint

Check spelling rule 2 on page 429.

Step 2. Changing Wrong Comparisons. Each of the following sentences uses a comparison incorrectly. Draw a line through the wrong word, and write in the blank space at the right the word or words that you would use to make the sentence correct.

EXAMPLE

He runs the most fastest on the team. *fastest* _____

1. My father is more smarter than anyone else I know. _____

2. Herbert Yee is the difficultest to understand. _____

3. The clown on the left is most silliest. _____

4. Don is the more creative of all the writers. _____

5. Of those two shirts, I prefer the most brightest one. _____

Step 3. Your Own Comparisons. Use correctly, in a sentence of your own, each of the following words or word groups. Use separate paper.

1. most
2. better
3. least

4. more softly
5. worse

● Formal and Informal Language

Formal English is the language of professional journals, formal speeches, and most serious college writing. Informal English (the English you speak each day) is found in parts of novels, short stories, letters, books, most newspapers, articles for general readership, and advertisements. *Colloquialisms* (informal expressions used in speaking but generally not in writing) and *slang* (vivid words or phrases used because they are brief, "loose," and colorful) mark informal language and are perfectly acceptable in informal situations. Although it may be appropriate to use such informality for special effects in your writing or as part of the quoted words you show someone speaking, for the most part informal language should be avoided in your compositions. And very often informal expressions change so rapidly that acceptable words one year are no longer used at a later time.

But be careful! Do not substitute for an informal expression something stuffy, unnatural, and jarring to the ears. Usually, however, students are too *in*formal in their writing.

Here are some informal expressions used in student themes and some alternatives that could be used.

INFORMAL	EXAMPLE	MORE FORMAL EXPRESSION
cool; awesome; wicked; radical	It was an *awesome* party.	excellent; exciting; remarkable; incredible; superior
fun (used to describe); sick	We had a *fun* time. The party was *sick*.	enjoyable; uproarious; amusing; hilarious
sort of (a) kind of (a)	That policeman was *kind of* strange.	rather; somewhat
a couple of	Bring me *a couple of* books.	some; several; a few

bum out (around)	This weekend I'm going to *bum around* the house in my old clothes.	relax; rest
lousy	What a *lousy* time we had.	dull; depressing
psyched; enthused	The singer is *psyched* for tonight's concert.	enthusiastic about or over; excited
a lot, lots of	I have *lots of* time.	much; a great deal
a fix; a mess	What a *fix* I got into with this car!	complication; trouble-some time; awkward event; punish
myself yourself himself } used as subjects	Mary and *myself* were late.	I you he
real; totally; awfully; plenty	He was *real* annoyed at me.	very; extremely; strongly
faze	It didn't *faze* me in the least.	bother; disturb; annoy
sure; yeah	*Sure* I wanted to leave the house.	certainly; indeed; surely; absolutely
drag; bummer	Biology is a *drag*.	boring; uninteresting
to ditch	My girlfriend *ditched* me for a football player.	left; betrayed

Hint

If you want to use some informal word occasionally for special effect, put the word in quotation marks:

Because of so much construction and repairs, no one but the builders can "dig" Atlanta any more.

• Using Contractions •

Putting words together by replacing letters with an apostrophe helps writers record accurately the words people speak. Thus, hearing *can't, isn't, it's, could've,* and other contractions, writers attempting to produce on paper a direct quotation would write exactly what they hear.

Contractions are also acceptable in informal writing, even when no speaker is being quoted. Therefore, in newspapers, popular magazines, and textbooks aiming for a conversational tone, contractions work well—though never when they are excessive.

However, most formal writing for your college course demands that you avoid contractions wherever you can. Use the two words that led to the contraction rather than the abbreviated form of the word. Here are some examples:

Informal	Formal
She *didn't* look up from her page of notes.	She *did not* look up from her page of notes.
They'd have phoned if they *could've.*	They *would have* phoned if they *could have.*

Instead of the Contractions	Write the Words Out
I'm	I am
isn't	is not
wasn't	was not
weren't	were not
aren't	are not
don't	do not
couldn't	could not

Step 1. Informal to Formal. Rewrite each of the sentence examples of informal usage on pages 326–327 into more formal language. Be careful not to make your new sentences sound too high-flown. Use separate paper.

Step 2. More Informal Sentences. Here are several more sentences using informal language. Discuss how you would change them into sentences that would be acceptable in a formal writing activity. Do not write anything too stiff.

1. Those guys are real cool but my old man thinks they're a couple of jerks, so I didn't hang out with them.

2. For sure, that scene was so outrageous we all got kinda wasted.

3. This gig is heinous, but I really need the bread, so I won't cop out.
4. I was totally psyched to have a fun time, but then my girlfriend ditched me, so it was a bummer.
5. Dude, the babes were hot and the music was rad.

Step 3. A "Square" Dictionary.   Write your own dictionary of several more informal expressions (slang, colloquialisms) that you define for someone who might not "dig" your language. Write a definition for each word; use each word in a colloquial sentence that you might speak or write; give one or two alternative words that could be used for the same effect; then, rewrite your original sentence in more formal English. You might want to define colloquial and slang expressions like *dough, kookie, wicked, uptight, with it, right on, boss, bread, gig, gross, airhead*. Make a chart like the one below. Follow the example.

A "SQUARE" DICTIONARY

INFORMAL EXPRESSION	DEFINITION	MY OWN SENTENCE	ALTERNATIVE WORDS	MORE FORMAL ENGLISH
uptight	nervous	I was all uptight about the driving test.	anxious, worried, troubled, nervous	I was nervous about the driving test.

● Fragments

A *fragment* is an incomplete part of a sentence used as though it were a sentence itself. Here are some fragments that are easy to recognize.

1. Over the curb and into the street.
2. Pushing angrily through the crowds.
3. Just to play his radio quietly.
4. Usually exhausted from lifting heavy cartons.

None of these fragments makes any real sense. Since a sentence contains a complete thought and has a subject and a verb (see the Sentence Review Chart on pages 403–405), the word groups above are not sentences.

Fragment 1 has no subject or verb. *What* is being done over the curb and into the street? *Who* is doing it?

Fragment 2 has no subject (*Who* does the pushing?) and only a part of a verb—the word *pushing*.

Fragment 3 has no subject (*Who* plays the radio?) and only part of a verb—the infinitive *to play*. (You may recall that if *to* is used like this, what results is merely the starting point of a verb, not a verb itself.)

Fragment 4 has no subject (*Who* was exhausted after lifting heavy cartons?). The word group would also need a word like *is* or *was* in order to be complete. Here *exhausted* without a helper is no verb.

Each fragment, 1, 2, 3, 4 above, separated from the sentence that comes before it, is easy to recognize because it really makes no sense. But now look at the fragments as they appear as parts of paragraphs and read the explanations alongside.

FRAGMENT	EXPLANATION
1. *a.* In a square of pavement down the block a small dog played with a rubber ball, but it rolled out of his reach. *b.* He rushed after it. *c.* Over the curb and into the street.	Here a student might think that the subject *he* and the verb *rushed* in sentence *b* would also serve as subject and verb in word group *c*. But that is not the case. Word group *c* is a fragment because it lacks its own subject and verb. The capital letter in *over* and the period after *street* indicate that the writer thought the sentence a complete one.
2. *a.* Holiday shopping is always a difficult task. *b.* Every store I visit overflows with noisy shoppers. *c.* Pushing angrily through the crowds. *d.* I'll try to shop earlier next year.	Here, a student might think that the word *shoppers* in sentence *b* would serve as the subject in word group *c*. But word group *c* must have its own subject. Furthermore, the word *pushing* is not a verb: if *is* or *was* appeared before it, or if the word were *pushed* instead of *pushing*, it would be a verb. But as it stands, word group *c* is also a fragment because it lacks a verb.
3. *a.* It is important to understand that teenagers often require privacy. *b.* For an hour or two a boy wishes to be left alone in his room. *c.* Just to play his radio quietly.	Here, it is possible that an inexperienced writer would imagine the word *boy* in sentence *b* serves as the subject in word group *c*. But word group *c* must have its own subject to be complete. In addition, *to play* is no verb. We need to add a word such as *wants* or *likes* before the infinitive. Sometimes the infinitive can be changed to a verb: *plays, played,* or *is playing.* As it stands, word group *c* is also a fragment since it lacks a verb.

4. *a.* My mother works very long hours to support our family. *b.* She trudges home at eight o'clock every evening. *c.* Usually exhausted from lifting heavy cartons. She falls asleep by nine-thirty.

Here, the writer gives no subject in word group *c.* Furthermore, *exhausted*—as it is used—is only a part of a verb. It must have *is* or *was* or some such word before it. So, word group *c* is also a fragment because it lacks a verb.

Fixing Fragments

Knowing that sentence fragments lack subjects or complete verbs, or both, you should not find this kind of sentence error difficult to correct.

1. Add a subject and a verb to make the sentence complete.

CORRECT THIS FRAGMENT

THIS WAY

Over the curb and into the street.

The dog jumped over the curb and into the street.　[added subject] [added verb]

Pushing angrily through the crowds.

They are pushing angrily through the crowds.　[subject] [word added to make verb]

They push angrily through the crowds.　[-*ing* word changed to verb]

Just to play his radio quietly.

He just wants to play his radio quietly.　[subject] [word added to make verb]

He just plays his radio quietly.　[infinitive changed to verb]

Usually exhausted from lifting heavy cartons.

She is usually exhausted from lifting heavy cartons.　[subject]
[word added to make verb]

Step 1. Completing Sentences.　The last word group in each item below is a fragment. Rewrite the fragment in the space provided, and add a subject or a verb, or both, in order to make the sentence complete. You may wish to change an -*ing* word or an infinitive to a verb; or you may wish to add a new verb as a helper.

1. Ryan turned on the TV. Hoping to stay awake to see his guests.

　　_____

　　_____

2. Imagine my disappointment when I went to the refrigerator and looked for the apples. Already eaten by my brother Juan.

_____

_____

_____

3. Sally was finally accepted into law school. After waiting for three years.

_____

_____

_____

4. Millions of people are now exercising and watching what they eat. To stay fit and healthy.

_____

_____

_____

5. Lucy squinted her eyes. To try to see the words written on the blackboard.

_____

_____

_____

2. Another way to fix the fragment is to connect it to the sentence that comes before it. In that way you legitimately give the fragment the subject and verb it needs by using words of another sentence. Notice how the last two sentences in 1, 2, and 3 on page 330 may be joined together to eliminate the fragment:

CORRECT THE FRAGMENT

He rushed after it. Over the curb and into the street.

Every store I visit overflows with noisy shoppers. Pushing angrily through the crowds.

For an hour or two a boy wishes to be left alone in his room. Just to play his radio quietly.

THIS WAY

He rushed after it over the curb and into the street. [small letter] [no period]

Every store I visit overflows with noisy shoppers, pushing angrily through the crowds. [no period] [small letter]

For an hour or two a boy wishes to be

left alone in his room just to play his radio quietly. [no period] [small letter]

3. A fragment may be corrected by attaching it to the sentence that comes after it.

CORRECT THE FRAGMENT

Usually exhausted from lifting heavy cartons. She falls asleep by nine-thirty.

THIS WAY

Usually exhausted from lifting heavy

cartons, she falls asleep by nine-thirty. [comma] [small letter]

Hearing the photographer talk about his travels through Alaska. Audiences responded with enthusiasm.

Hearing the photographer talk about his
[comma]
travels through Alaska, audiences responded with enthusiasm. ＼ [small letter]

Hint

When you open a sentence with a fragment that contains an *-ing* verb part or an *-ed* verb part, follow the fragment with a comma.

Step 2. Correcting the Fragment. Each of these groups contains at least one fragment. Correct the error by adding the fragment either to the sentence that comes before or to the sentence that comes after. Write your new sentence in the blank spaces alongside.

Hint

Make sure that the new sentence you have written makes sense.

1. Going into the twentieth inning. I thought I would faint. Staring at the scoreboard. I actually wished the other team would hit a home run.

2. Just thirty minutes of yoga a day will keep you in good shape. Without too much strain. You will feel more alert, too.

3. It's no wonder people find it hard to be independent. Everywhere we turn someone gives us orders. At home, in school, on the job.

4. Each month Marla puts aside some money to buy a jeep. Which will be very expensive. She hopes her brother will lend her a little money as well.

5. In America everyone recognizes
   the extent of teenage unemployment. Even the President and the
   members of Congress. But they
   cannot agree on how to end it.

   _____

   _____

   _____

   _____

   _____

Finding Fragments

Here are some suggestions for learning to recognize sentence fragments of the type described in this chapter.

1. Read your paragraph aloud. Learn to tell the difference between pauses between words and stops between sentences. A pause often requires a comma. A full stop requires a period or one of the other end marks, a question mark or an exclamation point. A semicolon may also indicate a complete stop between sentences.

2. Read the sentences of your paragraph from the last to the first. In that way you'll be listening for complete thoughts that make sense.

3. Look for an -*ing* word used incorrectly as the verb in a sentence.

4. Make sure every sentence has its own subject and its own verb. (See item 7 in the sentence review, page 405, for "understood" subjects.)

5. Make sure every sentence expresses a complete thought by itself.

6. Watch out for these "Fragment Stop Signs: Group I" because they are expressions that often open word groups that fail to include subjects and verbs.

Fragment Stop Signs: Group I

just	especially
for instance	for example
such as	like
also	mainly

If you open a sentence with one of these words or word combinations, be sure that a subject and verb come later on in the sentence.

Study the review chart below before moving on to the next steps.

• A Fragment Finder •	• A Fragment Fixer •
1. Read aloud. Listen for incomplete thoughts.	1. Add subject or verb, or both.
2. Look out for *-ing* words, especially when they start sentences.	2. Add fragment to sentence that comes before or sentence that comes after. Make sure final sentence makes sense.
3. Look for subject and verb in each sentence.	3. Change an *-ing* word to a verb by using *is, was, are, were, am* in front of it. Or, change *-ing* word to a verb.
4. Read paragraph from last sentence to first. Stop after each sentence and ask: Is it a complete thought?	4. If you put an *-ing* fragment or another "verb-part" fragment in front of a complete sentence, use a comma after the fragment.
5. Know Group I of the Fragment Stop Signs:	5. Change an infinitive to a verb by removing "to" and by using the correct form of the verb. Or, put one of these verbs before the infinitive: *like(s), want(s), plan(s), try(tries), is, was, were, are, am.*

just   *mainly*
especially   *for instance*
for example   *like*
also   *such as*

Example

Fragment	Corrected
John works on week-ends.	*John works on week-ends.*
To earn money for college.	*He* earns *money for college.*

OR

John works week-ends.
He likes *to earn money for college.*

Step 1. Eliminating Fragments. Most of the sentence groups below contain *one or more* sentence fragments. Correct the fragments by using any of the methods you have learned so far. Cross out words, add words, change or remove punctuation. If the set of sentences is correct, mark it *C*. Use a separate sheet of paper.

1. Shana shouted, "Go team!" Watching the Bruins game on TV. She was glad she could watch football without leaving her own living room.

2. Use patience in explaining something to a child, even though you might feel angry or tired. Hold your temper.

3. A great many men were outstanding leaders. For example, the Roman states-man Caesar. The head of one of history's greatest empires.

4. Old people face many terrible problems. For example, their dependence on fixed incomes. Poor medical care in nursing homes. Also, neglected by their own relatives.

5. I have stopped smoking. Also I now exercise regularly. I hope that these steps improve my health and fitness.

6. Longing for his mother's baking. He daydreamed about her pies. Especially her pecan pies.

7. My boyfriend and I love sailing. Feeling the spray of the sea on our faces. Enjoying the sun and the clear blue sky.

8. Many athletic events attract large crowds only because the sports are violent and bloody. Such as ice hockey and boxing.

9. Our plane soared through the sky. Like an eagle in flight. The captain rang a bell. To let us know we could take off our seatbelts.

10. The South is unlike the other sections of our country. In many ways. Its magnificent architecture is a blend of the past and the present. Modern skyscrapers soaring over quaint, wooden townhouses.

Step 2. Avoiding the Fragment Error.   Use each of these word groups to open a sentence of your own. Complete the sentence in the space provided.

> **Hint**
>
> If you follow the word group with a complete sentence, use a comma after the opening word group.

1. To learn ice skating

_____

_____

2. Stalled in rush-hour traffic

_____

_____

3. Crying for her mother

_____

_____

4. Stung by a bee

_____

_____

5. Staggering to the finish line

_____

_____

Step 3. Correcting Fragments: A Review.   Each of the following passages was written by a professional writer but has been altered to include sentence fragments. In each selection, correct the fragments, using any of the methods discussed in this chapter. Ask your instructor for a copy of the original passages to compare with your corrections.

1. This morning I got a note from my aunt. Asking me to come for lunch. I know what this means. Since I go there every Sunday for dinner and today is Wednesday, it can only mean one thing . . . .

    —*Walker Percy*

2. Sula would come by of an afternoon. Walking along with her fluid stride. Wearing a plain yellow dress . . . .

    —*Toni Morrison*

3. Just as he started to turn off the lamp. He thought he saw something in the hall . . . He leaned over. To look for something to throw.

    —*Raymond Carver*

4. He was at his letter-writing desk. Again in the morning. The little desk at the window was black. Rivaling the blackness of his fire escape . . . .

    —*Saul Bellow*

5. Once down at the creek. Blinking at the yellow-birds that fluttered and disappeared and reappeared above their heads. With his back against the big oak as usual. The old man would relax.

    —*Joyce Carol Oates*

Step 4. Review.   Read this paragraph for errors with fragments like those you have learned about so far. Correct mistakes directly on the page. There are nine sentence fragments.

The Last Ski Run

A light December snow speckles my ski goggles as I gaze down the experts' slope on Buttermilk Mountain. At the powdery whiteness below. The sun is dipping behind the jagged mountains. Surrounded by feathery clouds. Like a peacock's tail. The skiers in blue and red ahead of me start their graceful slide down the slope. Quickly disappearing in the late afternoon shadows. Exhausted after a full day on the slopes. I watch my warm breath turn into vapor in the brisk mountain air. To start my last run of the day. I finally plant my poles in the soft powder and surge forward. Realizing that my wife is probably beginning to worry about me. My legs stiffen in fear and sweat drips from under my hat. Especially at an icy patch or a sudden bump. At last I reached the bottom of the lift. To discover that I am the last skier on the mountain.

—Mark Kent

● Fragments with Subordinators

The technique of subordination that you learned in Chapter 3 is an essential characteristic of effective writing style. Used incorrectly, however, subordination gives rise to another type of *sentence fragment*. It's important to use the subordinating word group only when it can join on to a complete sentence, a word group that can make sense standing alone. These fragments appeared on student papers because the students forgot that subordinators must *join* ideas together:

1. **When** an empty shopping <u>cart</u> <u>soared</u> down the aisle.
2. **Who** really <u>looked</u> ridiculous.
3. **Unless** our <u>government</u> <u>gives</u> financial assistance.

The words in dark print are *subordinators*. Each one indicates that a major and complete idea will be expressed either earlier or later on in the sentence.

In number 1, the reader wants to know *what has happened* **when** that empty shopping cart soared down the aisle.

In number 2, the reader wants to know **who** looked ridiculous.

In number 3, the reader wants to know *what will happen* **unless** the government gives financial assistance.

It is true that each of the word groups does contain a subject and a verb (they are underlined in each case). However, the use of the *subordinator* means that connection to a complete thought must be made for a correct sentence.

But these subordinator fragments are easy enough to recognize in isolation. Now look at them as they appear in parts of paragraphs.

FRAGMENT

a. (1) Parents should leave their children at home when shopping must be done. (2) One afternoon at the A&P I stood minding my own business at the corn counter. (3) *When an empty shopping cart soared down the aisle.* (4) I knew some little brat was to blame.

EXPLANATION

The word *when* here is a subordinator. It must connect all the words that follow it to a complete sentence. Since word group 3 is standing alone and *is not* connected to a complete thought, it is a *fragment*. The reader needs to know, within word group 3, what happened *when an empty shopping cart soared down the aisle.*

b. (1) All the children in the third grade danced in snowflake costumes on the auditorium stage. (2) Over to the left stood my cousin Tyrone. (3) *Who really looked ridiculous.* (4) He was covered with a big white sheet and he moved more like a hippo than a snowflake.

The word *who*, as it is used here, is a connector. It must join all the words that follow it to a complete sentence. In addition, the sentence that uses the word *who* must also identify the person that *who* refers to. It's not enough to use *Tyrone* at the end of sentence 2. Since word group 3 is standing alone and is not connected to a complete thought, it is a *fragment.*

c. (1) Our country's Olympic teams will be defeated. (2) *Unless our government gives financial assistance.* (3) American athletes cannot afford the time to train and compete.

The word *unless* is a subordinator. It must connect all the words that follow it to a complete sentence. Since word group 2 is standing alone and is not connected to a complete thought, it is a *fragment.* The reader needs to know, within word group 2, what will happen *unless our government gives financial assistance.*

• Fixing the Subordinator Fragment: Method I •

Join the fragment to the sentence before. In *a,* above, join 2 and 3.

One afternoon at the A&P I stood minding my [no period] own business at the corn counter when an empty [small letter] shopping cart soared down the aisle.

In *b,* above, join 2 and 3.

Over to the left stood my cousin Tyrone, [comma] [small letter] who really looked ridiculous.

In *c,* above, join 1 and 2.

Our country's Olympic teams will be defeated [small letter] [no period] unless our government gives financial assistance.

Hint: A comma may be required when a subordinate word group is added at the end of a complete sentence. See pages 86–94.

Step 1. Adding Fragments On: Method I. Correct the selections below by adding the fragment on to the sentence that comes before it.

1. It is very important to get a good night's sleep. When you have a test the next day.

2. I greatly admire my Uncle George. A man who taught me to love the simple things in life.

3. I soon loosened my hold on the leather straps. As I grew accustomed to the ride.

4. Adjusting to a new city is not difficult for me. Because we often traveled when I was a child.

5. I never believe what I read in the newspapers. Until I can check a second source.

• Fixing the Subordinator Fragment: Method II •

Join the fragment to the sentence after. In *c*, page 339, add 2 and 3.

Unless our government gives financial assis-
[comma]
tance, American athletes cannot afford the time to train and compete.

In *a*, page 338, add 3 and 4.

When an empty shopping cart soared down the aisle, I knew some little brat was to blame.
[comma]

Hint: When a subordinate word group comes first in a sentence, use a comma between it and the complete sentence that follows.

Step 2. Adding Fragments On: Method II. Correct the selections below by adding the fragment to the sentence that follows it. Add commas where needed.

1. When I was finally able to sleep. I had nightmares of doctors sticking me with needles.

2. Provided we bring our thermos of water. It is safe for us to walk on the nature trail in such hot weather.

3. Because Hector is such a fine dancer. He will surely receive a scholarship.

4. As we searched the soft, wet sand. We felt relief.

5. An event that I'll never forget. The day the first astronauts landed on the moon was a great achievement for all citizens of the earth.

Hint

In trying to decide whether to add the fragment to the sentence before or after, first decide which way makes more sense. Add the fragment to the sentence to which it is most closely related in meaning.

• Fixing the Subordinator Fragment: Method III •

Add a new subject-verb word group to the fragment.

In *a*, page 338:

[added word group]

When an empty shopping cart soared down the aisle, I had to jump out of the way. I
[subject] [verb]

knew some little brat was to blame.

Step 3. Adding Words to Fragments. Add the necessary words to these fragments and rewrite the correct sentence on the blank lines below. Remember punctuation.

1. If the drought continues. _____

   _____

2. That nearly won first prize. _____

   _____

3. Unless the legislature acts quickly. _____

   _____

• Fixing the Subordinator Fragment: Method IV •

Sometimes you can take out the subordinator and some accompanying words in order to correct the fragment.

In *a*, page 338:

[Remove subordinator]

When An empty shopping cart soared down the aisle.
[capital letter]

Sometimes it is necessary to add a new word, which will serve as the subject.

In *c*, page 339:

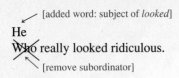

[added word: subject of *looked*]

He
~~Who~~ really looked ridiculous.

[remove subordinator]

Hint: Use this method only when all others fail. It's best to incorporate the fragment into a complete sentence. In that way you will be improving your writing style by using subordination.

Step 4. Dropping the Subordinator.   Correct these fragments by removing the subordinator.

1. Although I applauded the actors and actresses.
2. The woman who owns the hardware store.
3. While Julie looked around the museum.

FINDING THE FRAGMENT

You can see that the only way to spot the subordinator fragment is to be thoroughly familiar with the list of subordinators you were asked to experiment with earlier in this chapter. Here again are most of the subordinators, this time in Stop-Sign warning charts. If you memorize these words, you'll know what causes most students to write fragments.

• Fragment Stop Signs •

I		II	
as long as	how	what	that
after	provided	which	whoever
although	if	who	whomever
as	since	whose	whatever
as if	so that		
as soon as	though		
because	unless		
before	until		
whenever	when		
once	where		
while	whether		

Hint: Remember, do not avoid using these words. When used correctly, they add variety and clarity to your style.

• Review Charts: The Subordinator Fragment •

A Fragment Finder

1. Learn the list of subordinators that frequently give rise to fragments (see above).

2. Read the sentences aloud; do not confuse a pause for breath (which may or may not be indicated by a comma) with a complete stop (indicated by a period, a semicolon, or some other end mark).

3. Read your sentences from the last one to the first, stopping after each sentence to see if a complete thought has been exposed.

A Fragment Fixer

1. Join the fragment to the sentence that comes before.

2. Join the fragment to the sentence that comes after.

3. Add a new subject-verb word group.

4. Remove the subordinator. Add any new words.

Step 1. Correcting Fragments.   Most of the selections below contain fragments of the subordinator type. Correct the fragments in any of the ways you have learned. If the selection is correct, mark the sentence *C*.

1. After living in Nice for ten months. She spoke French quite fluently.

2. Motor skills are important for a child. Because they are needed for proper muscular development.

3. Travelers' checks are very safe. Wherever people travel. Their money is secure. Even if it is lost or stolen.

4. Diets high in sodium are unhealthy. A special problem for people who have high blood pressure. Who have to watch salt intake.

5. *Gone with the Wind* is still very popular. A book that shows the horrors of the Civil War. That presents complex but appealing characters.

6. Many people fear that learning to use a computer is very complicated. Which it can be. But a good teacher can help you over the rough spots.

7. Because AIDS is a serious health problem, we read and hear about it often. But many doctors believe that the public's fears of catching the disease are exaggerated and irrational.

8. The fawn stood very still. As I loaded my camera. A rustle in the grass frightened the animal and it ran away.

9. My stepfather was late for work. Since he missed the bus. He had to walk to the office.

10. Many people praised WABC-TV. The station that first reported the story. That showed the events of the crime.

Step 2. More Practice with Fragments.   Study the fragment review charts on page 343. Then follow directions.

1. Write two sentences to tell something that you do each morning when you wake up. Use the words *when I get out of bed* in one of your sentences.

   _____

   _____

2. Write one complete thought about a person who is always helping you. Use the words *who always helps me* in your sentence. _____

   _____

   _____

   _____

3. Write two sentences that tell how you study for a final exam. Open one of your sentences with either of these word groups: *whenever I have a final exam* or *before a final exam.* _____

   _____

   _____

   _____

   _____

4. Write a sentence that tells what you do when you meet someone for the first time. Start your sentence with one of these words: *when, if,* or *while.*

   _____

   _____

   _____

5. Write a sentence or two about cleaning your room. Use the words *to clean my room* somewhere in your sentence. _____

   _____

   _____

   _____

6. Write a sentence about some difficult course that you will have to take in college. Use the words *which is difficult* in your sentence. _____

   _____

   _____

7. Write two sentences about a TV program you enjoy watching. Use the words *that I enjoy* in one of your sentences. _____

_____

_____

_____

8. Write three sentences about people you know. Use one of these word groups in each sentence: *who always waves to me, who tells me all her problems, whom I have not seen in a long time.* _____

_____

_____

_____

9. Write a sentence about a relative who looks like you. Use this word group in your sentence: *whom I greatly resemble.* _____

_____

_____

_____

10. Write a sentence or two about some changes in your lifestyle as a result of your learning to drive. Use one of these word groups somewhere in your sentence: *because I learned to drive* or *since I learned to drive.* _____

_____

_____

_____

Step 3. Look at Step 1 on page 343. For each word group that is not a sentence, write a complete one by adding and/or changing words.

● Mirror Words (Homophones)

The following exercises focus upon words that are especially difficult to spell because they look and sound so much like other words with different meanings. Words that look and sound alike but have different spellings and different meanings are called *homophones*.

● It's Its ●

it's: it is it has	*It's* too quiet. Tell us if *it's* true *It's* been a week since I saw her.
	Hint: You must be able to use the words *it is* or *it has* whenever you want to use *it's*.
its: possession or ownership by some nonhuman thing	The Raggedy-Ann doll lost *its* stuffing. As winter approached, the tree lost *its* leaves.
	Hint: If you can use *his* or *her* and the sentence gives a sense of ownership, you can use *its*.
	The tree lost *his* leaves. (*His* gives the sense of ownership; since trees have no male or female qualities, *its* should be used.)
~~its'~~	This form does not exist! *Do not use it.*

Step 1. *It's* or *Its*?   Write the correct word, *it's* or *its,* in the blank spaces below.

1. _____ been only three days since they bought this typewriter, and already _____ broken.

2. Although _____ easy to read a poem, _____ meaning is often difficult to understand.

3. When _____ five o'clock, our parrot taps _____ beak on the water dish.

4. _____ clear that the cat is freezing; notice how it rubs _____ fur against the bark of the old maple tree.

5. _____ interesting to watch an ant carry _____ food.

• Two   Too   To •

two: the number 2

too: 1. One meaning is "very," "more than enough," "excessively," or "in a great degree."

  The color is too dull.
  My cousin is too tall.

  2. *Too* means "also" as well.

  Let me go, too.
  Will the mayor, too, speak at the luncheon?

Hint: When you use *too* [meaning "also"] at the end of a sentence, you must use a comma before it to indicate a pause and to give emphasis to your statement.

I shook Senator Carter's hand, too.

to: 1. *To* is used to show direction. It means "toward," "for," or "at."

  Carry the milk to the refrigerator.
  To me he is always fair.

  2. *To* is used as part of the infinitive. An infinitive is the starting point of any verb used in a sentence. In the sentence "He likes food," *likes* is the verb whose infinitive is *to like*. All infinitives are preceded by the word *to*. These two sentences use infinitives correctly: notice the word *to*.

  [infinitive]
  They like to fish in a stream.
  To run in track meets, you must begin to train your legs.
  [infinitive]   [infinitive]

Step 2. *To, Two, Too.*   Fill in the blanks below with the correct form: *too, two,* or *to*.

Listening _____ the _____ men arguing outside about a parking

space was _____ much _____ put up with. It was hard enough

having _____ finish this essay in just _____ more hours, but listening _____ these _____ cursing each other was starting _____ drive me crazy, _____. I guess it's my fault; after all, I should have listened _____ my father when he told me _____ start the assignment _____ weeks ago. Instead, as usual, I got _____ involved with other things and waited until _____ in the morning _____ begin writing.

Step 3. Using *To, Two, Too* Correctly.   Follow directions. Use your own paper.

1. Write a sentence that uses *too* to mean "also."
2. Write a sentence that uses *to* as an infinitive.
3. Write a sentence using the word *two*.
4. Write a sentence using *too* to mean "very."
5. Write a sentence that uses *to* as a direction word.

● *There*   *Their*   *They're* ●

there: a place   Was it *there?*

Hint: *There* often starts a sentence. It is sometimes followed by *are, were, is,* or some other verb.

There are three birds.
There was a good movie at the Rialto.
There sat two children playing.

their: ownership (possession) by a group   It's *their* car.

Was it *their* house that burned?

they're: they are

Hint: If you can say *they are,* you can use *they're.*

They're late again!
If *they're* tired, they should sleep.

Step 4. Listening for *Their, They're,* and *There*.   Read the brief paragraph below, noting the use of *their, they're,* and *there*. Then on separate paper, write the paragraph as your instructor dictates it.

In the past my mother and father loved their apartment, but they're just not happy there anymore. There is no longer room for all Dad's trophies, and Mom's plants lie cluttered over the entire living room. My folks are starting to look for a new place that they're both going to enjoy as much as their old apartment. There must be an apartment building in their area that has large rooms to hold many precious belongings. I'm going to look in today's paper. An apartment must be listed there that my parents will find right for their needs.

● *Your*   *You're* ●

---

your: ownership. It means "belonging to you."

Is that *your* car?
Give *your* theme a lively title.

you're: you are

Hint: If you can say *you are,* you can use *you're.*

You're late.
When *you're* out of town, call.

Step 5. *Your* and *You're*.   Circle the correct words in the parentheses.

1. (Your, You're) trying to make me angry!
2. (Your, You're) back is getting very sunburned.
3. If (your, you're) uncertain of the date, check (your, you're) calendar.
4. (Your, You're) parents won't let you drive (your, you're) own car?
5. When (your, you're) computer is down, (your, you're) right to call for help.

● Who's   Whose ●

who's: the contraction for *who is* or *who has*

Who's at the door?

Tell him *who's* on the phone.

Who's been to El Paso?

  Hint: If you can say *who is* or *who has,* you can use *who's.*

whose: possession. It asks a question (*Belonging to whom?*) or it refers to some
  person or thing named earlier in the sentence.

Whose dime is that?

The man *whose* briefcase was lost offered a reward.

Step 6. Sentences with *Who's* and *Whose*.   Complete the following sentences so
that they make sense.

1. I wonder whose _____
2. Please tell us who's _____
3. The squirrel, whose _____, darted behind a
    large bush.
4. Whose _____
5. Who's _____

● Quit   Quiet   Quite ●

quit: to stop

I *quit* my job last week.

quiet: silent; without noise or movement

A *quiet* room is restful.

quite: completely; rather

He was *quite* disturbed at the accident.

Step 7. *Quit, Quiet, Quite?* Fill in the blank with *quit, quiet,* or *quite* so that the sentences make sense.

1. "That's _____ a _____ automobile you have there," the gas station attendant said with a grin.

2. In a _____ voice, he mumbled that he would _____ as of tomorrow.

3. "I'm just looking for some peace and _____ ," he wearily told the desk clerk.

4. The first-grade teacher was _____ amazed at how _____ her class remained throughout the day.

5. It's _____ a drive to Helena from Great Falls but perfect for a _____ Sunday morning trip.

● *Principal*   *Principle* ●

principal:

1. a head person at a school

   The principal *speaks to the students each day.*

2. a major sum of money

   The principal *he invested earned $1,250 interest.*

3. a descriptive word that means "most important"

   Rice is still the principal *food for many people.*

principle: a rule, a major belief, a basic idea or truth

One principle *for success is hard work.*
As a man of principle, *he refused a bribe.*
The principle *of atoms and molecules goes back to the early Greeks.*

Hint: Princi*ple* and ru*le* both end in *-le*: if you use princi*ple*, make sure it means ru*le*.

Step 8. Using *Principle* and *Principal*. Fill in the blanks with the letters *-le* or *-al* so that the word *principle* or *principal* correctly suits the meaning of the word group.

1. The princip_____ critic
2. Stick to your princip_____s.
3. the high school princip_____
4. princip_____s of architecture
5. the princip_____ text in this course

6. the princip_____ of the matter
7. a critic with princip_____s
8. lost interest and princip_____
9. a speech from the princip_____
10. my princip_____ goal in life

● Loose   Lose ●

loose: rhymes with *moose.* It means "not tight, freer"; sometimes it means "set free."

A *loose* shoelace is dangerous.
You should *loose* the brake before driving your car.

lose: rhymes with *whose.* It means "to misplace" or "not to win or keep."

If you *lose* the registration form, you will have to pay another fee.

Step 9. *Lose* or *Loose?*   Write in the correct word, *lose* or *loose,* so the word groups make sense.

1. a _____ plank on the bridge
2. _____ your wallet
3. a _____ -leaf notebook
4. The child's tooth is _____ .
5. _____ your place

6. _____ -fitting jeans
7. turn it _____
8. _____ the championship
9. _____ your temper
10. Don't _____ your way in the woods.

● No   Now   Know ●

no: negative; not any

I have *no* information about it.

now: at this time

Now you can understand his reasons.

know: to understand, to be acquainted with

I *know* the principles of chemistry.
They *know* the family next door.

Step 10. *No, Now, Know* **for Proper Meaning.** Fill in the blank spaces with the correct word, *no, now,* or *know.*

Many people _____ do not _____ where their ancestors came from. Yet _____ one can resist the urge to _____ his or her true beginnings. Men and women everywhere _____ longer ignore the past and _____ that if they ask questions _____ amount of effort is too much _____ to uncover family origins. To _____ one's past is to _____ oneself.

• Were   Where •

were: the past tense plural form of the verb *to be*

Hint: *Were* rhymes with *her.*

We *were* searching for our car.
They *were* laughing.

where: a word that tells a place or asks "in what place?"

Hint: Pronounce the *wh* at the start of the word. *Where* rhymes with *care.*

In the city *where* I grew up many changes now appear.
Where did all that noise come from?

Step 11. *Were* and *Where* **in Action.** Fill in the blanks with the correct word, *were* or *where.*

1. I know _____ they _____ going.
2. _____ are the jackets that we _____ wearing?
3. It is a place _____ everyone is scared to go.
4. Is it true that they _____ late?
5. _____ both answers to the problem correct?
6. Tell them _____ to park.
7. The mosquitoes _____ really biting last night!
8. _____ they playing tennis in the rain?
9. _____ _____ the police officers when we needed them?
10. Why _____ you laughing?

● *Piece*　　*Peace* ●

---

piece: a part or portion of something

One *piece* of glass cut his finger.

peace: without war; a state of restfulness

Peace is one of our noblest goals.

Step 12. *Piece* or *Peace*?　Fill in the blanks with *piece* or *peace*.

1. a _____ of chicken
2. _____ -loving
3. world _____
4. two _____s of chicken
5. a _____ mission

6. _____ of mind
7. _____ of pie
8. _____ in the Middle East
9. a broken _____ of the desk
10. a _____ officer

● *Then*　　*Than* ●

---

then: at a certain time

The folksinger performed, and *then* we left the party.

than: a comparing word

She is taller *than* her brother.

Step 13. Using *Then* and *Than*.　Fill in the blank spaces with the letter *e* or *a* to make *then* or *than*, whichever the sentence requires.

1. a car newer th____n yours
2. Th____n Jane spoke.
3. more th____n you know
4. larger th____n life
5. more votes th____n her opponent

6. could not leave just th____n
7. I saw her just th____n.
8. first lightning, th____n thunder
9. looked thinner th____n her sister
10. "I'll see you th____n."

• *Lead*   *Led* •

lead:

1. rhymes with *weed*. It means "to show the way."

    A good instructor will lead *you to discover important values.*
    The boy who leads *must know the forest path.*

2. rhymes with *fed*. It is a grayish metal.

    A lead *pencil contains graphite and no* lead *at all.*

led: rhymes with *fed*, too. This *led* is the past tense of *lead*. It means "showed the way."

    He led *us through the back alleys of Los Angeles.*

Step 14. Making Sense with *Lead* or *Led*. Fill in the blank spaces with *lead* or *led*, whichever makes sense.

1. Who will _____ the expedition?
2. The hostess _____ us to a booth near the window.
3. When we dance the waltz, I _____ ; when we dance the rhumba, she _____ s.
4. Who _____ the discussion of Fowle's new book?
5. Do felt-tipped pens _____ the _____ pencil in popularity?

• *Knew*   *New* •

knew: had knowledge about; was familiar with

They *knew* each other from childhood days.

new: the opposite of old

That *new* car has all the safety features.

Step 15. *Knew* or *New* in Word Groups.   Write in *knew* or *new* so that the selection makes sense.

As soon as we entered Ed and Sally's apartment, we _____ nothing would ever be _____ in their lives. There was not one _____ piece of furniture anywhere. It was as if they _____ their lives would never change. We had hoped so much that this _____ place would be a _____ beginning for them.

● *Cloths*   *Clothes*   *Close* ●

---

cloth: woven or knitted material used to make a variety of items

cloths: pieces of cloth

Dry the dish*cloths* before using them.

clothes: what you wear

The *clothes* of today are lively and imaginative.

close: to shut; near

Please *close* the door. Stand *close* to me.

Step 16. *Cloths, Clothes,* or *Close?*   Underline the correct word in the parentheses below.

1. If you have picked out your (clothes, close), please (close, cloths) your closet door.
2. Cover the table with one of the lace (clothes, cloths, close); then change your (clothes, cloths, close).
3. If your (close, cloths, clothes) are dirty, light (cloths, clothes) may be used to wipe off the dust.
4. If you (clothes, close) the garage door, put the oil-soaked (cloths, close) outdoors.
5. To save energy, make sure to (clothes, close) the (clothes, close) drier door tightly.

Step 17. Reviewing Troublesome Words. Fill in the blanks with proper letters in the sentences below.

There is nothing qui____ so annoying as a high school princip____ who claims to ____ow everything about keeping order in a school. When each ____ew student received a p____ce of paper entitled "____ew Princip____s of Order at Melville High," we ____ew something was very wrong. It was bad enough that there w____re ten more hair and cl____s regulations th____n last year, but the regulations w____re also full of corny old sayings. One said, "L____se lips sink ships." My dad said it was something from World War II. The ____ew regulations told us there was n____ talking in the halls, ____o slamming doors, and n____ wearing jeans to assemblies. He was practically telling us w____re to sit. Th____n, when the Handi-Wipe cl____s started showing up near bathroom sinks, I thought I would l____se my mind! It's one thing to want p____ce and qu____ in a school, but attending Melville High was beginning to cl____ in on me. It was enough to make me want to qu____ school altogether. Well, to sum it all up, we got tired of being l____d around by our noses; ____ow we're taking the l____d and calling a strike until the princip____ changes his princip____s. After all, we've got nothing to l____se.

● Misplaced Modifiers

Words or word groups must stand as close as possible to whatever words they are describing. Words like *only, just, even, almost, hardly* affect the meaning that the writer wishes, depending upon where they are placed in the sentence. Look at the word *just* in five different places in the same sentence below and examine the explanations of the meanings.

Just he suggested that we leave early.
(This means he was the only one who spoke.)

He *just* suggested that we leave early.
(This means that he merely told of one idea. It also means that he made the suggestion only a short while ago.)

He suggested *just* that we leave early.
(This means that he made no other suggestion.)

He suggested that *just* we leave early.
(This means that he meant nobody else should leave early.)

He suggested that we *just* leave early.
(This means that he felt we should do nothing else but leave early.)

Words placed too far from the words they describe (*modify*) often create confusing sentences. *Misplaced modifiers* are words or word groups that, because of faulty placement, do not describe the words they intend to describe.

Our neighbor sold dresses to my sister without buttons.
(The *sister* has no buttons?)
At the age of five the doctor administered a smallpox vaccination to me.
(The *doctor* was five years old?)
I watched as an old car was pulled down the street that had a flat tire.
(The *street* had a flat tire?)

Here are the sentences with the describing words in the proper places.

[This word group describes *dresses:* put
it close to what it describes.]

1. Our neighbor sold dresses *without buttons* to my sister.

[This word group describes *me:* put
it close to what it describes.]

2. The doctor administered a smallpox vaccination to me *at the age of five.*

3. I watched as an old car *that had a flat tire* was pulled down the street.

[This word group describes *car:* put
it close to what it describes.]

Step 1. Explaining Placement.   Discuss the meanings created by the italicized words in the sentences below.

1. From the ship's deck we *only* saw the sea for miles.
2. From the ship's deck *only* we saw the sea for miles.
3. From the ship's deck we saw *only* the sea for miles.
4. From the ship's deck we saw the sea *only* for miles.
5. From the ship's deck *only,* we saw the sea for miles.

Step 2. In the Right Places.   Add the italicized word group in the right place in the sentence so that it expresses a logical and clear idea. Rewrite the sentences in the space provided. You may want to rearrange words.

1. *in a sudden flash*

   Lightning crossed the sky where the children played with their toys.

   _____

2. *that I had planted*

The roses and the tulips looked beautiful growing next to the house.

_____

3. *last year*

In history class I did not see why the settlers struggled westward in covered wagons to cross the desert.

_____

4. *in the soup*

Father stirred the vegetables for our dinner guests.

_____

5. *that it had begun to snow*

A cold chill ran up my spine and sent a message to my brain.

_____

Step 3. Changing Faulty Placement. In the sentences below, words or word groups do not appear close enough to the words they describe. On your own paper, rewrite each sentence by putting the words in their proper places. If the sentence is correct, mark it *C*.

1. My sister only eats after ten in the morning.
2. He saw the airplane approaching from the window of the airport terminal building.
3. Mr. Jones is a handsome man; he has a wide forehead, a straight nose, and long brown hair with glasses.
4. At the zoo, I felt sorry for the monkey with the pink nose that couldn't leave its cage.
5. I agree that a college diploma these days is only worth the paper on which it is written to a certain degree.
6. The functioning of the heart and respiratory system in our society has traditionally been the basis for proclaiming death.
7. I read about the progress of nineteenth-century homesteaders in moving westward every Saturday morning.
8. In biology we saw a movie about the growth of a baby to an adult which lasted until the end of class.
9. The high-calorie, high-fat, high-sugar, low-fiber American diet is typical in most households.
10. I watched while Spot played with Dad barking and rolling on the ground.

● Parallelism

> ● What Is *Parallelism?* ●
>
> Parts of a sentence with the same function generally need the same form. When you place sentence elements in a series or when you use certain types of connectors in pairs, you must use parallel form. *Parallelism* is a quality of correct sentence structure that balances connected parts by using the same form for ideas joined equally.

Balancing Connected Parts: Keeping the Same Form

Words or word groups in a series must match in form.

Hint

You can often recognize a series by commas and the words *and, but, or, nor.*

The homemaker liked to bake, to sew, and to cook.

[all infinitives]

NOT

The homemaker liked to bake, to sew, and *cooking*.

We prefer dancing and singing.

[both *-ing* words]

NOT

We prefer dancing and *to sing*.

[verb] [verb]

We heard that the President spoke to his advisers, contacted reporters, and then made his announcement to the public.

[verb] NOT

We heard that the President spoke to his advisers, contacted reporters, and *of his announcement to the public.*

Step 1. Making the Parts Fit.   Add a word group that completes the series with a balanced part.

1. On our vacation we wanted to ski and_____

2. José likes swimming, diving, and _____

3. Mike knew he'd been caught when the teacher asked him to stand and _____

    _____

4. On Tuesday, Mrs. Kuo worked at the lab, cooked dinner, and _____

    _____

5. To wake my son, I banged on his door and _____

    _____

Balancing Connected Parts: Repeating the Series Opener

Often you need to repeat, for each part of the series, the first word in the opening item of the series. The sentences on the right are clearer because they repeat the opening word.

NOT

They approved his plan because it was logical and it promised to succeed.

He spoke out for the party, for its leaders, but not its principles.

BUT

They approved his plan *because* it was logical and *because* it promised to succeed.

He spoke out *for* the party, *for* its leaders, but not *for* its principles.

• Some Series Openers That Often Need Repeating •

because, for, of, by, to, at, that, so that, a (an), who, which, could

---

Step 2. Balance through Repetition. On separate paper, rewrite the incorrect underlined portion in each sentence so that it balances with the rest of the series. Look at the example.

EXAMPLE

The coach announced that athletes need special diets, that sweets add needless fat and calories, and <u>we should avoid chocolates at all costs.</u>

that we should avoid chocolates at all costs.

1. To fix the tire, you need a jack, <u>spare tire</u>, and <u>pump</u>.
2. He decided to write a book, <u>get</u> it published, and hope he made enough money to support himself.
3. Mr. Dunbar's new wonder feed could be used for cattle, for pigs, and <u>chickens</u>.

4. I watched my son running down the field and <u>tried</u> to score a goal.

5. It is a long journey which is made by steps forward and <u>falls downward</u>.

Balancing Connected Parts: Paired Words and Matching Forms

A special effect of balance in sentences comes about through certain connectors that work in pairs. These paired connectors must be followed by words that have the same form. In the sentences below, connectors are in boldface. *X*'s appear over words that do not match in form. Underlined words show matching forms.

The registrar is **either** <u>working</u> at his desk **or** <u>visiting</u> the dean.

NOT

XXXXXXXXXXXXXXXXX

The registrar is **either** working at his desk **or** on a visit with the dean.

I wondered **whether** to <u>make</u> the telephone call **or** <u>to see</u> her in person.

NOT

XXXXXXXXXXX

I wondered **whether** I should make the telephone call **or** to see her in person.

WORDS THAT WORK IN PAIRS

either . . . or	whether . . . or
neither . . . nor	not only . . . but also
both . . . and	if . . . or

Step 3. Paired Words and Forms That Match. Add a word group to each sentence below, making sure that what you add matches the underlined segment.

EXAMPLE

We saw not only <u>all the movies he directed</u>

but also the television commercials he wrote.

1. Our grandpa always brings us either <u>candy</u> or

2. The dog is both <u>growling</u> and

3. Geoff wondered <u>if he should make stew for dinner</u> or

_____

4. I didn't know whether <u>to call him</u> or

_____

5. Those trees are neither <u>green</u> nor

_____

Step 4. Balanced Sentence Ideas: More Practice.   The sentences below contain errors in parallelism like those explained in the previous pages. On separate paper, rewrite the sentences so that they are correct.

1. If you want to exercise in the winter, try taking an aerobics class, skiing cross-country, or to swim at an indoor pool.

2. Titian is a painter of great skill and who uses color in dramatic ways.

3. Each summer, we like to travel through the West by train or we drive by car through New England.

4. We not only missed our bus but forgot to walk the dog.

5. He enjoyed the movie for its ideas on modern life but not the photography; most, he liked the scene between a business executive and elevator operator.

6. There are clothes to wash, formulas to make, diapers to change, and just the general playtime also.

7. There are three aspects of my life which I recognized as signs of the end of my childhood: my treatment of my parents, my relationships with my friends, and school.

8. The car had a broken window, rusty body, and missing a headlight.

9. The three articles agree that the aftermath of rape can be traumatizing, humiliating, and scars the victim mentally.

10. Parakeets make great pets because they eat very little, a beautiful chirp, and always knowing where they are.

● Plurals

Although the usual method of plural formation involves the addition of an -*s*, there are several variations. Study the review charts below, which show examples and state rules.

Regular Plurals

Add -*s* to the singular for most plurals

boy + -*s* = boys
pencil + -*s* = pencils
tree + -*s* = trees

Words Ending in *y*

1. If a consonant comes before the *y*, change the *y* to *i* and add -*es*.

   cit⟨y⟩ + -s = cities
   part ⟨y⟩+ -s = parties

2. If a vowel comes before the *y*, add only -*s*.

   day + -s = days
   key + -s = keys

Words Ending in *f*

1. Most words ending in -*f* form plurals by adding *s:*

   roof—roofs
   chief—chiefs

2. Some words ending in *f* change to *v* and add -*es:*

   leaf—leaves   wife—wives
   elf—elves   self—selves
   wolf—wolves   half—halves
   knife—knives   calf—calves
   shelf—shelves   loaf—loaves

Plurals That Add Syllables

If another syllable is added when you pronounce the plural, add -*es*. Words ending in *s, ss, ch, sh, tch, x, z* add another syllable and therefore add -*es*.

fox + -es = foxes
church + -*es* = churches
glass + -*es* = glasses

Words Ending in *o*

1. Add -*s* to most words ending in -*o*.

   piano + -s = pianos
   radio + -s = radios

2. Exceptions:

   echoes   heroes   mulattoes
   potatoes   Negroes   mosquitoes
   tomatoes   torpedoes   mottoes

-*en* Plurals

Some words add -*en* to make plurals.

ox—oxen
child—children

Inside Plurals

Some words show plurals by changing letters within the word:

mouse—mice
man—men
louse—lice
foot—feet
tooth—teeth
goose—geese

Plurals That Stay the Same

Some words are the same in plural and singular:

cattle	series
deer	sheep
bass	wheat
corps	means
cod	dozen
	swine

one deer, many deer

a series, three series

Words from Other Languages

Some words still keep the plural of the foreign language from which they originated:

alga	algae
oasis	oases
alumnus	alumni
alumna	alumnae
parenthesis	parentheses
thesis	theses
basis	bases
bacterium	bacteria
medium	media
phenomenon	phenomena
axis	axes
criterion	criteria
radius	radii
fungus	fungi
datum	data
stratum	strata

Combination Words

1. If a word is formed by combining two or three words, make a plural of the main word.

    son-in-law = sons-in-law   man-of-war = men-of-war

    editor-in-chief = editors-in-chief

    commander in chief = commanders in chief

2. If the combination is written as one word, add -*s* to the end.

    suitcase = suitcases

    cupful = cupfuls

Hint: Check a dictionary for plurals of combination words.

Step 1. Plurals.   Write the plurals of these words:

1. bush	10. beauty	18. halo
2. deer	11. clue	19. child
3. soprano	12. fistful	20. medium
4. focus	13. valley	21. task
5. woman	14. mouse	22. crisis
6. dwarf	15. wheat	23. father-in-law
7. church	16. belief	24. torpedo
8. Negro	17. shelf	25. Wednesday
9. bacterium		

Step 2. Selecting Plurals.   Change the words in parentheses to their plurals, and write them in the spaces provided.

1. Hosts at both (party) _____ served (cod) _____ with two (dozen) _____ different (loaf) _____ of bread.

2. Those (woman) _____ who are (alumna) _____ of the University of Texas are (editor-in-chief) _____ of their county newspapers.

3. The ship-to-shore (radio) _____ informed the marine (corps) _____ of the (torpedo) _____ headed their way.

4. The scientific (datum) _____ on the study of (mouse) _____ show that they can kill (themself) _____ by eating (spoonful) _____ of a known poison.

5. The (economy) _____ of many (nation) _____ are tied to changing political (crisis) _____ and (phenomenon) _____ .

6. The (wolf) _____ attacked the (sheep) _____ , but the ranchers leaped to their (foot) _____ and became (hero) _____ by scaring the (animal) _____ away.

7. Although she is best known as one of Hollywood's prettiest (woman) _____ , Marilyn Monroe was also among the best dramatic (actress) _____ of her day, as many of her more serious (movie) _____ prove.

8. The New York (Yankee) _____ defeated the Los Angeles (Dodger) _____ in two consecutive World (Series) _____ .

● Possession

a. It is the *car of the man*.

b. It is the *car belonging to the man*.

c. It is the *man's car*.

In sentence *a*, the car belongs to the man. Ownership is shown with the words *of the man*. The car is owned. The man owns it.

In sentence *b*, the car belongs to the man. Ownership is shown with the words *belonging to the man*. The car is owned. The man owns it.

In sentence *c*, the car belongs to the man. Ownership is shown by using an apostrophe *s* (*'s*) after the word that tells who owns the thing. The car is still being owned. The man still owns it. But in this sentence the owner is named *before* the thing that he owns. And the only way we know the owner is through the apostrophe *s*.

                           [owner]

It is the man's car.
                    [thing owned]

Sentence *a* sounds clumsy and unnatural. You would rarely say or write such a sentence. Sentence *b* is more natural, but it is wordy.

Sentence *c* is the most convenient and most usual way of indicating ownership. When we speak of *possession,* it is usually this form of showing ownership that we mean. And, because of the misunderstood apostrophe, this method often causes many difficulties.

As you practice with possession, keep in mind that ownership involves two separate ideas.

1. Somebody or something is the owner. That word will contain an apostrophe.

2. Somebody or something is being owned. That word usually comes soon after the word with the apostrophe.

Step 1. Owner and Owned.   In each sentence below, circle the word that indicates who or what owns or possesses something. Put an X over the word that shows what (or who) is being owned.

EXAMPLE

           X   X

The (child's) toy fell into (Mother's) waiting arms.

1. The senator's aide spoke gently to the children's parents.

2. Dr. Asher's patients asked whether the nurse was a friend's sister.

3. The restaurant's policy was to take reservations only upon a customer's request.

4. Suzanne's only birthday wish was that Jorge's mother would leave them alone.

5. The government's problem over the next few years is to encourage our citizens' awareness of the value of saving money for the future's sake.

● How Not to Use Apostrophes ●

Do not use apostrophes to show plurals. Form plurals by adding *-s* or *-es,* or by any one of the special methods explained on pages 363–365.

For example, a familiar error is one like this:

The store sells pencil's and paper's.

If an apostrophe *s* is used at the end of a word, it means that the word owns something. What, according to the sentence, do the pencil and the paper possess? Nothing belongs to either of the two words written with apostrophes. The student who wrote the sentence wants only to indicate more than one pencil and more than one paper, so the sentence should be:

The store sells pencils and papers.

There is a minor exception, one case in which you do use an apostrophe to show plural. When you write numbers, letters, or symbols and you need to pluralize them, you use an apostrophe. (For example: "The word *membership* has two *m's.*") However, this use is rare enough for you not to worry about but to remember instead that apostrophes do *not* usually indicate plurals.

Step 2. Spotting Wrong Possession. Correct any incorrect use of possession in each of these sentences by changing the word to its proper plural form.

1. The kitten's in the pet shop's window's looked cuter than Anne's old cat.

2. The morning's dampness reminded Barbara of the soggy vacation's she had spent at Joe's cottage in the Oregon hill's.

3. The guitarist's instrument's had not arrived although there were thousand's of fan's screaming for the band's first number.

4. As Amy's old Chevy stalled, all of the car's and truck's behind her honked their horn's loudly.

5. Leah's boyfriend worked as one of the extra's in two film's made about water sport's.

● How to Form Possessives: Two Simple Reminders ●

Reminder I for Possession

If the word that names the owner *does not* end in *s*, add an apostrophe *s* (*'s*).

girl   The girl's dress ripped.
        [apostrophe *s*   [This is owned by the girl.]
        added to
        girl]

senator   The senator's campaign failed.
        [apostrophe *s*   [This is owned by the senator.]
        added to *senator*]

   Hint for Reminder I: It does not matter if the word is plural or singular. If the word does not end in *s*, add an apostrophe *s*.

[This word is plural, ⟶ *men*   The men's cars crashed.
even though it does   [apostrophe *s*   [These are owned
not end in *s*.]   added to men]   by the men.]

Step 3. Possession Reminder I in Sentences. Change the words below so that they indicate ownership. Then write your own brief sentence to use the word correctly.

EXAMPLE

city   *city's*   *The city's roads are crowded on weekend mornings.*

1. Mr. Chan   _____   _____

2. company   _____   _____

3. child   _____   _____

4. media   _____   _____

5. women   _____   _____

Reminder II for Possession

If the word that names the owner *does* end in *s*, add only an apostrophe (').

boys   The boys' bicycles broke.

[an apostrophe   [These are owned
added to *boys*]   by the boys.]

governors   The governors' meeting ended when the leader fainted.

an apostrophe   [This is owned by
added to   the *governors*.]
governors]

Hint for Reminder II: It does not matter if the word is plural or singular. If the word ends in *s*, add only an apostrophe.

[This word is singular: *Doris*   Doris' trip was canceled.
it ends in *s*.]

[apostrophe   [This is owned
added to   by Doris.]
Doris]

See page 398 for an alternative method of showing possession for *names* that end in *s*.

Step 4. Possession Reminder II in Sentences.   Add apostrophes to the words below so that they indicate ownership. Then write your own brief sentence to use the word correctly.

EXAMPLE

nurses   *nurses'*   *The nurses' caps blew off.*

1. mosquitoes _____   _____

2. Mr. Harris _____   _____

3. horses _____   _____

4. Nikos _____   _____

5. authors _____   _____

• Four Special Cases with Possession •

I.   Compound Words or Word Combinations

Only the last word shows possession.

brother-in-law   My brother-in-law's cat sleeps all day.
              [apostrophe *s* to show possession]

A compound word is a combination of words that name one thing.

secretary of state   A secretary of state's position is important.
                          [apostrophe *s* to
                          show possession]

II.   Time and Money Words

Words that indicate time values, in certain uses, are said to show ownership.

hour   One hour's rest is too much.
                          [apostrophe *s* added
                          to *hour* (Reminder I)]
[This word is thought of as
"possessing" the rest.]

minutes   Five minutes' rest is all you need.
                          [apostrophe added
                          to *minutes* (Reminder II)]

Words that indicate money value, in certain uses, are said to show ownership.

                          [apostrophe *s* added
                          to *quarter* (Reminder I)]
quarter   A quarter's worth of apples will not feed many children.
       [This word is thought of as
       "possessing" the worth.]

dollars   He bought three dollars' worth of chocolate.
                          [apostrophe added to
                          dollars (Reminder II)]

III.   Two People as Owners

When both people are thought to be equal owners of the same thing, only the last word shows possession.

McGraw-Hill's textbooks

Standard & Poor's Index

If two people own things individually, show possession for both words.

Harry's and Jerome's cars crashed.

IV.   Pronouns and Ownership

Pronouns never have apostrophes to show possession.

his book	NOT	*his'* book
That is *hers*.	NOT	*hers'* or *her's*
The pen is *yours*.	NOT	*yours'* or *your's*
Those are *ours*.	NOT	*ours'* or *our's*
Is it *theirs*?	NOT	*theirs'* or *their's*
The cat hurt *its* paw.	NOT	*it's* or *its'*

Hint: Look at the mirror words, pages 345–357.

Step 5. Practice with Special Possessives.   Underline the correct words in the parentheses.

1. In a (minutes, minute's, minutes') time, (Carlos' and Maria's, Carlos and Maria's) son will arrive with (his, his') new wife.

2. The (bride-to-be, bride-to-bes, bride-to-be's) gown would arrive in ten (days, day's, days') time.

3. When I was a child, we used to go to (Anna and Pop's, Anna's and Pop's) candy store to buy three (cent's, cents') worth of licorice.

4. Not two (months, month's, months') time had elapsed, and the public was demanding the (secretary of interior's, secretary of interiors') resignation.

5. When (Nora and Aldo, Nora's and Aldo's, Nora and Aldo's) car slowed, they put in two (dollars, dollar's, dollars') worth of gasoline.

• If You Think a Word Needs an Apostrophe •

1. See if you can figure out what is being owned.

2. See if the word in which you want to use an apostrophe is the owner of something. Usually, the thing owned appears in the sentence soon after the owner.

   Exceptions

   It is David's.
   We ate at Carl's.

Here the thing owned is not specifically mentioned, but understood.

David's (book)
Carl's (house)

3. Sometimes the owner is more than one. Make sure the word shows plural with the right ending.

   a. If the word does not end in *s*, add an apostrophe *s*.

   b. If the word does end in *s*, add only an apostrophe.

Examples

   a. You want to show that a boy owns books. The word *boy* does not end in *s*. The possessive is shown this way:

   the *boy's* books
          ↑ [add apostrophe *s*.]

   b. You want to show that many boys are the owners of books. The word *boys* ends in *s*. The possessive is shown this way:

   the *boys'* books
             ↑ [Add apostrophe after *s*.]

Step 6. Adding Possessive Endings. In the blanks at the ends of the words below, add *s*, *'s,* or simply an apostrophe (') so that the sentence is correct. For some words you need to add nothing.

1. Three children played on the patio at their Uncle Les _____ house while their cousin _____ patted the neighbors _____ dog.

2. Both adding machines _____ on Clyde Stevens _____ desk work more quickly than yours _____ .

3. Shirley _____ and Jesus _____ children brought toy _____ to school; mine brought only a book and two pen _____ .

4. Because the electric company _____ rate _____ are increasing, many elderly people will not be able to heat their homes _____ this winter.

5. It is neither Carlos _____ nor Mai _____ fault that their parents _____ are getting divorced.

Step 7. Possession Review. Add apostrophes wherever needed in the sentences below. Numbers in parentheses tell how many apostrophes to use.

1. Its too soon to take the childs temperature because the aspirin has not yet made its way to his bloodstream. (2)

2. Because her sister Karens dresses did not fit, Jen borrowed Mrs. Davis daughters dress. (3)

3. Charlie and Muriels daughters wedding was a big hit with all the relatives. (2)

4. This appliance stores catalog shows that its lawn mowers are less expensive than other stores lawn mowers. (2)

5. My sister-in-laws father works at Davis and Hargoods Department Store. (2)

6. Joan Rivers acts always make my sisters laugh. (1)

7. We were invited to our neighbors pool soon after they installed it. (1)

8. Phyllis cat lost its bell so if youre able to get her another, her mother will pay you five dollars. (2)

9. My cousins boss accidentally paid him for six hours work on Tuesday when he worked for eight hours. (2)

10. Mothers-in-laws advice often makes their sons wives best intentions seem selfish. (3)

● Pronouns as Subjects

● Pronoun Chart I: Subject Pronouns ●

Singular Pronoun Subjects		Plural Pronoun Subjects	
I	it	we	you
he	you	they	
she	who		

You remember from your work in subject-verb agreement that the pronouns that appear above may be used as subjects of verbs.

_____ *run(s).*

Any of the pronouns you see in the chart could be used in the blank space in the sentence above.

EXAMPLE

I run.

He runs.

They run.

Although you would never say or write *Me run* or *Him runs*, when you use two subjects (one of which is a pronoun) for the same verb, you may forget to use the subject pronouns from this chart. The following sentences from student papers fail to use pronouns correctly. Alongside the incorrect sentence you will see the sentence written with the right subject pronoun.

INCORRECT

1. My father and *me* never got along.

2. *Him* and *me* watched fireworks from across the bay.

CORRECT

1. My father and *I* never got along.

2. *He* and *I* watched fireworks from across the bay.

● Hints for Correct Pronouns When You Use Two Subjects for the Same Verb ●

1. Always pick a pronoun you want to use as a subject from Pronoun Chart I on page 374.

2. Test each subject *alone* before you decide which pronoun to use. For example, suppose you do not know whether to use *her* or *she* in the blank space in this sentence:

   Her mother and _____ *rushed into the house.*
   First say:
   a. *Her mother* rushed into the house.
   Then say:
   b. *Her* rushed into the house.
   That does not sound right. Then say:
   c. *She* rushed into the house.
   That is correct. Now combine the two subjects from *a* and *c.*

   Her mother and *she* rushed into the house.

Step 1. Speaking about Two Subjects. Combine any one of the subject pronouns (*he, I, she, it, we, they, you, who*) with the name of someone you know to tell about a place you recently visited. Speak your answers aloud.

EXAMPLES

Suzette and he bought a house in Seattle.

My father and I drove into Waco last night.

Step 2. Filling In Pronoun Subjects. Fill the blank spaces with any pronoun subjects that make sense to you. Use different pronouns in each sentence.

1. Diego and _____ dance well together.
2. _____ and her friends went to the movies.
3. My family and _____ go to California every summer.
4. His father and _____ share all the cooking.
5. _____ and the children love to watch the sun set behind the mountains.

• Pronouns after to Be •

$\qquad$ /[part of *to be*]

a. Everyone thought it <u>was</u> her.

b. Everyone thought it <u>was</u> she.

If you had to choose between *a* and *b*, you would probably select *a* as the sentence that you hear more frequently. However, sentence *b* is correct, and in writing, you want to remember this suggestion:

After a form of the verb to be *use a subject pronoun.*

The verb *to be* has many forms, a number of which appear below:

am	has been	should have been
is	have been	should be
are	had been	could be
was	will be	may be
were	must have been	could have been

Hint: The expression *It's me* (It is me) is not correct formal English: Formal writing requires *It is I*. However, *It's me* is used in conversation and is acceptable.

Step 3. Pronouns After *To Be*. Complete each sentence below by writing a correct *pronoun* after the verb. Circle the pronoun you use. You may add any other information you like.

EXAMPLE

It was (he) *who sang.* _____

1. The child we saw was _____

2. The winner is _____

3. It could have been _____

4. It will be _____

5. That should be _____

Step 4. Selecting Pronouns. Choose *subject pronouns* in the parentheses below to make the sentences correct.

1. The driver and (she, her) argued fiercely on the street corner.

2. It is (she, her) who plays the piano at all of our parties.

3. The other patients and (he, him) refused to wait any longer.

4. (She, Her) and (me, I) had the same elementary schoolteacher.

5. Both (he, him) and his roommate knew it was (they, them) who stole the money.

6. Not only (he, him) but his entire family believed it was (they, them) who started the argument.

7. If the other students are lazy, it will be (her, she) who gets the best grades.

8. Dr. Wells and (we, us) are convinced that classical music or soft jazz will soothe the babies.

9. (He, Him) and (they, them) formed their own rock band.

10. Charlotte Yip and Ken Long ran for school council, and the winner was (she, her).

● Pronouns as Objects

• Pronoun Chart II: Nonsubject Pronouns (Objects) •

Singular	Plural
me	us
him	them
her	whom
whom	

Hint: The words *it* and *you* may be used as subject or nonsubject pronouns.

The pronouns above are not subject pronouns and do not appear as subjects in sentences. Yet these words are usually found in two important sentence positions.

1. *Pronouns After Verbs*

    [verb]   [pronoun]

Give **me** the book.

       [verb]   [pronoun]

Bonnie *selected* **him** as her dancing partner.

          [pronoun]

You *told* **whom** about the riot?
[verb]

Although you would never write

Give *I* the book

    OR

Bonnie selected *he* as her partner.

whenever you use *two* words after the verb (one of which is a pronoun), you probably have some difficulty selecting the correct pronoun. Look at these sentences; is *a* or *b* correct?

          [verb]

a. The instructor praised Harriet and *I* for our creativity.

          [verb]

b. The instructor praised Harriet and *me* for our creativity.

You remember that *I* can be used only as a subject. In sentence *a*, the subject is *instructor* (for the verb *praised*). Since the pronoun you need comes *after* the verb *praised*, select the pronoun from the chart above. Since *me* appears in the chart, sentence *b* is correct.

● Hints for Correct Pronouns After Verbs ●

1. Select the pronoun from Pronoun Chart II, page 377.

2. If two words must come after the verb, test each word alone before you decide which pronoun to use. Suppose you do not know whether to use *he* or *him* in the blank in the sentence:

   The teacher praised his brother and _____ *for their cooperation.*
     First say:
   a. The teacher praised *his brother.*
     Then say:
   b. The teacher praised *he.* (That wouldn't sound right.)
     Then say:
   c. The teacher praised *him.*
     That is correct. Now combine the words after the verb in *a* and *c*.

   The teacher praised *his brother* and *him* for their cooperation.

Step 1. Writing Pronouns After Verbs.   On separate paper, write sentences for any ten of the following verbs. Use *two* words after each verb, one a noun and the other a correct pronoun. Write about things that really happened, and use as many different pronouns as possible. Look at the example beneath the list of verbs.

pushed	called	carried
hurried	begged	threw
needed	replaced	asked
allowed	punished	shocked
left	helped	chased

EXAMPLE

The movie left my sister and me with an unpleasant feeling.

Step 2. Choosing Pronouns After Verbs.   Select the pronoun in parentheses that correctly completes each sentence.

1. Our parents left my sisters and (I, me) home when they went to pick up our new TV.

2. Mr. Wang hired Charlie and (she, her) on the same day.

3. The judge accused Roberto and (they, them) of disrupting the peace at a political rally.

4. I found her brother and (she, her) sitting by the rippling pond.

5. The editorial insulted you and (us, we) terribly.

2. *Pronouns After Connecting Words That Show Relationship*

Aside from their use after verbs, the pronouns in Chart II are used after certain connecting words, called prepositions, that relate one word or word group in the sentence to some other sentence part. First, look at some of the connecting words that show relationship.

a. We read a *book* **about** *teenagers*.

The word *about* relates the words *book* and *teenagers* to each other by showing the kind of book.

b. Charlene *ran* **toward** *David*.

The word *toward* relates *ran* and *David* by showing where the action was performed. Now, if you wanted to use a pronoun instead of *teenagers* and instead of *David,* you would need a word from Pronoun Chart II (page 377):

We read a book **about** *them.*

Charlene ran **toward** *him.*

Connecting words that show relationship like *about* and *toward* are called *prepositions.* You've already seen many of these in the exercise on expanding sentences and changing word order (pages 164–166).

● Some Connectors That Show Relationship (Prepositions) ●

about	along	across	within	up	through
by	among	on	beside	before	along with
beneath	of	upon	since	like	because of
inside	except	into	as to	below	by way of
above	under	after	toward	between	on account of
for	onto	to	in	next to	in spite of
over	at	with	beyond	by means of	in front of
outside					

Step 3. Remembering Connectors. Study the connectors above. Then, on separate paper, write from memory as many as you can.

You probably would not have trouble writing *one* correct pronoun after the connector words mentioned above. No one would write

Give the book to *I*.

OR

The boy ran toward *he*.

But as soon as *two* words are used after the connector, you can have difficulties.

Give the book **to** Mary and (I, me).
The boy ran **toward** the child and (he, him).

Since the pronoun you need comes after a connecting word that shows relationship (*to* and *toward*), you must select a pronoun from Pronoun Chart II. The words *I* and *he* are not correct because they are subject pronouns (Pronoun Chart I) and must be used as subjects of verbs. Correctly written, the sentences above become

Give the book to Mary and *me*.
The boy ran toward the child and *him*.

● Hints for Pronouns After Connectors That Show Relationship ●

1. Select the pronoun from Pronoun Chart II, page 377.

2. If *two* words come after the word that shows relationship, test the words one at a time before you decide which pronoun to use. If you don't know whether to use *I* or *me* in this sentence:

   The dean spoke about Joe and _____
   First say:
   a. The dean spoke about *Joe*.
   Then say:
   b. The dean spoke about *I*.
   That doesn't sound right Then say:
   c. The dean spoke about *me*.
   This is obviously correct. Now combine the results in *a* and *c* above.
   The dean spoke about *Joe* and *me*.

Step 4. Pronouns for You to Choose. Fill in both blanks in each of the following items. Use a pronoun in at least one of the blanks. You can use a noun *or* another pronoun in the other blank. Look at the example.

EXAMPLE

toward _____*him*_____ and _____*me*_____

1. between _____ and _____
2. after _____ or _____
3. except _____ and _____
4. from _____ and _____
5. near _____ and _____
6. because of _____ and _____
7. in spite of _____ and _____
8. in front of _____ and _____
9. between _____ and _____

Step 5. Writing Sentences with Connectors That Show Relationship. Use five of the subject-verb combinations below in sentences of your own. After each subject-verb combination, use correctly one of the completed word groups from Step 4 above.

you speak	they included	she sat
he walked	the truck swerved	he watched
they drove	an eagle soared	everyone bowed

EXAMPLE

They drove toward him and me. _____

1. _____
2. _____
3. _____
4. _____
5. _____

Some of the words listed as connectors that show relationship may also act as coordinators or subordinators. You remember that coordinators and subordinators (see pages 12–15 and 86–94) introduce subject-verb groups that are connected to complete sentences. So, it *is* possible to find a subject pronoun after one of the words listed as connectors that show relationship. But notice how differently the word is used in each of these sentences:

A

My brother ran <u>before</u> me.

B

Before I ran <u>away, my</u> brother left home.

In *A*, the word *before* is a connector that relates the words *ran* and *me* by showing where the action took place.

In *B*, the word *Before* is a connector that subordinates the subject-verb word group *I ran away* to the complete thought *my brother left home*.

Step 6. Connectors in Two Ways.   Fill in each blank after the connector with the correct pronoun from either Pronoun Chart I or Pronoun Chart II.

1. Milly and _____ asked Bill and _____ to the dance.

2. The civic agency distributed the food equally among _____ and _____ .

3. Between Stauros and _____ there is a special bond of friendship.

4. Stacy and _____ decided to finish our project before we ate dinner.

5. We were very thirsty, for my brother and _____ ate hot sauce.

6. After Pete and _____ left work, we went out for ice cream.

7. I thought someone was following my cousin and _____ .

8. The operator finally connected Edwina and _____ .

9. Inez gently placed the blanket over _____ .

10. Mr. Jacobs and _____ chatted about our college days.

● Pronoun Agreement

a. The girl kissed <u>her</u> mother.
b. The boys brought <u>their</u> gloves.

In these two sentences, the underlined word is a pronoun that takes the place of the noun to which the arrow is drawn. In sentence *a*, the word *girl* is singular and the pronoun that refers back to it must be singular (*her*). In sentence *b*, the word *boys* is plural and the pronoun that refers back to it must be plural (*their*). It is easy to see that *boys* is plural and *girl* is singular.

c. She kissed <u>her</u> mother.
d. They brought <u>their</u> gloves.

In sentences *c* and *d*, the underlined pronoun takes the place of another pronoun. *Her* takes the place of *she*: since *she* is singular, *her* must be singular. *Their* takes the place of *they*: since *they* is plural, *their* must be plural too. But with words like *boys, girls, they,* and *she*, it is easy to decide whether the word is singular or plural. Several pronouns—although they may look plural—are always singular. If another pronoun later on in the sentence refers back to one of these special singular pronouns, that pronoun must be singular too.

• Special Singular Pronouns •

anyone	everyone	someone	one
anybody	everybody	somebody	neither
each	either	no one	none
			nobody

Hint: If a pronoun refers to one of these words, the pronoun must be singular.

Everyone   should bring   *his* own assignment.

Each   of them packed   *his* own bag.

Anybody   may raise   *his* own hand.

Either   of the boys can drive   *his* own car.

Anyone   can love   *his* own country.

One   of them sold   *his* own camera.

None   of them helped   *his* own country.

[This pronoun refers to one of the special singular pronouns.]

• His *or* Her? •

His is used as a pronoun even when the group contains men and women. *Her* is used when the group is clearly all women.

Everyone of them drove *her* own car.

Either of them can make *her* own clothes.

Many writers who are sensitive to sex stereotyping try to avoid using *his* to refer to mixed groups that contain men and women. Sometimes plural forms help avoid choosing *his*.

Examples

Singular	**Plural**
Everyone should bring his own assignment.	*All* the students should bring their assignments.
Each of them packed his own bag.	*They* all packed their own bags.

Some writers use the form *s/he* to refer to mixed groups, but it has not won wide popular approval.

Step 7. Selecting the Right Pronoun.   Write in the blank spaces the correct word in the parentheses. Or rewrite the sentences so that they use plural forms.

EXAMPLE

Everyone sharpened _____*his*_____ pencil (his, their).

1.   None of the gardeners remembered to clean _____ tools (his, their).
2.   Each of the children picked out _____ own clothes (their, his, her).
3.   Each of them should have driven _____ car more safely (her, their).
4.   Everybody likes to take _____ time when making important decision (their, his).
5.   All the drivers started _____ engines at the same time (their, his).

Pronouns That Point Out: Demonstrative Pronouns

This book is mine.

These papers ripped.

That girl fell.

Those cars sped along the highway.

Only *this, these, that, those* point out. Don't use *them* to point out.

NOT   *Them* windows look dirty.

BUT   *Those* windows look dirty.

Since *this* and *that* are singular, the words that they point out must be singular.
Since *these* and *those* are plural, the words that they point out must be plural.

[singular]   [singular]

This kind of book is stimulating.

NOT

[plural]   [plural]

These kinds of cars save money on gasoline.

[plural]   [singular]

These kind of books is stimulating.

Step 8. Pointing Out with Pronouns.   Fill in the blanks with *this, that, these, those,* or *them.*

1.   We like _____ paintings the best.
2.   _____ clock is very old.

3. With _____ sort of friend, you never need enemies.

4. _____ kinds of people buy many books but never read them.

5. _____ kind of sandwich is too filling.

• Review •

Pronoun Chart I
Subjects

I	we
he	
she	they
it	
you	you
who	

After *to be,* use subject pronouns.
Use *this, that, these, those* to point out.
Don't use *them*!

    these boys

      NOT

them boys

Pronoun Chart II
After Verbs and After Connectors
That Show Relationship

me	us
him	
her	them
it	
you	
whom	

If you need a pronoun as one of two words, try one word at a time.

He asked Barry and (I, me).
He asked *I.* [wrong]
He asked *me.* [right]

Then: He asked Barry and me.

Hint: Use a singular pronoun to refer to a special singular pronoun like *anyone, everyone, anybody, someone, no one, neither, either, each.*

Using the Pronoun *You*

In informal writing, where the writer is actually addressing the reader, the pronoun *you* works nicely. However, it sometimes creates problems in style when *you* includes the reader unintentionally. In the second of the two sentences below, the writer addresses the reader as if the reader were present.

My room is a restful place. When you look out the window, you can see tall pines against the gray sky.

The use of *you* in the second sentence is too informal and, hence, not appropriate to essay writing. The *you* assumes that the reader can join the writer in the actual experience.

One way to avoid the informal *you* is to use *I* (or *we,* if it works), a more accurate pronoun under the circumstances.

My room is a restful place. When *I* look out the window, *I* can see tall pines against the gray sky.

Although American writers (as opposed to British, say) do not always feel comfortable with the pronoun *one, one* can serve well for more formal effects than *I.*

My room is a restful place. When *one* looks out the window, *one* can see tall pines against the gray sky.

Another solution is to use a word like *person* or some other noun that works in the sentence.

My room is a restful place. When a *person* looks out the window, *he or she* can see tall pines against the gray sky.

Finally, a writer could combine sentences to eliminate the pronouns for a smoother, fuller, more descriptive sentence.

My room is a restful place; beyond the window, tall pines nestle against the gray sky.

Step 9. Avoiding *You* in Sentences.   Rewrite the sentences below for formal papers by removing the pronoun *you.*

Hint:
If you use *one,* make sure that your new sentence does not sound too formal or strained.

1. Hospital conditions during the Civil War were terrible. You could die in bed as easily as on a battlefield. _____

   _____

2. The cathedral in Reims, France, is a superb example of gothic architecture. You can see the stained-glass windows just above your pew if you look to your left. _____

   _____

3. This restaurant is an excellent one. You always leave feeling stuffed, though.

   _____

   _____

4. When you open the classroom door, you see the desks and chairs lined up in

   neat rows. _____

   _____

5. If you are a Richard Gere fan, you should see the movie *An Officer and a*

   Gentleman. _____

   _____

For the steps below, use the review chart on page 386. Make sure that you know the prepositions listed on page 380.

Step 10. Pronouns in Your Sentences. On separate paper, use the following word groups correctly in sentences.

1. my father and me
2. the mechanic and I
3. the author and us
4. these kinds
5. Sandy and me

6. she and I
7. Maria and who
8. Carla and me
9. him and me
10. he and I

Step 11. Reviewing Pronoun Usage. Write on the blank lines the correct pronouns you select from parentheses. Look at the example.

Is College Worth It?

_____*I*_____ Sometimes I wonder if college and (me, I) were meant for each other.
1. _____ These days, many people say that a college diploma is worth only the
2. _____ paper it is written on. (Them, Those) people may be right. My father tells
3. _____ me that all his friends and (he, him) have done just fine without college
4. _____ degrees. In many ways he and (them, they) are very successful. To
5. _____ anyone who measures (their, his) success by big cars, large houses, and
6. _____ fancy clothes, a college degree may not be worth (his, their) time.
7. _____ However, for my friends and (I, me) success means something else.
8. _____ Every one of us wants more for (his, their) life than just material things.
9. _____ Sure, (them, those) symbols of status are very nice and comfortable, but
10. _____ against (it, them) we'll compare even one finely tuned mind. So, al-
11. _____ though we may never have Cadillacs and diamonds, the people whom I
12. _____ respect and (me, I) will always have our knowledge. (You, One) can lose
        (your, one's) riches, but knowledge always remains.

Step 12. Pronouns in Review. Circle the correct pronouns in the parentheses.

1. None of the actors forgot (his, their) lines.

2. Mathilda invited my sister and (I, me) for New Year's dinner.

3. Was it really (her, she)?

4. Elizabeth borrowed (them, those) compact discs from Jerry and (I, me).

5. Maria and (I, me) love to sketch people in the park.

6. The doctor and (he, him) agreed on the diagnosis.

7. Between you and (I, me), this child is very spoiled.

8. (Those, Them) tomato plants wilted in the sudden freeze.

9. Dina and (she, her) knew it was (they, them) who would have to clean up the shed.

10. Someone slipped and broke (his, their) leg on these stairs.

● **Punctuation**

● Aids to Punctuation: End Marks ●

The Period (.)

1. Use a period after a sentence that makes a statement.

I watched a crow circle over a twisted oak.

Everyone was tired.

2. Use a period after a sentence that makes a mild command.

Take the bus into Austin.

Buy United States savings bonds.

3. Use periods after initials.

Robert E. Lee

John F. Kennedy

The Question Mark (?)

1. Use question marks at the end of sentences that clearly ask questions.

Who wrote A Farewell to Arms? ←— [question mark; end of question]

"Can't you hear me?" David shouted.
[end of sentence: no question mark]

The Exclamation Point (!)

1. Use the exclamation point at the end of a sentence that shows strong emotion, sharp surprise, forceful command, or strong emphasis.

I hate all men!

I don't believe it!

Call the police!

I meant what I said!

2. Certain words and expressions, like *what, oh, alas, hurray, bravo,* often introduce exclamations.

Oh! What am I going to do?

What! You stole that car?

The Period (.)	**The Question Mark (?)**	**The Exclamation Point (!)**
4. Use periods after most abbreviations.	2. Some sentences, though they mention that a question is being asked, do not ask the question themselves. Such *indirect questions* are not followed by question marks.	3. Only the individual writer can determine which sentences are spoken with strong emotion. *Do not overuse the exclamation point.*
Ph.D., N.J.		
Exceptions		
1. Most government agencies use no periods in abbreviations.	*She wondered why he did not call.* ← [period]	
FBI, CIA	*He asked who brought the station wagon.* ← [period]	
2. tv or TV		
3. Business companies		
IBM, A&P		

Step 1. A Variety of Endings.   Put in correct end marks in the paragraph below. Use a capital letter to show the start of a new sentence.

My Fear of Flying

Why was I boarding this massive TWA jet that loomed ahead of me on the icy runway did I really have to fly to Washington, DC, on such a stormy day of course I did I couldn't miss my own sister's wedding she would never forgive me for not attending I wonder why I didn't take the train at least they were showing during the flight highlights of the NFL game of the week although an old W C Fields movie would have made me more relaxed, I could not concentrate on any movie Oh God I was scared suddenly the captain's voice said, "Please fasten your seatbelts" in any case, I was trapped my body tensed, my eyes stared straight ahead, and my clammy hands squeezed the armrests we landed safely, but I would never fly again

● Quotation Marks (" ") ●

1. Use quotation marks to show someone's exact words.

   "Roller skating is great!" Jane shouted excitedly.

   "When I'm in a big city," she admitted, "I miss my father's farm."

   "Why is the sky blue?" his son asked.

   Hint: The exact words may be repeating what someone said in speaking; or the exact words may be a statement quoted from a book. In any case, quotation marks are needed.

2. Use quotation marks to set off the names of short stories, poems, chapters, articles, or essays that are parts of books, magazines, or newspapers.

   I read a column called "The Presidency" in Time *magazine.*

   The anonymous poem "Frankie and Johnnie" appears in Understanding Poetry *by Brooks and Warren.*

● Underlining (Italicizing) ●

Underlining is used in handwritten sentences to show when italics are needed.

1. Underline all titles of books, magazines, movies, TV shows, and newspapers to show that these titles should be in italics.

   Most people still enjoy Hemingway's novel, <u>The Old Man and the Sea</u>.

   If the sentence were printed, it would look like this:

   Most people still enjoy The Old Man and the Sea.

2. Underline names of ships, trains, and airplanes.

   Explorers have finally found the ship <u>Titanic</u> off the coast of Canada.

Step 2. Quotation Marks and Italics. Put in quotation marks or use underlining where required in the sentences below.

1. Jean said Crimes and Misdemeanors was a great movie, but my favorite of Woody Allen's is still Annie Hall.

2. Is traveling on the Orient Express still as elegant as it used to be? my aunt asked.

3. When you go to the store, said David, please buy some oranges.

4. On the Merv Griffin show, Peter Benchley, author of the novel Jaws, discussed an article that appeared in Life magazine.

5. John Updike's short story A & P, which appears in the collection Pigeon Feathers, is especially appealing to young adults.

● Using Semicolons (;) ●

1. Use a semicolon to separate two complete sentences that are closely related.

    The landlord painted the fence; now he is painting the steps.

2. Use semicolons instead of commas to separate items in a series if some of the items contain commas themselves. See pages 302–303.

    [comma]   [comma]

    At our picnic Lynette brought a whole chicken which, because of deep frying,
       [end of first item in series;
       semicolon used because commas
       already appear within the item] [end of second item in series]

    was a rich golden brown; two pounds of potato salad that her mother prepared; and a basket of cold, ripe apples.

3. Use semicolons instead of commas occasionally before coordinators that join complete thoughts that already contain commas.

    [semicolon instead of comma]

    The landlord painted the fence around my patio; but, even if he agrees to fix the plaster and repaint the whole apartment, I still intend to move.

• How to Use the Colon (:) •

1. A colon is used

    a. after the opening in a formal letter.

    Dear Ms. Stevenson:

    Gentlemen:

    Use a comma after informal openings.

    Dear Steve,

    b. between the hour and the minute when you write the time in numbers.

    The plane left at 6:18 P.M.

    c. between the numbers of the chapter and the verse in the Bible.

    Matthew 6:12 is inspiring.

    d. in a title, to separate the main name of the selection from a subtitle (see page 389 for example).

    e. between act and scene in a play.

    Macbeth II:iii

2. Use a colon when you introduce a long or detailed list of items.

    [colon]

    Remember to bring to registration the following: two sharpened pencils with erasers, your admissions letter, your IBM registration card, and a check for $36.00 for student fees.   [Commas separate items in series.]

    Hint: Don't use the colon for a simple listing.

    [no colon]

    We bought shoes, gloves, and jeans.

3. Use a colon whenever you want to force the reader's attention to the statement that comes after the colon. That statement usually explains or clarifies the opening part of the sentence.

    [Colon pushes emphasis to what comes after.]   This part of the sentence explains the first part.]

    Of this I am sure: I do not want any more life insurance.

4. Use a colon before you introduce a formal quotation.

    [colon]

    About greatness, Ralph Waldo Emerson said: "Every human being has a right to it, and in the pursuit we do not stand in each other's way."

Step 3. Semicolons and Colons in Practice. Use the semicolon or colon correctly in each sentence below. Be prepared to explain your answer.

1.   Our class ends at 810 I will not be able to stay until the end.

2.   In Shakespeare's *Hamlet* ii, Hamlet speaks these famous words "The play's the thing wherein I'll catch the conscience of the king."

3.   Always keep this rule in mind if you play tennis keep your eye on the ball.

4.   Before you begin painting your apartment, make sure to have the following items available a large drop cloth, brushes of various sizes, rollers and pans, wooden or plastic stirrers, and, of course, a few gallons of paint.

5.   The pastor referred us to Matthew 83 he felt it would give us something to think about.

6.   Gentlemen

Kindly send me three red, all-wool long johns two navy-blue, 100%-cotton kerchiefs and one green-plaid, chamois shirt.

● Parentheses ( ) ●

Parentheses are used to set off words or word groups that are not so important as the rest of the sentence. *Parenthetical expressions* add information and/or make some side comment on or about the material in the sentence.

[The information in parentheses is a side comment that adds information.]

Abandoned automobiles (and there are thousands throughout the country) line our roads and highways.

[The information in parentheses is a side comment.]

If you have seen Woody Allen's *Zelig* (certainly you have), you know how important a good director is.

[The information in parentheses adds information about the author's birth and death.]

Dylan Thomas (1914–1953) read his own poetry brilliantly.

Hint: 1.   Although parentheses indicate less important information, do not ignore or fail to read what appears in parentheses.

2.   Commas also set off parenthetical information, but commas give the material more importance.

   a.   *That old man (a carpenter) works hard.*
   b.   *That old man, a carpenter, works hard.*

   The words *a carpenter* are parenthetical in both sentences, but the commas in *b* make the parenthetical information more important than it is in *a*.

3.   Don't use parentheses too often in your writing.

Step 4. Your Statements in Parentheses. Add your own parenthetical information to the blank spaces in the following sentences. Use parentheses (or commas) as explained above.

1. The Federal budget deficit _____ has many citizens alarmed.

2. Our city's downtown area _____ is awaiting state funds for urban renewal.

3. The inflation rate _____ rose sharply in 1979.

4. The fields of corn _____ filled the Oklahoma landscape in every direction.

5. Our natural resources _____ may be seriously depleted by the end of the century.

● The Dash for Interruption and Summary ●

1. Use a pair of dashes to set off a sudden shift in thought or structure of the sentence.

[This question breaks into the complete thought expressed in the sentence.]

That old maple—did you see it?—lost all its leaves in June.

Hint: Parentheses could be used here as well. But the dash makes the information more important and stresses its sudden break into the main idea of the sentence.

2. Use a single dash before a summary of details mentioned earlier in the sentence.

Running a mile each day, exercising in a careful program, choosing food thoughtfully—these are the ways to keep weight down.

[This part of the sentence briefly summarizes the meaning of the details in the first part.]

3. Don't use the dash too often in your writing.

Step 5. Using the Dash. Use dashes correctly in the sentences below.

1. That newspaper is how shall I put it too offbeat for my tastes.

2. Daily exercise, a good diet, emotional stability these are essential ingredients for remaining healthy.

3. The airplane crash a horrible thing to witness destroyed three private homes.

4. Lowering taxes, increasing defense spending, lifting government regulations these were all part of the President's economic program.

5. *E. T., Star Wars, Close Encounters* each one was a staggering financial success.

• The Hyphen as Divider •

1. Use a hyphen to separate parts of certain compound words (words that are made by putting together other words).

time-consuming	*president-elect*
thirty-one	*well-bred*
self-assurance	*brother-in-law*

2. Use a hyphen to divide a word when there is no room on the line to finish the word.

    [hyphen]

    After the union leaders approved the con-
    tract, the members voted it quickly into effect.

3. Use a hyphen to separate the years of birth and death of some important figure.

    Rudyard Kipling (1865–1936)

When dividing words, observe the following:

1. Don't separate the word if you can avoid it.

2. Do put the hyphen at the end of the first line, *never* at the beginning of the next line.

approved the con-	NOT	approved the con
tract		-tract

3. Do separate the word at the end of a syllable and nowhere else.

be-lieve	NOT	beli-eve
re-call	NOT	rec-all
per-mit-ting	NOT	pe-rmit-ting

Hint
Check a dictionary for proper syllables in words (see page 436, How to Read a Dictionary Entry).

4. Do divide the word, if pronunciation allows, so that a consonant starts the part of the word that appears on the next line.

writ-ten   stop-ping
            BUT
leop-ard   knowl-edge

5. Don't divide words of one syllable: *laugh, called, brought.*

6. Don't leave just one letter of a word at the end of the line. Write the entire word on the next line.

NOT   He tried to e-   BUT   He tried to
        rase his mistake.   erase his mistake.

7. Don't carry over to the next line brief word endings like *-ly* (happi*ly*), *-ed* (hint*ed*), or *-ing* (sing*ing*).

8. Don't divide people's names.

Harry, Barbara   NOT   Har-   Bar-
                              ry   bara

9. Do leave a space at the end of a line rather than fill the space with part of a word that is incorrectly broken.

10. Do learn the difference between hyphen and dash.

IN WRITING BY HAND	IN TYPING
The hyphen is a short line (-). The dash is a longer line, about the length of three hyphens (—).	The hyphen is a short line (-). The dash is typed as two hyphens with no spaces before or after them (--).

Step 6. Breaking Up Words.   In the blank spaces, rewrite the words that appear below to show where you would use hyphens to break the word at the end of a line. Put an X after those words you would not divide.

1. proposal   _____   4. spectacle   _____
2. innocent   _____   5. phenomenal   _____
3. trapped   _____   6. sport   _____

7. occurrence _____   9. Sarah   _____

8. truly   _____   10. knowledge   _____

● Three Uses for Apostrophes (') ●

1. Possession (see pages 367–374)

   a. If a word *does not* end in *s*, in order to show ownership add an apostrophe *s* ('s).

   > *boy + 's = the boy's hat*
   > *men + 's = the men's club*

   b. If a word *does* end in *s*, in order to show ownership add only an apostrophe (').

   > *ladies + '*   *The ladies' coats were soiled.*
   > *boys + '*   *The boys' bicycles all fell down.*

   Hint: If a person's name ends in *s* and the name is to indicate possession, add *either* apostrophe *s* or just an apostrophe. Whichever you choose, however, be consistent throughout your writing.

   Doris' book   OR   Doris's book

2. Contractions

   To show where letters are omitted in words that are combined in contractions, use an apostrophe.

   > *it's = it is*   *I'll = I will*
   > *doesn't = does not*   *you're = you are*
   > *hasn't = has not*   *I've = I have*

   Hint: Contractions are usually informal words and should be avoided in formal compositions. Write out the two words in your themes.

3. Special plurals

   To show the plurals of numbers, letters, and symbols, use an apostrophe *s* ('s).

   > *There are two t's in committee.*
   > *Our address has three 5's in it.*
   > *All &'s should be written as* and.

   Hint: Aside from these special cases, *do not* use apostrophes to show plurals.

Step 7. Correct Apostrophes.   For each word in parentheses, add an apostrophe or apostrophe *s* so that the sentence is correct, and write the new word in the blank. If the word needs no apostrophe, put an *X* in the blank.

1. _____ (Youre) buying an expensive car, but _____ (its) not one of the safest.

2. The _____ (Mens) Club meets monthly at _____ (Russ) house.

3. The preschool child practiced writing her _____ (m) and _____ (w).

4. The _____ (women) letters of protest _____ (werent) even read by the _____ (committee) chairperson.

5. Ms. _____ (Jones) mother _____ (couldnt) climb the stairs to our apartment because _____ (shes) a woman in her _____ (nineties).

Step 8. A Punctuation Review.   Use correct punctuation in the following paragraph. Although the ends of sentences are indicated by periods, sometimes you will have to change them to exclamation points or question marks. The following list indicates what punctuation you will need. Do not add commas.

colons: 3	underlining (italics): 3
quotation marks: 4 pairs	hyphens: 2
exclamation points: 1	apostrophes: 3
question marks: 1	dashes: 1 pair
semicolons: 2	parentheses: 2 pairs
periods: 4	

Conrad's Photographic Eye

One of the masters of sensory images is Joseph Conrad 1857 1925. Pictures rich in color and sound, pictures of the sea in all its beauty these fill the pages of Conrads works. Born in Poland, he settled in England in the 1890s at the age of thirty seven. Conrad came to love about the English language its musical qualities its sweet, yet harsh, sounds its rich, lively, fluid motion. Conrad knew no one can deny it the importance of the senses in creating word pictures. *My task which I am trying to achieve is, he wrote, by the power of the written word to make you hear, to make you feel—it is, before all, to make you see.** How could that be more clearly expressed. It is Conrad's power to make readers see what has led many MA and PhD students to study his novels like Lord Jim and Nostromo. What marvelous use he makes of the language. In the description of a railroad changing from the short story Heart of Darkness he says *A slight clinking behind me made me turn my head. Six black men advanced in a file, toiling up the path. They walked erect and slow, balancing small baskets full of earth on their heads, and the clink kept time with their footsteps. Black rags were wound around their loins, and the short ends waggled to and fro like tails. I could see every rib, the joints of their limbs were like knots in a rope; each had an iron collar on his neck, and all were connected together with a chain whose bights swung between them, rhythmically clinking.** It must be a scene like this that John Galsworthy who, incidentally, was a writer and fellow traveler journeying on Conrads ship the Torrens thought of when he wrote *Conrads eyes never ceased snapshotting; and the millions of photographs they took were laid away by him to draw on.**

*Start of quote.
**End of quote.

● Quotations

One way of adding life to your paragraph is to use the words spoken by a person who plays some part in your narrative. It's usually more realistic and more lively to use the person's specific words rather than an indirect quotation, a statement that only summarizes what was said. Look at the difference:

1. My father said that I might be a good basketball player, but that he wanted me to study for my exam tomorrow.
2. My father shouted, "You might be a hot-shot basketball player, but I want you to study for that exam tomorrow!"

Sentence 2 has more force because it is a direct quotation; it lets the reader hear the person's exact words. Now, of course, if you are writing about a moment that occurred a while ago, it's impossible to remember *exactly* what a person said. Still, if you recall the general idea of the person's words, you can construct a sentence so that the reader hears it as a quotation.

Correct punctuation of quotations—exact words—is sometimes tricky. Remember that most quotation sentences have two parts: one part tells who is talking and how the person says the words; another part tells what is being said. These parts must be separated by punctuation. Study the charts below.

• I. Exact Words at the End •

[quotation marks]
[Capitalize first spoken word.]

My father shouted, "You might be a hot-shot basketball player, but I want you to study for that exam tomorrow!" [quotation marks]

[comma]   [end mark inside; period, question mark, or exclamation point]

Hint: If the same person speaks another sentence—without being interrupted—right after the first one, *don't* use another quotation mark. Put the last quotation mark after the very *last* word any one person speaks.

My father shouted, "You might be a hot-shot basketball player, but I want you to study for that exam tomorrow. I won't put up with any more failing grades."

Step 1. Correct Quotations.   Put in the correct punctuation for these sentences.

1.   Coach Martinez shouted get the lead out
2.   Will Rogers said I never met a man I didn't like
3.   The basketball star insisted I never give interviews
4.   The astronaut explained it was like nothing I ever felt before
5.   The police officer asked did you see the car's license plate

• II. Exact Words at the Beginning •

[quotation marks]
[capital letter]   [small letter]

"You might be a hot-shot basketball player, but I want you to study for that exam tomorrow," my father shouted. ← [period]

[comma, question mark, or exclamation   [quotation marks]
point inside quotation mark: no period]

Step 2. Writing Quotations.   Put in the correct punctuation for these sentences.

1.   This will hurt me more than it hurts you my father said
2.   Nobody ever likes the workout coach Davis complained
3.   May I take your order the waitress asked

4. I hope Dad comes home soon my sister said

5. Doesn't anyone care about me anymore he snapped

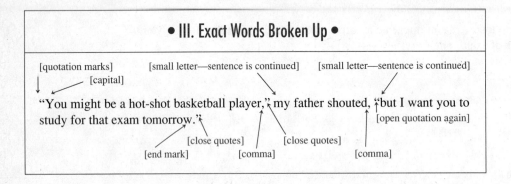

Step 3. Punctuating Quotations. Punctuate these sentences correctly.

Hint

A question mark goes at the end of a complete question.

1. Didn't you know Barbara asked that the third baseman is in the hospital

2. I would have been on time my aunt said but the traffic was very heavy

3. Never mind the dessert Don said where's the salad

4. If Paul were here Richard said he would know what to do

5. For to write good prose Maugham said is an affair of good manners

Step 4. Practice with Exact Words. Write three sentences you have heard spoken recently. Then rewrite each sentence with correct punctuation to show who did the talking. Sometimes a word like *shouted, muttered, whispered,* or *cried* is more vivid than *said*. In other sentences, *said* is adequate because the words in the quotation itself tell the tone the speaker is using. In one sentence, use the spoken words at the beginning; in another, use the spoken words at the end. In one sentence, break up the spoken words as in Chart III, above. One of each appears in the examples below. Use separate paper.

EXAMPLES

1a. *"Are you serious about joining the track team?"*

1b. *Trying to stifle a laugh, my friend, Che Hsin, asked, "Are you serious about joining the track team?"*

2a. *"Hey, we'd better move or we'll be late for class."*

2b. *"Hey, we'd better move," Marlene insisted, "or we'll be late for class."*

3a. "*This cafeteria coffee is poisonous!*"   *3b.* "*This cafeteria coffee is poisonous!*"
                                                gasped Peter, frowning.

Step 5. Punctuation Review. Punctuate these sentences correctly. Both direct and indirect quotations are included.

1. Every night at nine my five-year-old son crawls out of bed and cries I want some apple juice

2. In ten years as a gymnast Lydia insisted I've never seen a person as agile on the parallel bars as Terry

3. I've been told that when I was two years old my father threw me into the water and suggested that I learn how to swim

4. Roy screamed from his room who took my magazine

5. Come on up and see for yourself Henry shouted in front of his booth at the county fair

● A Sentence Review

The chart below will help you review some basic sentence elements.

• Writing Complete Thoughts: A Sentence Review Chart •

1. To be a sentence, a word group must contain a subject and a verb and must express a complete thought. In the following sentences, the verb is underlined twice and the subject once.

Our teacher gave us an assignment.
The men work hard.

Hint: To find a verb, try these tests:

a. Put *yesterday, today,* or *tomorrow* in front of the sentence. The word that changes is the verb because only verbs show tense—time change.

The children *laugh* while playing hide-and-seek.
Yesterday the children *laughed* while playing hide-and-seek.

Laugh changed to *laughed* with the word *yesterday.* Only verbs change in this way. *Laugh* is the verb.

Tomorrow the children *will laugh* while playing hide-and-seek.

Laugh changed to *will laugh* with the word *tomorrow*. Only verbs change this way. *Laugh* is the verb.

b. When you have the word you think is a verb, put *he, she, we, it, you, I,* or *they* in front of the word. If you've created a word group that makes sense with one of these subject pronouns (see page 374), you have a verb.

Word	**Test**	
work	I work, they work	verb
sings	he sings, it sings	verb
laughter	I laughter, they laughter	no verb
is	she is, he is	verb
seldom	I seldom, you seldom	no verb

c. Some words are *always* verbs, no matter how they are used in a sentence. Often working along with other verbs, these *auxiliaries*—helping verbs—are worth memorizing. When you see them, you know that they are verbs; and you know also that they may be signaling other verbs soon to follow in a sentence. Here are some of the most important helping verbs:

have	has	will	might	had	am	was
may	does	can	do	should	is	were
could	did	shall	would	must	are	been

2. Some sentences have verbs made up of more than one word. Notice how *had, should have,* and *were* are helping other verbs in these sentences:

Our teacher had given us an assignment.

Those men should have worked hard.

They were laughing aloud.

3. Some sentences have more than one verb for the same subject.

Those men worked and laughed.

4. Some sentences have several sets of subjects and verbs joined together.

Those men worked, but because they laughed, the job was finished late.

5. Some word groups, although very brief, are grammatically correct and are considered complete sentences because they express complete thoughts.

He ran.

It fell.

You might logically say, "We do not know who *he* is nor what *it* is. Aren't those sentences incomplete?" However, from a grammatical point of view, these word groups, because they contain subjects and verbs and express complete thoughts, *are* sentences. You might need more information to understand fully the correct meaning of the sentence, but often that information appears in sentences that come earlier or later on.

6. Some sentences have more than one subject for the same verb or verbs.

   My <u>brother</u> and <u>sister</u> <u>attended</u> the concert.

   <u>Mr</u>. <u>Holmes</u> and his <u>son</u> <u>went</u> to Boston but <u>returned</u> today.

7. Some sentences express complete thoughts, although the subject does not actually appear in the sentence.

   <u>Walk!</u>

   <u>Go</u> down the steps quickly!

   In both these sentences, the subject is understood to be the word *you*.

8. Some words can be either a subject or a verb, depending upon how they are used in a sentence. However, the guidelines above will help you decide if the word is a verb. If you are still uncertain, check a dictionary.

   Cats cry outside my window at night.

   (Here *cry* is the verb: yesterday, cats *cried*.)

   A cry awoke me.

   (Here *awoke* is the verb; tomorrow the cry *will awake* me. *Cry* is the subject: What awoke me? The cry.)

9. Some describing words often separate parts of a verb when the verb is more than one word. Don't be confused into thinking that words like *only, not, never,* and others are verbs simply because they appear near or because they break up verbs.

   The crow <u>could</u> not <u>flap</u> its wing.

   They <u>had</u> never <u>seen</u> so strange a sight.

   In the first sentence *could flap* is the verb. (*Could* is one of the helpers; and both *could* and *flap* work in the test with subject pronouns: *I could, I flap*.) The word *not*, though it appears between the two words that serve as verbs in the sentence, is not a verb: *I not? They not?* Similarly, in the second sentence *had seen* is the verb; *never*, despite its position in the sentence, is not a verb. Both *not* and *never* describe the verb and are called *adverbs*.

Step 1. Sentence or Nonsentence?   Only some of the word groups below are complete sentences. Read each item aloud; then, using the principles suggested in the Sentence Review Chart, pages 403–405, write *s* before each word group that makes a complete sentence and *ns* before each word group that is not a complete sentence. For each *ns* you write, explain how you would make the word group complete so that it qualifies as a sentence.

My Pen was

ns 1. Beyond the teacher's desk.

I was

ns 2. Lying in a lounge chair under the blistering sun.

s 3. Jeffrey fed the chickens before dawn.

He Das

ns 4. Running all the way home from school in the rain last Thursday.

s 5. The officer listened carefully and wrote our testimony on a sheet of yellow paper.

ns 6. For example, our swim team. *lost the championship.*

s 7. They listened.

s 8. Stop!

s 9. Leave these premises immediately.

He's

s 10. My only true love.

Step 2. Verbs and Subjects.   Among the words below, only eight may serve as verbs. Circle them. From the words remaining, select subjects that make sense with the verbs. Then write six sentences of your own, including in each a correct subject-verb combination. Use separate paper.

EXAMPLE

Sparrows fly swiftly.

radiator	draw	flutter
dim	hisses	light bulbs
stairs	listen	creak
children	sparrows	airplanes
(fly)	artists	engine
applaud	noises	audiences

Step 3. Finding Subjects and Verbs in Sentences.   Using the pointers in the Sentence Review Chart, pages 403–405, find the subjects and verbs in each sentence below. Underline the subjects once and the verbs twice.

EXAMPLE

After I had fallen, an old man helped me to my feet.

1. Since she left for college, the house has felt empty.
2. Janet voiced amazement at how spotless the Toronto stations and trains are kept.
3. Always revise your writing, or your paper may contain several grammatical errors.
4. The scent of sweet rolls filled the kitchen as Uncle Raol made coffee.
5. Arlene put her son at a window seat on the bus so that he could see the desert cactus in bloom along Route 10.
6. Because of the high crime rate in New York City, many people think all of New York is unsafe.
7. If you look out your window, you will see the fireworks explode against the dark sky.
8. Never forget your homework when you leave for class.
9. Hanging on the line, the red sweater flapped lazily in the summer breeze as Pedro put out the rest of the clothes.
10. Some people cry when they are happy.

● Verb Tense

Every verb has three main forms, called *principal parts,* and from these all the different tenses are made. The present tense, the past, and the future you usually have little trouble using; but other tenses are not so simple. Look for a moment at the verb *to laugh* and its three main parts. Beneath them, you will find an explanation of the tense that is made from each part.

• To Laugh •

I	II	III
laugh	laughed	laughed
The Present Tense	*The Past Tense*	*Tenses That Show Continuing Action*

They *laugh* too loudly.
She *laughs* softly.

I *laughed* also.
They *laughed* aloud.

He *has laughed* without stopping.

The Future Tense

They *will laugh* tomorrow.
I *shall* laugh too.

(This action began in the past, but may go on into the present.)

She *had laughed* before they arrived.

(This action began in the past but was over before another action in the past.)

Before next week she *will have laughed* at all the dull jokes in the book.

(This action will be finished before some definite time in the future.)

Hint: To form tenses that show continuing action:

1. Always use the third main part of the verb. (You will see later the main parts of many other verbs. These parts are always arranged in the same order as those above.)
2. Always use a helping verb:

has	had	will have
have		shall have

For *most* verbs (like *to laugh*), the principal parts are easy. All you need to know is the infinitive. If you take away the word *to*, you have the first main part of the verb (and you can form the present and future tense). If you add *-d* or *-ed* to the first main part, you have *both* the second and third main parts, and you can form the past tense and all the tenses that show actions that continue. Here are two other examples:

	I	**II**	**III**
		(add *-ed*)	(add *-ed*)
to talk	talk	talked	talked
	They talk.	I talked	She has talked.
	She talks.	They talked.	They have talked.
	We will talk.		She had talked.
	I shall talk.		They will have talked.
		(add *-d*)	(add *-d*)
to dance	dance	danced	danced
	They dance.	I danced.	She has danced.
	She dances.	They danced.	They have danced.
	We will dance.		She had danced.
	I shall dance.		They will have danced.

Step 1. Writing Main Parts of Verbs. From each infinitive below, make the three main parts in the same way as in the examples *to talk* and *to dance*. Write the verb parts in the columns listed.

	I	II	III
1. to love	_____	_____	_____
2. to wish	_____	_____	_____
3. to smile	_____	_____	_____
4. to skate	_____	_____	_____
5. to decide	_____	_____	_____

Troublesome Verb Parts

Unfortunately, a number of verbs do not form their parts as easily as the ones above. These verbs—called *irregular* because they are different from the usual— also happen to be among those we use most often, so it is not surprising to hear and to see a number of mistakes with them in spoken and written English. Although the list below does not include *all* the irregular verbs, it tries to indicate those most frequently used incorrectly. The starred verb is not irregular, but it still confuses many writers.

THIRTY-THREE HEADACHES: IRREGULAR VERB PARTS YOU NEED TO KNOW

I	II	III
TODAY I	YESTERDAY I	FREQUENTLY I HAVE
am	was	been
begin	began	begun
break	broke	broken
bring	brought	brought
burst	burst	burst
choose	chose	chosen
come	came	come
do	did	done
drink	drank	drunk
drown*	drowned	drowned
eat	ate	eaten
fly	flew	flown
freeze	froze	frozen
give	gave	given
go	went	gone
know	knew	known
lend	lent	lent
ring	rang	rung
rise	rose	risen
run	ran	run
see	saw	seen
sing	sang	sung
sit	sat	sat
speak	spoke	spoken
steal	stole	stolen
swim	swam	swum
take	took	taken
teach	taught	taught
tear	tore	torn
think	thought	thought
throw	threw	thrown
wear	wore	worn
write	wrote	written

• Some Advice in Making Tenses •

1. If you can say *now, today, at present* before the verb, select the form from Column I.

   Examples
   Now I take *French.*
   Now they will write *a letter.*
   At present she swims *well.*

2. If you can say *yesterday* before the verb, select the form from Column II.

   Examples
   Yesterday I wore *a black tie.*
   Yesterday they swam *at sea.*

3. If you can say *frequently* or *often* and one of the helpers (*has, have, had, shall have, will have*) before the verb, select the form from Column III.

   Examples
   Often I have done *good work.*
   Frequently they have stolen *bicycles.*

Step 1. Saying Aloud Correct Verb Parts. Many people do not use verb parts correctly in their writing because the correct forms sound incorrect to the ear. Speak aloud each sentence below so that you learn the sound of the correct verb—no matter how strange it sounds to you.

1. Sandy *lent* her favorite sweater to her best friend.
2. A cat *drowned* in Hyat's Creek yesterday.
3. After he *had swum* thirty laps, he was exhausted.
4. They already *have drunk* a case of cola.
5. My sister always waits until the phone *has rung* four times before she will pick it up.

Step 2. Correcting Students' Errors. Cross out any incorrect verb part in the sentences below. Put the correct verb part in the blank space to the left.

_____ 1. We have chose to go to Virginia Beach instead of to Florida.

_____ 2. The lifeguard swum the length of the beach.

_____ 3. The plumber done his job well.

_____ 4. The announcer brung us up to date on the news.

_____ 5. She drunk four cups of coffee this morning.

_____ 6. He should have took the job at Chemical Bank.

_____ 7. I seen that movie last week.

_____ 8. Did you ever have a pen that busted and leaked ink?

_____ 9. Frequently I have ate at the sidewalk cafe.

_____ 10. Nobody could have sang "Summertime" as well as Billie Holiday did.

Using *Has* or *Have* with Verbs

You use *has* or *have* with a verb form from Column III if you want to show an action that started some time in the past but is still continuing.

She *has laughed* for five minutes.

       ↖ [She began in the past but is still laughing now.]

    If the action began in the past and ended in the past, use the past tense (Column II verb form).

She *laughed* for five minutes.

       ↖ [She began in the past, but ended before now.]

Step 3. Verbs with *Has* or *Have*. For each infinitive in parentheses, write the correct form of the verb in the blank space on the left.

Hint

If *has, have, had, will have,* or *shall have* appears before the verb, pick the form from Column III on page 410.

_____ 1. That actress has (to speak) out against drug abuse.

_____ 2. By this afternoon, I will have (to eat) four dozen clams, and Jim will have (to drink) ten cans of cola.

_____ 3. Rosalita has (to choose) to attend the University of Nebraska.

_____ 4. The truck driver has (to ring) your doorbell twice.

_____ 5. My aunt has (to give) me so much; how can I repay her?

_____ 6. For the past three years, a child has nearly (to drown) in the ocean each summer.

_____ 7. Esteban has (to come) to class late every Friday since September.

_____ 8. A lively discussion has (to bring) the issue into clear focus.

_____ 9. It is so cold that the lock has (to freeze) solid and the pipes have (to burst).

_____ 10. For three days he has (to think) that it would rain.

Had as Verb Helper

If a sentence expresses two actions in the past and one of the actions came before the other, the verb that names the earlier action needs *had* as a helper.

The man thought that he *had seen* a ghost.

    [This is one ↗   ↖ [This past action came
    past action.]   before the man had the
                     thought.]

Step 4. Using *Had* Correctly as Verb Helper. Complete each sentence below by using *had* with the correct form of the verb in parentheses and any other words you need to complete the thought. Study the example.

EXAMPLE

(to come)   Yesterday we heard that you *had come late to class.* _____

(to steal)   1. Fortunately we visited the museum before thieves _____

                      _____

(to rise)   2. The convict disappeared before the sun _____

                      _____

(to give)   3. I found out that my brother _____

                      _____

(to drink)   4. I brushed the stallion's coat after he_____

                      _____

(to write)   5. Sonia was thrilled because the magazine accepted the story she

                      _____

Will Have, Shall Have with Verbs

Use *will have* or *shall have* with a verb part if you want to show that an action will be finished before some definite time in the future.

By tonight, I *will have made* twelve telephone calls.

Hint

In formal writing, *shall* is used only with *I* and *we*. *Will* is used with any subject.

Step 5. Your Sentences with *Will Have* or *Shall Have*.   Use three of these word groups in sentences of your own. Use separate paper.

EXAMPLE

By tomorrow I shall have seen your employer.

shall have spoken	will have taken
will have written	shall have seen
will have swum	will have dressed

Shifting Tenses

When you write, be careful not to switch back and forth unnecessarily from present to past tense. If you are telling about an event that occurred in the past, use the past tense. Look at this sentence:

I saw my friend Thomas and he asks me, "Where are you going?"

Saw is a past-tense verb.

Asks is a present-tense verb and should be replaced by *asked*, a past-tense verb.

Are is not incorrect, even though it is in the present tense, because the writer is quoting someone's exact words.

The correct sentence would be

I saw my friend Thomas and he asked [*not asks*] me, "Where are you going?"

Step 1. Tense Shifts.   Correct the tense shifts in each sentence below. Write the verbs correctly in the spaces on the left. Write *C* if the sentence is correct.

_____   1.   When I told her I found her lost bracelet, she screams and hugs me.

_____
_____   2.   I wanted a small pizza, but he brings me a large one and hands it to me. I decided to keep it.

_____   3.   I feel the softness of the tulip petals as they brushed the back of my hand.

_____ 4. Just as the car was about to hit the man, it swerves away, just missing him.

_____ 5. After he awakens, he prepares breakfast before he showers and dresses for work.

Some Confusing Verbs: *Lie* and *Lay*

The words *lie* and *lay* are two different verbs.

To lie means "to rest or to recline."

To lay means "to put or to place something."

Here are the three main parts of *to lie* and the tenses that are made from them.

LIE	LAY	LAIN
I lie in bed.		
The book lies there unnoticed.	He lay down for a nap.	The cat has lain in the driveway for hours.
Tomorrow we will lie in the grass.	She lay there quietly.	She had lain in bed for hours before the doctor arrived.

Hint

The past tense of *to lie* is the same as the present tense of *to lay*. That is the source of much of the confusion. Also, *to lie* means "to tell an untruth." The principal parts of this verb are *lie, lied, lying*.

The *-ing* form of *to lie* is *lying*.

The flowers *are lying* on the table.

A cat *is lying* in the yard.

Here are the three main parts of *to lay* and the tenses that are made from them.

LAY	LAID	LAID
I lay the pencil on the desk.	The cowboy laid his gun on the bar.	She should have laid the carpet on the hallway floor.
The child usually lays his head on a small pillow.		After Lynn had laid out the map, directions were easier to follow.

Hint

There must always appear after the word *lay* or any of its forms the thing that is being put somewhere. Also, if you can use the word *put* or *place* for the verb you want, select a form of the word *lay*.

The -*ing* form of *to lay* is *laying*.

He *was laying* out his clothes on the bed.

Step 1. Using *Lie* and *Lay*.   Follow directions. Use your own paper.

1. Use the words *has lain* correctly in a sentence.
2. Write a sentence using the words *he lies* to mean "he rests."
3. Write a sentence in which you use *lay* to mean "put" or "place."
4. Use the word *laying* correctly in a sentence.
5. Use in a sentence the word *lay* so that it means "rested" or "reclined."
6. Use the word *laid* in a sentence so that it means "put" or "placed."
7. Use the words *has laid* correctly in a sentence.
8. Use in a sentence the word *lying* to mean "resting."
9. Use *had lain* correctly in a sentence.
10. Use the words *I lie* correctly to mean "I rest."

Some Confusing Verbs: *Raise* and *Rise*

Raise means "lift up."

Rise means "get up" or "go up."

> **Hint**
>
> There must always appear after the word *raise* or any of its forms the thing that is actually being raised.

Here are the main parts and the tenses of *to raise*.

RAISE	RAISED	RAISED
[thing being raised] ↘		
He raises his hand.	She raised our scores.	He has raised enough
I raise the flag at	[thing being raised] ↗	money to start a
dawn.	[thing being raised] ↗	business.

-*ing* form: raising

The farmer *was raising* beans.

Here are the main parts and some of the tenses of *to rise*.

RISE   ROSE   RISEN

Everyone rises when the   He rose to shake our   The sun has risen earlier
  judge enters.   hands.   than usual.
I will rise when he
  speaks.

-ing form: rising

We were just *rising* to leave.

Step 2. *Raise* and *Rise*: Which Is Right? Pick out the correct word in the parentheses, and write it in the blank space.

_____ 1. As the two Army officers passed in the street, each (rose, raised) his arm to salute the other.

_____ 2. An eagle (rose, raised) higher in the sky as it searched for its prey.

_____ 3. Even before the circus was under way, the little boy had (risen, raised) eagerly from his seat.

_____ 4. Stephen's temperature (rose, raised) to 103°F in the past two hours.

_____ 5. The feminist movement has (raised, risen) the consciousness of men and women alike.

Some Confusing Verbs: *Sit* and *Set*

Sit means "to take a seat."

SIT   SAT   SAT

I sit in the last row.   They sat in the office.   The dog has sat there
She sits quietly.   without moving.
                                                          She had sat down before
                                                            they asked her to.

Set means "to place" or "to put."

Hint

There must always appear after the word *set* the thing that is being put somewhere.

SET   SET   SET
   [thing being
   put somewhere] ↘

I set my dictionary   Yesterday she set her   By the time he had set
   where I can reach it   coat in the closet.   the pot on the stove,
   easily.   we were not hungry
                     ↗   anymore.
               [thing being   [thing being
               put somewhere]   put somewhere]

Step 3. Completing Sentences with *Sit* or *Set*.   Write the correct form of *sit* or *set* in the blank spaces below.

1. After Rosa had _____ in her seat, she remembered that the oven was still on.

2. Five minutes after I had _____ the vase of flowers on the table, my Mom arrived.

3. You are the first person to _____ in that chair since I refinished it.

4. If you had _____ your glass down while you poured, the juice would not be all over the floor.

5. Let me _____ awhile before I leave.

Some Confusing Verbs: *Leave, Let; Stay, Stand; Can, May*

To let means "to allow."
To leave means "to go away from."

Let me speak to you.   We want *to leave* early.

     NOT

Leave me speak to you.

To *stay* means "to remain."
To *stand* means "to be in a straight up-and-down position."

I *stayed* in bed with a cold.

     NOT

I *stood* in bed with a cold.

I should have *stayed* home.

     NOT

I should have *stood* home.

Can asks whether or not you are able to do something.
May asks whether or not you will get permission to do something.

Can I drive the car?

(This question means: Do I have the ability to drive the car?)

May I drive the car?

(This question means: Will you give me permission to drive the car?)

Step 4. *Leave, Let; Stay, Stand; Can, May.*   Circle the correct words in the parentheses.

1. (May, Can) we come shopping with you?
2. If you (let, leave) your sister alone, you will (stand, stay) home when the rest of us go out.
3. When he (leaves, lets) you off from work, go directly home.
4. I (stood, stayed) in the house waiting for your call.
5. (Can, May) I (leave, let) my car on this side of the street?

A Minibook of Eight Special Skills

●

● **1. Improving Spelling**

● How to Be a Better Speller ●

1. Keep a list of the words you usually have trouble with: write the word correctly spelled; underline the troublesome letters; and make up some way of remembering the word. Start your list on page 434 after you examine the sample.

2. Write troublesome words several times, saying the letters aloud.

3. Trace the letters with your fingers after you think you know the spelling.

4. Use a dictionary to find correct spelling. Note the syllables.

5. If you cannot find the word in a dictionary, don't assume that the dictionary left out the word you are looking for. Try as many possible letter combinations as you can. For example, let us imagine that you had trouble spelling *conscious*. You look first under the letter *k* (it often makes the same sound as *c* at the beginning of a word), but when you find no *kon* combination, you have to look for another possibility: *con* starts many words. If you had trouble with letters after *con*, you might look next at *sh* (it makes the same sound as *sci* here). But when you find no *consh*, you need to think of other possibilities: maybe even *consch*. If you follow these suggestions, you will often locate the correct spelling. When you find the spelling that looks right to you, *read the definition* to make sure that the spelling offered is the correct one for the word you want.

6. Learn the spelling demons, words most frequently misspelled by many people. One hundred and fifty appear below.

7. Learn spelling rules for the most difficult problems.

Spelling Demons: Group A

1. *abundance*   Have <u>a</u> <u>bun</u>; then <u>dance</u>.
2. *accommodate*   two <u>c</u>'s, two <u>m</u>'s
3. *achievement*   <u>i</u> before <u>e</u>
4. *adolescence*   -<u>sc</u>ence
5. *allowed*   Look for <u>all</u>.
6. *analyze*   -<u>yze</u>
7. *apparent*   double <u>p</u>; -<u>ent</u>
8. *appreciate*   double <u>p</u>; -<u>iate</u>
9. *arrangement*   Don't drop the <u>e</u>.
10. *attendance*   two t's; end in <u>dance</u>
11. *available*   <u>Ail</u> is in this word.

12. *becoming*   Drop the <u>e</u> in <u>become</u>; one <u>m</u> only.

13. *benefited*   Look for the <u>fit</u> after <u>bene</u>.

14. *business*   The <u>bus</u> is <u>in</u> so add -<u>ess</u>.

15. *category*   an <u>e</u> between <u>cat</u> and <u>gory</u>

16. *cigarette*   two <u>t</u>'s surrounded by <u>e</u>'s

17. *competition*   Make the last <u>e</u> in <u>compete</u> an <u>i</u>; add -<u>tion</u>.

18. *conscious*   <u>sc</u> + <u>ious</u>

19. *cruel*   <u>u</u> + <u>e</u>

20. *dependent*   -<u>ent</u> ending

21. *dilemma*   Emma has a <u>dilemma</u>.

22. *discipline*   -<u>sci</u>

23. *eliminate*   <u>e</u> + <u>lim</u> + <u>i</u> + <u>nate</u>

24. *environment*   <u>nm</u> combination

25. *exaggerate*   two <u>g</u>'s

26. *existence*   <u>exist</u> + <u>ence</u>

27. *familiar*   The word <u>liar</u> is in fam<u>iliar</u>.

28. *grammar*   Hint: <u>ram</u> and <u>mar</u> are the same letters reversed.

29. *guiding*   Drop the <u>e</u> in guide.

30. *hoping*   only one <u>p</u> in hope

31. *independence*   -<u>ence</u> at the end

32. *jealousy*   Jea<u>lousy</u> is <u>lousy</u>!

33. *loneliness*   lonel<del>y</del>*i* + ness

34. *management*   Add <u>ment</u> to <u>manage</u>.

35. *mischief*   The Indian <u>chief</u> does mis<u>chief</u>.

36. *organization*   Drop the <u>e</u> in organize; add -<u>ation</u>.

37. *particular*   i c u are parti<u>cu</u>lar.

38. *persuade*   Add -<u>suade</u> to <u>per</u>.

39. *precede*   pre + <u>cede</u>

40. *presence*   If you are <u>present</u> make your <u>presence</u> known.

41. *proceed*   The church n<u>eeds</u> the proc<u>eeds</u>.

42. *receive*   <u>i</u> before <u>e</u> except after <u>c</u>

43. *rhythm*   <u>rhy</u> + <u>thm</u>

44. *satisfied*   -<u>fied</u>

45. *separate*   Sepa<u>rate</u> means <u>part</u>.

46. *sincerely*   Keep the last -<u>e</u>.

47. *succeed*   two <u>c</u>'s, two <u>e</u>'s

48. *thorough*   a <u>rough</u> word to spell
49. *thought*   -<u>ought</u>
50. *un<u>nece</u>ssary*   two <u>n</u>'s, two <u>s</u>'s

Step 1. Practice with Group A Words. Fill in the blanks with correct letters to complete the words below.

1. We must all pro_____ d to el_____ m _____ te the un_____ c _____ ary pollution of the env_____ n_____ nt if we are ever tho_____ r_____ ly to ap_____ c_____ te our ex_____ st_____ ce.

2. Because he a_____ ow_____ d it to continue, Mr. Powell did not seem con_____ i_____ s of how cr_____ l his son's m_____ ch_____ f was, or else he would have th_____ t twice about it.

3. Jazz often consists of se_____ ate r_____ t_____ ms combined in a p_____ rti_____ lar ar_____ g_____ ment.

4. A f_____ l_____ r dil_____ ma of adoles_____ n_____ e is a choice between the need for ach_____ v_____ t and ind_____ p_____ ce on the one hand and for dis_____ pline and comp_____ t_____ t_____ n on the other hand.

5. We rec_____ ve complaints annually about ci_____ ar_____ tes from those trying to p_____ rs_____ de us to stop smoking in public places.

Spelling Demons: Group B

1. *a<u>cc</u>ep<u>t</u>ance*   accept + <u>ance</u>
2. *a<u>cc</u>ompan<u>ied</u>*   two c's + -<u>ied</u>
3. *a<u>c</u>quain<u>t</u>ance*   <u>ac</u> + quaint + <u>ance</u>
4. *adverti<u>se</u>ment*   <u>tise</u>
5. *a<u>ll</u> right*   two words like "all wrong"
6. *a<u>nn</u>ually*   double <u>n</u>
7. *app<u>ear</u>ance*   An <u>ear</u> is part of your app<u>ear</u>ance.
8. *a<u>pp</u>roach*   a double p before the <u>roach</u>
9. *artic<u>le</u>*   -<u>le</u> ending
10. *a<u>tt</u>itude*   double <u>t</u>
11. *bas<u>is</u>*   ends in <u>is</u>
12. *beha<u>v</u>ior*   Don't forget the <u>i</u>.
13. *breath<u>e</u>*   We breath<u>e</u> to take a breath.
14. *car<u>ee</u>r*   two <u>e</u>'s
15. *certainly*   <u>cer-tain-ly</u>
16. *comin<u>g</u>*   Drop the <u>e</u> in come.
17. *condem<u>n</u>*   Don't forget the silent <u>n</u>.

18. *convenience*   con + ven + ience
19. *deceive*   i before e except after c
20. *description*   des
21. *disappoint*   dis + appoint
22. *discussion*   discuss + ion
23. *embarrass*   two r's, two s's
24. *equipment*   Look for the quip.
25. *excitable*   Drop the e in excite; add -able.
26. *experience*   -ence at the end
27. *fascinating*   sc after the a and before the i
28. *guaranteed*   guar as in guard; two e's at the end
29. *height*   -ei in the middle
30. *hungrily*   Make the y in hungry an i; add -ly.
31. *intelligence*   Can you tell he has intelligence?
32. *knowledge*   Did you know the ledge was there?
33. *losing*   Drop the e in lose.
34. *marriage*   marry + age (i)
35. *morale*   Ale will lift a soldier's morale.
36. *parallel*   Are all lines parallel?
37. *peculiar*   A liar is peculiar.
38. *pleasant*   Drop the e in please and add an ant.
39. *preferred*   Start with pre; double -r at the end.
40. *principle*   A principle is a rule.
41. *psychology*   psy to open
42. *recommend*   one c, two m's
43. *ridicule*   rid + i + cule
44. *schedule*   s + ch
45. *significance*   -ance
46. *studying*   study + ing
47. *surprise*   no z in this word
48. *tragedy*   no d before the g
49. *valuable*   Drop the e in value, add -able.
50. *weather*   I can't bear the weather.

Step 2. Practice with Group B Words.   Unscramble the following list of jumbled letters in order to spell the words correctly.

Hint

The first letter of each word is in boldface; the second letter is underlined.

1. c e m e̲ r d m o n _____
2. a n n i̲ e s c i f i g c _____
3. l u̲ n i y **h** g r _____
4. l l e l a̲ r **p** a _____
5. a p̲ e r u l i c _____
6. e e̲ e v c i **d** _____
7. h o y g l s̲ **p** y c o _____
8. l e e d u c̲ h s _____
9. o̲ a r l e **m** _____
10. n̲ l e t **i** l i e g c n e _____

Step 3. More Group B Practice: Looking for Smaller Words.   In the Group B words, there are many words that contain another word of five letters or more. Write nine of these words below and underline the smaller word contained in each. Use your own paper.

EXAMPLE

dis̲c̲u̲s̲s̲i̲o̲n

Spelling Demons: Group C

1. *ac̲c̲i̲d̲e̲n̲t̲a̲l̲l̲y*   two c̲'s, two l̲'s
2. *ac̲c̲ustom*   double c̲
3. *admit̲t̲ance*   two t̲'s
4. *ag̲g̲ravate*   two g's
5. *amat̲e̲u̲r̲*   e̲ u̲ r̲
6. *apo̲l̲o̲g̲ized*   Look for the l̲o̲g̲; add i̲ z̲ ed.
7. *ap̲p̲ly̲ing*   two p̲'s. Don't drop the y̲ at the end!
8. *arg̲u̲ment*   Drop the e̲ in argue.
9. *athl̲e̲te*   Don't forget the e̲ in "let." No e̲ after h̲.
10. *audi̲e̲nce*   At such a bad show the audi̲e̲nce almost di̲e̲d̲.
11. *beaut̲i̲ful*   y̲ in beauty changes to i̲

12. *believe*   Don't believe a lie.
13. *brilliance*   two l's + iance
14. *carried*   double r
15. *changeable*   Leave the e in change.
16. *committee*   two m's, two t's, two e's
17. *conscientious*   A scientist is conscientious.
18. *criticize*   -cize
19. *definitely*   Look for the finite.
20. *difference*   two f's; ence
21. *disastrous*   no e between the t and r
22. *efficient*   -ient after c
23. *emphasize*   Does it emphasize your size?
24. *especially*   This word has something special: double l.
25. *exercise*   No -z here!
26. *extremely*   The m stands between two e's.
27. *genius*   -ius not ious
28. *guidance*   Put gui before dance.
29. *heroes*   Add es to hero.
30. *ignorance*   He ran in ignorance.
31. *interest*   in + ter + est
32. *leisure*   -ei + sure
                                    i
33. *magnificent*   magnify + -cent
34. *miniature*   mini + a + ture
35. *noticeable*   Was not ice able to freeze the lock?
36. *paralyze*   -yze
37. *performance*   -ance after perform
38. *possession*   two double s's
39. *prejudice*   Look for the dice.
40. *privilege*   Privilege is vile.
41. *pursue*   two u's
42. *relieve*   Lie down to relieve your pain.
43. *sacrifice*   sacrifice
44. *seize*   The -e comes before the -i.
45. *similar*   ilar
46. *sufficient*   double f; -cient
47. *transferred*   two r's

48. *unusually*   three <u>u</u>'s all in one word
49. *villain*   The vil<u>lain</u> had <u>lain</u> on the street.
50. *writing*   Drop the <u>e</u> in write.

Step 4. Group C Practice. In each of the following sets of words, one word is misspelled. Write that word, correctly spelled, in the space provided at the left.

_____	1. amateur	heros	beautiful	criticize
_____	2. writing	sieze	admittance	pursue
_____	3. efficient	possession	especially	athelete
_____	4. privilege	villain	argument	paralize
_____	5. performance	carried	definately	exercise
_____	6. ignorence	unusually	genius	leisure
_____	7. transferred	noticeable	aggravate	disasterous
_____	8. brilliance	beleive	conscientious	accustom
_____	9. interest	comittee	similar	apologize
_____	10. magnificent	miniature	sufficient	changable

Step 5. Mastering Spelling Demons. Fill in the blanks to complete the words (taken from Groups A, B, and C) in the following phrases.

1. not_____ble jazz r_____t_____ m
2. the sig_____fi_____ of the ar_____ment
3. it was a_____l r_____t to ap_____ch
4. an amat_____ ath_____ te
5. a successful b_____iness car_____r
6. appl_____ng the princip_____
7. a be_____t_____ ful des_____iption
8. con_____ us of his j_____lo_____y
9. to exa_____erate the d_____le_____ a
10. a d_____ast_____us exper_____nce
11. e_____ci_____ly high mo_____le
12. the p_____chology of human behav_____
13. to s_____ze val_____ble gems
14. her ap_____r_____t ability
15. a cr_____l ex_____t_____nce
16. a fa_____inating per_____m_____nce

17. we conde_____ pre_____dice
18. her magn_____cent appe_____nce
19. must have suff_____ent exer_____e
20. an eff_____ent sch_____d_____le
21. he was be_____m_____g too ex_____t_____le
22. un_____ally th_____r_____gh job
23. pl_____sant w_____ther
24. a di_____us_____ion about their her_____s
25. the e_____pment is gu_____ant_____ed.
26. to emb_____a_____s him ac_____dent_____y
27. to be_____ve the th_____g_____t
28. to p_____sue knowl_____e
29. con_____entious stud_____ing
30. a cigar_____te advert_____ement
31. to rec_____ve their indep_____nd_____nce
32. the lon_____l_____ness of adol_____c_____nce
33. his par_____c_____lar in_____est
34. an ext_____mely good env_____ro_____ent
35. hop_____ng to suc_____d
36. to sac_____f_____ce his pos_____e_____ion
37. They are def_____nit_____ly sim_____l_____r.
38. a chang_____ble a_____itude
39. the bri_____nce of a ge_____s
40. to pers_____de sin_____ly
41. sat_____sf_____d with his wri_____ng

SOME SPELLING RULES FOR DIFFICULT PROBLEMS

Rule 1. Solving *-ie* Headaches

1. *i* usually comes before *e*

   EXAMPLES

   f*ie*ld   y*ie*ld   ach*ie*vement   rel*ie*ve

2. If the letter immediately before the *-ie* combination is *c*, the *e* usually comes before the *i*.

   EXAMPLES

   dec*ei*ve   rec*ei*ve   conc*ei*ve

3. The *e* also comes before the *i* if the combination of letters sounds like the *a* in *say* or *clay*.

EXAMPLES

n*ei*ghborhood   w*ei*ght   *ei*ght

[This sounds like *a* in *say*, so the *e* comes before the *i*.]

• Exceptions for You to Memorize •

*ei*ther	l*ei*sure
for*ei*gn	sci*e*nce
s*ei*ze	h*ei*ght
n*ei*ther	effici*e*nt

The following jingle will help you to remember the rule:

i before *e* except after *c*,
or when sounded like *a*
as in *neighbor* and *weigh*.

Step 1. Using -*ie* Correctly.   Fill in *ie* or *ei* in the following words.

1. h _____ ght
2. rec _____ pt
3. s _____ ve
4. l _____ surely
5. w _____ rd
6. w _____ ght
7. sl _____ gh

8. n _____ ther
9. rel _____ ve
10. misch _____ vous
11. f _____ ld
12. r _____ gn
13. rec _____ ve
14. s _____ zure

15. n _____ ghbor
16. p _____ ce
17. for _____ gn
18. sc _____ ntific
19. w _____ ght
20. y _____ ld

Rule 2. Changing *y* to *i*

1. If a word ends in *y* and the *y* is directly preceded by a consonant (any letter other than *a, e, i, o,* and *u*), the *y* is changed to *i* before an ending (*suffix*) is added.

EXAMPLES

[This is the new ending.]

fly + *es* = flies   carry + *ed* = carried

[The *y* is preceded by the consonant *l*.]

2. However, when the ending begins with *i* as in *-ing*, the *y* is *not* changed.

EXAMPLES

study + *ing* = studying   try + *ing* = trying

• Exceptions for You to Memorize •

lay + *ed* = laid   say + *ed* = said   pay + *ed* = paid

Step 2. Adding to Words That End in *y*.   Using the above rule, add the suffixes indicated to the following words.

		-ed	*-ing*	*-(e)s*
1.	apply	_____	_____	_____
2.	spy	_____	_____	_____
3.	delay	_____	_____	_____
4.	carry	_____	_____	_____
5.	annoy	_____	_____	_____

Step 3. More Practice.   Add the indicated endings to the following words.

1. hurry + *ed* _____
2. destroy + *ed* _____
3. bury + *ing* _____
4. lonely + *ness* _____
5. donkey + *s* _____

6. fancy + *ful* _____
7. mislay + *ed* _____
8. portray + *ed* _____
9. rally + *ing* _____
10. deny + *al* _____

Rule 3. Words That Drop the Final *e*

1. Words ending in silent *e* usually drop the *e* before a suffix beginning with a vowel.

EXAMPLES

[vowel]   [silent *-e*]   [vowel]

use + *ing* = using   use + *able* = usable

[silent *-e*]

2. However, the silent -*e* usually remains before a suffix beginning with a consonant.

EXAMPLES

[silent -*e*] [consonant] [silent -*e*] [consonant]
use + *ful* = useful   care + less = careless

• Exceptions for You to Memorize •

argue + *ment* = argument   change + *able* = changeable
judge + *ment* = judgment   courage + *ous* = courageous
true + *ly* = truly   canoe + *ing* = canoeing
notice + *able* = noticeable   mile + *age* = mileage

Step 4. Working with the Final *e*. Using the above rule, add the suffixes indicated to the following words.

		-ing	*-ment*	*-able*
1.	arrange	_____	_____	_____
2.	achieve	_____	_____	_____
3.	state	_____	_____	_____
4.	refine	_____	_____	_____
5.	advertise	_____	_____	_____

Step 5. More Practice. Add the indicated suffixes to the following words.

1. trouble + *ing* _____
2. true + *ly* _____
3. argue + *able* _____
4. home + *less* _____
5. survive + *al* _____

6. judge + *ment* _____
7. judge + *ing* _____
8. outrage + *ous* _____
9. write + *ing* _____
10. notice + *able* _____

Rule 4. Doubling the Final Consonant

When you add a suffix to a word, the final consonant of that word is doubled if the following are true:

1. The suffix begins with a vowel.

    EXAMPLE

    let + *ing* = letting

2. The word is one syllable *or* is accented on the last syllable.

    EXAMPLES

    sit + *ing* = sitting   (This word is one syllable.)
    control (con-trol) + *ed* = controlled   (The accent is on the last syllable.)
    suffer (suf-fer) + *ed* = suffered   (The accent is *not* on the last syllable, and so the final consonant is *not* doubled.)

Step 6. Doubling Practice.   Add the indicated suffixes to the following words.

1. drop + *ing* = _____
2. big + *est* = _____
3. happen + *ed* = _____
4. begin + *ing* = _____
5. depend + *ence* = _____
6. fit + *ing* = _____
7. regret + *able* = _____
8. refer + *ed* = _____
9. stop + *able* = _____
10. lessen + *ing* = _____
11. plan + *ing* = _____
12. benefit + *ed* = _____
13. admit + *ing* = _____
14. slip + *ed* = _____
15. stop + *ed* = _____
16. hug + *ed* = _____
17. submit + *ed* = _____
18. visit + *ing* = _____
19. travel + *ing* = _____
20. forbid + *en* = _____

Step 7. Mastering the Spelling Rules.   Test your mastery of the preceding spelling rules by adding the indicated suffixes to the following words. The numbers in parentheses refer to the spelling rule that applies to that word.

1. ugly + *est* _____ (2)
2. judge + *ment* _____ (3)
3. deprive + *ing* _____ (3)
4. pay + *ed* _____ (2)
5. differ + *ence* _____ (4)
6. accompany + *ed* _____ (2)
7. inhibit + *ed* _____ (4)
8. ready + *ing* _____ (2)
9. unwit + *ing* _____ (4)
10. knowledge + *able* _____ (3)
11. annoy + *ed* _____ (2)
12. relay + *ed* _____ (2)

13. forbid + *en* _____ (4)

14. deny + *al* _____ (2)

15. revenge + *ful* _____ (3)

16. slip + *ed* _____ (4)

17. petrify + *ing* _____ (2)

18. concur + *ed* _____ (4)

19. canoe + *ing* _____ (3)

20. say + *ed* _____ (2)

21. argue + *ment* _____ (3)

22. offer + *ed* _____ (4)

23. beauty + *ful* _____ (2)

24. profit + *able* _____ (4)

25. dismay + *ed* _____ (2)

26. transfer + *ed* _____ (4)

27. entire + *ly* _____ (3)

28. arrange + *ment* _____ (3)

29. quarrel + *ed* _____ (4)

30. receive + *ing* _____ (3)

31. damage + *ing* _____ (3)

32. write + *ing* _____ (3)

33. cut + *ing* _____ (4)

34. true + *ly* _____ (3)

35. forget + *ly* _____ (4)

36. apply + *ing* _____ (2)

37. deplore + *able* _____ (3)

38. ship + *ment* _____ (4)

39. admire + *ing* _____ (3)

40. bury + *ed* _____ (2)

Fill in *ie* or *ei* in the words below. To check your spelling, refer back to Rule 1.

1. sh_____ld

2. aud_____nce

3. c_____ling

4. l_____surc

5. gr_____ve

6. dec_____ve

7. w_____ghtless

8. bel_____ve

9. s_____zure

10. f_____gn

YOUR OWN DEMON LIST: WORDS YOU MISTAKE

Fill in the columns on page 434, as indicated, with your own troublesome spelling words. Study the examples. Continue your list, if necessary, on your own paper.

WORD CORRECTLY SPELLED	CONFUSING LETTERS UNDERLINED	A WAY TO REMEMBER
you're	you're	you're = you + are
accommodate	accommodate	double c, double m

● 2. Learning Vocabulary

● How to Learn New Words ●

The following steps will help you build your vocabulary:

1. Look up new words in a reliable dictionary.

2. Read definitions carefully. Pick only definitions that explain words as you want to use them or as they are used in what you have read.

3. Write each word on a small index card. Put definitions on the other side.

4. Categorize study words in related groups: *size* words, *liberation* words, *space-age* words, and so on.

5. Study words briefly on many occasions rather than for long periods on few occasions.

6. Say words and meanings aloud.

7. Write sentences using the words.

8. Add new words to your speaking vocabulary.

9. Use new words in writing sentences.

10. In reading, if you see an unfamiliar word, try to figure out its meaning from

   the way it is used in a sentence

   the prefix, root, or suffix that you see

   the words that may be put together to make up the new word

   a smaller word you recognize within the new word

Step 1. Predicting Meanings.   Try to determine the meanings of the words below in any way that you can. Write definitions in the blank spaces.

1. underestimate _____

2. irreplaceable _____

3. keepsake _____

4. paramedical _____

5. dockside _____

6. warmonger _____

7. irrevocable _____

8. spittoon _____

9. For that <u>laudable</u> plan, you deserve all the praise and thanks that the committee can

 give. _____

10. He was so thrilled by her political ideas that he overcame his usual <u>apathy</u> and

 promised, "I'll join the campaign right now!" _____

● 3. Using a Dictionary

Most instructors encourage you to use dictionaries to check meanings and spellings even when you write a test or an essay in class. Although pocket dictionaries give simplified entries for the words, you still need to understand the several parts of each entry. Here are samples from the *New Merriam-Webster Pocket Dictionary:*

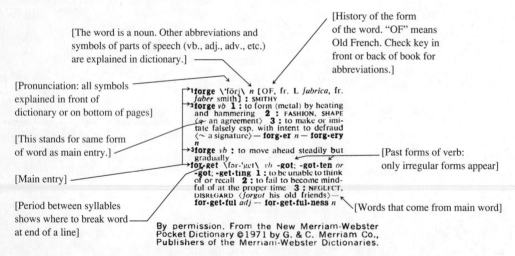

[The word is a noun. Other abbreviations and symbols of parts of speech (vb., adj., adv., etc.) are explained in dictionary.]

[History of the form of the word. "OF" means Old French. Check key in front or back of book for abbreviations.]

[Pronunciation: all symbols explained in front of dictionary or on bottom of pages]

[This stands for same form of word as main entry.]

[Main entry]

[Period between syllables shows where to break word at end of a line]

[Past forms of verb: only irregular forms appear]

[Words that come from main word]

By permission. From the New Merriam-Webster Pocket Dictionary ©1971 by G. & C. Merriam Co., Publishers of the Merriam-Webster Dictionaries.

Step 1. Understanding Dictionary Entries. Using the *New Merriam-Webster Pocket Dictionary* or some other handy pocket dictionary, look up the word *essay*. Use separate paper to answer the following questions.

1. What languages did the word come from?

2. What syllables make up the word?

3. What part of speech is the word?
4. How is the word pronounced?
5. What is an alternative pronunciation?
6. How many definitions appear?
7. What suffix can combine with it? What new word is created?
8. Which definition is new to you?

● 4. Using a Thesaurus

A *thesaurus* is a dictionary of synonyms. You can look up a word like *humorist* (given below), for example, and find fifteen or twenty words which are in some way related in meaning to that word.

• When to Use the Thesaurus •

when you repeat the same word too often

when a word does not sound right in your sentence

when you write slang or nonstandard expressions and you want more formal language

when you learn new words and you want to see other words used in a similar way

---

Two Hints for Thesaurus Use

1. Different methods of organization are used in preparing a thesaurus. One thesaurus groups synonyms according to ideas or subject categories. There, you look up words in the back of the book, find the section numbers in which the word you want appears, and then turn to a specific section which gives the synonyms that interest you. Other thesauruses are alphabetically arranged, like dictionaries.
2. Not all synonyms listed for any word have the same meaning. And the thesaurus rarely tells the difference in shades of meaning among the synonyms offered. Therefore, know definitions of any words you select. Don't pick words just because they are unusual, impressive in length, or new to you. Use a dictionary to check out differences in meanings.

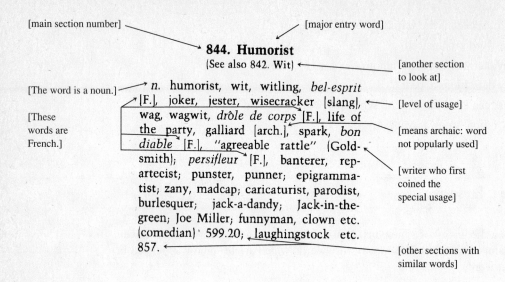

[main section number]

[major entry word]

844. Humorist

(See also 842. Wit)

[another section to look at]

[The word is a noun.]

n. humorist, wit, witling, *bel-esprit* [F.], joker, jester, wisecracker [slang], wag, wagwit, *drôle de corps* [F.], life of the party, galliard [arch.], spark, *bon diable* [F.], "agreeable rattle" (Goldsmith); *persifleur* [F.], banterer, repartecist; punster, punner; epigrammatist; zany, madcap; caricaturist, parodist, burlesquer; jack-a-dandy; Jack-in-the-green; Joe Miller; funnyman, clown etc. (comedian) 599.20; laughingstock etc. 857.

[These words are French.]

[level of usage]

[means archaic: word not popularly used]

[writer who first coined the special usage]

[other sections with similar words]

Step 1. Thesaurus for Synonyms. Use a thesaurus to look up the following words. For each word, select and write down three synonyms whose meanings you do not know. Then, using a dictionary, write definitions of the three new words. Look at the example. Use your own paper.

EXAMPLE

WORD	SYNONYMS	DEFINITIONS
happy	1. *opportune*	1. *coming at the right time*
	2. *auspicious*	2. *favorable; suggesting success*
	3. *joyous*	3. *full of delight*

1. compulsion

2. to observe

3. obedient

4. pleasant

5. gesture

● 5. Preparing a Résumé and Job Letter

Preparing a Résumé

When an advertisement for some good job appears in a local paper, the employer often receives hundreds of responses. If you are one of those interested in such a position, you will want to make sure that your response attracts the employer's interest. Your answer should be brief but to the point; and your qualifications should be clearly stated. A convenient method of presenting your qualifications is through a *résumé*, a statement of your particular accomplishments in summary form. In a résumé, a prospective employer can see at a glance just why you feel he or she should select you for the job opening.

Notice in the résumé on page 440 how the writer groups information together for easy reference to show clearly her qualifications as an accountant's assistant.

● How to Write Your Résumé ●

1. Include your name, address, and telephone number.

2. Sometimes an office will advertise several available positions, so make sure to indicate the job for which you are applying.

3. If you have a specific salary in mind, include it in the résumé.

4. Include honors or awards that show your qualifications for the job you want. Otherwise leave out this part.

5. Include all your job experience. Any job can give you skills that may be helpful in the position you are seeking.

6. Extracurricular activities show your interest in voluntary service and often reflect skills that might be handy on the job. Susan Davis' membership in the Business Honor Society suggests that her skills are advanced.

7. Show whatever specific training you have had that makes you eligible for the job.

8. List two or three references—their names and addresses—so that information about your character and abilities is easy to obtain. Make sure that you include people who know you well enough to give a fair evaluation of your character. It is a good idea to ask someone's permission before giving that person as a reference.

9. *Type* your résumé on sturdy typing paper. Avoid errors and erasures.

Résumé

Personal Data
Susan E. Davis
18-25 Deegan Road
Elmhurst, New York 11373
Telephone: (212) 481-9998

Career Objective: Junior Accountant

Educational Background: Long Island City High School (Commercial
Diploma: June 1986). LaGuardia Community College (Major:
Accounting; A.A.S. Degree expected June, 1989).
Major Courses: Accounting, data processing, statistics, insurance,
business organization and management, writing for business,
bookkeeping, business law, economics, stenography, typing.
Special Skills: Typing (65 W.P.M.); stenography (120 W.P.M.);
machine experience: IBM electric typewriter, IBM 029 and 129
Keypunch.
Honors and Awards: Perfect attendance award (1985-1986);
certificate for highest yearly average in bookkeeping (1985);
outstanding service award (1986).
Extracurricular activities: Business Honor Society (1984-1986);
Program Committee (1983-1985).

Experience

Pantry Pride Supermarket
82-86 Broadway
Elmhurst, New York 11373
Manager: Mr. Micelli

August 1984 to present
Cashier and Office Worker
Duties: Recording sales in
the ledger book.

F. W. Woolworth Company
976 Third Avenue
New York, New York 10002
Manager: Mr. Pastore

April 1984 to August 1984
Part-time Cashier
Duties: Pricing merchandise
and filling shelves.

Abraham & Straus
Fulton Street and East
Broadway
New York, New York 11201
Section Manager: Mr. Murray

November 1983 to January
1984
Sales Clerk
Duties: Recording cash and
charge sales and displaying
merchandise.

References
Mr. John Micelli, Manager
Pantry Pride Supermarket
82-86 Broadway
Elmhurst, New York 11373

Mr. John Weigel, Coordinator
Division of Cooperative Education
Fiorello H. LaGuardia Community College
31-10 Thomson Avenue
Long Island City, New York 11101

108 East 93 Street
Brooklyn, New York 11212
October 5, 1990

Mr. Harry Koster
Chief of Division of Receipts
Comptroller's Office of the City of New York
New York, New York 10007

Dear Mr. Koster:

Your advertisement in the <u>New York Chief</u> yesterday called for a
part-time accountant's assistant to help in the processing of city
income tax forms. Because of my interest in accounting and city
government, I think I am well qualified to apply for the job you
are advertising.

You will see from my résumé that I have had both training and
experience in the field of accounting. My course of study at
college is designed to qualify me as an accountant after
graduation. My interest and skill in mathematics contribute to my
qualifications for this job.

My schedule at college now requires me to attend classes late in
the afternoon; for this term I am available for work from 9 a.m. to
11:30 a.m. every day but Wednesday when I can work from 9 a.m. to
11:00 a.m.

May I please come for an interview any morning during the week? I
will telephone your office to arrange a time convenient to you.
You will find me an eager and cooperative worker.

Very truly yours,

Susan E. Davis

Susan E. Davis

Step 1. Writing Your Résumé.   Prepare a résumé about yourself on a separate sheet of
paper. Assume that you want to apply for a job for which you feel well qualified. Résumés
often include additional information, such as travel experience, military status, bilingual-
ism or other language skills, hobbies, involvement in sports; many of these may be
appropriate for your résumé. The kind of job always determines the range of information to
be included.

A Letter of Application

The letter that you send along with your résumé should be a brief and sincere attempt to arouse the employer's interest in you. Paragraphs in a business letter are often just three or four sentences long, making the letter easy to read quickly.

The first paragraph usually includes a statement about how the job came to your attention and expresses your interest in the position. The second paragraph mentions briefly the highlights of the résumé that you send along with the letter: if you are not planning to send a résumé, the second paragraph (and the third as well, if you need more space) should indicate all your special qualifications for the job.

Another paragraph can indicate any special conditions you may have to present. If you are not sending a résumé, name your references in this paragraph. Another brief paragraph should show your willingness to come for an interview—suggesting a convenient time and a day. On the facing page appears the letter that will accompany Susan Davis's résumé. Use the format of the letter to write your own business letters.

● 6. Writing a Summary

Much college writing—especially brief reports and homework questions—is summary writing. A summary gives a brief idea of material you have read. It is usually a statement you write from your notes or from your underlining. Good summaries focus on main ideas, major subtopics, and only *important* details.

● For Clear Summaries That Make the Point ●

1. Read carefully. Take notes as explained on pages 260–262. Look up words you do not understand.

2. Your first sentence should state the main idea of the selection you are summarizing.

3. Use your own words in repeating details. Use the author's exact words for certain key ideas.

4. Repeat information accurately.

5. Follow the author's development in the selection you are summarizing. If information is arranged chronologically or by importance; if material is presented through comparison-contrast, narrative, several examples—your summary should reflect the author's pattern.

6. Revise your first draft so that your sentences flow smoothly. Use subordination to tighten ideas.

7. Summaries should be brief, usually not more than a third of the total number of words in the original.

Here is a summary of the selection by Maude White Katz on page 76.

Summary of "Racism in Education"

Racist beliefs make many Americans view Negroes as "subhuman or only semihuman." The Establishment (higher education and mass media) is responsible for this philosophy. Yet Blacks *are* educable, in spite of dishonest intelligence-test results. Although valid reasons appear for intelligence differences among white children, Blacks are said to differ from whites for genetic reasons. Proofs of racism in education appear in the exclusion of Blacks—through craft union officials—from trade schools. The New York State Commission on Human Rights found guilty the Sheet Metal Workers Union Local 28 because none of its 3,300 members was Black.

—*Geoffrey Hunte*

● 7. Writing about Literature

Often in your courses you will have to report on assigned reading. In your English class you may have to give your responses to a novel, perhaps, a short story, a play, or a poem. As with all writing assignments your first step as part of prewriting activity is to limit your topic. Of course, there are many possibilities for writing that each piece of literature itself suggests, but with an idea of some *possible* approaches to take, you might find it easier to prepare an essay on a literary work. Below appear some suggestions that singly or in combination may help you focus your discussion.

Approaches to Writing about Literature

1. Write about the *theme*. The theme in a poem, novel, play, or short story is its main idea, the dominant point the writer had in mind for the work. Because the writer rarely states the theme outright—it is almost always implied—you have to figure out the main idea by thinking about the people, the characters, the events in what you have read. Is the writer trying to make a point about human behavior? about social conditions? about religion or morality? about personal psychology? about humanity's place in the universe? How does the work of literature reveal one or several of those points? Once you have an idea about the theme, you will have to support that idea with specific details drawn from the work itself.

2. Write about one *character* or about several of the characters. Explain what you think their motives are; discuss their behavior and the results of it; show how characters interact; examine their personal psychologies. Are the characters realistic? Do they change through the course of the work or do they remain constant?

3. Write about the *action*. Although you may need occasionally to summarize some details of the plot (the story line, the events that take place), writing a report that is almost entirely a summary is not a good idea because it reveals none of your abilities to evaluate. Therefore, in writing about action, you must avoid a simple plot summary. You might want to discuss the climax of the action, its major turning point; you might show how various incidents are connected to each other; you might show how characters are forced to behave in certain ways because of events; you might point out

the elements that cause suspense; you might show how the events are rooted in historical occasions.

4. Write about the *structure* of the work. How does the writer put the pieces together? How is the work similar to or different from other examples of literature like it? If you are writing about a love poem, for example, how does the poet conform to what readers expect to find in such poems? How does a writer make a work special, however? How do the different stages (or chapters or acts or scenes) interact with each other?

5. Write about the *tone* of the work. What is the writer's attitude toward the subject? Is it serious or mocking? What attitude does the writer show toward the characters? Is it admiration or dislike or pity?

6. Write about the *language* in the work. What is the quality of the writer's use of words? Are the images particularly clear and vivid? Are figures of speech used (see pages 184–187) with any special skill? Are there any patterns that you can figure out about the images? Does the writer have special talents in writing dialogue? Does the language portray actions clearly? Does any special strength lie in the use of details?

An Essay on a Book Character

The pages of novels and biographies are rich in unforgettable characters who make exciting topics for book reports. One approach to take to an essay on character is to select *two* dramatic moments that illustrate something significant about an important person in your book. Then, you can expand each moment in a body paragraph as you try to illustrate your proposal. Study the guidelines and the student model on the next pages before you write.

• Essay Guidelines for Book Characters •

1. Decide on some important personality trait of the hero in your book. Is the person *brave, mean, thoughtless, loving, pitiful?* Write a proposal sentence that indicates that personality trait.

2. Let each body paragraph relate one specific moment that illustrates from the book the impression you stated in the proposal sentence.

3. Select moments that are important in the growth and development of the hero. A moment that focuses on the hero in the midst of a crisis or a turning point (especially where some important decision must be made and acted upon) is especially emphatic for the reader.

4. Make the sounds and colors and smells of each moment alive. Show the actions of the character. What is he or she doing, thinking about, or saying?

5. Follow the suggestions on pages 121–125 for writing introductions: be sure also to include the author's name and the title of the book in your first paragraph.

6. Make sure that you use in your essay a quotation right from the book. This may be a sentence or two that describes an action or it may be something said by one of the characters.

In the student essay below, notice how the two body paragraphs effectively support the proposal sentence.

Antonia's Strength

History books are filled with words of praise for the pioneers who settled the West. But the struggle with personal hardships by the courageous families who cleared Nebraska and Kansas come to life in Willa Cather's *My Antonia*. In the novel the heroine, Antonia Shimerda, faces familial hardships with unusual strength.

She shows it first after her father's suicide. A girl in her early teens, Antonia loved her father deeply. When Jim Burden, the narrator of the novel, arrives at the house for the burial, Antonia rushes out to him and sobs, her heart almost breaking. But at the funeral she is much more controlled. Her dead father lies in the coffin with his knees drawn up. "His body was draped in a black shawl," writes Cather, "and his head was bandaged in white muslin, like a mummy's; one of his long, shapely hands lay out on the black cloth; that was all one could see of him." Yet Antonia, in spite of that awful figure, follows her mother up to the coffin and makes the sign of the cross on the bandaged head of her dead father. When Antonia's mother, a woman with little maternal softness, pushes her youngest daughter Yulka up to the body, the child cries wildly. After a neighbor insists that the child not touch the body, it is Antonia who puts her arms around the younger girl and holds her close. I'll never forget the warmth of that scene: Antonia, herself so sad, comforting her little sister as a fine, icy Nebraska snow falls outside.

That quiet moment of courage Antonia matches later on with physical strength. On an April afternoon after Mr. Shimerda's death, Jim Burden rides out to the house; he has not seen Antonia for three months. When he spots her as the sun drops low, he watches her drive a team of horses up to the windmill. She wears her father's boots, his old fur cap, and an outgrown cotton dress with sleeves rolled up. Antonia has taken upon herself to work the fields in her father's absence. Although she cries briefly at not being able to attend the sod schoolhouse, she states in her broken English, "I ain't got time to learn. I can work like mans now. . . . School is all right for little boys. I help make this land one good farm." Jim is disappointed at her mannish ways: She yawns at the table, eats noisily like a man, and boasts often of her strength and the chores she can perform. But this is just an outgrowth of what is really strength of character. To accept the challenge of the soil as a man in her father's place is certainly an act of courage.

Antonia's courage should be a lesson for women of today. Living the soft life, I and many of my contemporaries complain about the slightest trouble. We complain when the washing machine is broken or when we have to walk to the bus. We complain if we have to wash dishes by hand or if the garbage barrels need pushing out to the street. Antonia Shimerda would look these minor inconveniences in the eye and say, "I can work like mans now."

—*Phyllis Dubin*

• Other Approaches to Literature Essays on Character •

1. Compare and contrast two characters with different traits, showing a dramatic moment to illustrate each personality.

2. Show how the hero changes by relating two different instances, one from an early part of the book and one from a later part.

3. Show how the hero responds to a moment of crisis and then show how a moment in your own life was similar to or different from the hero's. Or, show how you would have behaved in the hero's place.

4. Show how a moment in a book compares with the same moment in a movie about the book.

● **8. Answering Essay Examination Questions**

Midterm or final examinations in college courses usually ask—in addition to short-answer questions—that you answer some questions in *essay* form. Although the word *essay* in this sense is used loosely, it usually means some longer response to a question that requires extended thought and development.

Hint

If the exam asks you to answer more than two or three *essay* questions, a one-paragraph response is often adequate for each question.

If the exam asks you to answer only one or two questions, plan to write a four-paragraph essay to develop your responses.

• Making the Grade: How to Answer Essay Questions •

1. Think about the question before you write. Take clues for the development of your paragraph or essay from the question itself.

   a. If the question says *compare and contrast,* use comparison-contrast methods of development.

   b. If the question says *how,* show how something is done or how something works. If the question says *explain, tell, illustrate, discuss,* use any method of development that uses facts, statistics, paraphrases, or quotations in order to back up your point.

    c. If the question says *define*, write a paragraph or an essay that uses substantial details to illustrate the meaning of a word, an idea, or a theory.

    d. If the question says *list,* it is often enough just to write your answer by numbering 1 through 10, for example, and by writing some fact for each number. But you can also "list" ideas in paragraph form.

    e. If the question asks *why,* make sure that you understand what conclusions the instructor wants you to reach. Then, give as many details as you can to explain the *causes* for the result you are asked to explain.

2. Repeat the main part of the question in your topic sentence (for one-paragraph answers) or in your proposal sentences (for four-paragraph essay responses).

3. Your introduction and conclusion may be much briefer than those urged in other parts of this book. But do not abandon other requirements of the well-constructed essay.

    a. Make sure that the proposal sentence comes *last* in paragraph 1.

    b. Make sure to use clear transitions in the first sentence of each body paragraph.

    c. In your conclusion, summarize your topic; then, apply your topic to some general principles, if possible (see pages 126–128).

4. Use a number of details to illustrate or to prove whatever points you make in your paragraphs. In this book, you have learned how to use the following kinds of details and illustrations:

    a single moment from your life experience

    concrete sensory details

    figurative language and imagery

    statistics

    quotations and paraphrases

    illustrative moments from fiction

    cases

Step 1. Understanding Questions. These essay-type questions all come from college textbooks. Explain on a separate sheet of paper how you would go about answering them; tell what methods you would use in developing you paragraph or essay.

1. Discuss the growth of trade unions in the 1930s in America.
2. List the basic features of the open classroom.
3. Compare *realism* and *naturalism* in literature.
4. Explain Freud's Oedipal theory.
5. Compare and contrast Marxism in Europe and Latin America.

A P P E N D I X

A

Glossary of Usage

accept, except

accept—means to *receive,* to *welcome,* to *say yes.*

    We *accept* your offer of help.

except—means *leaving out, excluding.*

    Everyone *except* Barry ate together.

affect, effect

affect means

1. to *assume* or *pretend.*

    He *affected* a smile of agreement.

2. to *influence* or *act on.*

    Good study habits *affect* learning speed.

    Hint

    Think of the **a** in *affect* as a signal to act.

effect means

1. to *bring about.*

    His disposition *effected* a change in our mood.

2. *result* or *outcome*.

> The *effect* of her speech cannot be measured.

Hint

Think of the **e** in *effect* as a signal for result.

Hint

If *the* or *an* comes before the word, you must choose *effect*.

all ready, already

all ready—means *fully prepared*.

> The team was *all ready* to play.

already—means *by this time* or *before a set time*.

> When you arrived, I had *already* eaten.

among. See between.

amount, number

amount—refers to things in large masses, things that cannot be counted.

> A large *amount* of water filled the tub.

number—refers to countable things.

> He received a *number* of parking tickets.

bad, badly. See good, well.

barely. See hardly.

being that—avoid this expression Use *since* or *because*.

> *Because* (not "Being that") I felt tired, I went to sleep.

between, among

between—used to name relationships between *two* people or things.

> *Between* you and me the book is dull.

among—used to name relationships referring to *three* or more people or things.

> *Among the* students only Carol answered.

could have, could've, could of

could have—correct for all forms of written or spoken expression.

> We *could have* studied more carefully.

could've—a contraction, good for informal writing or speaking.

> "You *could've* been more careful," Sandra replied.

could of—incorrect! *Could've* sounds like *could of*, but this last form is not correct in writing. Also, use

> *should have*   NOT   should of

would have   NOT   would of
might have   NOT   might of

If you need a contraction, use *should've* for *should have, might've* for *might have,* and *would've* for *would have.* But remember, contractions appear most of the time in informal writing only.

different from, different than

different from—the preferred form, although *different than* is sometimes used when a subject and a verb follow it.

That pen is *different from* mine.

effect. See affect.

except. See accept.

fewer, less

fewer—used for things that can actually be *counted.*

He has *fewer* books than I have.

less—shows worth, quantity, or degree.

The cigarette has *less* tar than yours.

His car costs *less* than hers.

former, latter

former—between two objects, *former* refers to the first thing named.

latter—between two objects, *latter* refers to the second of two things named.

Neither the car nor the motorcycle would start; the *former* because of a bad carburetor, the *latter* because of faulty ignition.

> **Hint**
>
> If three objects are involved, do not use *former* and *latter;* use *first, second* (or *next*), and *last.*

A dog, a cat, and a horse appeared in the cartoon; the *first* did a tap dance while the *last* played a guitar.

good, well; bad, badly

good, bad—describe things or people.

A *good* movie is hard to find.

What a *bad* idea!

well or *badly*—describe actions named by most verbs.

She reads *well.*   not   She reads *good.*

She dances *badly.*   She dances *bad.*

Hint

After one of these verbs use *good* or *bad: is, am, are, were, have been, look, remain, appear, taste, smell, feel.*

She looks *bad.*
The soup tastes *good.*
The news was *bad* this morning.

If you want to indicate someone's health, use *well* or *bad* with one of the above verbs.
I feel *well* today.

hanged, hung

hanged—shows someone's life was taken by execution.
The mob *hanged* the criminal without a trial.
hung—refers to *things*, not to people.
We *hung* the mirror on the wall.

hardly, scarcely, barely

Since these words are already negative, do not use them with *never, not,* or with verb contractions ending in *n't.*
I *could hardly* breathe.　　NOT　　I *couldn't hardly* breathe.

hung. See hanged.

in, into

in—movement within one place.
He ran *in* the room. (This means he was already inside the room when the action began.)
into—movement from one place to a position within.
He ran *into* the room. (This means he was not already within the room when the action began.)

irregardless. Avoid! See regardless.

latter. See former.

learn, teach

learn—means *gain information* or *knowledge.*
teach—means *give information so that someone else learns.*
He *taught* me right from wrong.　　NOT　　He *learned* me right from wrong.

less. See **fewer.**

might have, might've. See **could have.**

myself
Use *myself* to stress the word *I* in a sentence or to show that the subject and the receiver of the action are the same.

I *myself* will judge.
I shaved myself this morning.

Avoid using *myself* as a substitute for *I* or *me.*

It was Larry and *I.*   NOT   It was Larry and *myself.*
She took Beverly and *me* to the Dean.   not   She took Beverly and *my-self* to the Dean.

number. See **amount.**

regardless, irregardless
Use *regardless* only; *irregardless* is incorrect.

Regardless of our suggestions, he voted in his own way.

B

Theme Progress Sheet

After your instructor grades and returns your themes, count up and enter the number of errors you make in each category listed on top of the chart. Before you write each following composition, study this sheet so that you know your errors and so that you can avoid them in your writing. The symbols for the errors and the page numbers on which to discover how to make specific corrections appear on the inside covers of this book.

													Date	
													Title of composition	
													RO	Grammar
													Frag	
													Agr	
													Vb	
													Pro	
													Ms	Mechanics
													Cap	
													It	
													Abbr	
													,	Punctuation
													;	
													'	
													"	
													./	
													!/	
													?/	
													:/	
													–/	
													( )/	
													-/	
													Sp	Spelling and vocabulary
													Voc	
													Us	Diction
													Ef	
													Var	Strong sentences
													Ord	
													//	
													mm	
													Dang	
													¶	Paragraphs and essays
													¶ Det	
													¶ Dev	
													E	

APPENDIX

C

Record of Teacher-Student

Conferences on Compositions

DATE	DISCUSSION POINTS	FOLLOW-UP ASSIGNMENT

Acknowledgments

Leonard Abramson, "Uncaring Women's Health Care," *The New York Times,* May 14, 1990. Copyright © 1990 by The New York Times Company. Reprinted by permission.

Robert F. Biehler and Lynne M. Hudson, excerpt from *Developmental Psychology,* third edition. Copyright © 1986 by Houghton Mifflin Company. Used with permission.

Suzanne Britt, "That Lean and Hungry Look," *Newsweek,* 1978. Reprinted by permission of the author.

Claude Brown, "Down South," reprinted with permission of Macmillan Publishing Company from *Manchild in the Promised Land* by Claude Brown. Copyright © 1965 by Claude Brown.

Nancy Bubel, "How to Make a Terrarium," originally published in *Blair & Ketchum's Country Journal,* December 1978, © Cowles Magazines, Inc.

Sarah Ferguson, "The Homeless: Us Against Them," as it appeared in the *San Francisco Chronicle,* May 6, 1990. © Pacific News Service.

Dorothy Canfield Fisher, "Theme Writing." From *Essays in Modern Thought,* Thomas R. Cook, ed.

"forge" and "forget," by permission, from *The New Merriam-Webster Dictionary,* © 1989 by Merriam Webster Inc., publisher of the Merriam-Webster dictionaries.

Ellen Goodman, "U.S. Kids Need More School Time," © 1990, The Boston Globe Newspaper Company/ Washington Post Writers Group. Reprinted with permission.

Christopher Hallowell, "About Men: Family Farm," *The New York Times,* September 8, 1985. Copyright © 1985 by The New York Times Company. Reprinted by permission.

Linda Hayes, "Boom Time for Brokers," *Fortune,* February 9, 1981. © 1981 Time Inc. All rights reserved.

Langston Hughes, "Mother to Son," from *Selected Poems of Langston Hughes* by Langston Hughes. Copyright 1926 by Alfred A. Knopf, Inc., and renewed 1954 by Langston Hughes. Reprinted by permission of the publisher.

Roger Kamien, excerpt from *Music: An Appreciation.* Copyright © 1990. Reprinted by permission of McGraw-Hill, Inc.

Maude White Katz, "End Racism in Education: A Concerned Parent Speaks." Reprinted from *Freedomways,* vol. 8, no. 4, 1968. P. O. Box 1356, Cooper Station, NY, NY 10276.

Doris Lessing, excerpt from *Particularly Cats* by Doris Lessing. Copyright © 1967, 1989 by Doris Lessing. Reprinted by permission of Alfred A. Knopf, Inc., Michael Joseph, Ltd, and Doris Lessing Productions Ltd.

Edna St. Vincent Millay, "Lament" by Edna St. Vincent Millay. From *Collected Poems,* Harper & Row. Copyright 1921, 1948 by Edna St. Vincent Millay. Reprinted by permission of Elizabeth Barnett, Literary Executor.

George Orwell, excerpt from "Such, Such Were the Joys" from *Such, Such Were the Joys* by George Orwell, copyright 1952 and renewed 1980 by Sonia Brownell Orwell, reprinted by permission of Harcourt Brace Jovanovich, Inc., the estate of the late Sonia Brownell Orwell and Martin Secker & Warburg Ltd.

Robert Phillips, "The Mole" from *Running on Empty: New Poems* by Robert Phillips. © 1981 Robert Phillips by arrangement with Wieser & Wieser, Inc., 118 East 25th St., New York, NY 10010. First Published in *The New Yorker.*

George Plimpton, "How to Make a Speech" from *The Power of the Printed Word* Series. Reprinted by permission of International Paper Company.

John L. Postlethwait and Janet L. Hopson, excerpt from "The Improbable Giraffe," *The Nature of Life.* Copyright © 1989. Reprinted by permission of McGraw-Hill, Inc.

Anna Quindlen, "Suicide Solution," *The New York Times,* September 20, 1990. Copyright © 1990 by The New York Times Company. Reprinted by permission.

David J. Rachman et al., excerpt from *Business Today,* 6th Edition. Copyright © 1990. Reprinted by permission of McGraw-Hill, Inc.

John Reid, "If It's Cute Enough, We'll Save It," as it appeared in the *San Francisco Chronicle.* July 15, 1990. © Pacific News Service.

Peter Mark Roget, "Humorist" from *Roget's International Thesaurus,* 4th ed., by Peter Mark Roget. Copyright © 1977 by Harper & Row, Publishers, Inc. Reprinted by permission of HarperCollins Publishers.

Berton Roueche, "A Walk Along the Towpath" from *What's Left?* by Berton Roueche. Reprinted by permission of Harold Ober Associates Inc. Copyright © 1962 by Berton Roueche.

Andrew Siscaretti, "What Am I? West Clapton and Flynn" from "Media Compositions: Preludes to Writing," by Harvey S. Weiner, in *College English,* February 1974.

Mark Twain, excerpt from *Mark Twain's Autobiography.* Copyright 1924 by Clara Gabilowitsch, renewed 1952 by Clara Clemens Samossoud. Reprinted by permission of HarperCollins Publishers.

James Vander Zanden, excerpt from *Sociology: The Core,* 2nd Edition. Copyright © 1990. Reprinted by permission of McGraw-Hill, Inc.

Eudora Welty, "The Little Store," from *The Eye of the Story: Selected Essays and Reviews* by Eudora Welty. Copyright © 1978 by Eudora Welty. Reprinted by permission of Random House, Inc.

Jade Snow Wong, "Uncle Kwok" from *Fifth Chinese Daughter* by Jade Snow Wong. Copyright 1950. Reprinted by permission of University of Washington Press.

Al Young, excerpt from *Kinds of Blue,* copyright © 1984 by Al Young. Published by Creative Arts Book Company, Berkeley.

Index